Coping and Defend

Processes of
Self-Environment Organization

Norma Haan

Institute of Human Development
University of California, Berkeley
Berkeley, California

WITH CONTRIBUTIONS BY

Paul Joffe
Richard F. Morrissey
Murray P. Naditch

Department of Psychology
Cornell University
Ithaca, New York

ACADEMIC PRESS   New York   San Francisco   London   1977

A Subsidiary of Harcourt Brace Jovanovich, Publishers

ACADEMIC PRESS, INC.
111 Fifth Avenue, New York, New York 10003

United Kingdom Edition published by
ACADEMIC PRESS, INC. (LONDON) LTD.
24/28 Oval Road, London NW1

Library of Congress Cataloging in Publication Data

Haan, Norma.
    Coping and defending.

    (Personality and psychopathology series ;   )
    Bibliography: p.
    1.   Personality.   2.   Ego (Psychology)   I.   Title.
BF698.H15   155.2   76-55746
ISBN 0-12-312350-X

Contents

Preface

Several germinal, but still relatively disparate lines of thought are taken up, put together, and pursued to build the personal—social psychology that is described in this book. The hope is that the simultaneous consideration and synthesis of these ideas will suggest ways for personology to become a psychology of people within situations. We can hardly escape the impression that personality—social research has been adrift for some time now, nor can we avoid our own self-inflicted criticisms and exhortations that personology is incomplete without a social outlook. Even though we lack commanding formulations and are unable to say in a general lawful way how people make something out of what situations make of them, these several ground swells suggest directions we might take:

1. The Freudian insights that made a deep impression on previous generations of psychologists still haunt us. The question is whether these should be ignored and forgotten or reworked to include and accord with what we now know about (a) undefended, rational, logical thought, (b) the mutable and dynamic qualities of situations and societies, and (c) biological functioning, most particularly the singularity of biological energy (as contrasted with separate id energies of sex and aggression and the latter day "ego energies" of Hartman, Erikson, and White).

2. The Piagetian description of cognitive structures and development and the cognitive theory of moral development have not yet been thoroughly exploited and extended to develop a personal—social psychology interlaced with cognitive and moral-social propositions. Yet it is obvious to many that this extension surely can and should be made.

3. Ways need to be found to make a personological account of people within situations that still does not become sociology. The interstice between person and situation has still not been made an integral part of our formulations. Our person is

still too much of an entity to be seen as a being who reacts, interacts, and transacts with situations in the strong sense of these terms. We either succumb to the easy, positivist idea that situations determine people or recoil and assume the superindividualist position that man decides and circumscribes his own milieux.

4. The power of the developmental, historical view, which has gripped the younger generation of child psychologists, has not yet resulted in a psychology of personal–social development. Logically, such an account of personality development should flow from the historical point of view, but as yet, we have few ideas about what its outline and structures might be.

5. The ramifications of the constructivist epistemologies of Quine, Piaget, and others for psychology's own social basis of knowledge are not well understood nor have their implications for psychological investigation been drawn yet. We increasingly find that we must understand the social character of experimentation to understand our subjects. A corollary benefit of this necessity may be our increased awareness that we need to reexamine the basis of our own "scientific" knowledge. If we were to do so, we might find that many of our technical-methodological disputes are moot.

6. As social scientists we seem to be experiencing a moral and a practical crisis about how we should relate to our subjects (and our patients)—especially when they have no self-expressed need of us—whether to hold them at arm's length, admit them into the social dialogue of experimentation and psychotherapy, or to move ourselves to ever more complex and careful forms of double blind.

7. Related to but distinct from the personal-moral crises of social scientists is the question of what model of valued, ideal man should be now selected to direct personality–social research and psychotherapy and to articulate our findings and clinical understandings. Past formulations have usually become ardently political—wantonly humanistic or beyond freedom and dignity—and defined by private preferences and formed in one of several images personally valued by psychologists themselves. Worse yet has been the inadvertently value-saturated supposition that personologists can proceed without a formulation of a well-functioning system.

This book presents a proposal that will not, by any means, answer all of these questions nor integrate all their implications, much less put controversy to rest. In fact, some aspects of the exposition may exacerbate the situation by calling attention to anomalies that now seem to exist. Instead a "middle level," bridging conceptualization, is presented: The personalities of people are most fruitfully and clearly formulated in terms of the processes used, and all else that is usually called personality is better regarded as something else. Thus, the argument will be made that processes and their organizations are the singular core of personality. When personality is regarded as such, the various issues mentioned above seem to form a coherent whole. In the end, readers will judge the adequacy, completeness, and success of this effort for themselves, but the formulation (a) rescues the most useful Freudian insights, (b) outlines a personality psychology that Piaget probably would not reject, (c) directly represents people interacting and transacting within situations in the strong sense of these terms, (d) suggests the form of a developmental–personality psychology that maintains proper respect and allegiance to the accepted knowledge of cognitive development, (e) makes it possible, and even necessary, to adopt a constructivist epistemology, (f) has something practical to say about the social nature of experimenters' transactions with subjects (and therapists' with patients), and finally (g) suggests a process formulation of valued ideal man as one who copes.

Parochially enough, a model of particular processes is described and used throughout this book, but from time to time the reader will find disclaimers to the effect that this particular array is the only one or that it includes all the processes there are. Nevertheless, the general idea of personality as process has importance since it works to make a whole first out of the intrapsychic and the social context and second, a whole out of intrapsychic structures, emotions, and motivations. Consequently, a number of intraindividual interregulatory matters—such as the processes' relationship to cognitive and moral structures—will be considered in later chapters, while other chapters concern the person's social contextual interchanges within social collectivities—such as families.

Thus, the scope of this book is broad, as it must be, because the middle-level nature of the process proposal works, or at any rate it is so intended, to consolidate subject matters that concern developmentalists, cognitivists, personologists, clinicians, and social psychologists, as well as sociologists and perhaps anthropologists. The decision was made early on to draw the implications of the process model of the person from many fields, rather than to narrow the focus and attempt to exhaust the detail of a single area. At the present time, psychology seems to need go-betweens, and this is the role that I suggest processes can take when their implications are fully exploited. For instance, personologists, who study the cognitive processing of stress, need to understand the processing of cognitive development, and cognitivists, if they are to deal fully with development, need to understand stress as it is processed while people are growing up. Social psychologists and sociologists need to understand the intraindividual processes whereby situations are constructed, while personologists need to understand the structure and process of groups and situations as they are constructed by the people within situations.

A formulation of the ways in which the Freudian and Piagetian insights (both oversimplified designations) can meet and coalesce clearly cannot be a strategy of simple addition. Both systems have to undergo revisions in order to make a whole. Very likely there are other ways than the present one, in which these main systems can be articulated and reconciled, and without doubt, we will be presented with them in time. Such efforts need to be made, because we cannot reasonably suppose that either account is the whole story, or that they are unrelated, or that the older system, psychoanalysis, lacked merit.

Necessarily, then, the present proposal is developed slowly. To build a detailed and explicit rationale for the process view, the first section of the book is devoted to past and present theories of ego, to the relationships of the present conceptualization to past ones, and to the difficult problems of the place of value in an empirical field. The first chapter presents an overview of the main formulation. Then the history and fiber of our usual thinking and suppositions about **personality** are critically examined in Chapters 2 and 3. A full presentation of the present proposal is first made in Chapter 4. Following this exposition the chronic problem of psychologists' values in conceptualization, research, and practice is taken up and eventually focused on the conceptualization of coping in Chapter 5. This explication becomes necessary once we admit that our knowledge of personality and society is based on social constructions, because then we can no longer think that psychological theorizing and research are value-neutral. However, we are left then with a new question: What kind of values *should* scientific investigation choose?

The next main section of the book, Chapters 7–12, is largely devoted to empirically based findings, after a preliminary development in Chapter 6 of the problems and methodologies of investigating processes. Empirical studies that concern the interregulations of processes and structures, the development of processes, stress and processing, and processing in families are presented in the later chapters. Some of these studies are new, while others have been previously published. After a concluding statement in Chapter 11, the final section of the book, Chapters 12 and 13, was written by former associates at Cornell University. Richard Morrissey summarizes and evaluates all research available to him that has used the present model of coping, defense, and fragmentation. Finally, Paul Joffe and Murray Naditch report their recent work in developing and improving coping and defense scales based on personality inventories.

Acknowledgments

I want to express my appreciation and gratitude to a large number of people who belong to several institutions. The people of the Institute of Human Development at Berkeley have permitted my eccentricities, taken fraternal joy in my accomplishments, and provided support beyond measure. I salute Rose Fox, June Aiman, Katherine Eardley, Christine Godet, Margaret Heick, Marjorie Honzik, Mary Jones, Vivien March, Tsipora and Harvey Peskin, Fred Rosenblatt, Judy Tiktinski, and many more whose support was more indirect. I especially want to thank Lilly Nakagawa who typed and read much of the manuscript. Her analytical mind forced me to become clearer than I would have been, left to my own devices. I have high appreciation for the intellectual companionship of Guy Swanson who criticized a number of these chapters. I had not discovered a satisfying formulation of the human group until my discussions with Guy Swanson, and I owe much to him in this regard. Dorothy Eichorn, principal investigator for the federal grants supporting the Institute's longitudinal studies (HD 03617-06 changed to AG 00365), which have permitted some of the data collection and many of the analyses described in this book, has been generous in her encouragement and aid. Various directors of the Institute—starting with John Clausen, then Brewster Smith, and now Paul Mussen—not only made space and time for me to develop the ideas and do the research for this book, but also provided more ineffable but indispensable support by their individually expressed suppositions that the basic conceptualizations were worthwhile and should be pursued.

The original understandings of coping and defense grew out of Ted Kroeber's and my joint work following the death of Else Frenkel-Brunswik with whom we both worked. She had said that psychology's next step would surely have to be the understanding, as she put it, of "coping mechanisms." At the time it seemed to be a very important idea and it still does. Other Berkeley people who have helped me include: Enrico Jones, Joseph Kuypers, Jonas Langer, Richard Lazarus, and Janice Stroud. All have read and criticized drafts of various chapters—sometimes in disagreement—I appreciate their interest and help.

I want to thank the people of the psychology department of Cornell University for inviting me to come as visiting professor to teach about ego psychology. There were many students and faculty who enriched my exposition by their questions, criticisms, disagreements, and probes. I am particularly grateful to Henry Alker, Margaret Gargan, Richard Darlington, Paul Joffe, Richard Morrissey, Murray Naditch, Joanne Newman, Ann Scales, Paul Schaffner, Carol Suhr, and Nanette Wiser.

I appreciate the California School of Professional Psychology's willingness to facilitate my securing a doctoral degree at a very late date. The dissertation that I submitted to the faculty contained some of the ideas that are further developed in Chapter 10, which concerns the family. I am particularly grateful to Richard Metz, Laurel Samuels, Murray Tondow, and Martha White.

Some analyses reported in this book are based on part of the data from the Youth and Moral Dilemmas project, an investigation only recently concluded. I thank the Board of Directors and the officers—William Bradley and Ann Hoblitzelle—of the Hazen Foundation for their financial support of this research and for their enthusiastic interest, as well as the staff of the project who joined me in an adventure of high excitement and importance: Abner Boles, Betty Lou Bradshaw, Phyllis Cohen, Harriet Curtis, Sandra Dobkin, Carol George, Louis Gomez, Bruce Hansen, Vicky Johnson, Linda Kastelowtiz, Cynthia Marshall, Della Mosley, Connie Phillip, Larry Sullivan, Darlene Tong, Rick Weiss, Lani Wilson, and Michael Wynne.

Finally, my husband, Aubrey Haan, has helpfully supported, tolerated, and cajoled as I ruminated over my ideas and reconsidered my words. My daughter and son-in-law, Mary and Paul Shinoff (both writers), have had close interest. Mary Shinoff also read and criticized Chapter 9, which concerns stress. Peter Haan, my son, has been willing to engage in philosophical disputation about the proper role of empirical science vis-à-vis the phenomenology of each man's mind; in the process I discovered several kinks in my thinking and borrowed several ideas from him.

Acknowledgment is made for permission to quote from the following sources:

pp. 10, 12, 26: From Freud, S., *Outline of psychoanalysis* © 1949, W.W. Norton, pp. 15–16, 110, 110–112.

p. 20: From Erickson, E., *Childhood and society,* 2nd ed. © 1963, W.W. Norton, pp. 273–274.

p. 26: From Freud, S., *New introductory lectures* © 1946, Hogarth Press, p. 106.

p. 57: From Piaget, J. Plays, dreams, and imitation in childhood © 1962, W.W. Norton, p. 251.

pp. 75–76: From Macklin, R. Mental health and mental illness: Some problems of definition and concept formation, *Philosophy of Science,* 1972, *39*:356.

p. 167: From Rosten, L., *Captain Newman, M.D.* © 1965, Harper & Row, p. 272.

p. 199: Courtesy of Swanson, G.S., unpublished manuscript, 1968, p. 12.

pp. 207–208: From Haan, N., Moral redefinition in the family as the critical aspect of the generational gap, *Youth & Society,* 1971, 2(No. 3):265–270, by permission of the publisher, Sage Publications, Inc.

p. 265 and Table 20, p. 266: From Gleser, G. and Ihilevich, D. An objective instrument for measuring defense mechanisms. *Journal of Consulting and Clinical Psychology,* 1969, *33*:52.

1. Preview

This work is about personality, although not in its usual global, wide-ranging, inclusive sense that encompasses almost everything that can be said about the person. Of all the various views that psychologists have held about human beings, their most immodest and vague have been those of personality; still, these constructs are among the most exciting. By way of amending this state of affairs, a case will be made that it can be conceptually clarifying and productive of greater truth to decide that personality, most properly and narrowly, refers to the fundamental and persistent organizational strategies that people use to interregulate various aspects of themselves—their cognitive and moral structures, their emotions, their constructions of durable or momentary social impingements, and their motives, viewed here as their intents and plans.[1] Thus the present definition is made comparatively tight and exclusive by its insistence that the processes are central to the idea of personality and that all else has a different history and taxonomy and should be relegated to other classes of conceptualization. In other words, I propose that personality should concern the processes that people use in their attempts to be "persons," the strategies they use to achieve a modestly sensible view of themselves. This view is constructivist by reason of its assertion that personality consists of organizational processes; however to build upon what has gone before,

[1] The word *structure* will be used precisely to mean "a set of any elements between which, or between certain sub-sets of which, relations are defined [Lane, 1970, p. 24]." Thus psychological structures are the products or conclusions of reason that arise out of constructed experience and represent wholes or totalities of relations that are logically prior to their parts. This meaning is different from the more informed definition of structure used by psychoanalysis to describe parts of the personality, for example, ego, id, superego, or by others as parts of the brain's functions, for example, perception, memory, and so on.

1

we had best call these ego processes, although the word *ego* has not always been used in a constructivist sense. This work, then, is concerned with ego processes— their definition, taxonomy, organization, functioning, development, effective and ineffective versions, and their interface with other aspects of the person.

The central aim is to describe people's synchronic and diachronic uses of self-constructed processes; both matters concern the question of "how?" or "by what means?" This goal contrasts with that of most personologists, whose eventual aim is to predict individual behavior, an activity that necessarily concerns the question, "why?" The more limited ambition of describing patterns and sequences of processes, used by people to solve the momentary or the persisting problems of their lifetimes, is based on the supposition that people's actions are not faithfully reproduced but are instead inventively organized on the spot. When prediction and eventual control of individual people's behavior is the goal, specific causes need to be believed in and discovered, in order to answer the version of the "why" question that asks "for what motives?" The aim of the present work is different; it strives for a network of implications that represents a different kind of explanation: "How did it come about?" Although this is a paler ambition than those usually held by social scientists, it follows from the proposition that processes are central and that people's constructions result in their doing the same thing for different reasons and different things for the same reasons. Regularity is to be found in the limited number of processes involved in the ways people bring about their own results. The goal of the enterprise is to seek general laws that describe the patterning and sequencing of developmental evolution. In this light, the hope of predicting individual people's behavior is inappropriate (and left to therapists, biographers, lovers, and nearest of kin).

This volume is, then, a radical, but paradoxically not an extreme, proposal that among the vast array of characteristics that people possess, personality as such "exists" only in a special and limited way. All we see that is specifically personality and not more clearly something else are the analyzing and synthesizing efforts that the person makes, moment by moment and within the framework of his own phenomenology, to make self-consistent sense out of himself and what others and the world make of him. Unlike a number of past proposals that take up the idea of "self," this proposal, which is still scientifically ambitious despite the above assertions, is not directly about the self. Instead, the self is taken to be an unknown that will never be fully or adequately described by the enterprise of science, which seeks to identify regularities across people. In this proposal, the self is still taken as the fundamental given and as a necessary postulate for the scientific investigation of process, but it is regarded uniquely organized by each person according to his own lights.

The nature and history of new proposals in psychology may have prepared the reader to expect that the foregoing statements place the ego system in the executive role. Such is not meant to be the case; in fact, we will see in subsequent explication that it is reasonable to think that much of the time the person's ego processing merely functionally expresses and follows his attained cognitive or moral stage development, that is, his achieved structural level. However these specific qualifications take us beyond this general discourse.

When the work of ego is defined in this limited but specified way, a taxonomy of ego processes can be identified and their various modes of operation charted. The taxonomy that will be described here was proposed by Kroeber (1963) and by myself (1963). Although this is not the time to describe this model in great detail, several aspects need to be brought out now to advance this preliminary discussion. First are the various sectors: Included are processes which, more than anything else, coordinate the presentation of cognitive structures; others concern the intraceptive, reflexive interchanges the person has with himself; others involve the regulation of feelings and, more forcefully, emotions and impulses; others concern the focusing of attention. No assertion is made that these functions (or this model) represent the definitive or the entire taxonomy of human ego capabilities.

Kroeber's and my earliest proposal included a fundamental and pivotal distinction between the defensive and coping modes of the ego, and I (Haan, 1969) later added a third mode, ego fragmentation, to describe some of the reactions of very troubled people and, likely, of all people some of the time, in very stressful situations. Originally the classical defenses of psychoanalysis provided an identification of ten such processes (or mechanisms, as they are usually called in psychoanalytic parlance). Taking the Freudian definition of defense very seriously, Kroeber and I thought to derive each coping function as a counterpart of a defensive one; thus both could represent the same generic process, but each member would have different properties. The concept of coping was formulated to describe not how the person defended and fortified himself, but rather how he acted when he led himself on and out. The fragmentary modes are common clinical labels used to describe disorganized, pathological behavior. When they, too, were seen to be processes, and ones that always represented the various generic actions, another mode could be added.

Although the entire array and organization is discussed in Chapter 3 and detailed definitions can be found in Appendix A, an example may help the reader at this point. Projection (the defensive mode) is a matter of sensitively reacting to others' thoughts and feelings (the generic process), as are empathy (the coping mode) and delusions or ideas of reference (the fragmentary mode). All three involve the same action of being concerned with others' thoughts and evaluations, but they can be distinguished one from another by the nature of the assessments that are made—their accuracy, purpose, and the character of the concomitant affect.

My experience suggests that the immediately post-Freudian generation of psychologists and psychoanalysts have difficulty supposing that coping, as it is defined here, really exists. (They have no problem with the defensive or fragmentary modes.) If they agree that it does exist, they often believe that it is unacceptably value-laden (see Lazarus, Averill, & Opton, 1974), or they state that it is a subcategory of defense (see Murphy, 1962, 1974) or that it merely describes a kind of functioning that occurs only in the most dire and stressful of circumstances and therefore has little to do with everyday life (see White, 1974).

I have come to the conclusion that these means of disposing of coping are only partly due to the value implications which troubled Lazarus and his colleagues. A more important obstacle may be that coping entails a changed view of the "successful" man. He is not primarily a winner, but merely an accurate, authentic negotiator with himself, others, and life. The postulate of coping does not mean that scientific neutrality must be recklessly discarded. In fact, common sense makes reliable, everyday judgments as to when people are accurately assessing themselves and their situations and when they are negating or distorting their judgments. However, the problem of value intrusion is subtle and complex and besets *any* social scientific formulation and particularly those that concern a "good" in man. The importance of these questions necessitates their full treatment in Chapter 5. For now, we can note that decisions about processes do not need to rely on culturally or personally bound criteria, and I readily admit that the present definition of coping is value assumptive in supporting the concept that it is "better" to solve problems accurately, within the terms of accurately knowing one's self and within the framework of intersubjective reality and logic, than it is not to do so.

To make coping a subcategory of defense, as Murphy and others do, results in defense itself being the central aim of man's ego strategies. The subordinate position of coping protects an idea shared by both psychoanalysis and behaviorism: that the untutored child is most importantly described as id-ridden (psychoanalysis) or unsocialized (behaviorism). The "revisionism" represented by the present formulation and others suggests that the instincts or unmodified drives are not a sufficient or the only basis for beginning the explanation of how development or functioning takes place. The formulation rests on the Piagetian evidence that the child's and the man's strategies are not solely or even most importantly protective of their wishes for drive gratification. Consequently a conceptualization of equally important, but qualitatively different, processes is needed. Finally, if the word *coping* is reserved for describing only those actions that arise in dreadful situations, as White suggests, we will mix coping actions and defensive actions, and we will tie the action to the stimulus rather than describe what people do. Moreover we will surely need still another word to describe people's nondefensive problem solving in less than dire conditions.

Coping may seem abstruse to some because its logical implications are quite different from those of the original definition of defense that we post-Freudians grew up with (however, the meaning of defense will be partially redrawn here too). As the ramifications of coping are followed, they invariably lead, at this time in the history of ideas, to a view of the restless person, incessantly engaging in a series of inconclusive choices. He or she is forever choosing, both synchronically for the moment and diachronically for a lifetime, sometimes in a grand Sartrean manner, but more frequently in the modest mode of assimilating and accommodating like a good Piagetian. A diminution of our usual views of the successful man is subtly implied by this view, and it troubles some people because no impressively competent nor final, stable, equable solutions are deified—even the analyzed and the well socialized are only better able to bear their everyday difficulties.

A logic underlying the ego process view of personality makes it necessary to consider constantly how development takes place and what difference it makes. Processes and development both occur in time, and an argument will be made in Chapter 4 that development is processed and processes follow development. Most concepts of dynamic personality do not require this concern, even though it is difficult to represent dynamic happenings—a well-recognized virtuous goal of any theory of personality—without direct and explicit representations of processes. Most systems have relied on constructs of drives or motives to explain dynamic movement and development; that is, the drive exerts the energy that instigates both behavior and learning. In contrast, both development and processes are the vehicles whereby life in progress continues to evolve by momentarily equilibrated states continuously becoming something a little bit different from what they were before. Thus the construct of drives is not of central importance in the present view. The view of personality development is larger than, but includes, the idea of children growing and changing between Time A and Time B. Represented here is a meta-historical view of personal history as it is changed and re-understood, not a deterministic view of the unqualified past determining the present. Thinking this way, the investigator's task becomes one of tracking and describing sequences of personal actions and transactions with environments, and later chapters will demonstrate this preoccupation in action.

Focus upon ego processes leads to concern for their situational contexts, not merely because personologists should pay attention to situations as sociologists and anthropologists do, but because the ego processes' work *is* interchange with internal and external situations and ego processes make no sense understood in any other way. Sometimes ego processes are self-actional in reaction to situations, but their work is more often situationally interactional and transactional, to use John Spiegel's (1972) series of useful distinctions of family interchanges in a different way than he may have intended. The Piagetian model of the assimilative–accommodative work of all biological functioning within ecologies will be proposed as a good general description of the activity of ego processes in contexts. The interactive features of ego processes make all psychological measurement difficult. Situations of data collection are social contexts, and people as subjects become cannily self-actional, interactional, and transactional as they do in all situations. As a result they do not always construct and present clear, true representations of themselves. They may decide that it makes the most sense to comply and opt for the socially desirable as the experimenter appears to be identifying it. Thus subjects can put experimenters in the classical double bind: "I am earnestly cooperating but don't be taken in by what I am letting you see."

An attempt will be made in this work to reconcile the Freudian and Piagetian views in several ways, but not without extending both and discarding and revising some assumptions of each. The signal triumph of the Piagetian system is its restoration of the common man's capabilities of logic and reason after the Freudian renunciation of the validity of his knowingness. However in their single-minded concern with these goals, the Piagetians have slighted the psychopathologies of everyday life. The signal contribution of the Freudian system was its recognition and elaboration of man's deception of himself and others. The political and scientific effects of this insight can hardly be overestimated. Political strategists' wish to devalue common man's insistence on the rationality of his own choices found a newly legitimized basis, and scientific theorists came to give rationality short shrift as they, too, concurred that men know little of the whys and wherefores of their enterprises. No other matter takes priority or poses a more knotty problem for the integration of Piagetian and Freudian theories than that of the place of both rational and irrational processes in the person's self organization.

From one viewpoint, the Freudian system is oversold on the omnipresence and centrality of pathological functioning but undersold on the importance of rational determinations in everyday life. The Piagetian system is oversold on the omnipresence of rationality and undersold on the facile willingness of people to twist, bend, and forego rationality when it suits them. This paradox suggests that intermediate concepts are needed, ones capable of making a coherent whole out of people's pathological and rational determinations. The ego processes—their taxonomy, organization, and history—are meant to be candidates for this work. Psychology has few intermediary concepts for describing people's mild clashes and reconciliations between the pulls and temptations of irrationality on the one hand and the social insistencies of rationality on the other hand. Regard the usual treatment of rationality within the context of conflict itself: Semantically, conflict almost always denotes a disturbance of considerable proportion and strength, usually a neurosis, that is typified by gross cognitive distortions. Or take the word disequilibrium, intended by the Piagetians to denote the person's confused state when he is stage transitional and is not quite able to assimilate and accommodate to a new class of information. A theory of personality for everyday life needs conceptualizations that will embrace these two—neurotic conflict and developmental disequilibrium.

One attempt to build a conceptual bridge between these two systems is the following, stated now in abbreviated, preliminary form: A defense is a process that people use to preserve a sense of their own integrity despite the expense of attenuating their usual allegiance to intersubjective logic and the consensus of others. The action usefully serves their own intrasubjective logic and order; that is, they feel they need the defense to prevent chaos that could debilitate themselves and possibly even others. Consequently it follows that a person who evokes a defense is for the moment (or if he is chronically defensive, for a considerable span of time) not all he can be in both a personal and a social sense. He is not "himself." We come to know the intersubjective imperatives of reality and logic in the presence of others and we come to share their views of logic and reality, but this knowledge is by no means all-encompassing nor is it necessarily compelling. As Freud showed, these social imperatives are readily bypassed for more pressing concerns. If the person is chronically defensive, it will be all the more difficult to know what he is functionally capable of being were his defensive needs to subside.

This formulation emphasizes and reifies the difference between capacity and performance and suggests such disparities abound—not a new idea, but often only an occasion for researchers to question the adequacy of data and its collection. Here the disparity is reified and made a pivotal part of the formulation. Such dysfunctions (often too strong a word) are involved in the typical experience of not acting like one's self or not living up to one's self. Figure 1, which includes ideas that will be the subject of more detailed analyses in Chapter 4, is introduced here to illustrate the parallel but different sequelae that are posited as characterizing coping and defended outcomes. As suggested in Figure 1, normative circumstances lead to structural activation and consequent affective evaluations that take the form of motive-plans. Both are then organized by coping processes, and the resulting coordinated action is a reasonably accurate representation of the person's level of structural development. Nonnormative circumstances also lead to structural activation; however the subsequent affective evaluation disrupts the sense of self so that defensive or fragmentary reactions are deployed which disorganize action and result in the person's level of structural development not being represented in his behavior.

The elevation of the discrepancy between performance and capacity from a methodological annoyance to a substantive construct makes it possible to accommodate two seemingly opposite concepts about the nature of ego action: (1) the Piagetian insistence that structures are irreversible, enduring developments that directly express themselves in action with (2) the Freudian insistence that defensive actions are typical. The proposed bridge suggests both can be true and both can be typical of the same person, but only in separate situations—the action of the defensive processes intervenes between capacity and performance to distort, but not to destroy, structural achievements. Psychoanalysis recognizes the disparity in its therapeutic work and explicitly intends to aid the analysand in discovering and

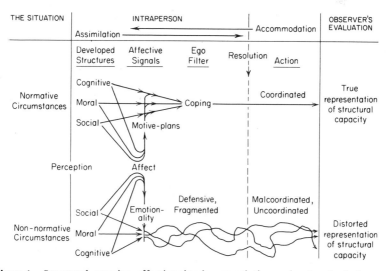

Figure 1. Structural capacity, affective signals, ego solution and action in single sequences of construction for normative and nonnormative circumstances.

actualizing his capacity, but then, in protection of instinct theory, compartmentalizes its practice and theory by the insistence that the recovered patient must be "well defended." Another conceptual culprit that perpetuates the idea that defenses are omnipresent is the Freudian view of the structure of society as immutable—properly and importantly repressive of the instinctual life, but nevertheless inimical to the self-expression of mature, well-analyzed individuals. As a consequence, humankind always needs its defenses.

Coping processes are expected to present accurately whatever structural stages of cognitive and moral development have been attained, when situations are primarily cognitive or moral in nature. If we knew more about the aspects of social development, we might then be able to identify intrapsychic structures of social meaning, ranging from understandings of love to understandings of institutions. If we were so informed, coping could then also be expected to present these social structures accurately and to coordinate them with the various other kinds of structures.

Emotions probably do not form structural stages or sequences of development since they are qualitatively and intrinsically diffused, intangible, and without form. However it is widely understood that feelings become more differentiated with development, that is, the child progressively comes to cognize different feelings and to discriminate among a wider range of feelings. As these developments take place, coping processes serve to coordinate feeling with its understood cognitive representation to inform the person and his companions of his disposition.

Drives are not particularly important or omnipresent in ordinary life and are not critically placed in this formulation. We have concluded that ego processes and cognitive representations are invariably part of any intent, including mild motivations which assert, "I am entitled to this satisfaction," or more forcefully, "There is no need for my ending up feeling like a sinner." At the same time, when biological drives are aroused, they must still be "processed" with the work of the ego.

Readers who are Freudian sophisticates will note that the present description of defensive functioning departs slightly but significantly from the usual psychoanalytic view. First, this formulation grants a constructivist intent to defense, that is, the person has his own intrasubjective logic and intends to preserve his integrity at whatever the intersubjective cost; secondly, the formulation imparts fluidity and changeability to the person's use of defenses. All ego processes, including the defensive and fragmentary modes, are viewed as being strategically evoked (although people do have preferences) and not as armor buttressing character, as in the psychoanalytic definition. Probably only *some* ego processes of some people in some homogeneous, limiting, and monotonous situations support the immutable brand of functioning that psychoanalysis calls "character." The present constructivist view also leads in the end to questioning whether neuroses or psychoses represent well-worn ruts—wherein people are solely preoccupied with questions of security and guilt—and instead focuses on an alternative formulation that troubled people go to great lengths to maintain self-integrity, even if they must reject intersubjective reality by psychoses.

All these matters are considered in detail in subsequent chapters. Since the proposal that personality is nothing more than the analyzing and synthesizing processes of the person significantly departs from many past and popular ideas, a brief history of ego conceptualizations is first needed (Chapter 2) and will be followed in Chapters 3 and 4 by examinations of the critical assumptions of two current formulations: first, that of ego as a state, and second, that of ego as processes.

2. Past Definitions of Ego

Freud's Main View of Ego

To know the shape of the current definitions of ego, we need to turn to its author, Freud, and first consider the view of ego he most frequently presented, that of the ego as a mechanistic state. As Holt (1967) commented, "In the flush of his youth [Freud] longed to be as scientific as possible, and in those days, mechanics seemed to him the very model of a modern science [p. 483]." Thus Freud would have needed to avoid all suppositions that the ego introduced anything new or emergent into the intrapersonal situation. In this regard, the Freudian and behavioristic theories have made common cause, which is hardly surprising since both grew up in the same, positivist climate of science. Late in his career, Freud still said:

> The principal characteristics of the ego are these. In consequence of the relation which was already established between sensory perception and muscular action, the ego is in control of voluntary movement. It has the task of self-preservation. As regards *external* events, it performs that task by becoming aware of the stimuli from without, by storing up experiences of them (in the memory), by avoiding excessive stimuli (through flight), by dealing with moderate stimuli (through adaptation), and, finally, by learning to bring about appropriate modifications in the external world to its own advantage (through activity). As regards *internal* events, in relation to the id, it performs that task by gaining control over the demands of the instincts, by deciding whether they shall be allowed to obtain satisfaction, by postponing that satisfaction to times and circumstances favorable in the external world or by suppressing their excitations completely. Its activities are governed by consideration of the tensions produced by stimuli within it or introduced into it. The raising of these tensions in general is felt as *unpleasure* and their lowering as pleasure [Freud, 1949, pp. 15–16].

Freud's view of ego can be seen, then, as centrally featuring nervous tensions produced by internal drives and by environmental threats. Both impinge on the ego.

For classical psychoanalysis, the intrapsychic impingements are sex and aggression; for behaviorism, they are at first the physiological drives of the baby, such as hunger and thirst, but eventually secondary motivations are derived. Both theories hold similar views that social impingements work to socialize the infant's original primitive state. Also common to both theories is the supposition that the lowering of these tensions is experienced as pleasure and their raising is experienced as unpleasure, as Freud states in the preceding quotation.

Freud essentially describes the nature of the ego's activity in responding to external and internal events as a matter of traffic control. The ego becomes aware of external stimuli, stores up memories about them, avoids their excess, adapts to moderate stimuli, and responds to the external world by modifying it when it can. In regard to internal events, the ego controls the instincts by permitting some to have satisfaction, and postponing or suppressing others. This description is not unlike the concepts of mediation that behaviorists adopted after they gave up their earlier, ultrapositivist commitments. Thus for both systems the ego is rather like a computer that controls traffic flow at an intersection without contributing to it in any way.

The contents of the intrapsychic stimuli, which are particularly important from the psychoanalytic view, are the direct representations or later derivations of sex, aggression, and the recently added, motive of competence (White, 1963). From the behaviorists' view, the contents are, first, representations of the primary drives and, later, their secondary derivatives. All in all, the ego is essentially a buffer state, and all its activities are directed toward self-preservation. As Freud (1960) analogized about the ego: If a rider is not to be parted from his horse, he is often obliged to guide the horse where the horse wants to go. Thus it is with the ego, which transforms the id's will (or for the behaviorists, more importantly society's will) into action, and the ego is only deluded in thinking the will is its own.

The widely held view of maturity for this formulation of ego is that of efficient, smooth control, which can only occur, however, after the ego has acquired a sufficient memory bank to do an effective job of associating stimuli with memories of previous responses that reduce tension. From the neobehaviorists' position, proper reinforcement works to produce the same efficient associations of new stimulus with prior response.

Later on various elaborations of ego as state were made so that more positive ego activities could be included in the account. Although the overall purpose of self-preservation was retained as the primary intent, the two major qualifications of the original definition have (1) added some form of self-expression to the fundamental idea of self-preservation (e.g., White's [1963] competence, or postulates representing constitutional capabilities, such as Hartmann's [1964] primary autonomy of the ego, that included memory, perception, intelligence), or (2) made provisions for self-expression to be drawn out of self-preservation at some late date in the developmental course by transforming the original intentions of self-preservation vis-à-vis instinctual and social pressures into ones of self-expression (e.g., Hartmann and Kris's [1945] secondary autonomy of the conflict-free ego sphere developed through eventual neutralization of the instincts). Whichever method the latter-day theorists used to expand the original view of ego, all agreed that the self-preservation invariably preempts self-expression.

Freud's Second View of Ego

Freud and the Freudians sometimes recognize ego as a kind of processing. Processes are more often emphasized in discussions of the therapeutic exchange, and states, in discussions of metatheory. When analysts act as therapists, their patients usually cause them to attend to, understand, use, and interpret the process aspects of ego. To paraphrase Erikson (1950), the doctor often goes beyond the scientist. Freud described in another part of the same text, already cited as evidence for his view of ego as state, the following process view:

> Its *constructive* function consists in interposing, between the demand made by instinct and the action that satisfied it, an intellective activity which, after considering the present state of things and weighing up earlier experiences, endeavors by means of experimental action to calculate the consequences of the proposed line of conduct [Freud, 1949, p. 110, emphasis added].

Thus Freud held at least two views of ego: as a buffer or mediating state and as a process that assimilates information and works toward novel, "experimental" actions and solutions. In recent psychoanalytic discussion these two disparate views have been regarded as evidence of Freud's ambivalence about whether the ego was subservient or autonomous (see Holt, 1967, for an extended discussion of Freud's various views of ego). This dichotomy does not completely or precisely express the distinction between the formulations of ego as state and ego as processes. More complicated contrasts are also involved—not only mechanical versus constructivist, but also arational versus rational, unorganized versus organized, solid versus mobile, regulated versus self-regulated. Perhaps all of the second terms—constructivists, rational, organized, mobile, and self-regulated—could be thought to add up to autonomy, but I think they do not, particularly when the psychoanalytic meaning of antonomy is examined. The core idea is that the ego can become only relatively but never completely free from the drives of the id and the tyranny of the superego, the representative of society's demands. These freedoms from the id and the superego do not tell the entire story of nondefensive functioning.

Formulations of the Positive Ego and Its Development

The view of ego as reacting, rather than initiating, has been a deterrent to psychoanalysts' understandable ambitions to make the system a general theory of behavior. Consequently various attempts have been made, as was briefly noted above, to repair the theory by adding more positive characteristics or by postulating that such characteristics appear at later points in development as precipitates of successfully resolved id—reality conflicts, particularly the oedipal.

Erikson's (1950) "ego victories" have appeared to be an exception, since they are integral to his developmental description of each stage's resolution and occur even with the earliest, preoedipal stages. However under careful scrutiny, this proposal does not revise the theory since the victories actually combine the two reform methods of extending or adding to the theory. Erikson added the positive achievements to particular negative consequences that were already stipulated by the analytic theory as occurring when particular stages of psychosexual development were not resolved. He extends the theory, as Hartmann (1958) had, by drawing the victories out of the stage resolutions, a method that can be warranted only to the extent that the stages exist and develop in the manner suggested. Thus Erikson merely points to a series of smaller id—reality resolutions that occur throughout life, which, if successfully negotiated, free energy. Erikson revises analytic theory more with his account of ego identity as the core and emergent achievement. As he commented, "The study of identity becomes as strategic in our time as the study of sexuality was in Freud's time [1950, pp. 282–283]." It is difficult, however, to analyze the meaning of ego identity because Erikson has more often been the proponent for youth than the rigorous theoretician. How the emergence of an identity can occur without granting constructivist powers to the ego is not clear. In any event, none of his proposals has put the core postulates about the instincts or the morally coercive role of society in jeopardy. All changes are reforms and within the confines of the basic structure of analytic theory.

The classical, and still not challenged, view of development, as explicated by both Sigmund and Anna Freud, was organized around a central idea: The ego is originally part of the id, and it develops as external influences curtail the id and result in the reality principle being substituted for the pleasure principle. As Anna Freud (1937) had commented, it is instinctual dangers that make human beings intelligent. Moreover, the id is never finally or permanently curtailed, so that the ego must maintain a constant vigil lest the id's wishes reassert themselves. Thus the central developmental question in the Freudian view of the ego is clearly that of effective control. As Freud said in *The ego and the id* (1923), the ego develops from perceiving to controlling and from obeying to inhibiting.

In the same volume Freud advanced a basic idea that later theoreticians carried further: Ego development involves desexualization, which permits the libidinal energies to be sublimated, that is, redirected toward other, more positive, aims. This stipulation has provided the foundation for the later psychoanalytic formulation that the positive ego arises from the negative ego. Hartmann (1958) elaborated this construct of energy transformation by proposing that both aggression and sex are neutralized, thereby freeing both kinds of energies, which are originally conflict-bound. Hartmann accompanied this postulate of "the secondary autonomy of the conflict-free sphere" with a second proposal: Not only could the ego achieve secondary, later autonomy from the instincts, but there must also be other aspects of the ego that enjoy primary autonomy. He suggested that perception, memory, and constitutional givens were examples of primary autonomy. He did not go on to elaborate or specify how these abilities were to fit in the context of the ego that he had already described as being critically oriented to id—reality conflicts. Questions arise as to interrelations and priorities: Do the primary autonomies fit into the secondary or do the secondary fit into the primary autonomies? To give an adequate account of the primary autonomies—their taxonomy, organization, development, and functioning—would be to answer the central questions of modern developmental psychology. Note that the Piagetian theory is almost entirely concerned with the constructs that Hartmann called primary autonomy. Hartmann never elaborated his proposal in any detail. If he had, psychoanalytic theory would have had to be radically revised in several ways, since the primacy of the instinctual conflicts would have been brought into serious question.

Primary autonomy interests Holt (1967), and he encourages the study of mnemic and perceptual factors at the physiological level to understand how the ego functions are related. As he says, the issue concerns the freedoms to *do*, as opposed to the freedoms *from* instinctual dangers. However this enterprise can only move as far as the understandings achieved by general biopsychology will permit. There are great and complex problems that psychology must solve for itself before a marriage with physiology can be contemplated. As it is now, the primary and secondary autonomies remain the central, although not highly articulated, explanations of the positive ego, which extend psychoanalytic theory by drawing further implications from already existing postulates.

White's (1963) motive of effectance as an "independent ego energy," which leads to the state of competence, is a prime example of adding another element to psychoanalytic theory while leaving it intact. In fact, White observed that his addition of this third energy to the drives of sex and aggression opposed Hartmann's postulates of energy transformations. Since effectance provides an explanation of positive ego functioning in itself, there would be no clear need to postulate the more convoluted development of the ego's secondary autonomy within a conflict-free ego sphere. Competence will be discussed in considerable detail in the next chapter because its stipulations of a positive motive of effectance (or curiosity, exploration, manipulation, etc.) and its description of ego as a state well represent the mainstream of contemporary personality research. Here we will note only that White is clear that the traditional instincts can preempt effectance at any time; effectance is a "gentle" motive and operates only in the child's "spare time." The mechanisms or processes for competence's expression are not spelled out, but its development is described as depending on successive experiences of mastery. Thus White's idea of ego is more than a matter of effective control; the positive ego is also competent.

The last psychoanalytically oriented proposal of positive ego development we will consider here is Loevinger's (1966a,b, 1973a,b), which is described in several theoretical papers but is more concretely represented by a sentence completion test that measures her conceptualization of ego development. As she says, "The case for my conception of ego development rests on rigor with respect to measuring operations [1973a, p. 16]." Although Loevinger has eschewed discussion of the positive ego, the higher stages of her system do represent more mature ego development. The descriptions of the lower stages, such as impulse-ridden, opportunistic, and conformist, are not positive in their connotations, while the fifth stage of autonomy is described as "coping with inner conflict and toleration of differences," and the integrated sixth stage as "reconciling inner conflicts and renunciation of the unattainable [1966a, p. 198]." Loevinger posits a universal sequence of ego development, specifically with respect to the longitudinal tasks of achieving impulse control and character development, as the fundamental means of achieving maturity. Individual differences are generated by people's varying stage achievements. The specific vehicle of ego development is described in a theoretical paper (1966a) as mastery through the reversal of voice—one is controlled, so one wants to control. Thus intrapersonal schemas come to duplicate commonly experienced interpersonal schemata, and we can conclude that social elements must play a crucial role in development of the positive ego through such conceptualizations as modeling and identification with the powerful or the aggressor. Loevinger observes that the ontogeny of sex drives was a major psychoanalytic contribution and that only a slight shift in point of view is needed to reveal ego development as an analogue, one concerned with the development and articulation of aggression. Altogether, Loevinger appears not to have revised psychoanalytic theory, but instead to have put extra emphasis on aggressivity and its vicissitudes as the mover of men and women.

Piaget's View of Ego

The word *ego* is not one that Piaget uses with frequency, and when he does, he seems to be referring to the "self" in two general but related senses: being aware of one's self and the self as a center of activity. In one of his earliest works, *The child's conception of physical causality* (1960), "ego," "I," and "self" are indexed as a single item. Later, in *Play, dreams and imitation* (1962), he refers to the ego's lack of awareness during infancy and sleep. He frequently uses "ego" as he writes of the various occasions of decentering that conclude infantile adualism as well as later egocentricisms, for example, the experience of coming to know one's self (in different ways at different levels), as one among many selves and as an object among objects. There is no advantage to be gained by hunting further for Piaget's idea of ego in his specific uses of the word. From his general position a conceptualization of ego directly follows: Rather than a state of personal being, the Piagetian ego would have to be a constructivist organization of processes that includes the intellective structures and their operations, the affective schemas, the social schemas, and more.

Some of Piaget's (1962) thoughts about the Freudian view of ego are made clear in the only elaborated criticisms—as far as I know—he made of psychoanalysis. He observes that the Freudian genetic psychology, despite its billing, is actually more a psychology of permanence than it is one of development and construction (hence its consistency, noted previously here, with the concept of ego as state). Piaget notes that Freudian theory posits: (1) permanent rather than reconstructed memories; and (2) the "lighting up of early and permanent associations," instead of the "constitution of thought which is the real constructive activity [1962, p. 189]." At the same time, or at least in this exposition, Piaget does not seem, entirely, to understand the Freudian central and potentially constructivist concept, that of defense. Although he observes that Freud's idea of repression is clear and important, he asks, in regard to censorship, which is a broad term for a kind of defensiveness, how can "consciousness be the cause of ignorance? [1962, p. 191]" When the defenses are regarded as constructivist in nature, we see that achieving conscious ignorance of many phenomena of the self and others is the precise intent of defending one's self. Erikson (1950), noted the inventiveness of defensiveness when he spoke of "the ego's tricky methods of overcoming feelings of anxiety and guilt [p. 151]."

Whatever the case, Piaget noted, it is a pity that the Freudians had little interest in intellective activity, which is for him, of course, the central question that we must address before we can understand man. I try in this volume, starting in Chapter 4, which is concerned with ego processes, to reorganize the essential implications of defense to make them compatible with the Piagetian account of constructivist, intellective activity. However central, even a complete description of intelligence cannot tell the whole story of personality. To accomplish this task, the Piagetian account will have to be extended and in some ways revised, and parts of the Freudian theory that make it too undifferentiatedly a psychology of permanence will have to be discarded or revised. If Piaget had decided to define ego—a task he would not set for himself, but one he would probably not reject as futile—its elements would surely be described as processes which are thoroughly constructivist.

3. Conceptualizations of Ego: State and Entity

Most conceptualizations regard the ego (or the intrapsyche) as a state, a predication that imparts solidity, content, and stasis to the construct. Some positions move even further toward thingness and refer to ego as if it were a material, substantive entity. Psychoanalysts sometimes speak of "the ego" and psychologists of "types" in this way. In a more differentiated, attenuated sense of psychological "thingness" there may be solid, durable ego structures, but with close scrutiny it appears that the commonly understood meanings of ego do not include the same properties as are included in structures, that is, wholeness, self-regulation, and capabilities of being transformed (Piaget, 1970). Definitive answers in this regard must await the eventual construction of a substantiated taxonomy of the mind, but an argument that ego structures per se likely do not exist is developed in detail in the next chapter.

Whatever the case, neither a general definition of ego nor that of ego as a state is clear or well established. Constructs of the same general meanings as ego go by other names, and the term ego is used for meanings some would reject as representing ego. In the midst of this state of confusion we will first describe Robert White's (1963) *competence*—an independent ego energy—as a widely accepted example of ego as state. Since all theories of personality are partial models at the present time, they have different limitations in representing the lively reality of people's personalities; consequently, the inherent constraints upon conceptualizations of ego states will be analyzed next. Following this explication, states of ego are considered with respect to six controversial issues that separate various theories from one another: the view of personal man as a mechanical or constructivist being, the role of rational and irrational processes, the centrality or dispersedness of personality organization, the means of personality growth as accumulation or development, and as either continuous or potentially discontinuous, and finally, the nature of personality description across time and situations. The same general plan of presentation will be followed in the analyses of ego processes which are considered in the next chapter.

Competence as an Example of Ego State

Competence appears to be a state. To quote White (1963), "It is an existing capability to interact with the environment that is largely the consequence of learning [p. 39]." If competence is such a capacity, it is reasonable to expect that it should be reliably manifested across many situations. In that case it can be measured, if and when it is activated. White logically suggests that there should be differences among people in the quantity and quality of their competencies and the speed of their presentations. If adult people differ in the various kinds of competency, an inventory of parts is a reasonable next move for the system builder to make. White (1963) suggests that social competency may be the most important kind, thereby hinting at a hierarchy of competencies; however he specifically excludes from competence the most intimate social interactions, such as having a sexual relation, loving children, or cherishing friends.

Since proposals of ego states lead to stipulations of what parts and how much of the state exists, developmental propositions that account for the sufficiencies or deficiencies in the achievement of the state easily follow. Competence is thought to be established by repetitive, clear experiences with mastery. This supposition has several implications. Since infants have not had extensive opportunities to learn, and no account of structural development is included, it follows that babies are necessarily incompetent. The lack of competence in adults—a pathological manifestation—must result from some deficiencies in the accumulation of these mastery experiences or in the ways they are stored. Thus incompetence is defined, in essence, as an insufficient acquisition of the capacity. Anxiety is brought into the account as a disturbing, preempting factor and therefore as a deterrent to the development and expression of competence. Anxiety is also viewed quantitatively—too much anxiety takes up the spare time activity that is necessary to build competence.

Since an achieved state is not imbued with movement itself, a separate means is required for its activation; otherwise the state can only await its stimuli. Alongside the classical Freudian instincts of sex and aggression, White places the independent ego energy, the motive effectance, as the prime mover of competence. Effectance is thought to be intrinsic, like sex and aggression, and to move the person toward stimulus seeking, while sex and aggression produce tension that must be reduced. Altogether, competence is a pale force as far as Freudian theory goes, since it is an ego rather than an id energy. Nevertheless, it is a motive and the necessary means for the learning and the activating competence.

Logical Constraints of Ego as State

This oversimplified and therefore inevitably unfair description of competence as an achieved ego state still provides a sufficient basis to consider the constraints exerted by such conceptualizations, whether they be competence, internal locus of control, or psychological health. We can ask:

1. Could there be *too much* of this capability? What is to prevent this waiting capacity from being applied too strenuously or inopportunely once it is activated? For instance, are people authentically loved when they are loved competently? Can one die competently, or is it grace that is needed?

2. Does anxiety invariably rule out competent solutions? Do not people sometimes arrive at viable solutions to situations and to lifetimes even though they may be beside themselves with anxiety? Are anxiety and competence actually reciprocal to each other?

3. Is ego always about mastery, or is it sometimes about nonmastery? Is the latter always pathological, or is it not sometimes rational and logical to lose and be mastered?

4. Is pathology always a deficiency, or can it sometimes be an elegant, complex, creative solution to an impossible set of circumstances?

5. How are transformations of functioning to be formulated? An achieved state suggests that behavior has a well-established, clear direction. How are radical re-routings, new organizations, or even manifestations contrary to previous habitual behavior to be explained? From whence do they come?

6. How are we to decide on the criteria of an achieved state across age groups, cultures, sexes, and situations and within heterogeneous societies, since difficult conditions determine different states? For instance, are women and men competent in the same ways? Or are we to posit as many achieved states as there are homogeneous groups of people in identical circumstances and situations?

7. Does the assumption that achieved states are activated by drive to reduce tension or to seek stimuli provide a sufficient description of the reasons for choice and action? Are not people sometimes rationally motivated to achieve elegant, or even just viable, solutions to their situations?

Neomechanical Personal Man

Most prior investigations of ego are dependent, whether this is recognized or not, upon Freudian and behavioristic notions of learned and achieved states resident within the person and activated by drive. Most neobehaviorists expect that states become manifest directly on stimulation without any intervening finesse or ado. Although the psychoanalytic position essentially agrees with this view of activation, it does not expect that drives are directly presented, because defense mechanisms are expected to intervene and stop, detour, or delay the expression of impulse. In psychological thought there have probably been three progenitors to the idea of ego as an achieved capacity: both the Freudian and the behaviorists' ideas of character and habit formations, Freud's division of psychological space into the substantialist entities of id, ego, and superego, and the machine as an apparatus that works only when some form of energy is delivered to it. Personality came thereby to be considered a conglomerate of achieved states that await drive and appropriate environmental stimuli, not only for their activation, but also for their development. Movement is achieved by the energies of external stimuli and internal physiological necessities. Altogether this view of the person is, in its essence, a mechanical one. People are made of different, workable parts that are quiescent in all important ways until energy is applied. Responses are directly set off along known pathways in accordance with a chain of events that produce known and predictable outcomes. Since people, but not machines, grow more efficient with practice, an explanation of the state's development immediately follows: People develop the state by practicing the behavior that it is.

Even Erikson has not escaped the interpretation that his eight stages are achieved states. He expresses a concern in a footnote, added to the second edition of *Childhood and society* (1963), that his eight stages of man have been misunderstood and misused, and he wants to absolve them of the "taint" of being regarded as achievements. However one might want to be persuaded by his attempt, it is hard to be convinced because his main account still gives the prime role to accruing ego victories, and no explicit analysis of the role of processes in personality development and functioning is made. Erikson does suggest obliquely that processes are represented in the interplay between the positive and negative aspects of each stage and more generally in the paradoxes, the tragic potentials, and eventual decay of each human life. To quote him directly:

> Some writers are so intent on making an *achievement scale* out of these states that they blithely omit all the "negative" sense (basic mistrust, etc.) which are and remain the dynamic counterpart of the 'positive' ones throughout life. The assumption that on each stage of a goodness is achieved which is impervious to new inner conflicts and to changing conditions is, I believe, a projection on child development of that success ideology which can so dangerously pervade our private and public daydreams and can make us inept in a heightened struggle for a meaningful existence in a new, industrial era of history. The personality is engaged with the hazards of existence continuously, even as the body's metabolism copes with decay. As we come to diagnose a state of relative strength and the symptoms of an impaired one, we face only more clearly the paradoxes and tragic potentials of human life.
>
> The stripping of the stages of everything but their "achievements" has its counterpart in attempts to describe or test them as "traits" or "aspiration" without first building a systematic bridge between the conception advanced throughout this book and the favorite concepts of other investigators. If the foregoing sounds somewhat plaintive, it is not intended to gloss over the fact that in giving to these strengths the very designations by which in the past they have acquired countless connotations of superficial goodness, affected niceness, and all too strenuous virtue, I invited misunderstandings and misuses.

However, I believe that there is an intrinsic relationship between ego and language and that despite passing vicissitudes certain basic words retain essential meanings [pp. 273–274].

Clearly many theorists do not subscribe to the strong version of personality as mechanically run—certainly Erikson does not, but there is probably no way to rise above the stasis implied by achieved states unless *direct* representations of functions and organizations are part of the model.

The conceptualization of stages could, conceivably, make the developmental account of states less mechanistic. At a minimum some systematic, self-instigated actions and transformations of being, although not necessarily wholeness, are implied by stage developments. If stages of various personality states could be identified, we would then need to know the rules of their coming into being and how each stage is subsequently changed or transformed into the next. In other words, we would need to identify the particular processes and structures typical of each stage as well as the history of their development and their relationships. However, if we knew all these facts, it seems likely that we would not be using the concept of states anymore. In any event, Erikson has not provided this detail, and to date neither has the theory of ego stages proposed by Loevinger, Wessler, and Redmore (1970).

Here, the construct of stage is used precisely to mean a homogeneous, structural, and functional whole that importantly defines the way that the person interacts with the world at any one time period. A stage should bear a logical relationship to the previous one—having been constructed and transformed out of it—and to the subsequent one, since the current stage is the ground for the development of the next. The organism—environment transactions critical to these kinds of developments must necessarily be quite systematic and orderly to account for stage evolutions to describe people in general. We have no biological evidence that there are anything like oral or anal drives or that any drives exert their force with sufficient regularity to account for stage development. Moreover, environments, in and of themselves, are far too unreliable to account for stage progressions.

Role of Rational Choice

Ego as achieved state encourages the view that manifestations of ego capacity will occur when activated, without interference from the person's rational intentions and constructions. Thus, conceptualizations of personality as existing capacity lean toward a conceptualization of the person as nonintellective and nonchoosing. He is the creature of his learned capabilities, which result from the effects of early experiences, according to psychoanalysis, and from the history of his reinforcements, according to the neobehaviorists.

This position is held by many who personally do not want to deny the validity of rational, intelligent choices. Thus, they require a citadel for the individual determinations of private man. Since a learned capacity does not easily accommodate to the idea of on-the-spot, individual choices, the citadel must be found elsewhere. Individual biological propensities provide such a refuge—ego energy level, intellective inheritance, perceptual style, speed of reaction, temperament, and so forth. Lionel Trilling's widely quoted little book, *Freud and the crisis of our culture* (1955), which was originally the Freud anniversary lecture delivered to the New York Psychoanalytic Institute and Society, served to reassure psychoanalysis that the biological self was the ultimate and obdurate refuge of individuality for citizens in a mass society. When Lois Murphy (1962) faced the problem of "good" functioning in *The widening world of childhood: paths to mastery,* she also ascribed various children's strengths to individual constitutional factors. Skinner's (1971) *Beyond freedom and dignity* allots rational choice to the biologically capable so that the many may enjoy happiness. A more complex positivist solution is proffered by Lefcourt (1973) who said, "while freedom and control are illusions, inventions of man to make sense of his experience, they do have consequences [p. 417]."

The confusions produced by the nonintellective ramifications of ego as learned state are well illustrated by White's discussion of the mother's reaction to the growth of the baby's competence. The baby's effectance urges him away from being mothered; however, the competent mother is activated to mother (as a manifestation of her state of competence), so that her state conflicts with the baby's state. Consistent with psychoanalysis' views of person's arationality, White deduces that the mother's encouragement of her baby's independence must be done with "a divided heart" (except in pathological cases where the mother dislikes her nurturing role). Clearly the underlying premise concerns the existing state of the mother's heart, not her head. She is thereby depicted as a person who mindlessly expresses her state rather than one who constructs solutions in terms of rational, empathetic considerations about her child and their mutual situation.

An interesting analogue to this line of reasoning has recently been the subject of discourse in the developmental literature. Children have been identified as being reflective, impulsive, or hyperactive. A dimensionalized state of maternal intrusiveness along with possible biological determinations are thought to be implicated in these behaviors. However, Campbell (1973) has recently shown that the behaviors of the mothers of all three kinds of children were mostly explained by (1) the nature of the tasks the children were performing in their mothers' presence and (2) the actual difficulties the children were having. In other words, the mothers reacted rationally and realistically to their children's situations instead of naively overriding the children's circumstances with their own personally driven states.

The limitations of ego as an achieved state will likely be better understood as soon as psychologists take full account of the significance that their investigatory situations have for subjects' sensibilities. The current national political concern with respect to the protection of human subjects may unexpectedly yield this substantive gain by encouraging investigators to consider their subjects' views of the situations of data collection more carefully. As Berlyne (1960) noted in the first sentence of *Conflict arousal and curiosity,* it has been a misfortune for psychology that human beings in experimental situations have been so obliging and compliant.

Hierarchy and Organization

The prediction of states has led to inventories of their various kinds and assessments of their differing strengths, but not directly to interest in personality organization. As a result, it is not clear how the person comes together as a unitary being at any one time or across his life span, even though we can argue that the understanding of personal integration would seem to be a special mission of a theory of personality. The main obstacle to formulating an organization is that states are thought to be determined and developed entirely by external forces—drives and the environment—which are inherently unorganized and far from unitary in their impact. As a consequence, neither can be counted on to provide systematic organization, and of course, little importance is given to the mind. Behaviorists expect that various environmental forces, such as parents, organize and unify the child's character, but so far no one has demonstrated that experience or parents are that orderly.

Making the understanding of organization even more difficult is the number of different states identified by inventive, energetic personality researchers. Although the number seems infinite, the intercorrelation among some segments of variables must be high. Since the conceptualization of state includes the expectancy that it emits reliable responses (rather than *constructs* reactions), measurement of strength is made easy and efficient by the means of personality inventories. A strong state is presumed to emit many scorable answers to the array of questions. Given the unity of people, their needs to maintain consistent views of themselves, and the standardization of testing situations (possibly as important as the standardization of the test), reasonable validity is frequently found. However we are not always clear about what is being measured validly, for example, the willingness to report anxiety in a test situation, or the state of anxiety itself, or both. One of the probable reasons that personologists continue to propose constructs of states is that they can be efficiently measured—clearly not a rational reason for advancing one scientific conceptualization over another (Rawls, 1971).

In any case, precision in measurement does not elucidate an organizational hierarchy of various states. The beginnings of a hierarchy could be had by actually demonstrating differential universal strengths of various substates. Personality inventories cannot provide that kind of information since assumptions that different states are measured in equal strengths are hard to meet. Questions must inevitably be couched in terms of contents, and there is an unknown universe of possible contents that might be emitted by each state. Furthermore, test responses are what people choose to report about the state; they do not directly represent the responses emitted by the state. In important ways, tests of states intervene between subject and investigator.

Another aspect of measurement helps defeat the goal of constructing hierarchical organizations, especially when valued or disvalued states are considered, which they surely must be if personality theory is to be viable. Measurement of some attributes, like achievement or intelligence, does not include these difficulties because there is greater clarity about the dimensions of growth. If having the state in great strength is "good" then having it in little strength must be "bad" (or vice versa with the disvalued state). However, as we asked earlier in "Logical Constraints of Ego as State," is it possible to have too much of a good thing like competence, self-control, or responsibility? Moreover, a canny test constructor tries to design scales, for obvious statistical advantages, that have normal distributions with few high and low scores and many scores in the middle range. This pattern of scores well fits the supposition that states have varying strengths. At the same time, it includes the corollary assumption that people's strengths and weaknesses lie on the same dimension. (This may not be plausible; the ego process formulation considered in this work is based on the assumption that it is not.) Whatever the case, people with "good" or "bad" scores will be few in number, so their organization, if it were known, might be quite esoteric and deviant. Moreover there are problems in understanding the numerous people with middle range scores: (1) Is their characterization to be a truly middling one (e.g., they are neither competent nor incompetent); (2) could some of the sample possess extreme tendencies, representing both ends of the continuum, that cancel each other out in the test response (e.g., they are competent in some content areas but incompetent in others); (3) is it possible that the state being measured is a matter of indifference to some people and that they respond to the necessity of answering first one way and then another? Altogether, the precision of measurement offered by personality inventories seems to be a snare and a delusion that has kept personologists from addressing the reality of their subjects in relationship to the constructs, an activity that might lead to questions of organization, if, in fact, man is a reasonably organized being.

A degree of organization might be introduced into theories of states if the means of activation—the drives, motives, or energy—were one instead of several. In reviewing White's (1963) study of competence, Holt (1964) wondered why White had not delivered the coup de grace to psychoanalytic instinct theory by positing only one master, independent ego energy, since he came close to doing so. As Holt observes, this step would have moved the theory closer to a unitary organization and made the energetics of psychoanalytic theory more nearly compatible with the understandings of modern biology. However White's avoidance of this step was probably solidly grounded in his theoretical position, since the idea of one energy is not only incompatible with psychoanalytic instinct theory but, more to the point here, incompatible with a view of personality as a topography of internal, separately acting entities, like ego, id, and superego, or as a conglomerate of states, like needs achievement, affiliation, approval, and so on. A single biological energy in itself could not be expected to activate the person in such divergent sectors and with such different manifestations without proposing additional constructs, such as an active, constructivist ego to bring about organization. White did not take this step, and he made it clear that he needed both id and ego energies. The stipulation of a single energy that serves to arouse separate, achieved states would begin to suggest a unitary being, but additions would be necessary to solve the problems of hierarchial organization of psychological elements.

Modern biology is clear that there is only one energy, and so it must be regarded as a a given; consequently its nature is not a central problem for psychology. Psychological questions more appropriately concern not the energy itself but the ways energy is deployed by the minds of men. When energy is regarded as an inherent expression of life in motion, detailed questions concerning its operation become the concerns of biologists, and personologists can refocus on the psychological enterprises of describing man's developments and organizations, given the energy. An understanding of the hierarchial organization of unitary man hopefully can flow from this effort, but separate energies exerting their force within separate principalities probably can never organizationally be more than a distressed bureaucracy without a flowchart. All that is required from a psychology of meaning systems, which the field of personality must preeminently be if any part of psychology is at all, is that its postulates not violate biological understanding. In the light of the present knowledge of alternative functional systems, redundancies, feedback loops, the operation of the reticular formation, and the like, it is difficult to think of a brain model that would be consistent with the representations of the ego as state and entity.

Some of psychology's most trying conundrums disappear when we recognize a single energy and move on to analyze the implications for psychology. It becomes possible (1) to dispense with questions of the activation of separate and sometimes contradictory energies, (2) to abandon the specter of separately operated capacities that await their signals to perform, and (3) to transform motivational questions from ones concerning drives into ones of intents, plans, and strategies that are organized and implemented with cognitive, moral, social, and affective considerations.

The Question of Development

The fundamental and central question of development from the psychoanalytic and behaviorist points of view is the acquisition of sufficient self-control vis-à-vis internal demand and social inhibition. The issue rests on the premises (1) that the state of the young is positively uncivil (not simply inexperienced or untutored) because of their instincts of sex and aggression and their primitive drives of hunger, thirst, pain avoidance, and so on, and (2) that the inherent needs and motives of societies make the young's uncivil state intolerable, so that social collectivities exhort the young to acquire control. In a nutshell, the reality principle must be substituted for the baby's pleasure principle. As Colby (1955) commented in *Energy and structure in psychoanalysis,* "Inhibitory functions remain of central importance in our views [p. 66]."

Two statements made by Freud give the details of the ego's development of control and restriction as it confronts the reality principle. When these descriptions are stripped of their lively language, the construct of ego can be seen to be very near to the behaviorists' ideas concerning the acquisition of habit family hierarchies.

> The ego has taken over the task of representing the external world for the id, and so of saving it; for the id, blindly striving to gratify its instincts in complete disregard of the superior strength of outside forces, could not otherwise escape annihilation. In the fulfillment of this function, the ego has to observe the external world and preserve a true picture of it in the memory traces left by its perceptions, and, by means of the reality-test, it has to eliminate any element in this picture of the external world which is a contribution from internal sources of excitation. On behalf of the id, the ego controls the path of access to motility, but it interpolates between desire and action the procrastinating factor of thought, during which it makes use of the residues of experience stored up in memory [Freud, 1946, p. 106].

Thus we see that the ego develops from special experiences wherein the reality of the external world *modifies* the id's demands, new responses are substituted for old (conditioned responses), and stored memories which are residuals of previous experiences are used. Thought is viewed as a procrastinating factor, but it appears, not in the guise of reasoning, but instead closer to a concept of mediation between stimulus and response which is boosted by associated memories from the storehouse. A second statement of Freud's describes more of the social setting in which the ego operates and develops:

> Just as the id is directed exclusively to obtaining pleasure, so the ego is governed by considerations of safety.... It makes use of sensations of anxiety as a signal to give a warning of dangers threatening its integrity.... Thus the ego is fighting on two fronts: it has to defend its existence both against an external world that threatens it with annihilation and against an internal world that makes excessive demands [Freud, 1949, pp. 110–112].

Thus the ego acquires its strength by learning about the safety of the middle ground, since the id pressures for expression, but the external world threatens the ego if it accedes to the demands of the id. Through development, the Freudians contend, safety must eventually become more pleasurable and rewarding than primary pleasure itself (secondary motivation).

White's proposed independent ego energy of effectance tempered to a degree psychoanalysis' preoccupation with control. This was a noteworthy step since psychoanalysis needs an account of the development of positive, uninhibited actions to become a theory of general human behavior. However, effectance as a vehicle of development cannot carry much of this burden, since White himself defined it as a gentle, spare time motive. Thus the child's serious workaday efforts of growing up are still concerned with the critical problems of id and social control and inhibition.

A special interest of Erikson's, demonstrated in *Childhood and society* (1950) and in his later psychohistorical analyses of great men, is developmental histories that culminated in near emergent, personal-social integrations. In this way Erikson moves beyond psychoanalysis by adding a positive note to the system. Still he revises it more by the mood he assumes than by any structural revisions or modifications he makes of its developmental stipulations. For example, he says in *Gandhi's truth* (1969), "Instinct has become an embarrassing term . . . yet in psychoanalysis it is not expendable. . . . If one abandons the term altogether, however, one neglects the energetic and the driven aspect of man's behavior [p. 427]." Moreover, he continues to accept the central core of psychoanalysis' view of the ideal developmental resolution, "Psychoanalysis offers a method of intervening nonviolently between our overbearing conscience and our raging affects, thus forcing our moral and our 'animal' natures to enter into respected reconciliation [p. 439]."

There is a range of positions, then, within psychoanalysis with respect to the development of the ego: from the simplest, most mechanical view that development involves the imposition and acquisition of self-control to Erikson's description of the nearly positive and emergent ego identity, which still turns out to be based on a forced reconciliation between animal id and moral control.

The control required to effect the reconciliation of id and the moral world is not achieved overnight, and the child's compromises are often undifferentiated and only sporadically used. Nevertheless, the development and maintenance of control is basically a quantitative matter, so clinicians speak of states of ego strength and behaviorists of habit strength. The main thrust of development is toward some quantitatively optimal state of control; thus there can be too much as well as too little control. This formulation of the central issue of development does not actually need an underlying stage sequence for its explication, and the behaviorists do not propose one. However psychoanalytic theory proposes two: the classical psychosexual stages—oral, anal, phallic, and oedipal—which unfold in embryonic fashion, supposedly under the impact of maturing biological imperatives, and Erikson's eight psychosocial stages, which incorporate the psychosexual stages but add concern for society's expectancies vis-à-vis the child's psychological and biological maturing. Both of these stage formulations are only indirectly concerned with psychoanalysis' view of the main difference between the child and the man, namely the difference in the effectiveness of their control (as the id pressures of each stage are transformed or neutralized, control is expected to improve, but the exact mechanism is not clear). As Macklin (1972) notes in a philosophical examination, psychoanalysis is a mixed model theory since it uses concepts of different classes to explain the same phenomenon. Furthermore, both formulations of stages make it clear that reasonably "healthy" adults may also have psychosexual and psychosocial problems that typify the young, so that the contrast between child and adult is not defined by their differences in stage achievements either. Thus the psychosocial and psychosexual sequences do not fall within the present definition of structural stages, and we must conclude that they lack the power to demarcate the differences between the adult and the child.

The classical psychosexual stages were probably originally needed to underscore the theory's allegiance to biology, particularly in regard to the libidinal drives, and to describe at the same time a chain of interests that children go through as they discover their bodies. Erikson later drew his parallel psychosocial stage designations from the interpersonal characteristics that seem to typify psychiatric patients with problems centered around various psychosexual conflicts, for example, the oral question, "Will I be fed?" being seen as the emotional equivalent of "Can I trust?" Although these matters are of interest, it is not altogether certain whether they are associated with the main developmental thrust of achieving control by reconciling the warring forces of our animal and moral natures. Erikson does not directly treat the development of moral concerns, so that the morality of psychoanalysis remains, as it is for neobehaviorism, the internalization of social control. All analytic theorists agree that drives are universal givens; they are both class-fair and sex-fair and do not undergo psychological development themselves.

To strip Erikson's developmental accounts of their poetry, clinical insight, and humanity diminishes them unduly, but the issue is drawn to point out that conceptually the civil, rational, sensual, wise aspects of man must still be wrought developmentally by a series of reconciliations between warring forces, and that the main developmental thrust for Erikson is still that of control and compromise. The lack of concepts to describe the development of the "good" in man, except in the most convoluted, tortured terms, is undoubtedly related to the climate of ideas experienced by the early proponents of psychoanalysis and behaviorism. Since the science of the psyche was young and religious explanations of man were preeminent, early psychologists were most certainly concerned that they be scientists and not vitalists, wedded to the will-o'-the-wisp of men's minds, which seemed at the time to defy empirical study.

Discontinuity and Continuity in States

Existing, achieved states cannot be expected to shift their expression readily or markedly; they are learned, hard won, and finally accumulated usually over a considerable length of time; consequently theories involving ideas of states have difficulty in dealing with dynamic phenomena of change. Developmental investigators who work with constructs of states most often search for stabilities and avoid designs that address questions of change and transformation (see Kagan & Moss, 1962, for example). The psychoanalytic concepts that represent marked change are regarded as "mechanisms" that are primarily concerned with controlling the direction of instinctual expression—neutralization, sublimation, reaction formation, and turning the passively experienced into the actively expressed.

However as Holt (1964) and White (1963) moved near to criticizing instinct theory, both questioned whether energy radically shifts its direction, as these mechanisms and the Freudian metaphor of hydrodynamics suggested.[1] If these functions were banished from the system, however, it would be even more difficult for psychoanalysis to account for discontinuity in personality development and functioning. They provide one of the few ways that marked shifts can be described.

Although both Erikson's and Loevinger's theories of ego stages are about discontinuity, neither is specifically or directly concerned with these kinds of developmental transformations. Instead discontinuity is merely the by-product of moving from one stage (or state) to another. Since the stages are qualitatively different from one another, one could infer, ex post facto, that a marked change had occurred. Unlike the Piagetian system, neither theory provides the critical observations or rules of change whereby one stage is changed or dissolved and is replaced or transformed into the next. Moreover Erikson stipulates that the nuclear conflicts of each stage remain a problem if they are not resolved. The biological, psychosocial problems of the next unfolding stage make it necessary for the child to deal with the new tasks even though some of his energy is still bound up with the conflict of the previous stage. Thus there is movement to the next stage even though the problems of the prior ones remain, and some provision is made for developmental discontinuity.

Still personality theory needs conceptualizations to account for the garden-variety shifts observed in everyday life, such as the sudden "goodness" in naughty children, personality shifts during development, sharp improvement in psychotherapeutic patients, transference phenomena itself, and the sudden formation and disappearance of symptoms. How a state, as a capacity laboriously acquired, can be made to describe these fluidities is not clear; presumably change can only occur by the more tedious process of relearning.

Applicability across Time and Cultures

A good theory of personality is one that can aspire to the possibility of describing human enterprises across a diversity of personal and historical times and social-cultural locations. This does not mean that the role of external conditions must be diminished conceptually, but rather than such a personality theory should encompass the common forms of reaction to the fundamental elements of social interdependence that all people take into account in their maturing and their living. Needless to say, the achievement of this goal for personality theory is a long way

---

[1] Parenthetically, we should note that energy is never directly expressed in a raw form, since it must be first filtered through some kind of resolution or decision process. Neither Holt nor White took into account the power of ego processes to change the course of action. In the present view, sublimation, reaction formation, and likely neutralization are, carefully speaking, processes and functions, not mechanisms.

off, but the aim seems reasonable and proper and it seems to be a criterion to apply to proposed conceptualizations even at this primitive stage of understanding. By their nature, some constructs are more likely to stand the test of general applicability than others.

The content of people's behavior, which states are likely to represent, shows great variation across conditions—whether they drive a camel, a Ford, a Rolls Royce, a tricycle, or walk, or whether they wet nurse, breast feed, bottle feed, or cup feed their babies—still people's propensities to transport themselves and feed their babies are universal. Greater generality across time and culture is more likely achieved with conceptualizations of processes and structures. Piagetian investigation indicates that some of these forms represent people's universal understandings of the physical world, and possibly of the social world, in the case of moral structures (Kohlberg, 1969; Piaget, 1965). Thus we have some knowledge of the common structures of cognitive development, but we are clearly less certain about the identity or existence of social forms whereby men relate to each other and to their collectivities. The fundamental fact of human interdependency suggests that these too may be identifiable and limited in number.

When we come to intrapersonal personality structures and processes, we are still mystified. The early hypothesis of the unversality of the psychosexual stages has generally not found support in anthropological study. Erikson's and Loevinger's stages are meant to be general to mankind, but no empirical structural analyses have been done of them so the stages may each represent an intercorrelation of states, in other words, types. Self-evident in the Erikson scheme is movement toward greater self-differentiation and in the Loevinger scheme toward more effective and later refined self-control. According to Erikson the early stages, for instance trust versus mistrust, remain problems for man throughout his life course (and it would seem that the regulation of impulses would as well); consequently these stages cannot be structural in the present definition because they lack the properties of being irreversible, organized resolutions of knowing, which characterize the logical structures concerned with the physical world. To be trustful or nonimpulsive in all situations is clearly neither rational nor logical, but it is logical and necessary for all men to come to understand, for instance, the conservation of physical matter.

Another difficulty with achieved states is that they involve more content than form, so that culturally specific social valuations are involved in identifying a state's presence and strength. Since contents are also likely to be situationally specific, the number of possibly identifiable states must be great. Still another problem is raised when statements of comparative value are made between people in different situations. We could try to warrant logically the idea that all reasonable men would have to agree that it is better for a person to be competent than incompetent in whatever role his society assigns to him. The criterion, however, is still limited by social valuation—some ascribed roles in all societies are defined as inherently incompetent in one or more areas of social participation, for example, slaves, usually women, children. Surely we would not be impressed with the psychological effectiveness of one who performed his role of slave well. Moreover, as Erikson complains, the success ideology of this society results in most valued states being ones of achievement that must necessarily be supported by avid goal seeking. In contrast, others point out that it is meritorious to be able to know when one is sated and then to be able to stop (Kubie, 1958). Altogether then, it appears that conceptualizations of states are poor tools for the personologist who might want to make his theory descriptive of people across time and situations.

Summary of Arguments in Regard to Ego as State

Although most formulations of ego represent it as a state, arguments were made that these constructions are faulty. Ego states view man as mechanical, composed of disparate entities that await arousal by drive or external stimuli to perform, irrespective of their holder's rational choices or his situation. Various contents are introduced into the state by society's teachings and by the nature of different drives. The latter expectancy is incompatible with modern biology's understanding of the life processes, and the former is incompatible with psychology's increasing understanding of man's constructivist propensities. Dynamic movement and, therefore, the organization of ego states, is entirely due to the determination of forces outside the ego—id instincts in psychoanalytic theory and the pressures of environment in the behavioristic theory. Since instincts and environments are clearly not highly organized themselves, no clear or strong explanation for man's unitary functioning can be achieved with these provisions. All that can be done, without positing the greatest of mythologies that organization is entirely imposed on the ego states from the outside, is to assume differential strengths of various internal states, some being stronger than others. The assumption that states have quantitative strengths has led to numerous attempts to measure states, and socially valued and disvalued ends of continuums have been viewed as reciprocals of each other. Substantive arguments about whether this latter supposition faithfully models man was deferred to the next chapter. Several methodological difficulties at the empirical level were suggested; all seem to arise from the distance between the researcher and his subjects.

The contemporary expression and long-term development of states are essentially the same phenomena. In both instances there is activation by inner biology and/or environmental demand, and the ego states' response is reinforced from both sources to bring quantitative increments of ego or habit strength in either adult or child. The stasis and solidity of a state make dynamic, discontinuous actions or developments most difficult to explain. Change can only occur through the tedious processes of relearning. Such a view of man implies a complementary social psychology that portrays societies and adults as necessarily intolerant of the young and intent on shaping them. Consequently the most important ego habits that the young must acquire are those concerned with the control of the self. The argument was drawn further to illustrate that achieved states reflect the content of particular societies' values, so that they cannot reasonably be applied across situations and time except to persons in equivalent social roles and in identical social circumstances.

By way of summary, we should note that the conceptualization of personality as composed of states permeates much current psychological thinking of psycho-analysts, personologists, and developmentalists. In making the arguments in regard to states, distinctions among various points of view were often slighted. The intention here was to pursue the conceptualization of state wherever it was used, and not to review the theories themselves.

4. Conceptualizations of Ego: Processes, Functions, Regulations

The view of ego to be developed here is that it is exclusively processes, specifically the ceaseless acts of people assimilating new information about themselves and their environments and accommodating to these assimilations by constructing actions that attain and re-attain an unremitting series of dynamic equilibriums. Although this description of the ego's work will follow Piaget's account of cognitive development and functioning, it includes much more. Ego processes are directly involved with but are not the same as the subject matters that we usually call emotions, motivations, interpersonal and social reactions, and moral considerations. Ego actions can be variously regarded: in the broadest sense as *processes* to indicate the most general actions of moving forward or continuing on by assimilating and accommodating; in a more specific sense, as *functions* to refer to actions which are suited to particular conditions and occasions; in a different specific sense, as *regulations* to refer to actions that are especially involved in ordering emotions, impulses, and feelings.

The concept of *operations* is near to these ideas; however operations suggest that some specific principle is being carried out in practical application. For instance, in the Piagetian system, concrete operations are the practical applications of principles that represent concrete structures. Here the argument will later suggest that ego processes represent the person's general intent or principle of attaining and maintaining a consistent sense of self. But I will not use the word *operations* to refer to ego processes for two reasons: First, there are reasons to think that ego processes do not directly represent specific structural principles, a point that will be elaborated shortly; second, conceptual distinctions between what is ego and what is more properly the cognitive aspect of people's activities will need to be made, so that the term needs to be reserved to refer to matters that are more purely cognitive.

In accordance with the tenor of psychoanalytic theory, many use the term *mechanism*. However further clarification and development of the implications of processes will make it clear that there are vast differences between mechanisms and processes, functions, or regulations; the first term ascribes unbidden and routinized characteristics to the ego activities of people while the second set makes it possible to ascribe constructivist characteristics. The concept of mechanisms did give early personality theory some possibility of describing persons' movements. But as Mischel (1969) says, "generally, however, these processes have been viewed in dimensional and dispositional terms and quickly translated back to fit the consistency assumptions of traditional global trait and psychodynamic theory [pp. 1016–1017]." The implications of mechanisms better fit the constructs of ego states, which were described in the previous chapter. The idea of ego as processes will undergo considerable elaboration in this chapter, so we will let the preferred meaning grow with the explication rather than attempt any further definitions at this point.

Ego Processes: Coping, Defense, and Fragmentation

TAXONOMY

The model of ego processes described here first included coping and defense functions proposed by Haan (1963) and Kroeber (1963), and later elaboration (Haan, 1969) added ego fragmentations to the array. Its taxonomy is composed of 10 generic processes, each having 3 possible modes of expression—coping, defense, or fragmentation (see Table I for the organization of the array, Appendix A for a detailed manual for rating, and Appendix B for a listing of Q sort items representing the processes). The three modes of coping, defense, and fragmentation are distinguished one from another by a set of formal properties which are shown in Table II. Coping involves purpose, choice, and flexible shift, adheres to intersubjective reality and logic, and allows and enhances proportionate affective expression; defensiveness is compelled, negating, rigid, distorting of intersubjective reality and logic, allows covert impulse expression, and embodies the expectancy that anxiety can be relieved without directly addressing the problem; fragmentation is automated, ritualistic, privatistically formulated, affectively directed, and irrationally expressed in the sense that intersubjective reality is clearly violated. In effect, coping processes continue an open system, defenses produce particular closures of the system, and fragmentations signal temporary or more enduring dysfunctions that reject intersubjective realities that contradict important private formulations.

As an example of a generic process and its three modalities, the model is so structured that a coping function like *empathy,* a defense function like *projection,* and a fragmenting reaction like *delusional ideation,* comprise a trio with the

Table I
Taxonomy of Ego Processes

Generic processes	Coping	Defense	Fragmentation
		Cognitive functions	
1. Discrimination	Objectivity	Isolation	Concretism
2. Detachment	Intellectuality	Intellectualizing	Word salads, neologisms
3. Means–end symbolization	Logical analysis	Rationalization	Confabulation
		Reflexive-intraceptive functions	
4. Delayed response	Tolerance of ambiguity	Doubt	Immobilization
5. Sensitivity	Empathy	Projection	Delusional
6. Time reversion	Regression-ego	Regression	Decompensation
		Attention-focusing functions	
7. Selective awareness	Concentration	Denial	Distraction, fixation
		Affective-impulse regulations	
8. Diversion	Sublimation	Displacement	Affective preoccupation
9. Transformation	Substitution	Reaction formation	Unstable alternation
10. Restraint	Suppression	Repression	Depersonalization, amnesic

Modes

Table II
Properties of Ego Processes

Coping processes	Defense processes	Fragmentary processes
1. Appears to involve choice and is therefore flexible, purposive behavior.	1. Turns away from choice and is therefore rigid and channeled.	1. Appears repetitive, ritualistic, and automated.
2. Is pulled toward the future and takes account of the needs of the present.	2. Is pushed from the past.	2. Operates on assumptions which are privatistically based.
3. Oriented to the reality requirements of present situation.	3. Distorts aspects of present requirements.	3. Closes system and is non-responsive to present requirements.
4. Involves differentiated process thinking that integrates conscious and pre-conscious elements.	4. Involves undifferentiated thinking and includes elements that do not seem part of the situation.	4. Primarily and un-adulteratedly determined by affect needs.
5. Operates with the organism's necessity of "metering" the experiencing of disturbing affects.	5. Operates with assumption that it is possible to magically remove disturbing feelings.	5. Floods person with affect.
6. Allows various forms of affective satisfaction in open, ordered and tempered way.	6. Allows gratification by subterfuge.	6. Allows unmodulated gratification of some impulses.

quintessential, generic meaning of interpersonal *sensitivity,* that is, behavior that is attuned to formulating and understanding another's unexpressed or partially expressed thoughts and feelings, however accurately this might be done. These three modes of *sensitivity* may be distinguished one from another in terms of the properties shown in Table II.

The model and its taxonomy were designed with a number of considerations in mind. Kroeber and I thought there was clear need to represent the rational, logical, productive, wise, civil, loving, playful, and sensual aspects of people's ego actions. Such formulations needed to be more direct and parsimonious that various psychoanalytic concepts that had already been proposed to deal with such considerations, that is, (*1*) the convoluted and long road whereby id eventually becomes neutralized to produce the secondary autonomy of the conflict-free ego sphere (Hartmann, 1958); (*2*) other formulations whereby a "good" ego energy is added, but as a lesser power, to those representing the primitive id (White, 1963); (*3*) the necessity that the single ego mechanism of sublimation carry the entire burden of expressing civilized impulses (Fenichel, 1945); (*4*) the undeveloped notion of primary autonomy, which supposed that people's effectiveness was basically due to constitutional factors (Hartmann, 1958; Murphy, 1962).

Since all the classical definitions of the defenses included some element of negating intersubjective truth and reality, Kroeber and I reasoned that additional forms of ego actions, which do not negate truth and reality, were needed to describe human functioning. To illustrate, in the commonly used language of the clinic, the following denotations are made: isolation negates the logically indicated connecting relationships among things; intellectualization negates the same relationships, but more particularly the affective concomitants of cognitive propositions; rationalization negates the reality of a chain of causal events; doubt negates the person's necessities and capacities to make decisions; projection negates the person's own evaluation of himself; regression negates the reality of the person's age and time within his own life span; denial negates the perceptual reality of the person's present circumstances; displacement negates the object or the situation of his affective reactions; reaction formation negates his socially uncivil reactions; and repression negates the reality of his affective reactions by erasing their cognitive representations.

Despite clinicians' sensitivity to the distortions of reality and logic wrought by defensive functions, they seem to be reluctant to raise the questions about what ego functioning would be like if it were not defensive. A corollary question follows: does negation of intersubjective and intrasubjective reality and logic typify only the defensive functions of people seeking psychological help, or is it more widespread? The unsatisfying answer seems to be that the successfully analyzed become well defended, but patients and other people frequently negate reality and distort logic.

To deal with these problems, a short step was taken beyond the defensive processes. The coping functions were constructed in accordance with the assumption that the defenses represent just one *mode* or facet of generic processes that people use to solve their general problems of living. With this assumption in hand, the generic processes as well as their coping modes could be identified. Thus the defensive intents of the ten classical mechanisms lead by logical extension first to the identification of the generic and coping processes and later to the fragmenting functions, which were derived in the same manner and on the same grounds after these various clinical terms, often used to describe psychotics, were also seen to be processes (Haan, 1969).

Although coping-defense-fragmentation trios were constructed on the rational grounds just described, their intraassociation can be empirically examined. Alker (1967) studied the cooccurrence of defensive projection and coping empathy, as Powers and Alker (1968) did for coping suppression and defensive repression. Both studies lend support to the postulate that there are basic generic processes (in at least these instances), with either coping or defensive modes becoming manifest in immediate transactions.

The ego model is divided into four sectors according to functions that are primarily cognitive, reflexive-intraceptive, attention-focusing, or affective-impulse regulating. These divisions are conceptual conveniences, which cannot actually exist as pure forms given the psychological unity of the person. Obviously, cognition is always informed by affective reactions even at the purest of logical situations, just as affective reactions must be informed and represented by cognitive formulations and symbolizations. Still their separation represents a partial reality, and empirically attained results in various studies utilizing this model suggest that the distinctions are useful and practical.

The cognitive sector generally represents the active, outer-directed, instrumental aspects of man's problem-solving efforts and involves extensive extrapsychic accommodation. Three generic and general strategies are included: discrimination, detachment, and means–end symbolization. Conceivably all three can be brought to bear on any one problem, but people approach problems with different and preferred patterns of strategies. The generic affective regulations are also three in number and represent the supposition that when feelings and emotions are not directly and primitively expressed, which they almost never are except by the infant, they can only be accommodated by diversion, restraint, and transformation. The reflexive-intraceptive and attention-focusing sectors probably bear more explanation. None of the generic reflexive-intraceptive functions of delayed response, sensitivity, and time reversion represent people's activities as moving forward and intending to accomplish some end. Instead they reflect the person's assimilatory engagement with his own thoughts, feelings, and intuitions. Although the attention-focusing characteristics of concentration are probably self-evident, some clinicians may be surprised by the definition of denial as a process of focusing attention. However, careful analysis of denial will probably convince the reader that its ineffectiveness results from the person's selective focusing of attention rather than from some more efficient and complex means of negation. Denial is a way for the person to say, very simply, that a troublesome or unpleasant perception is not there, so that he need not take further action. He may focus instead on the pleasant side of the matter—the cloud's silver lining. Since nothing much is definitively changed by denial, either in the person's formulations or in his external situation, he may very well be plagued again if the problematic condition persists.

Most of the coping functions are represented by commonplace ideas (with the exception of substitution and regression in the service of the ego, or ego regression, as it will be called for short). All the defensive and fragmenting processes are well known to clinicians. However their individual meanings and arrangements need further emphasis. In the listing below the generic processes are generally defined, while various direct comments that might occur in a conversation are given for each of the individual processes. Affective regulations are not often represented by succinct verbal statements because they represent patterns of action, so general descriptions are given for these processes.

Cognitive functions

Discrimination: Separates idea from feeling, idea from idea, feeling from feeling

Objectivity:	*"I am of two minds about this problem."*
Isolation:	*"I can't see the forest for the trees."*
Tangential concretisms:	*"This tree is the only one; there is no forest."*

Detachment: Lets mind roam freely and irreverently, speculates, analyzes

Intellectuality:	*"My past economic insecurities have led me to a degree of petty stinginess."*
Intellectualizing:	*"My stinginess can be explained by my anal character."*
Neologisms, word salads:	*"An anality is the site of the parallel."*

Means–end symbolization: Analyzes causal texture of experiences and problems

Logical analysis:	*"Let's start at the beginning and figure out what happened."*
Rationalization:	*"I was trying at first, but then one thing after another happened."*
Confabulation:	*"The atmosphere spread and debilitated the family."*

Reflexive-intraceptive functions

Delayed response: Holds up decisions in complex, uncertain situations

Tolerance of ambiguity:	*"There are some matters that can't be resolved when you want them to be."*
Doubt:	*"It's the decisions that get me; I don't know what will happen if I choose to do it."*
Immobilization:	(under pressure from questioner) *"I just can't move."*

Sensitivity: Apprehends others' reactions and feelings

Empathy:	*"I think I know how you feel"* (second person agrees that first speaker does).
Projection:	*"Don't think I don't know what you have in mind"* (second person surprised and mildly guilty).
Delusional:	*"You'd be surprised if you knew what plan I have prepared for you"* (grandiosity).
	"You want to do me in; I can see it in your eyes" (persecution).

Time reversion: Recaptures and replays past experiences—cognitive, affective, social

Regression–ego:	*"Let's brainstorm this for a while."*
Regression:	*"I just can't deal with such situations; I'll just have to give up."*
Decompensation:	(Person acts out his helplessness, incompetency, harmlessness more than he speaks about it)

Selective awareness:

Attention-focusing functions

Concentration:
: *"I intend to work on this job now, and I'll worry about that later."*

Denial:
: *"Since every cloud has a silver lining, it's best to pay attention to that."*

Fixation, distraction:
: *"I listen only to the one true voice in the world"* (or person's attention flits from one intense matter to another).

Affective-impulse regulations

Diversion: Affectivity expressed in diverse ways and situations

Sublimation:
: Person expresses affectivity, both positive and negative, toward objects, people, and activities in relevant and understood ways

Displacement:
: Person displaces his affective reactions from the instigating situation to express them in another situation of greater safety, for example, taking it out on his dog, sexualizing children, animals, or great concern for a body part.

Preoccupation:
: Person reacts affectively and intensely to a random assortment of people, situations, and objects.

Transformation: Primitive affectivity transformed to more complicated forms

Substitution:
: Person appears to have thoroughly and comfortably transformed uncivil feelings into their socialized forms.

Reaction formation:
: Person's reactions are so socialized that they seem strained, excessive, and brittle.

Unstable alternation:
: Person vacillates back and forth between the most uncivil, primitive expression of feelings and the most excessive civilities.

Restraint: Affectivity restrained

Suppression:
: Person restrains his affective-cognitive reactions when their expression would be dysfunctional, but he knows what he feels and what he is doing.

Repression:
: Person curtails his cognitive knowledges and reactions, irrespective of his condition and the situation, but his affectivity is free-floating.

Depersonalization, amnesic:
: Person restrains his affective reactions to the point that he loses track of where he is cognitively and has little sense of who he is.

Although this taxonomy includes most of the commonly used ego processes, it is likely not complete and may even be wrong in some ways. For instance, the defensive function of undoing, its likely coping counterpart of reparation, and its fragmentary form of restorative ritualisms have not been included in most presentations because it is difficult to observe these processes in most research settings. The actual application of this model to a person's ongoing ego processing leads to observations of various patterns of ego functions. Most people move up (or down) a hierarchy of preferred or situationally indicated functions to deal with knotty problems; moreover under close scrutiny most people are seen to be neither wholly defensive or wholly coping. Various combinations and patterns of ego functions also account for complex chains of ego actions. As an example, take the clinically complex phenomenon of counterphobia: first, denial is invoked as a simple negation of the original fear; second, projection leads to the secret supposition that it is another, rather than the self, who is afraid; third, displacement permits the negated reaction to be expressed and lived out.

The unusual features of the taxonomy are its overall organization of previously disparate ideas, its attempt to distinguish the three modes of ego processes within a single genre, and its specification of the various sectors of functioning—cognitive, intraceptive-reflexive, attentional, and affective. As was previously understood and commonly agreed with respect to the defensive processes, none of the functions is necessarily conscious or unconscious; rather their operation is best regarded as "silent" or preconscious. They are known by their actions, and if they are "unconscious," it is not an insurmountable task to help their users to become aware (as in psychotherapy) that they persistently employ particular methods to solve problems.

ORGANIZATION

The processes are not in themselves organizations, but their most general purpose is that of facilitating the person's momentary and lifelong organizations. Several features of the present ego model make this work possible. First, there is the attempted comprehensiveness of the ego taxonomy itself which includes cognitive, reflexive-intraceptive, attentional, and affective functions. Although we are immediately concerned at this point with the person as a self-actional system, all of the processes are expressed in interpersonal as well as intrapersonal contexts. Second, and in parallel to the first point, is the fact that various situations instigate complementary intrapersonal hierarchical organizations of ego actions, however short-lived or mild the circumstances might be. More enduring contexts, such as a research career in physics, facilitate special, more durable kinds of organization. Third, and more separately, is the proposition that the person's everyday organizing attempts imply his larger, single enterprise of making self-consistent sense to himself. Fourth, the three general modes—coping, defensive, and fragmentary—form another kind of hierarchical organization. They represent a utilitarian hierarchy. The person will cope if he can, defend if he must, and fragment if he is forced, but whichever mode he uses, it is still in the service of his attempt to maintain organization. Whether he copes, defends, or fragments depends on his possibilities for maintaining a degree of equilibrium with the aid of his internal resources vis-à-vis the demands of a particular situation or a series of life situations. His coping does not insure his situational success nor do his defending or fragmenting entail his failure. Whatever mode he employs or whatever outcome he achieves depends on the nature of his situations; some may actually encourage defending or fragmenting reactions, for example, the so-called schizogenic family.

Many personality theories depend on sources external to ego processes to provide whatever organizational push is deemed necessary, as was noted in the last chapter. Psychoanalysis depends on the thrust of the id or superego, and behaviorism, on the effects of consistent external reinforcements from parents and the world. In the present formulation ego functions are the vehicles whereby organization is enacted, but the cause for synthesis lies in man's need for a degree of self-consistency. If there is merit in this proposal, the model of ego functioning does not need stipulations of physiological drive, id instincts, and perhaps not even traditional motives to explain most instances of dynamic, consistent functioning, and development. Instead, plans, intents, and enterprises may be sufficient to describe people's coherencies.

If this description of the nature of people's organizational efforts should prove wrong, it creates no great problem for the model. Its focus on ego processes makes it catholic in regard to motivation since all such thrusts must still be filtered through processes of ego decision. The model is also catholic with respect to terminal achievements, such as competence, self-actualization, or principled moral judgment, since whatever the outcome, ego processes are the midwives. Its coping mode makes it hospitable to the "new" stimulus-seeking motivations. Curiosity, exploration, intrinsic motivation, and the like are all intents of open systems that are experience-seeking, self-exposing, and information-gathering. All of these activities must be processed as well. Its defensive and fragmentation modes could be seen as simple intents to reduce the tension of drives in unbearable situations. If motivations to seek stimuli or to reduce drive tension turn out not to be literal or separate from ego plans themselves, these kinds of behaviors can then be ascribed, as they are here, to the intrinsic activity of men wishing to maintain a degree of togetherness as evolving beings. Altogether, diversity and complex individuation in both motivation and outcome are permitted by the present formulation since commonality is sought in processes. Just as there are alternative ego manifestations of the same drive, the same outcome can be achieved by diverse ego routes and for different reasons.

The Logical Constraints of Ego as Processes

The explication provided by this conceptualization of ego processes is circumscribed. Only the person's interchanges with his situation are in focus, whether these are with himself, with one other person, or, more broadly, with his ecology. Strictly speaking, the processes are without content, although we must admit that separation of content and process—a goal all structuralists hold—is more often an ideal of model building than a realizable achievement. The ego model is essentially descriptive and does not in itself include causative explanations. Processes are "implicatory" by nature in that one person's attack on a problem suggests a second's reaction, for example, a child's *denial* of wrongdoing may reciprocally imply his parents' logical analysis as they attempt to persuade their offspring that his perceptions are inconsistent with the facts of his behavior. Even though the persistent use of coping functions, with their general property of objective, social, and emotional accuracy, should *lead* to viable solutions and developments, coping does not directly cause these solutions. Objective, external circumstances have much to do with the nature of resolutions. Thus coping does not entail socially successful final states, such as a competence or self-actualization, but refers more simply to ongoing, open organizations. A person may cope, but the deleterious aspects of his situation may still bring social failure. Since coping implies contending on equal terms, it does not attach effectiveness to more aggressive modes of achievement. Some may feel that the model is flawed or at least flavored by a degree of pessimism for these reasons. In a sense this is true, since processes represent neither man's triumphs nor failures but can only describe how he arrived at either state.

No basis exists for assuming that ego functions move through stages of development in and of themselves, separate from particular effects wrought by stage changes in cognitive, moral, and social structures. Some kinds of ego processes are clearly not possible for the infant, for instance empathy or intellectualization; but it is not necessary to posit structural stages of evolution for the ego processes themselves to account for the later appearance of some functions. Since this particular point is complex, we will leave it for later discussion. Suffice it to add now, ego processes are far broader, more mobile, but less deep in their representation of human affairs than are structural stages as these are presently and commonly defined.

Constructionist Man

The conceptualization of processes leads to an organic view of man as using his past, engaged in his enterprises, and anticipating his future. In other words, the person does not reproduce his past in exact replica, but instead constructs both his past and his future in terms of his present. He seldom engages a new task with the exact same pattern of ego skills that he has used before. Instead, he constructs new organizations suitable to his present enterprise. He does not anticipate his future solely in terms of his past. Instead, he constructs suppositions and plans that the future will be different in some ways and in some ways the same. All of these constructions occur with the character in which "each of us commits himself to the world with but a part of his being and each of us holds back from the world that function of the self which remains secretive and dormant [Natanson, 1970, pp. 3–4]." Altogether, ego processes engage the problems of living by *constructing* resolutions to changing situations instead of reproducing learned responses emanating from achieved states.

The issue of whether people's behavior can be viewed in constructivist or mechanical terms is an old and bitter debate in psychology. I would hardly dare resurrect it here if it were not for the fact that its resolution in favor of a constructivist position is central to the present formulation. The next chapter, which is concerned with value choice in building personality models, will include an examination of current epistemological thought and an argument that subjects are not the only ones who construct formulations and actions, psychologists do too. Essentially the question of mechanical versus constructivist concerns what ontology to believe in now. As Quine (1963) says, that question stands open and "the obvious counsel is tolerance and an experimental spirit [p. 19]." In many clinicians' views, observations of ego at work provide the prime, persuasive evidence of human constructivism. An unending variety of combinations, sequences, and organizations of ego processes are consciously or subconsciously invented by people as self-actional, interactional, and transactional reactions to match the complexities of their everchanging situations. In the end the controversy that has gripped psychologists for years boils down to whether newness—in response or organization—occurs in some measure at the behest of and by the invention of people. In the present view newness is not necessarily tied to "goodness," as it has often been when questions were posed by constructivists as to how to account for man's creative products. Clinicians see amazingly inventive instances of pathology as well, although once invented, symptoms are often persistently held.

When I was a clinician I worked intensively for 2 years with a boy who, at the beginning, was 4 years old. He was not a personally troubled child, but he had constructed a rule for himself that he was not to speak with anyone outside of his immediate family, including playmates, near relatives, teachers, milkmen, and so on. He did not permit me to become his conversation partner either. Nobody knew and nobody ever found out why he had made this arduous stipulation for himself, but with members of his family he was loquacious and for the most part rather cheerful. However his rule, which he assiduously followed without making the slightest error, enraged most of the adults in his life. Although he clearly could talk, he *wouldn't*. Most everyone who was associated with him tried at one time or another to maneuver him into talking by tricking, seducing, bribing, or threatening him. The nursery school decided he might talk if they threatened to flunk him, but he remained silent, so he had to be flunked. Not being caught up in his everyday life, I could afford to wait and watch. After a time he began to report to me in various nonverbal ways with toys and the like, even though he had learned to read and write well before the expected time, that he was talking with first one person and then another. By the end of treatment he talked readily with everybody but me. No mechanical response this! Instead, a personal invention of power and impressiveness.

Clearly enough, repetitions of ego constructions do occur, and for a number of reasons. Not all spring full-blown from the head of Zeus. Constructions are re-used when they have proven useful, but likely not in exact replica since situations are never identical. The more the person assumes identity between situations, the more likely it is that he is defending his own private reasons for defining Situation B as identical to Situation A. Information about the situational usefulness of an ego process comes back to the person and allows him to suppose either that he is on target or that he had better shift his strategies, a process which has quite different implications than being positively or negatively reinforced. Nevertheless, problems at one time and another are similar; even though no two situations are identical, no situation is entirely new; consequently we can expect a degree of repetitiveness. Normatively the child is presented with situational sequences of steadily accruing dissimilarity over the years, so it follows that his reactions from one time to another will have similarity and dissimilarity. Studies of segments of the life span indicate that abrupt situational changes are likely to be times when most people construct new forms. Tryon (1939) showed in longitudinal study that the movement from junior high to senior high was such a time; Haan (1974b) found that considerable change had occurred in Peace Corps volunteers after their overseas tour of duty. However most situations that psychologists use to collect their data are much alike, for example, the experimental, laboratory, and psychometric. The consistency of behavior within similar situations has lent support to the impression that personality is preeminently a collection of durable achieved states that reliably emit responses on demand. The alternative constructivist explanation is that man very often constructs the meaning of a research situation as one where it makes sense to be polite to experimenters and compliant to their standardized situations.

Common sense sees evidence of man's constructivism everywhere—in his creativity, flexibility, developmental progressions, and in his own beliefs about himself. The difficulty is that the definitive experiment to prove the constructivist supposition or its contrary, that man acts in accordance with his past history of situationally reinforced behaviors (see Langer, 1969, for a discussion related to this point), probably cannot be done. The hypothesis of constructed activity requires evidentiary proof that response constellations are new, or new organizations of the old. The critical observations are almost impossible to make given the unfathomable number of experiences that people as young as 3 or 4 years old will have already had. The hypothesis of reproductive behavior also requires evidence that is impossible to obtain; the emitted response must be shown to be nothing more than a replica of the old. A quizzical resolution was recently offered. Lefcourt (1973) suggests that maybe it does not really matter where the truth lies, since there is evidence that man is better off for holding the belief that he has a hand in determining his actions and fate.

The Place of Rational Choice

Phillip Rieff (1959) observed in regard to Freud, "He surpasses even the Romantics in his deprecation of mere intellect. He calls into question all self-sight, intuitive as well as intellectual [p. 69]." Paradoxically, Freud's own enterprise was the hard-headed, intellectual investigation of human behavior, both theoretically and therapeutically. The patent contradiction is still not resolved and contains a two-fold implication about human behavior: a shocking dismissal of the common man's rationality along with the embarrassing supposition that only the analysts and possibly the analyzed have sufficient command of rationality to understand and criticize the theory. As Ricoeur (1970) comments, apologetically, in the preface of his definitive work on the Freudian system, "It is taking a gamble, no doubt, to write about Freud without being an analyst or having been analyzed [p. xi]."

The real stuff—the primitive variables, Rudner (1966) calls them—of the common man's dynamics in the psychoanalytic and behaviorist view is not his rationalities but his feelings. This position foreshadowed the insignificant role that rationality occupies in most modern theories of personality and likely paved the way for the variety of anti-intellectual, feeling cures now being offered to the public which is already persuaded that rationality gets one nowhere in an over-rationalized society. The Freudian theme of the common man's irrationality particularly runs against the grain of Piagetian theory. More than any other, this supposition has made it difficult to integrate the two systems despite the obvious advantages and wishes and attempts of many to do so. Piaget himself (1973) could apparently think of only a few obvious parallelisms between the two bodies of work in a recent careful and courteous address to the American Society of Psychoanalysis. At the same time the view that man is ever ready to forego rationality was the Freudian position's greatest insight.

If the power of the Piagetian findings is to be aligned and integrated with the insights of Freudian thought to produce a more complete description of the person than either can achieve alone, provisions will have to be made (1) for the development and role of authentic rationality and (2) for its subversion. Neutralization, the primary or secondary autonomies of the conflict-free ego sphere, sublimation, or the eventual manifestations of innate abilities—all Freudian explanations of why rationality develops—are insufficient accounts of the genetic epistemology that Piagetian research has developed.

At the same time and less certainly, there are the faintest rumblings among cognitive developmentalists that the person's presentation of his reasoning, at whatever stage, cannot always be simply ascribed to the pristine operations of logical structures. For instance G. Steiner (1974) observes that the problems presented by cognitive experiments are "prestructured" by subjects. He suggests in consequence that the Genevans do not observe pure structures because subjects make ad hoc elaborations. Another study (Haan, 1975) also found discrepancies between moral structures used in reasoning about real life and those used in response to hypothetical moral dilemmas. The variations accorded with differences in people's personalized constructions of themselves, particularly as these could be extrapolated to how they might act in a situation involving a real moral dilemma. Both sets of results suggest that the presented form of structural capacities can be modified by ego functioning.

The full account of how the two theories may be amalgamated, with ego organization providing the bridge, is taken up in the next several sections. I will argue that even though personality may disturb the presentation of rationality, rationality cannot be a precipitate of personality, as it is in the Freudian and neobehaviorist theories. Instead, personality is circumscribed and defined by the core developments of rationality. Dember (1974) has made a related suggestion, but he is more concerned with the deleterious effect that unbridled ideation might have on personality functioning. For all these reasons it must be argued that operations involving rational, logical choices need direct and central representation in any personality theory. If rationality is reduced to other terms, such as motives of effectance, habits, or mediation, its existence as a fundamental aspects of personality is denied. Rationality usually refers to the selection of means in relation to their relevance to particular ends; therefore it is not plausible that behavior should be determined solely by motives or by the environment.

The model of ego processes includes functions that represent rationality at work (i.e., objectivity, intellectuality, logical analysis, concentration, tolerance of ambiguity, empathy, regression in the service of the ego); but rationality also enters the account in two other critical ways: (1) in a positive sense, a number of the properties of coping add up to a supposition that it is better to reason than not; (2) in a negative sense, the defensive and fragmentary actions are based on the supposition that their users operate according to intrasubjective determinations that seem rational to them. even when these constructions could not pass muster as intersubjective rationalities.

Hierarchy and Organization

GENERAL ORGANIZATIONAL WORK OF EGO PROCESSES

Ego processes are more than the direct operational expression of structures, and structures are more than ego processes. Ego functioning is characterized by mobility, inventiveness, and changeability, while structures, being based on consolidated and irreversible principles of knowing, are stable, integral, and certain. When these widely accepted differences are stated, we can see that it is highly unlikely that there are structural stages of ego development per se.

There may, however, be *phases* when special patterns of ego processes are evolved or heavily used. Such occasions may arise from interactions between new structural attainments and societies' expectancies. These possibilities could be investigated. For instance the classificatory abilities first developed by the child at the stage of concrete operations are permitted by his decentering and coming to view his world in discriminative and objective ways, as he has not been able to do before; consequently the generic ego process of discrimination and its three modes of objectivity, isolation, and concretism should be especially facilitated at this point in development. If the child who is able to perform concrete operations were severely stressed, his classificatory structures would not be destroyed, but his performance would temporarily become more egocentric and intrasubjective. As an example, a phase of especially heavy and extensive use of particular ego processes is illustrated by the classical asceticisms of some adolescents, which can involve early rising, much reading, impecuniousness, taciturnity, and the like. These characteristics are based, if coping, on suppression of affect and an enhanced position of the ego-cognitive functions, again permitted by the recent decentration and liberation of thought that are inherently part of formal operations (an excellent account of this period from the cognitive point of view is given by Inhelder and Piaget, 1958). Ego processes are probably best regarded as simply what they appear to be: commonplace strategies that people use to solve significant and trivial problems of living.

The organizational work of ego processes can be generally described, as noted previously, by the same properties of exchange that characterize biological functioning and intellectual functioning within the Piagetian system, namely, assimilation and accomodation. Both are evident in the ego's ceaseless work of absorbing and integrating ongoing experiences to already existing constructions (assimilation) and of constructing particular reactions and responses (accommodation—to these experiences. When this two-fold interplay is considered and observed in ego terms, it can be seen to be the essential core of the ego's work as it is commonly described during infancy, old age, dreaming, waking, and psychotherapy, where both assimilation and accommodation are carefully and deliberately studied by patient and therapist alike.

The organizational work of ego processes does not require a specific vehicle of activation, as do constructs of achieved states and constitutional givens, but appears as the nature of life itself once it is underway. Some with different views have seen the ego as executor; for instance, Loevinger (1966b) has said that the ego is "the master trait." Rather than being master, the present view suggests its being "handmaiden," and rather than trait, the ego processes are seen as strategies of problem resolution with respect to the self, to others, and to the world and its essential social logic and immutable physical structure. There is a temptation, once the importance of the ego's organizational work and its integral relations to cognitive operations are recognized, to enter the ego into the personality system as the modern homunculus. But it cannot be. Ego work is more simply an incessant series of likely resolutions. Lenneberg (1967) has called attention to the temporal, moment-by-moment, ordering of decision patterns in the flow of language selection. Miller, Galanter, and Pribram (1960) suggested a TOTE unit (Test–Operate–Test–Exit) as a model of brain functioning that likewise emphasizes the work of ongoing decision, rather than the definitive, final determinations of a master.

EGO PROCESSES' HIERARCHY OF UTILITY

The patterns of balance between assimilation and accommodation vary for the coping, defense, and fragmentary modalities, not only during synchronic events, but also during diachronic sequences. Coping processes are likely to be employed synchronically when assimilation and accommodation are either quite evenly matched or the person experiences no pressure about the imbalance, for example, he's enjoying his daydreaming or he wants very much to acquire a new skill. Coping occurs diachronically, during times of stage or experiential balance. Defensive strategies are needed when marked imbalances between assimilation and accommodation occur either during stage transitions or during environmental disjunctures. For instance overaccommodation can be compelled by strong or uniform environmental pressures, or assimilation may be prolonged in monotonous or overindulging environments that do not include sufficient opportunities or expectancies for the person to accommodate (sensory deprivation, dreaming, overprotection). The person's defensive processes are brought into play, developmentally, then (1) when an insensate environment countervenes his ongoing course, making sufficient assimilation impossible, (2) when the environment disengages itself, failing to support or to expect achievement from him, (3) when he himself requires accommodation beyond his assimilated understanding, a hallmark of stage transition, and (4) he himself continues to cherish his assimilating activity to the detriment of his accommodatory possibilities.

Fragmentation, as a retreat to privatistic assimilatory modes, occurs as an accommodation to stress and as a solution to a situation or to a likely developmental movement, where and when the required accommodations are not only beyond the person's capability, but also irrefutably contradict and confuse his self-constructions and make intrasubjective reality preferable. More commonplace are the momentary fragmentations of ordinary people when events are surprising (unpredictable), inextricably complex, or inimical to their sense of their own integrity. When these qualities consistently characterize important experiences, fragmentation may become chronic. Whatever the environmental circumstances, the person's intent (traditionally, motivation or drive) is general, and in the terms of this present formulation it is merely that he be able to continue with a degree of self-determination, whether he copes or whether he defends, or fragments. Thus the three modes form an organized hierarchy of utility in supporting, deterring, or forcing shifts in his actions.

Coping is then very simply the *normative* mode. When all other matters are equal, the person will cope, and the extent of his logic, wisdom, productivity, civility, and sensuality will accurately and authentically reflect his structural stages of development, enriched and flavored by the special affect related to particular situations. If the subject's perceptions and constructions inform him that a situation is beyond his assimilatory or accommodatory capability—either because it is objectively so or he believes it to be—then he can invoke nonnormative defensive strategies that entail some negation or a distortion of the task. This is not an unusual occurrence. There are surely no wholly or continuously coping people, nor do great numbers of situations facilitate or even permit coping (as Argyris, 1975, has recently pointed out). The nonnormative strategy of fragmentation may sometimes be evidence of a momentary retreat, particularly when it is an inadvertent occurrence. When fragmentation is a stable strategy and supports a chronic psychosis, it may still be evidence of a "private victory" but nonetheless, a social failure, since the psychotic has systematically negated his social connectedness. In contrast, the more socially compliant neuroses often represent social victories and private failures. The view of fragmentation as a solution—a method to the madness—is in line with recent work and thought about nonorganic psychoses (e.g., Singer & Wynne, 1965a,b). Thus another general aspect of the organization of ego functions is suggested by this hierarchy of utility, wherein first coping, then defense, and finally fragmenting strategies are brought into play.

COORDINATION OF COGNITIVE, MORAL, AND SOCIAL STRUCTURES

If ego processes are not the functional equivalents of structures and only indirectly represent structures, we need to explicate the exact character of their relations with the cognitive, moral, and social structures. The role of affect within the overall organization will be subsequently examined. The history of man as a more or less rational being makes it self-evident that cognitive structures must take a central role in any theory of personality, all other matters being equal. Of course, there are aspects of man's history that indicate all manner of irrationalities, and other matters are often not equal. To consider the relationships between cognition and personality we will first assume a rational condition and a normative situation.

If the character of men's intellect is critical in determining their fate, then the level, specifically the stage, of cognitive development must be both a limiting and permitting condition of normative personality-ego expression. If a child is not capable of formal operations, he plainly cannot, no matter how effectively he copes, use ego functions that are predicated on formal, cognitive structures. Likewise a formal view of social interdependency, emphasizing its holistic, principled, mutually regulative character, could not be held if formal, cognitive structures had not been attained. One empirical study (Kuhn, Langer, Kohlberg, & Haan, in press) has suggested that cognitive level is the necessary but insufficient condition of moral development. Altogether then, cognitive structures seem to play the preeminent role within the person's hierarchical organization.

However, strong arguments can be made that cognitive structures, in and of themselves, do not entirely account for the manifest organizations presented by people in everyday life. First, even though the characteristic feature of a structure is its equivalent operation, whether or not it is presented in accurate form is subject to the vagaries of the person's occasional or chronic needs to defend himself or fragment in any particular situation. These conditions occur in everyone's life more than infrequently. Consequently frequent *disparities* between structural capacity and performance occur. Second, no or few situations are solely cognitive in character. They "pull" social, moral, and affective responses as well; consequently *coordination* of reactions and actions are needed even when intrapsychic and extrapsychic conditions permit structures to be accurately presented. What one's cognitive, moral, and social structures and what one's affective responses might lead one to do or think do not always agree. Third, people cannot consider or respond to social, moral, or affective issues without a degree of thinking. Still, this inextricable link between thought and nonthought does not mean that fully articulated cognitive structures invariably participate in all resolutions. Some cognitive activity is simply a matter of representing content information. Piaget (1969) in a like vein has recently distinguished between operational memory and imagined memories. Either there are elaborations of cognitive structures that are not yet identified, or not all cognitive is structurally organized (see Bruner, Oliver, & Greenfield, 1966, for a discussion of this point). With this more differentiated and elaborated view of the person's resolving processes and subsequent actions, we can see that the processes we identify as ego must often take the role of presenting and coordinating various forms of knowing, whether or not they do so with accuracy and efficiency.

The work of the ego functions is then to assimilate all these various sorts of information, at whatever the stage of structural development, to work toward an equable balance between the self's assimilation and possible accommodations. In many instances it is clear that all other matters are not equal and cognition may not accurately reflect structural capability.

COORDINATION OF AFFECTIVE REACTIONS

Feelings are another kind of informational signal and do not determine action without first being filtered cognitively (except possibly in the youngest infants). People are also frequently rationally motivated and make choices that complement or even counter their feelings and impulses, such as getting up in the morning to go to work or taking a moral action despite its emotional cost. Having made these two very general statements, we need now to present the formulation of emotion and motivation that is consistent with the present view of ego organization.

Emotions appear unbidden and automatically, but in fact they are cognitively evaluated (Peters, 1969; Pribram, 1967). In the adult they follow upon instances of mismatch between intrasubjective and situationally appraised intersubjective realities. Whether emotions are negative or positive from the person's point of view depends on whether the situation seems good or bad for him. Examples: "How could I be so lucky that he could fall in love with me?" (potentially leading to expanding, advancing, and disclosing one's self) or "How can I maintain my self-respect if he is to regard me in this way?" (potentially leading to withdrawing and protecting one's self).

The initial appraisal involves the ego processing of the objective, cognitive elements of the situation in terms of its likely social, personal, and affective implications. As this assimilatory activity is rapidly summarized, emotion begins to be experienced prior to the first definitive accommodations (this makes emotion seem to be unbidden, instantaneous, and "automatic"). Information in regard to emotion is not necessarily more "unconscious" than other assimilatory activities—

these almost always appear to be unconscious too—and it need not be an intuitive (preconceptual) appraisal. During sequences of appraisal, schemata of perceptions, memory, and cognitive constructions can be sharpened and heightened or distorted and negated, first by the affective schemata and secondly by invoking ego processes of coping, defense, or fragmentation. Laboratory stress research (Lazarus, 1966) has shown that subjects' emotional reactions, both psychological and physiological, can be manipulated by the cognitive information given to them; most research has concerned only "decrements" in response, like Lazarus' "primitivization," but there is little doubt increment can occur as well. Earlier experiences, acquired figurative memories, and affective schemata—both positive and negative—are likely more involved in emotions than in motivations. However, the person can be seen to experience "self-transcendence," that is, to cope and go beyond what he has hitherto postulated or formulated as the organization of his intrasubjective reality and logic. The latter is not meant to be self-actualization in the Maslowian sense, but is rather more momentary and situationally specific.

Subsequent or decisive appraisal may induce emotions to evolve into motives as cognitive plans of action (see Pribram, 1967). Motives have a de facto relationship with emotions since motives follow emotions and both rest on an imbalanced ratio between intersubjective and intrasubjective reality and the consequent—either avoidant bad or anticipatory good—formulation of self-consistency. When the person has assessed the situation as good for him, his accommodative coping reaction to his emotions is likely to enhance his plan of action by making it more decisive, differentiated, and intergrated. (Of course, some people cannot tolerate prosperity and may need to deny and undo what they themselves see as good for them.) When a person assesses the situation as bad for him, he may still accommodate and cope with a decisive, integrated, plan of action that makes whatever is possible out of an impossible situation, that is, he may "overcome." However, he may accommodate, defensively or by fragmenting, so as to protect his intrasubjective organization at some or great expense to intersubjective coherency and integrity. In these instances he chooses to compartmentalize himself to avoid disintegration of his intrasubjective reality. In this event, assimilatory actions predominate and distort accommodatory actions.

The development and differentiation of emotions follow the general development of the child in most ways. Initially the baby experiences gross feelings (not emotions) that follow physiological reactions that are biologically and immediately good or bad for him, for example, hunger or satiation, comfort or pain. These reactions are no different from any other mammal's (Arnold, 1969). As the child matures cognitively, socially, and morally, he comes increasingly to differentiate among evaluations of his emotions and among the situations that are good or bad for him. He acquires a history—a repertoire—of situations and appraisals that have been good or bad for him in the past (Melden, 1969). His formulations of these past situations are schemata that include varying degrees and kinds of affective, cognitive content as well as structural, operative evaluations. Faced with new but similar situations, he has varying readinesses to generalize or differentiate the new from the elements of his old schemata depending on their important similarities and differences and the affective overload. In general, affective overloads cause people to evoke ego processes of overgeneralizing or quite in contrast, overspecifying.

Emotion itself is of a different class from cognitive, moral, and social structures. It is adjectival rather than structural and catalytic rather than substantive, but the term is falsely applied to older children's and adults' affectivity when cognitive determinations are not recognized and included in the formulation. Emotions may be more "unconscious" in the child than are other assimilated aspects of his functioning. The mark of the infant and the young is their comparative inability to conceptualize their experience and develop motive-plans that would reestablish the intersubjective–intrasubjective balance. They are less able to carry out a plan that results in a return to equilibrium or in the establishment of new self-transcending equilibriums. Moreover, children's repertoires of historical schemata are likely to be more figurative than cognitive and thus more difficult to convert to motive plans. Figurative elements are highly individualized and particularized (Piaget, 1969), so they are less socialized, standardized, and communicable and hence appear to be more unconscious. However they are merely farther away from being accommodated.

Several additional organizational principles of ego processes have thus been suggested: In the normative condition, coping operations serve cognitive structures, which are themselves informed by social and moral structures and affective reactions; in nonnormative circumstances, defensive and fragmenting operations distort cognitive structures by negating information, or affective reactions immobilize the cognitive and prevent clear plans of action from forming. The structures themselves cannot be known and can only be deduced from representative actions. The veridicality of their presented form is always subject to the choice and nature of the ego regulations, whether these be coping, defensive, or fragmenting. If these are coping, the structures will be accurately reflected; if defensive, they likely will not be, at least not for the time being; if fragmenting, they certainly will not be. In this light, the evocation of defensive or fragmenting operations is still regarded as representing choice, even if they result in slavish compliances or the most socially objectionable psychoses, since the person will merely have socially retrenched to save his own integrity. Thus the hierarchy of ego processes accounts for his sensitive responsiveness to situations, but there is no need to contend that he is the creature of situations.

PREFERENTIAL USE OF PARTICULAR EGO PROCESSES

A more specific aspect of ego organization is the hierarchy of ego processes preferred by individual people, a phenomenon often called "choice of defense" by clinicians. A preference in function means that a particular ego process is more readily brought into play than another, when both are equally plausible ways of resolving the situation; thus the chosen function can be regarded as occupying a higher place in the person's hierarchy of preference. Although all the generic ego processes—whatever they turn out eventually to be—are likely available to all people, the research concerned with this model as well as with the various bipolar processes such as leveling–sharpening, field independence–dependence, repression–sensitization, internal–external locus of control suggests that people's actual uses of the various ego processes are skewed by their preferences.

To understand the genesis of preference we need to note that particular situations "pull" different functions and that when certain life conditions are continuously experienced, preference in ego functions may eventually become endemic. For instance, the tendency of lower-class persons to deny, first documented by Miller and Swanson (1960) with adolescent males, is not only an understandable, but also a reasonably functional accommodation to the all but irrevocable conditions of poverty. Being a psychologist likewise makes for a degree of intellectualization about the state of one's own psyche. Lags can be observed when people enter new situations: The lower-class boy with a college scholarship and the psychologist faced with a bona fide crisis of psyche may continue for a time with their usual methods of resolution—the boy denying the forthcoming examination and the psychologist intellectualizing his depression. The intrapsychic genesis of preference in ego operations is considered in the next section.

The Question of Development

There are two separate and different matters to be considered in regard to development: (1) the ego processes' ancillary relationship to the central thrust of the child's structural development; (2) the development of the ego processes themselves.

EGO PROCESSES' ANCILLARY RELATIONSHIPS TO STRUCTURAL DEVELOPMENT

I have previously advanced the argument that ego processes are not structures, so they cannot undergo structural transformations, but increased structural sufficiency will be reflected in the character of various ego functions. To develop these thoughts further, we must consider additional facets of the formulations presented in the last section, conducting the analysis this time within the context of action.

The Piagetian system regards all cognition, both prior to and after the advent of representational thought, as action in itself. In view of present parallel suppositions about brain mechanisms and the impressive body of cognitive developmental research, there is good reason to accept this supposition. According to earlier suggestions, cognition equals action when ego functions are coping. However there is a corollary question: Is all action *nothing more* than a direct and true expression of structures? From our knowledge of the operation of defensive and fragmenting actions we would have to answer no, since it appears that action is often more complex and frequently much more than a direct expression of developed structures. In fact, if the answer were "Yes, actions do equal structures," the phenomena of defensive maneuvers would have to be discarded as a mythology, and all differences between people's sufficiency and comprehensiveness of actions could be ascribed to their stages of structural development. (Some cognitivists actually seem to take this position.) Structures are probably not so simply manifested: Particular functions may not always by entailed by particular structures, but instead may be complicated, not only by other structures, but also, as we noted previously, by broader ego strategies that the person invents for the occasion.

Piaget (1973, p. 47) as well as Langer (1973) has recently said that affectivity does not modify cognitive structures. This would seem to be true except in extreme circumstances, such as deteriorative organic psychoses, given the person's irrefutable conviction that his attained structural knowledge is correct (one cannot convince a child that conservation does not occur after he understands it). How then can we entertain this position and still account for the unfaithful reflections of structural development that occur when people in emotional thrall invent exceptional excuses for themselves—when they can't see the forest for the trees, fiddle as Rome burns, or decide their enemy is the barbarian outside? If the solidity of structures as resolved organizations of knowing is to be respected, we must suppose that differences between the levels of structural capability and action performance sometimes occur in situations of stress, confusion, and uncertainty. In these instances, we might say persons are temporarily not themselves—that is, not what they could be—although the integrity of their structures is maintained and can still be expressed on other occasions.

When these circumstances are taken into account we can see that the orthogenesis and pathogenesis of ego processes cannot be developmentally symmetrical, as they are in the Eriksonian scheme of trust versus mistrust, autonomy versus shame, and so on. Instead, the defensive functions must be seen as qualitatively, rather than quantitatively, different from the coping functions. If the differences were quantitative, the Piagetian and psychoanalytic theories could probably be readily amalgamated, since their respective descriptions of orthogenetic and pathogenetic developments would be symmetrical and complementary. The present view suggests that the development of the coping operations quietly serves the child's evolving structures and the construction and reconstruction of his understanding of himself and the world. However the necessities of the child achieving some form of equilibrium, despite his insufficiencies in cognitive structuring and his limited strategies for dealing with affect, require the services of defensive and sometimes fragmentary functions.

Figure 1, which was first discussed in Chapter 1, depicted sequences of reaction and action between situation and person in order to illustrate the intrapersonal constellation of structures, affect, ego functions, and actions just discussed in great detail. Although graphic presentations of complex phenomena are inevitably limited, the figure indicated the variety and sequence of systemic elements that register and are finally represented in the manifest outcome: most importantly here, the asymmetry of the conditions for defense and coping, the primary and pivotal role of the structures as the form and means of knowing, the secondary role of affect, and the tertiary role of the ego processes' work in resolving the action. Only single linear sequences were shown, but clearly there are all manner of intermediate feedback loops (interactions) within the person and between the person and his situation.

The ego functions' integrative purposes need to be considered further with respect to the equilibration of structures when assimilations and accommodations are balanced and coping expresses the outcomes. I take it that a person's sense that he is integrated—that he's "got it together"—is not identical to his being structurally equilibrated, but that more is meant. The person must be seen as a larger enterprise than can be described by the idea of an equilibrated structural organization, as has been argued previously. The enlarged view of his state of dynamic balance may be regarded as self-integration, to distinguish it from equilibration, and would additionally include a sense of the self as integrated with one's self and with the situation.

A kind of self-integration, a consolidation, is also achieved, irrespective of structural equilibration, by the use of some kinds of defenses that work to close the system and permit integration by temporary or durable compartmentalizations. We might call this phenomenon a false equilibration. A solid solution can be achieved, for example, by deciding, projectively, that the barbarian is not one's self but some other fellow. To study moral development, for instance, is to become respectful of the lengths to which determined people will go in the way of defensive negation and distortion to reconcile their sense of moral "goodness" with evidence that indicates the contrary (see Haan, 1975, for instance). Thus the more complex defenses such as reaction formation, isolation, and repression, which work to relieve the person from further consideration of his situation, are invoked to achieve integrations that may not be based on the equilibration of structures. An occasional psychotic also gives the appearance of integration, as long as his self-explanations go unchallenged. Finally, equilibration of structures may be neither sufficient nor relevant to achieving integration in nonlogical, unrealistic situations. But in logical situations, within the person's coping capability, equilibration and integration may be one and the same.

DEVELOPMENT OF EGO PROCESSES THEMSELVES

All three modes of ego processes—coping, defense, and fragmentation—are affected by the development of cognitive structures, that is, they become progressively more differentiated, integrated, and complexly organized as they mirror the accrued capabilities of higher-stage structures. Thus the baby may defend by refusing to look or recognize, or by turning away from a situation that he cannot assimilate and accommodate as a simple form of denial. When he is older he may evoke the considerably more complex but similar strategy of defensive isolation to implement his decision that the unassimilable is not germane or it is information of a different or narrower class. The stressed baby may panic and cry, but the fragmented responses of the older person will bear the mark of his higher developmental level; consider for example the convoluted complexities of neologisms and confabulations. Thus defensive and fragmenting operations are not necessarily primitive constructions, as they are thought to be by most theories of pathology, but are rather as complex and inventive as their user's stage of development permits, although still typically strained and distorting of logic and reality.

Piaget's running accounts of his interviews with children include many examples of childish defense. We offer a few from *Play, dreams, and imitation* (1962).

When working with a 12-month old, Piaget opened and closed his eyes:

[F]irst she blinked, opening and closing her mouth at the same time, as if she were unable to distinguish the two schema from the motor and kinesthetic point of view, then she covered her face with a pillow. . . .

[A]t 1;0 (16) she again opened and closed her mouth when I opened and closed my eyes, and covered her face with the pillow. . . .

It was not until 1;2 (7), i.e., during the fifth stage that L clearly imitated this gesture without covering her face [p. 39].

In regard to a 37-month old:

[H]er father had died, her mother and J had been run over by a car, and an aunt was in charge. At about 3;1 (17) everybody in the games was naughty, which led to a distortion of the usual scenes [p. 129].

In regard to a 72-month old:

at about 6;0 there was little evidence of animism, except in affective reactions. For example at 6;5 (21) she screamed with fright when the door of the hen-house, blown by the wind hit her back. Then crying, she said: *"The wind's horrid, it frightens us—But not on purpose?—Yes, on purpose. It's horrid, it said we were naughty—But does the wind know what it does? It knows it blows"* [p. 251].

We can see in these accounts several different circumstances wherein the young evoke self-protective, defensive strategies: In the first a rudimentary denial is evoked to accommodate a developmental unreadiness to assimilate and accommodate to Piaget's invitation to imitate; in the second, displacing, projective functions are brought into play in an attempt to assimilate an unequilibrated, traumatic interpersonal event; in the third, the sudden impact of an incomprehensible phenomenon of the physical world is resolved by an explanation that involves a temporary, animistic projection and cognitive regression. In each account, affective reactions override the cognitive, and the defensive processes themselves become more complex along with the children's increasing cognitive differentiation.

To counter the widespread tendency among the psychometrically oriented to think in bipolar terms of dimensionalized good and bad, we need to underscore the evident fact that these defenses were probably very useful to these children in these conditions. As Anna Freud suggested in her classical work, *The ego and the mechanisms of defense* (1937), defenses can serve as "holding" functions which enable the developmentally changing person to work through a period of transition. Turiel (1974), in recent description of the transitional period between conventional and principled moral reasoning, reported typical responses of adolescents that I would regard as defensive. Even though the cognitive insufficiency and developmental movements of children likely provoke more occasions for defensiveness than they do in adults, the latter also find themselves in situations where defensive strategies may not only be useful but are perhaps the only methods of solution that they can employ. The literature of stress research, particularly with respect to terminal illness, gives many such examples.

In regard to the question of the development of the ego processes, we can now order the following parts of the problem:

1. Although we possess much of the detail that is needed to trace the cognitive-coping functions' evolution as a corollary of cognitive and moral development, this is not the case with the intraceptive and affective functions. Whatever developmental structures or differentiations exist in intraceptive and affective realms, none has been so thoroughly investigated that we can readily move on to investigate the adjunctive nature of ego coordinating actions. There are a few partial exceptions: Swanson's (1974) work with family decisions and the child's level of cognitive operations, Selman's (1971) work with moral stage and role taking, and Haan's (1974a) with the adolescent cognitive characteristics of later adult coping and defense.

2. We know almost nothing about the evolution of the nonnormative processes of defense and fragmentation. We can assume: (*a*) the degree of their differentiation goes hand in hand with cognitive development, (*b*) their construction and activation is specific to certain environments and developmental circumstances; (*c*) their more enduring integration into the total system of acting as "character" is probably related to the constancy of inimical environments; (*d*) children's use of defensive and fragmentary processes is likely more frequent than adults', given the insufficiency of the young's structural developments, but then pressures on them to accommodate are also less.

Continuity and Discontinuity

There is no problem from the ego process view in representing continuity and discontinuity during the life span since the formulation is itself one of stragegy, movement, and action vis-à-vis changing situations. However the investigative task of establishing the dialectic development of the ego processes is considerable and should include the following considerations: (*1*) the timing of the various processes' initial appearance in their rudimentary forms in concert with the development of cognitive, social, and moral structures, so as to provide a baseline for the processes' underlying continuity and discontinuities; (2) the differentiation and elaboration of the various ego processes during the developmental course within different environmental milieus; (3) the developmental interludes and situational conditions wherein the defensive forms of ego functions appear rather than the coping, both at early and later points in development; (4) the conditions of the ego processes' continuity and discontinuity once structural maturity is achieved.

The central strategem of research in personality development is that of *tracing* personality variables through the vicissitudes of change while keeping track of their main threads of continuity. The choice of developmental variables will determine the nature, complexity, and eventual fruitfulness of this task. Since the birth of the computer, most researchers have thought that the richness of personality could and should be expressed with multiple variables. However the strategy proposed here is different. The ego process formulation suggests that there are fewer generic variables—"primitive" elements as Rudner (1966) called the fundamental taxonomy of a system—that they are abstract in nature, and that they assume many forms. Thus richness is not found in the number of separate variables considered, but rather in the many different forms that a small number of generic variables take (1) in normative and nonnormative circumstances, (2) at various developmental periods, and (3) in relationship to other aspects of the person.

Discontinuity does not imply the biologically untenable idea of disappearance; it rather indicates that an aspect of functioning has assumed a qualitatively different form or role in the person's overall hierarchical organization (see Haan and Day, 1974, for a study of transposed and emergent changes, as well as stabilities, in Q sort items, describing longitudinal subjects at four different time periods over a 35-year span). In general, the use of coping functions should facilitate the expression of transformed structural achievements, while the use of the defensive and fragmenting processes distorts or impedes the expression of these achievements in particular ways. In general, psychotherapy is meant to encourage discontinuity by substituting more effective for less effective means of problem resolution.

One of the most dramatic forms of discontinuity in the development of ego functioning is the child's evocation of reaction formations when he is pressed by his intimate adults' and his peers' formulations about civility in eating, bowel training, general cleanliness, aggression, and so forth. The messy eater, the incontinent baby, the grubby and aggressive preschooler suddenly turns to the opposite actions and becomes fastidious and equable. Else Frenkel–Brunswik (1942) described the phenomenon as the "affinity of opposites," finding it particularly useful in describing the authoritarian personality's oscillatory preoccupations with good and evil.

The younger child would probably have to have some rudimentary grasp of the structures of class inclusion to construct reaction formations (although he could be "good" prior to that time by simply complying). Antinomic action implies the existence of a class formation make up of "good" and "civilized" behaviors expected of children by adults. Since it is a common observation that preschoolers are able to evoke reaction formations with relative ease, it seems possible that developing cognitive structures are first applied to situations of greater affective-social meanings with the aid of ego processes. That structures are first used in situations of great personal meanings has been frequently suggested and was empirically documented by Gounin–Décarie (1966) who found that babies' behavior shows that they attain object permanence for their mothers earlier than they do for physical objects.

In this ego model, the coping counterpart of reaction formation is designated as *substitution,* that is, a "good" reaction formation; the operationalization and evaluation of this function requires a degree of social valuation. Decisions are required as to the wishes and expectations of the subjects' society and family in order to identify the content areas where reaction formations or substitutions might appear. Rapaport (1954) first suggested that "good" reaction formations exist, after observing that some people's reaction formations do not "break down" and reveal their uncivil underpinnings even after years of careful and expert analysis. This phenomenon has been an important ingredient of the psychoanalytic account of character formation; however it may be culturally specific. Reaction formations probably become substitutions when they serve self-integration and equilibrium and all fundamental questions of the self's relation to society are equably settled.

Clearly societies have different assumptions about the noxiousness of various uncivil behaviors and the amounts of time that should be allotted to the developing child before he must become civil. Many modern parents in this society seem to be attempting to discover their child's "natural" timing, that is, one compatible with his cognitive–social–moral development.

Across Time and Cultures

The argument was presented earlier that ego states do not form and describe a taxonomy that can be comfortably applied across cultures and history, since these constructs primarily reflect accrued content. However all men must solve common problems of their daily living and social interdependencies, and irrespective of content, the forms they use—the processes, functions, regulations, and structures—are probably finite in number and may be universally manifested. This assertion is based on several pragmatic suppositions; some have been suggested with different intents by Piaget (1970,1971) and by modern constructivist epistemologists (e.g., Quine, 1969): (*1*) for all practical and scientific purposes, there is an objective reality to the world which all men attempt to know and verify by intersubjective consensus; (*2*) the structure of this reality is determined and can be analyzed by intersubjective logic; (*3*) the biologically based intellect of all men defines, both limits and permits, the nature and the number of the forms they may use; (*4*) the logic and structures of situations and the intellective structures of men (developed from their social interdependencies and their subsequent commitment to intersubjectivity) also suggest that there are a limited number of ego processes.

This proposal that there are general, universal forms of ego action seems within the realm of empirical possibility. Evidence is accruing that cognitive and moral structures may evolve in the same invariant sequences in different cultures and generations. I propose that ego processes can also be identified that will represent a finite number of possible ways that man can act, given the human condition and its physical location. Consider these examples: Should any human baby want to prevent his adult caretaker from overtaxing him (as described by Piaget in the example cited earlier), about all he can do is to turn away or cry. About all a man may do with his emotions is to express them, divert them, restrain them, or transform them. All men, if they are to solve cognitive problems, have a limited number of general ego strategies available to them—make discriminations, detach themselves from the problem, engage in means—end reasoning, and focus their attention. If they fail to arrive at a solution with the use of these strategies, about all they can do is delay their responses and live with the uncertainty, reconsider the problem in a nontemporal, nonlinear, intuitive way, or consider the position of the other person as he contributes to the puzzle.

Although there are undoubtedly other such general methods, it is clear enough that these particular generic processes do not depend on the social content of any one society or any particular point in history. In fact, some will undoubtedly find this array of methods too general to satisfy their needs for precision. The Piagetian hypothesis of universal structures is extended by the present proposal to suggest the possibility that the resolving actions of ego processes may also be observed in all cultures and times. However, different settings undoubtedly optimize or minimize certain functions or patterns and sequences of functions in forming hierarchical organizations of ego processes. The priorities I used in ordering the above examples of common ego solutions likely reflects my sense of my culture's hierarchy of preference and my time in history, for example, I mentioned intuitive solutions last.

As noted previously, some processes of coping can result in failure in nonsupportive circumstances or in failure as it is defined by some segments of any society. For instance, humor and playfulness (a matter of coping regression in the service of the ego) has served many socially oppressed groups well, but it has not directly led in this society to their material, social progress.

Coping is not covertly supported by a Rousseauian supposition that men possess "natural goodness"; it is merely what people prefer to do when they can. There is no empirical reason or basis for assuming that the pristine state of the neonate is coping, or even potentially so, since coping only ensues as interaction. The neonate can only be seen as inexperienced and undeveloped. Compared to defensiveness or fragmenting, coping is simpler, more likely to solve problems, and more likely to bring self-integration rather than an uneasy, convoluted compartmentalization of the self in its wake. The values underlying coping, as well as other proposals for describing good in man, are analyzed in the next chapter.

Summary of the Arguments in Regard to Ego Processes

An attempt has been made to integrate the Piagetian and Freudian theories to develop an account of the person's efforts at organizing himself by means of ego processes. This project has necessarily involved the logical extension of the Piagetian system in order to consider: (1) nonnormative circumstances where logic, objectivity, and rationality do not hold sway, (2) circumstances where affective reactions and social and moral structures are more salient than cognitive structures, and (3) circumstances where self-integration is a more critical thrust of the person's activity then is the equilibration of his structures. Revision of Freudian concepts has also been necessary. The most thoroughgoing and liberating modification was to discard instinct theory along with the behaviorists' companion supposition that personality is primarily about the history, use, and manifestation of affect. When personality theory is rid of instinct theory and its derivations, ego processes can be regarded as the vehicles men unceasingly use to make up their minds, choose their actions, and resolve their insignificant and their magnificent conflicts. Constructed, rather than merely reproduced, solutions can be recognized when processes take these roles, and the common man's rationality is re-legitimized and made a central part of his personal system. Moreover, the meaning of defensive strategies changes. Defenses become constructions whereby men choose self-compartmentalization rather than disorganization. Another persisting problem of psychoanalytic instinct theory—the naive search for hedonic satisfaction—is placed in proper perspective as an occasional and sometimes nonprudent pursuit.

This integration of the two systems required several important new assumptions: (1) When defensive and fragmenting reactions are evoked, the ego functioning and actions of the person do not accurately represent his structures, but this does *not* mean that his structures have deteriorated or that they have been destroyed; rather the person is temporarily not "himself"; (2) although action is cognition, that is, cognition is contained within action, ego action almost always includes more than cognition. Ego processes not only coordinate social, moral, and cognitive structures with the last being the most influential, but they also usually include motive-plans, flavored with affective concerns; (3) the person's most general and persistent intent is to preserve self-consistency within a reasonable range, whatever the mode of ego processes he uses and whether or not he appears objectively to do so in the eyes of observers; self-integration may contain the equilibration of structures, but it often includes more and sometimes represents a "false" equilibration.

The argument was made that these considerations suggest a hierarchical organization of ego processes for the study of the unitary person at different points in his life. However ego processes do not form structural stages since they do not have the durable, irrefutably resolved character of knowing that characterizes structures; they are instead more mobile and inventive. Consequently the thrust of cognitive, moral, and social attainments are only indirectly conveyed through ego processes.

However, ego processes can never be more complicated or integrated than their user's developed structures permit.

Finally, support for the idea that formulations of ego processes apply across cultures and time was developed on the bases that ego actions are the common, content-free, and logically possible ways that human beings solve their problems given the human condition and its physical location. Coping does not insure personal success, and defensiveness and fragmenting reactions do not entail failure. Both outcomes depend on the hospitality and needs of various societies and situations for particular patterns of reaction. Societies, groups, and families support varying patterns of solutions within the coping, the defensive, or fragmenting modes. Nevertheless, the utilitarian hierarchy of coping, defense, and fragmentation rests on the practical premise that the reality of the world and self, which ultimately rests on intersubjective consensus, is knowable by man. To cope is to know reality and to understand its social logic and how it makes a difference to you. The premise of defensiveness and fragmentation is that people wish to preserve a modicum of self-consistency in deciding what is good for them, even if they must sometimes negate or twist reality and the social understandings they ordinarily share. Consequently both defensiveness and fragmentation are, in some degree, retreats from commitment to intersubjectivity. The proposal was made that these means generally underlie coping, defense, and fragmentation in all cultures and times.

Finally, a number of the features of the ego process formulation must at this time, be taken as proposals rather than verified stipulations since there is no agreement about the fundamental taxonomies of social contexts or of the mind, either in the structural or the processed sense, and there is even less agreement about the definition of personality in general. It will be a long time before there is.

5. Immanent Value in Personality Theory

Personality theories, more than other areas of psychology, are about people's values and inevitably reflect the value commitments of their creators, a matter that has been noted and extensively discussed (e.g., Jahoda, 1958; Smith, 1969, 1974). However in this chapter the values immanent in most social scientific theorizing are considered from a different point of view. The essential message of most past examinations was that values should be chosen openly (so that people will be able to decide if they ascribe to the same values) and that the values should be "good" ones—humane, democratic, and fair. No psychologist—citizen would disagree with such recommendations. However, the argument, and the ultimate exhortation made here, is drawn differently and includes something more. The main questions addressed are: What are scientifically *workable* grounds for choosing certain immanent values over others? How does the epistemological ground of social science determine what values can and should be chosen? Are some classes of values more viable for the scientific enterprise than others? No strenuous effort will be made to argue that readers should shift their ontological commitments to mine; instead the task is circumscribed by a pragmatic question: What working agreements can we achieve?

Since personality has no known material, physical basis, scientific description must proceed by initially choosing constructs that are based on common meanings and then advancing to defining possible interconnections among the common meanings with the result that new, more general or supraordinate, constructs may be identified. All of these are acts of creative imagination that acquire reality only as they conform to others' reality. In other words, social agreement is one kind—social scientists' kind—of truth. As a result, the models we construct inevitably imbue our varying value suppositions in different ways and in different degrees. Under the sway of the ultralogical positivists, we pretended that these circumstances did not need to obtain if psychology would strictly confine itself to sense data. If value intrusion were admitted, it was regarded as nonscience. Now, neither pretense nor embarrassed admission is necessary. Still, we do need to be clear and, for the sake of science, vigilant, and we need greater sophistication about the precise nature of value intrusions and how they can and should be handled. On the one hand, confusion about the role of values is increased because there is no widely accepted theory of personality with a verified base; on the other hand, one of the reasons that there can be no consensual theory, it seems to me, is that the questions of value in personality and social psychology have not yet been fully analyzed. I will argue, as Smith (1959, 1961) has, that lucidity about the kinds of values that are immanent in our theories is needed, but the main thrust of the present discourse is that we need to know first, precisely how various values behave within the framework of different personality models, second, what are the consequences for scientific progress of the various roles that values play, and finally, what consequences psychologists' ignorance of their own value intrusions may have for society.

Although values will be considered generally, more specific attention will be given to those that define the "good" life, rather than the "bad" or "poor" life. However, to the extent that values are implicated in defining various pathologies, some of the same arguments would apply. Views of both the good and the poor life involve pressing, practical questions of social policy and therapeutic endeavor (see Smith, 1969, 1974, for collections of papers concerning psychology's moral dilemmas in these regards). These political predicaments posed by underdeveloped and unverified theories and pressing social responsibilities have not gone unconsidered; in fact, there has been lengthy, concerned, and rigorous discourse. They form a backdrop but are not the subject of this discourse.

Most comprehensive and clear was Jahoda's (1958) early examination of mental health, which she also discussed as a value. Her conclusions, which Smith (1959, 1961) has shared, were aimed at both application and theory: that there should be a "democracy" of many values espoused, and that more research was needed. However, the recommendation that psychology should permissively accept many values solves neither the dilemmas of what values a researcher had best choose nor how any one researcher might persuade the other 39,000 members of the American Psychological Association that a testable theory of the good life or a lucid view of pathology is at hand; but open, public agreement and verification are the essential requirements for the advancement of any scientific study, and these are clearly even more incessant and pressing concerns when meaning systems like personality are the target. Since Jahoda's review, mental health as a utopia has increasingly fallen into disrepute as a will-o'-the-wisp that implies only one certain matter—the absence of mental illness, if indeed the latter can be said to exist after Szasz's (1961) onslaught. Moreover, the consensus characterizing the days of psychoanalysis' hegemony as the generic theory of personality has disappeared. From the utopia of his self-actualizing model, Maslow (1962) suggested that White's (1963) competence would not be acceptable to a Hindu, Frenchman, or a women, and White criticized Erikson for assuming that the family oedipal drama preempts all the child's play, since in White's view, play is the opportunity par excellence for achieving competence. All in all, theorizing subsequent to Jahoda's explication has made it clear that whether or not there should be many definitions of positive mental health, many exist and are vigorously defended. The questions posed in this chapter are then: How can the scientific enterprise become more knowledgeable and skillful in its discussion and use of utopias? Can we find more modestly defined utopias to which we might all be able to subscribe?

After a general consideration of the role of values in personality theorizing, I will propose criteria, not yet in support of certain values but addressed to the prior question of the *ways* that immanent values should be chosen by psychologists when they are acting as social scientists and not as citizens. For instance, consensus might be achieved if values were based on *weaker* or *thinner* assumptions than on the strong assumptions used in constructing past utopian proposals. Weak assumptions are not to be thought of as sickly or frail; instead they should be thought of as modest and practical strategies for eliciting preliminary working agreements, so that the work of scientific description and, occasionally, discovery can proceed. (Rawls, 1971, has recently demonstrated the advantages of using weak, thin assumptions in formulating his theory of justice.) Strong assumptions underlie Freud's psychological man, Maslow's self-actualization, White's competence, Rogers' organic life force, as well as the garden-variety criteria of happiness, adjustment, mental health, and normality. Later the underlying value assumptions of these systems will be examined; clearly these models have been examined in the past, but perhaps some advantages will be gained by reconsidering them in the present context.

There are, additionally, the more covertly valuing, positivist systems that attempt to build their entire boat while at sea rather than constructing and reconstructing it bit by bit (the analogy is Neurath's, as reported by Quine, 1969). For example Mischel (1968) notes, apparently in agreement with the present position, that terms such as mental illness and statements about adjustment and socialization refer to social judgments; however he draws different conclusions from these observations. He urges that analyses done by social behaviorists should be (and therefore can be) immune to social contextual influences, and "requires elaboration of just what is being referred to and of the consequences of the described behavior to the person [p. 199]." Still he had noted previously, in an apparently disparaging and ironic vein, that "clients are not necessarily more immune than psychologists to theoretical preconceptions, and they too tend to put their constructs before their behavior [p. 199]." The positivists' as well as the humanists' attempts to construct objective, rigorous models of personality end up afoul of the question of immanent values. They, too, must ultimately recognize some basis for their theorizing or suffer the consequences of meaningless or nihilism as the definition of man's ontology. The positivists' selections most often represent the most conventional variants of social adjustment that follow "affective" socialization, and therefore represent culturally bound values. As Smith (1961) has urged, and Rudner has said, "to refuse to pay attention to the value decisions which must be made, to make them intuitively, unconsciously, or haphazardly, is to leave an essential aspect of the scientific method scientifically out of control [1966, p. 6]." I would add that the choice of nihilism first waits in the wings, and when it comes on stage its failure is usually followed by clear plans to bring order out of chaos, for example Skinner's *Walden II* (1948) and *Beyond freedom and dignity* (1971).

We need, Rudner (1953) noted, to become precise about what value judgments are being made, or, more challenging and to the point for the present discourse, about "what value judgments *ought* to be made [p. 353, emphasis added]." During the very early controversy surrounding the work on the *Authoritarian personality*, Else Frenkel–Brunswik (1954) made a like recommendation concerning the "ought" character of the personality–social psychologist's task: "there are richer and poorer, more efficient and less efficient orientations or ways of dealing with reality, and as scientists we are not entitled to obscure or to circumvent this fact [p. 468]." An even more radical argument will be advanced later: A model builder's inevitable selection of immanent value, which he will invariably have to make in order to identify the "good" and "poor" personality as it is structured by his system, is in itself a kind of moral choice. Thus he also needs to consider deliberately the moral grounds and warrants of his decisions. The Rudner and Frenkel–Brunswik positions imply this much.

Is a Value Choice Inevitable for the Personality Theorist?

Many areas of psychological research do not require a close examination of value assumptions because the immediate targets of investigation rest on material realities that may have nearly invariant relations with the behavior of some species, for example, the link between sex behavior and hormonic balance in birds. Work in still other areas of psychology is based on the supposition that physical systems that underlie and determine psychological actions will be eventually discovered, for example, studies of some aspects of perception or early ideas that intelligence might be related to cortical myelinization. However, as soon as words like "more intelligent" are used, a social-psychological construct is created by an active effort of imagination. People are not only individually selective about the acts that they regard as intelligent but they are even more so about what they call "more intelligent." For instance, there is an incipient argument brewing between the Piagetians and the psychometricians as to whether a high test IQ is more intelligent and better than being able to reason with formal operations (they are not synonymous, as will be shown in Chapter 7, "Configurations of Ego Processes and Cognitive and Moral Structures"). Only eventual intersubjective agreement can save such concepts.

Since much of psychology is about meanings, there is greater call for psychologists to work to make their constructions clear, veridical, and logically coherent than there is for them to seek physical bases and "neurologize" prematurely (Brunswik, 1950). If systems of psychological meaning were to become logically consistent and verified, they would not be overthrown by physiology; instead each field could serve to correct the other and both might then be able to converge. As Piaget (1969) recently noted, a complete psychology would be the best preparation for testing the plausibility of some of physiology's findings.

These matters of interdisciplinary priorities aside, the lack of a material target makes the personality psychologist's constructions personal and prescientific to the extent that he departs from common parlance and understandings of others. The safeguards against his personal—political intrusion and for the scientific ethic lie in the publicity that his choices receive: The progress that his constructs of meaning make as scientific vehicles—their usefulness and truth in the eyes of a generation of scientists—can only be due to the consensus they marshal. There is no need to despair that social science is any the less scientific for its value problems or for its constant needs to check its consensual base. As Quine (1963) notes, although the sum total of our knowledge at any one time is the sum total of our beliefs, we need not leap to the fatalistic conclusion that we are stuck with the conceptual schemes we grew up with, since they can be changed "bit by bit and plank by plank [p. 78]."

To summarize the implications of the discussion to this point, we can note that these matters are not pressing issues in the minds of some psychologists: (1) because their targets of research, even though not materially based, are clear and consensual (e.g., industrial psychology's acceptance of the research criteria of greater efficiency and more production with greater work satisfaction), or (2) because they think they have identified durable and universal psychological elements, such as cognitive, moral, or linguistic structures, that can be described both synchronically and diachronically in terms of development. The empirically verified description of the maximized, developed form of these structures can be an operational definition for criteria of "greater maturity," a kind of goodness that could guide both research and social policy, or (3) because value intrusion goes unnoticed and the model of personality is constructed by the psychometric mariner at sea, and the technician's values are unwittingly optimized.

At the present time personality—social psychologists have neither criteria of consensus (as do industrial psychologists) nor universal structural elements (as do the cognitive stage theorists) to form their taxonomies of personalities. Erikson (1950) and Loevinger (1966b) have proposed taxonomies of stages of personality development. But since neither system rests on consensual definitions or identified structural elements, these stage sequences may represent relatively parochial "goods." Since no one has yet identified personality structures that equal the cognitive in clarity and certainty, we are not able to evaluate whether or not these systems are substantive. Moreover arguments were made in the previous chapter that the personality, as it is defined here, is not structural.

Still, societies that are stable, progressive, integrated, or surviving, and people who are normal, healthy, adjusted, competent, self-actualized, or coping are regarded as "better" by various constituencies. However, so far, we cannot point to widely accepted elements of personal-social functioning, which in their developed or maximized form, represent public theories of good. We must either attempt to find (1) a "good" to serve as the basic presupposition of value to which all serious people would agree, or (2) universal structural elements of personality that develop in an orderly progression to a state of maturity, evidence that would permit the good to be defined empirically as "more structurally mature," or (3) some combination of the two.

A basic decision about the nature of personality research underlies these recommendations: a "good" theory is one that aspires, even though it must fumble along the way, to make a general, universal description of personality. In other words, an assumption is made, in disagreement with the relativists, that all men have some kinds of personal commonalities, but whether these general, catholicized elements exist and what their nature might be is not yet clear.

The next section will begin to suggest a compromise solution for psychology's difficulties with public and private theories of the good, a solution wherein personality theories are so designed that every man can be seen to entertain his own private theory of the good at the same time that he can be described in general and universal terms.

Goals as Criteria for Immanent Value in Personality Theory

Most theories of the good and enviable life embed value choice in finalistic, achieved states, for example, being competent, self-actualized, socialized, happy, or successfully analyzed. (In passing we can note for now that valued states, which are not goals, but more loosely achievements, have also been posited, for example, normality, adjustment, and mental health.) An attempt will be made in this section to show that this solution for registering immanent value in finalistic states does not make good science and that much of the personologists' scientific confusion and disagreement follows from values being embedded in ends. Subsequently a preliminary argument is made that it will make better science if value choice is introduced into systems prior to the introduction of goals—in the processes that people use to reach goals—and that this solution alleviates the necessity of making strong value assumptions; however, weak ones are still required. Finally, a proposal is made of four specific criteria for entering value into theories. These criteria might provide a starting point for consensus and solve the moral dilemmas of the researcher as a person among people.

There are probably two ideological ancestors, one religious and the other "scientific," for our thinking that final achievements are a reasonable definition of ideal states: Heaven was once such an ideal goal for many who expected they could reach this valued state if they prepared themselves correctly. As a consequence, life had purpose and a certain goal. The scientific ancestor is found in the earlier meanings of drive and motive as answers to questions of "why?"—meaning "toward what end?" White demonstrated this tradition by stipulating that the motive of effectance was needed to account for the achievement of competence (or he may have first considered the matter in reverse). Thus psychology assumed drives and the fruitions of drive were "natural" results. However, the nature of scientific explanation—no matter what the science—has increasingly come to be understood, not as a determinate matter of "what motive?" but rather as one of tracking law-like regularities to answer the question, "How did it come about?" In other words, "Why?" has come to be answered by chains of implications rather than by the discovery of single, determinate causation. Since psychology attaches importance to man's striking and obviously telic activity, it is understandable that final culmination of these strivings would appear to be the plausible candidate for the utopian role.

Rudner (1966) declares that a main mix-up in social science is the confusion between statements of contingent and analytic idealization. The former are empirical statements that are subject to disconfirmation. On close examination, valued goals can be seen to be examples of analytic idealizations, which can be entirely true even though they do not describe anything empirical and cannot be disconfirmed, for example, "All unicorns have horns [p. 58]." Their use in mature sciences rests on their deductibility from the contingencies of verified theories. When value is embedded in the end goals, the stipulation follows that men's activities are explainable on the basis of their striving to reach the goal of being, for instance, competent or self-actualized. This may be entirely true in some very general sense, but I argue that it designates no actuality and certainly not one that is testable.

As a child or a person is solving a problem, he is acting because he wants to solve this problem, or one in the near future, in such a way that its solution is congruent with his own private theory of what is good for him. He is almost never especially saying "I want to solve this problem because I want to be competent; moreover, its solution will lead to my eventual competence." All men are telic, but they are individually so, and when we designate the same content goal for all, we fail to take into account that my theory of what is good for me cannot be generalized to you. The privatistic qualities of theories of finalized good do not make for good science, even though they describe individual aspirations.

Goals represent the contents of individual people's lives; individual people strive for their own intrasubjectively defined goals in terms of their own particularistic, private contents and do not care a whit about the theoretician's formulations. Perversely enough from the researcher's point of view, the temporary goals of people acting as subjects may be to fit in with the researcher's goals, a problem that has received much attention recently in social scientists' discussions about the social nature of experiments. To rid the goal of its particularized content and to say more simply that goal striving in itself is the utopia does not take the discussion of which positive value to choose very far. Moreover, no great act of empathetic construction is required in order to see that psychotics are also goal striving within the terms of their own intrasubjective logic. We might even say that immobilized depressives have the goal of not commiting themselves to any course of action. Altogether, individual women and men want to optimize the good, but according to their own theories of the good, and within their own lifetimes, because it is clear to each, whatever their spiritual beliefs, that he or she can only live this particular life once.

Some psychologists—the clinicians and the humanists—are anguished by the thought of relinquishing their potential of describing all the rich details of people's individual goals. However to entertain this aspiration is to expect that science can model all of reality. As Rudner (1966) urged, it is not the task of science to reproduce the concrete details of reality—and, I would emphasize, certainly not the detailed, living reality of individual psyches—but it is rather to describe more general realities in reasonably economic, systematic, and abstract detail. As Einstein commented (according to Rudner), describing the taste of chicken soup is not the same as tasting chicken soup.

I have been arguing that personality psychology cannot find researchable commonality in the goals of individual women and men. Instead we must choose middle-level constructs that lie somewhere between the grand analytic idealizations of people as moved by a single purpose and the reproductive fallacy (Rudner, 1966) of planning to describe all there is to people. Moreover, it is morally hazardous for the researcher to assume that the description of soup is the same as tasting it since postulating a common desirable goal, for example, self-actualization, diminishes the individual choices and purposes of the single person. We have seen a depressing example of how private theories of the good can defeat social policy's setting of a common goal. The Johnson administration's Great Society programs operated with the presupposition that all lower class people surely held, or should hold, the valued goal that their children should become competent readers. However much money the Great Society granted to achieve its goals, the recipients' own theories of what was good for them took priority—they did not formulate their thories to be altered by someone else. Had the recipients determined their own goals, and had social policy decided to support that process, the results might have been different.

We need to back off and consider the question of what kinds of human actions or characteristics, other than goals, might better register the values that necessarily underlie formulations of ideal personality. The previous explication makes it appear that the telic activities of people need to be dissected and then described, instead of being simply postulated, to answer the modern version of the "why?" question: "How did personality come about?" From this perspective, consensual, immanent value must be introduced prior to goals and into the common processes that women and men use to do whatever their own private theories of the good lead them to want to do. Thus I will be arguing that consensual, immanent value should be registered *prior* to men's goals and in people's processes and that it cannot represent the contents of men's behavior.

Criteria for Choosing Values in Personality Theory

Having argued against idealized goals as a basis for achieving consensus, I want to suggest four specific criteria of value assumptions:

1. To mobilize the consensus needed, values will have to be based on thin or weak assumptions, since one man's ideas of the good life can turn out to be anathema to another.

2. To recruit agreement, *all* serious men and women would have to regard the value as being potentially supportive of their own prudentially considered theory of what would be good for them. (The statement is qualified by "potentially" because a vote for or against relevance will never actually be taken, but instead will be the consensus of the scientific community based on its logical analysis and knowledge of findings and implications, irrespective of any one society's actual limitations in permitting its citizens to enjoy a particular value.)

3. Values cannot be tied to the contents of people's lives or to their knowledge and acceptance of the contents of any society's sanctions. Latitude must be given for the supposition that each person would prefer, if he could, to choose his own good. To achieve the generality needed, values will probably have to represent the forms of personality, for example, processes and/or structures.

4. Finally, the values should represent the theorist's moral reciprocity with his subjects in recognizing that they have the same interest in choosing their good as he has in choosing for himself. The safeguard of reciprocity is demanded by the fact that personality theory is not physically based and is instead a system of meanings chosen by psychologists.

These criteria are proposed in addition to the usual hallmarks of any good scientific theory: correctness, comprehensiveness, logical consistency, and capability of being tested. But admission of the inevitability of the theoretician's value choice could clear the way for personality theory to achieve all of these with greater speed and lucidity. A traditional and additional criterion, left over from the positivist philosophy of science, that no a priori propositions should be made, is not met, since two such assumptions, necessary to the construction of meaning systems, are made: (*1*) each person surely would, if he could, choose his own good, defined as whatever his experience leads him to believe is a course of action that leads to his good; and (*2*) that psychologists *should* see that it is irrational to regard subjects as preferring *less* of their own good than psychologists require for themselves. (It is also untenable to think that well-informed people would unreasonably demand more than their share of good, since clearly negative consequences ensue; suggested by Rawls' formulation, 1971.)

Examination of Various Utopian Personalities

Up to this point the discussion has not drawn a distinction between the conceptualizations of ideal personality within theoretical systems and their use in the workaday clinical world, but there is a gap. The barrier between theory and practice is the lack of a generally accepted, comprehensive theory of personality that adequately solves the problem of "desirable" standards, as Macklin (1972) repeatedly points out in her recent and careful philosophical analysis. Ultimately there should not be such lacunae, as theory and practice correct each other. For the time being, clinical decisions are ostensibly made in the negative terms of the patient's lack of mental health, normality, happiness, and adjustment or adaptivity.

Treatment plans are almost never couched in positive-goal terms of the patient's need for competence or self-actualization, except for the affluent and sophisticated who can choose the luxury of treatment in accordance with current popular suppositions that people *should* be self-realized. This divergence between clinical practice and theoretical supposition would not be troublesome if treatment could be correctly and completely defined as an activity that involves *nothing more* than the alleviation of difficulties or symptoms. Many behavior modifiers feel that they do just that and they thereby escape implicit questions of value. Their own moral position is that treatment should be restricted to a social contract that stipulates only that particular symptoms will be alleviated (London, 1964). One result is that behavior modification is largely a "poor man's therapy," since the poor cannot afford to expect more, and only present themselves for treatment when their symptoms and situations have become unbearable. Another result is that the desirable standard for behavior modification is to be symptom-free.

Most clinicians do expect to affect their patients' positive well-being; furthermore psychological difficulties (or physical illnesses for that matter) probably cannot be alleviated without the person's positive attributes being facilitated, given the unitary qualities of life functioning. The nature of the desirable standards varies from theory to theory. In the classical Freudian view it is a critical fringe benefit that is achieved as various obstacles are identified, understood, and removed; in the self, life force theories, good is expected to be a direct benefit of the patient's growth in treatment.

Whatever the instance, a symmetry between positive and negative states (which may or may not be true) is implied. The most obvious example is that the absence of mental illness implies the presence of mental health. The assumption of symmetry has not been useful in defining ideal personality, since it is a definition by negation. The concept of mental health is an empty one and so meaningless that both Jahoda (1958) and Macklin (1972) were able to use it as the superordinate designation of a positive state of ideal personality under which they could subsume something of the idea of mental health itself, self-actualization, functional and structural integrity, normality, full use of capacities, and so forth. Moreover, its vagueness has permitted clinicians to operate with a comfortable sense that they are nonevaluative. Empirically, people are probably always mixtures. As Jahoda (1958) says, what of the strong man with a bad cold? I will argue late in this chapter that the only feasible position for the therapist to take with respect to his patient and to the question of desirable standards is one of facilitating the patient's coping.

Although other clinical criteria—normality, happiness, adjustment, or adaptivity, have clearer referents, they all have difficulties that have been widely recognized since Jahoda's (1958) explication. All suppose that extant social conditions are invariably right and good. However all, paradoxically, define the individual person as separate from social circumstances but still determined by these same benign social conditions, a model of parallelism between self and society rather than one of interaction. The use and force of these criteria has not waned, so each is now implicitly represented in more sophisticated theory. We turn now to focus on the class of values each of these criteria represents.

THE CRITERIA OF NORMALITY

Normality places value in whatever personality type exists in greatest number (a statistical nonentity if all mankind is the denominator). More informally, the clinician's understanding of normality is the modal, valued personality of his time and culture. Clearly the first value elevates the middleman, whatever his nature, to the position of favor, while the second variant is more susceptible to definition, and various attempts have been made to research it.

A statistically complex model of ideal normative personality defined by professional clinical psychologists was proposed recently and given two labels: "optimal adjustment" (Block, 1962; Siegelman, Block, Block, & von der Lippe, 1970) and "psychological health" (Livson & Peskin, 1967; Peskin, 1972). Both sets of researchers employed the same 100 Q-sort items (California Q Sort, Block, 1962) and had clinical psychologists (four sorters in the case of the Livson–Peskin study, and eight in the Siegelman study) sort their own definition of the optimally adjusted or psychologically healthy person. The composited scores for the 100 Q items of each group of sorters provided quantitative definitions of each conceptualization. Reliabilities among the judges in each project were high (raw $\overline{X}$ agreements of .82 for psychological health, .78 for optimal adjustment and .95 and .97, respectively, for their composited reliabilities). Since agreement between the two criteria was high (.91), we can probably conclude that the procedure defined an ideal, normative personality.

Later work (Haan, 1974a) showed that the same procedure of sorting done by eight young, and mostly counterculture, nonpsychologists had similar levels of agreement: the $\overline{X}$ of the raw intragroup reliabilities was .76 and when composited, .96. The nonprofessional sort correlated with the two professional sorts, .84 and .88, almost as high as they had with each other. However, the nonpsychologists were instructed to describe "a hypothetical, optimally adjusted person as he would be viewed in this society; remember, he may or may not be a person that you would like as a friend."

Apparently two conclusions can be drawn: The psychologists' information about ideal normative personality was not privileged, and normative personality in its second sense is understood by members of this culture, even when they do not endorse its values.

Jahoda (1958) notes that both the first and the second sense of normality must be culturally or subculturally specific, since no universal normative men can be said to exist. She rejects the second sense of normality as being defined with circularity: In the instances just described, the normative definitions of optimal adjustment and psychological health are what is valued in this culture, and what is valued "ought" to be psychological health and optimal adjustment. However, from the perspective of modern methods of science, temporary circularity is not anathema as long as it is recognized as such and does not continue indefinitely as a closed loop. A greater and more precise difficulty is that normality in both its first and second senses operates in a more specifically circular way that equates the normative "is" with "what ought to be," and thereby empirically puts a ceiling on what desirable standards there should be. Moreover, normality, like mental health, is an empty concept; it suggests nothing substantive and could be about any content, process, or structure. As an example, the Q sort researchers cited above were not concerned about the particular nature of the items that defined their normatively valued person.

Thus we can see that the values embedded in normality do not match our criteria on several counts: Although normality does not directly make strong, overt value assumptions, few men would agree that their good would be supported by the criterion that they should be like other people. Normality is clearly tied to society's sanctions, and few theorists would themselves be content if they were regarded as merely normal or that they represented the ideal norm of their society. Most would like to be more interesting.

THE CRITERIA OF HAPPINESS

We must set aside happiness for some of the same reasons. As Jahoda (1958) briskly observed, the proposal that happiness should represent the ideal condition reveals "a naive belief in the social justice of all conditions [p. 20]." Furthermore, as a psychological postulate in unelaborated form, happiness minimizes social concern and optimizes personal salvation, irrespective of social context, and by so doing places society, either as a force for good or bad, in an unimportant role. Taken alone, happiness also suffers from a lack of substance, but in its more sophisticated successors—those theories that emphasize a finalistic self-realization— substance is added by expectancies that the ideal person will be happy to the extent that he is realized. In Rogers' (1961) writings, realization was the full expression of an organismic wisdom; Maslow (1962) says self-actualization is the "acceptance and expression of the inner core of self [p. 197]." The social separatism of the self-realization models does more than ignore people's inherent embeddedness in social collectivities, it also tends to preclude examination of the social-consensual nature of model building itself. When the importance of the social world is denied, the theorist's interdependence with the world and his colleagues is also refuted, and his private knowledge is protected. There is some tendency for him to be regarded as being both wise and good, that is, he becomes a guru.

In further evaluation, I can do no better than to quote Macklin's (1972) conclusion (she uses the term "mental health" as a working designation for any concept of positive functioning, but she also rejects its inherent meanings):

> The assumptions about man's nature or essence cannot be accepted uncritically, and the difficulties of formulating a testable concept of man's "potentiality" (as a generic trait) are well-known. To the extent that a concept of mental health adopted by these theorists rests on the foregoing assumptions, we cannot expect much in the way of criteria that meet the requirements of empirical testability and confirmability . . . . As attempts to provide a basis for constructing a clear and workable *concept* of mental

health, the self-realization theories fail to satisfy the demands of conceptual clarity and empirical testability [p. 356].

To make self-realization theories testable, two corrections need to be made that would revise the theories beyond recognition. As noted above, the theories cannot logically be aloof from social feedback, but a second related difficulty, which self-realization theories do not adequately address, is the question of the *correctness* of the realized person's self-regard. Clearly the individual ought not to depend solely on his own criteria to form his self-realization, since he may be defensively negating noxious aspects of himself to himself, or he may be fully aware of his own negative aspects but rationalize, nevertheless, with egocentric, megalomaniac values, that these importantly and acceptably contribute to his self-realization. The very idea of correctness reveals the social nature of personal integrity, since one comes to understand the meanings and necessities of accuracy only in the presence of others. Consequently, to add the idea that self-regard should be aligned with social assessment to the self-realization models is not a simple matter, since their total structures would be affected. Correctness is based on a supposition that "reality" exists; in personality theory and most of social science "reality" can only be defined by a socially achieved and intersubjective consensus. Altogether, the emphasis of the self-realization models seems misplaced, since people can only realize themselves within social contexts and by social interchange, with all the complexities and conflicts these entail.

Since the immanent value of the self-realization theories optimizes self-concern at the expense of social concern, it makes a number of strong assumptions about the nature of man's social relationship. Even though these formulations, if true, could be universally applied, it is unlikely that all would assent—particularly not those who need special social care—that the system potentially supports their theory of the good. However, self-realization is contentless and is certainly not tied to society's sanctions. The moral position of the researcher is peculiar in that he gives all latitude for his subjects' individuality but then subtly takes away its protection as he threatens the social fabric by denying his own and his subjects' obligation to consider community consensus.

THE THEME OF ADJUSTMENT

The simple version of personal adjustment as criteria for positive personality can be quickly dismissed. In the 1930s and 1940s, it was an unexamined, common dictum that parents and teachers should bring about children's synchronization with social conditions; but subsequent sophistication about contradictory social demands and alienation from inadequate social institutions made the value of simple social compliance untenable and even foolish. However, adjustment as a criterion persists in a more sophisticated, differentiated form, most notably in psychoanalysis, since the theory, still held by many, represents a particular view of the individual person and entails a complementary character for society.

Given Freud's wish to maintain scientific objectivity and rigor and most of his followers' like commitments, psychoanalysis has been most chary of attaching explicit value to a formulation of ideal personality. As a matter of fact, Hartmann (1960) claimed that psychoanalysis was value-free. Freud's offhand comment that people should be able to work and to love is often quoted, but it is too simple to be the subject of our analysis. The theory's original preoccupation with pathology and its neglect of positive functioning has occasioned a lengthy series of attempted reforms (but few radical revisions) some of which were extensively considered in Chapters 2 through 4. I will not review this history of reform, which runs roughly from Adler to White and Loevinger. Instead, I will attempt to make a statement that highlights the core of the implicit values embedded in the metatheory. In so doing, I will be leaning heavily on Rieff's (1959) analysis and summarization of Freud's views, which was by no means an unfriendly effort.

The privileged role of the unconscious and the manner in which its entailments are constructed (e.g., the necessities of defense, the position of the sexual and aggressive impulses, the initial hedonism, and the necessary, limiting, and repressive role of society represented by the superego) determine the implicit definition of the ideal personality. As Rieff notes, in the end, the liberation offered from these warring forces is a modest one. Since unconscious conflict is virtually inevitable, optimal persons must almost always be those who have been successfully analyzed. However, the demands of the unconscious are never entirely quelled, so analysts themselves are enjoined to be re-analyzed from time to time. The liberated person has achieved mastery of his past, his sexual impulses, and his childish needs for hedonism, and he has come to see that he alone must choose for himself if the choice is to be authentic, but in the end he can only grow equable (Reiff's word). He should not hope for more, since the necessary repressiveness of society is given and immutable. The Freudian value thus emerges as a highly articulated variant of the adjustment theme: It is not a simple adjustment *to* society's terms that is valued, as in the naive definition, but rather adjustment to one's biology and to society's necessities by the means of a self that has grown scrupulous, self-centered (Reiff's words), and capable of canny negotiation.

Since society cannot be changed and its repressiveness is necessary for people's coming to terms with their hedonisms and assessing their realistic possibilities, all that is left for one to do, after he has rid himself of his childish neurosis, is to adjust. His social criticism and protest are suspect (as were the student activists' during the 1960s for a number of Freudians, for instance Freuer and Bettelheim). Fervent criticism most always reflects the acting out of neurotic rather than social problems. No ingrained social ills are reified, only insensible personal ills.

The unrelieved form of Freudian social psychology, in featuring an immutable society, produces a personal elitism based on special understandings of one's unconscious or on the salubriousness of one's first few years of life. Beyond these two ameliorations for the embattled self, psychoanalysis' value can only be to adjust to the necessary (society) and come to intelligent and wary protection of the private bastion. There is no assurance in the value for others and for society that the private intelligence of the successfully analyzed will include sufficient moral concern, since morality is left to early and nonrational internalizations of society's authority, however principled or unprincipled these might be. Noting the lack of human connectedness, Reiff (1959) comments, "Freud never understood the ethics of self-sacrifice. The omission leaves his human doctrine a little cold, and capable of the most sinister applications [pp. 55–56]." The value optimized by Freudian theory is clearly a version of individualism, one that highlights the Nietzschean mastery of self along with the supposition that other people—that is, well-functioning people—will surely do the same.

Clearly our criteria of value registry are not met: Strong assumptions are made about the nature of man but, more importantly, about the nature of society that would not be acceptable to many. Again those who need social concern would not see the system as potentially supporting their theory of the good; the theory is tied to specific contents (id instincts, oedipal drama, etc.) and strongly to society's sanctions. The privileged knowledge of the analysts and the analyzed about the nature of the good diminishes the system's moral reciprocity and makes it difficult for it to submit to publicity.

MULTIPLE CRITERIA

Aside from the theoretical inelegance of a conglomeration of multiple or mixed criteria, this permissive approach poses a number of problems, although it was recommended by Jahoda (1958) and supported by Smith (1959, 1961) as an earlier, practical, and presumably interim solution to the inability to choose in accordance with a verified theory. If the fundamental presupposition of this chapter has validity—that no description of positive and, likely, of negative functions can be made without value presumption—then it is evident that multiple criteria of positive personality only compound the difficulties. Instead of one value, there are many, and most people would immediately weigh some parameters more heavily than others. Another related problem concerns the internal consistency of multiple criteria. If they were internally consistent, we would be able to name the whole, but we cannot because the different criteria have relevant and important differences, as well as various similarities. As matters are now, the same person could receive a different diagnosis of positiveness or one of pathology or deficiency from the same data. The competent person may not be self-actualized: The self-actualized may not be viewed as competent; the Freudian private man cannot be said to be happy. As Macklin (1972) said, "Deviation from one such norm might count as mental illness, while the same person might be termed mentally healthy according to some different set of norms whose ideal he fulfills or closely approximates [p. 355]."

One study (Haan, 1974a) cross-tabulated subjects' identifications as being optimally adjusted, according to the Q sort criterion previously described, or as being primarily coping and defensive, according to ratings. Both designations were derived from the same interview material. Cutting points were established: (1) A correlation of .50 between the subject's actual description and the optimal adjustment criterion was used to identify the optimally or nonoptimally adjusted; (2) a mean split was used to identify the copers and defenders. All nonoptimally adjusted people, 19 men and 20 women, were identified as defensive. However, the cross-tabulation between coping and optimal adjustment produced different results. Only 50% of the 14 male copers and only 30% of the 10 female copers were identified as optimally adjusted. The nature of the disagreement, which could only be assessed in a clinical sense because of the small Ns, suggested that the coping, nonoptimally adjusted subjects were relatively unconventional people. These results imply that there is greater understanding and consensus about pathology than there is about positive states—an observation made many times without the aid of quantitative analysis.

Clearly the differences between all the various criteria could be empirically analyzed in similar fashions to draw out their important similarities and differences, if their primary variables could be operationalized, a task of uncertain outcome with most of these criteria. Even then, the results might very well be similar to those just described. Altogether the use of multiple criteria seems not to be even a reasonable interim solution.

PROCESSES AS CRITERIA

We turn now to the ego model of coping, defense, and fragmentation to examine its value implications. Although I obviously believe that this particular model has advantages, much of the argument I will make could apply equally well to other process criteria. Although the ego model has previously been described in great detail, several of its features need to be reiterated for this analysis of value:

1. The derivation of the coping from the defensive processes should have minimized but not ruled out intrusions of private theories of the good.

2. The area staked out for analysis and explication is limited; the processes were assumed to work to sustain the person as a "center of activity [Piaget, 1970]," within a range of internal consistency by coordinating other aspects of his person: (a) attained stage of structural capacities, (b) his affective reactions, (c) the contents of his individualized experiences that lead him to suppositions about who he is, what he believes, and what he likes and dislikes—altogether, his constructed appraisals of what is prudential and good for him.

3. The three modal processes of coping, defense and fragmentation are organized according to a hierarchy of utility, so the person will cope if he can, defend if he must, and fragment if he is forced to do so. Whatever processes he uses will depend on his possibilities for reaching a solution, given his internal resources and the nature of the immediate situation. However, coping does not insure success, nor do defending or fragmenting entail failure, since outcomes depend on matches between situations and resources.

Unlike some of the systems previously discussed, coping (as would also be true of other processes) does not depend on content nor is it tied to success. Processes can deal with any content, for example, aggression or love. They are catholic in permitting the achievement of any individualized goal, since they are positioned in the system prior to the goal. If a person should see his own good as involving the achievement of competence, or self-actualization, or a good vacation, presumably coping will help him achieve it. However processes are not without social knowledge since they are inherently responsive to situations. They do not involve naive assumptions that men should fit in with society, whether or not it is just, or whether or not its normative values can be regarded as "good." However coping cannot develop separately from social interaction.

All of these matters should make it possible to achieve the preliminary agreements that are necessary first steps for building a consensual personality theory: processes' lack of content and their focus on form, their permissiveness with respect to end goal, and their situational interactivity, which permits men's social embeddedness to enter into both diachronic and synchronic accounts. While the process of coping insures their awareness and commitment to social accuracy, the individuality of people's own theories of the good and their telic efforts within diverse situations are preserved; consequently the researcher's moral dilemma of permitting his subjects as much interest in attaining their own good as he expects for himself, is solved. Moreover, the role of the therapist is suggested by this analysis. He can hardly expect to do more than facilitate his patient's processes of coping—which includes their coping with their defenses—by knowing them or changing them. This is the intent of most reflective therapists. If they start the job of revising their patients' goals, two events usually ensue: They assume the mantle of the guru, and/or the patient does not return for his next appointment.

Now we need to ask, "What is the underlying value of coping, and is this value sufficiently general and weak that reasonable people could be persuaded to subscribe to such a working model?" The presumptive value underlying the model is that it is better to know one's intrasubjective and intersubjective situations accurately and to act in that framework, than it is to distort or negate one's appraisals and actions. The value is then one of accuracy in intrapersonal in interpersonal interchange, and to know that value is to match social and personal reality as it is defined by common, practical agreements about the nature of our mutual experiences.

All the properties of coping presented in Chapter 4—choice of action, flexibility, proportionate expression of feeling, and reality adherence—rest on the value of accuracy and can be deduced from it. To grow accurate and to be accurate is to know one's changing situation, oneself, and both these in interaction—altogether; it is to decenter and recognize one's own social embeddedness and indebtedness.

Clearly this proposition has both epistemological and value implications that we will consider, but as a psychological variable, accuracy has partial ancestry in Freud's reality principle and in clinicians' workaday espectancies that a patient's reality testing can be assessed and that therapy will improve it. Freud's meta-theoretical principle, however, represented the person's coming to learn how and in what ways his primary hedonism must be restricted and limited by external experience, rather than his coming to understand his context objectively in all its nuances and himself as an object among other objects. However, the working clinician assumes pragmatically that he and his patient can discover reality, that it is consensually knowable, and that it is critical to do so, not only in their interaction but also for the patient in his dealing with his world.

There are both survival and enhancing values that arise from accurate inter-personal exchanges and intrapersonal interchanges. Any person or society that consistently fails to recognize his social interdependency and to honor expectancies of accuracy in intrasubjective or intersubjective interchanges is eventually fated to chaos and disorder. We can say then, since coping usually works better for people than not, it is what they will prefer to do and in fact "should" do, in terms of their own rational self-interest. To grow accurate is to decenter—in Piaget's terms, by committing one's self to the world's perceptions rather than solely to one's own. Piaget (1950) observes that the child first becomes truthful and logical in the presence of others. Swanson (1968) makes a like stipulation from a sociological perspective: People require of each other that they be what they publicly allow themselves to seem to be.

As a primary, immanent value for personality theory, the accuracy requires no grand assumptions. This particular good carries no guarantee of certain outcome, nor does it rest on a cosmic spirit embedded in the universe or in society. Rather, man is viewed as engaged in an endless series of negotiations of uncertain character and outcome. For the time being, this good seems reasonably workable and almost empirical, and it does represent a middle ground between the grand assumptions of humanists about the nature of man and the prematurely rigorous assumptions of the neobehaviorists that man has no knowable nature.

Confusion about the omnipresent social backdrop of coping sets in when more individual, subjective activities like creativity, introspection, and daydreaming are considered. The ego processes are not exclusively toward solving the immediate problems of social living; the intraceptive functions are particularly concerned with assimilatory, intrapersonal activity. However when individual intrasubjectivity is not articulated within a framework of intersubjectivity, and assimilatory activities are preponderant, man grows increasingly odd and narcissistic. The artist's work becomes adualistic and therefore noncommunicative without an audience and critics. Hence a child's artwork, except by infrequent accident, never qualifies as a masterpiece because the child does not yet fully grasp so cannot express his social embeddedness.

The epistemological position represented here is a pragmatic, constructivist one that regards psychology as a component chapter of epistemology and epistemology as a component chapter of psychology, a position wherein both philosopher and psychologist recognize that their position in the world is no different from that of their human subjects (Quine, 1969, p. 83). Consequently no prior epistemological grounds can be stipulated, and no clear or marked difference can be found between a scientific observation and one that the community sees eye-to-eye on. "An observation sentence is one that is not sensitive to differences in past experience within the speech community . . . and [they] are the sentences on which all members of the community will agree under uniform stimulation [Quine, 1969, p. 87]."

Still there will be ontological relativities among people, but as Quine also notes, "We can reconcile all this with our neighbor's verbal behavior, by cunningly readjusting our translation of his various connecting predicates so as to compensate for [his] switch of ontology [1969, p. 47]."

Personality psychologists, led to suppose by the logical positivists that scientific data must be sense data and that it must exist prior to the subject's construction of meaning, themselves moved early to construct "traits" as the nearest they could possibly come to sensation. Later epistemological nihilism, which set man adrift with no possibility of a priori grounds for knowledge, has produced a psychological nihilism that undoubtedly repelled humanistic psychologists like Maslow, Rogers, and White. As a consequence they counterattacked with unabashed, strong assumptions of man's intrinsic possibilities of being richly textured and potentially "good." There is no need for such ardencies or abandonments. The new epistemologies of Quine and Piaget end the infinite regress of nihilism in practical working observations about the nature of human communications and agreements. As Quine says, when we fully appreciate the social nature of the institution of language, "We can see there cannot be, in any useful sense, a private language [1969, p. 27]," or, "When I correlate your sentences with mine by the simple rule of phonetic correspondence, I find that the public circumstances of your affirmations and denials agree pretty well with those of mine [1969, p. 5]."

For the time being, it seems to me, a working psychology of theory and application may proceed with its work knowing that valid knowledge and reality need not be based on prior assumption, nor need it be baseless, since it rests instead on the community consensus. As for coping, its underlying value is not that reality should be understood fully, broadly, or completely, but only that whatever there is between people that must be communicated, or whatever there is within an individual person that he needs and wants to know, should be understood accurately.

Thus the criteria for value immanence (which, of course, I myself set earlier in this chapter) is met: Coping is based on the weak assumption that it is better to be accurate and therefore socially reasonable than not; most serious and rational men would probably agree with the value of coping processes because it potentially supports each person's theory of his own good; coping is not tied to the content or sanctions of society although it develops hand in hand with people's understandings of men's social nature and commitments; it permits the researcher to take a morally reciprocal position with his subjects permitting them to pursue their own theories of the good, providing both agree that it is better to be accurate than not.

Conclusion

The argument was made that value is immanent in the construction of all meaning systems, but most strikingly in those concerned with theoretical models of personality. Consequently the frequently stated recommendation that value assumptions should be made explicit was followed in the analysis of a number of familiar systems, as well as in the analysis of the ego process model of coping, defense, and fragmentation. The idea that valued processes provide a "better" basis for the value assumptions of social science than do valued contents or valued end goals, was advanced. Processes are not only reasonably content-free, but are registered in models *prior* to finally achieved states. The latter feature allows variation in people's own theories of the good without jeopardizing common observations that men and women pursue their own finalistic states according to their own private theories of the good. Criteria of workable values were proposed for personality model construction, which were importantly based on the contention that the immanent values should rest on weak or thin, rather than strong, assumptions about man's nature, because they can apply across diverse contents and are able to recruit the baseline agreements we must achieve to proceed with our work. These criteria were thought to be necessary because personality theories can only rest on consensus since they are systems of meaning and without material base. Since the personologist must choose, not merely in his prescientific state, but in his scientific activity as well, he himself faces without exception the moral question of whether to award his subjects and his model men the same "natural" right of being interested in optimizing their own self-interested, rationally based good as he requires for himself. In other words, the scientist decenters so as to recognize that even in his scientific activity he is a person among people. Those personologists who are about to abandon their positivist base are reassured by the example of Piaget and the analyses of the epistemologist Quine that we do not necessarily "need to be struck with the conceptual schemes we grew up with [Quine, 1969, p. 78]." Although our realities are always changing in some degree, pragmatically they are knowable.

6. Investigating Ego Processes: Problems and Perspectives

The Nature of Research Verification

Since we have no direct access to intangible psychological or social things like dimensions, stages, traits, and processes—as was argued at length in the last chapter—our research effort is: (*1*) to fit patterns of our own making to established social realities, and (*2*) hopefully, thereby to increase our grasp of their coordination within other aspects of life so that we can then (*3*) deepen and extend our understanding and eventually (*4*) be able to characterize people's taxonomies and organizations more accurately and abstractly. The thesis that the personalities of people can be economically, usefully, and correctly characterized and understood by the patterns of their preferred processes has no privilege in this regard. Assessments of processes must also be shown to accord with already recognized social facts, and their analyses should extend and elaborate our understandings of their coordinations with other attributes of people and with their social circumstances. To be accepted and useful, the results of these analyses must so deepen, order, and accord with our experience that the worth of the process formulation becomes self-evident. Elaborating the argument, we can say: If processes are typical features of personality, then they must have at least weak implications for all areas of living and strong implications for others, because both personality and the processing of social realities are ceaseless.

Subsequent chapters in this book sample the role of processes within exemplary realms of living—both intrapsychic and social—contextual—and report findings that explicate empirical bases for the process formulation. The intrapsychic realms include the relationships of processes to cognitive and moral structures and to diachronic spans of ego functioning itself. To exemplify the international zone between the intrapsychic and extrapsychic, another chapter considers the role of processes in dealing with various kinds of stress and distress, both the unexpected emergency and the ordinary wear and tear of development and daily existence. Ego processing in the primary social—contextual area of family life is the focus of still a later chapter. Thus the remainder of this book provides bases for evaluating whether several main theses have merit and whether others of less importance elaborate what we already know. The main theses include: (1) the processes of coping can be regarded as normally expected actions, (2) the defenses and fragmentary actions are variously employed deviations from coping, and (3) this hierarchical pattern of use corresponds to already recognized social formulations of the ways that people actually experience and act.

Observing Processes

OBSERVING PEOPLE WITHIN SITUATIONS

Unlike traits or states, which are generally expected to manifest themselves at one point in time, processes occur, and are optimally observed, *across* an interval of time. The macroview of processing is the diachronic span of development, for instance, across a period such as adolescence. The diachronic view of identity formation regards the processes the adolescent uses as an extended regression in the service of the ego, undertaken to recapture, rework, and reorganize various self themes to attain a new, emergent self-definition. In contrast, the microview of processes is within the time frame of an immediate dynamic happening—the synchronic event. Since both micro or macro processes occur in time, their observation is best made over time—short in span for the microview of dynamic sequencings and interchanges, and long in span for developmental processes. Thus, parallelisms are posited between the processes preferred for dealing with a life epoch and those of an immediate event, a theme that will be developed in Chapter 8 concerned with the development of ego processes. The temporal nature of processes affects the nature and design of the research that is needed and the choice and understanding of the measurements that are to be made. Processes accord with our common experience that the nature of life and living is dynamic, but a dynamic occurrence can only be observed longitudinally, over time, or at least within a framework of implied time. The latter kind of observations is, of course, more frequently made because it is less expensive.

Psychological measures only roughly correspond to researchers' operational definitions, not so much because of their ignorance, but because subjects do not merely ingest information, they process it. Their responses represent partly what the researcher had in mind to observe; but, more critically, they include how they have processed and resolved the researcher's stimuli and how they have resolved their usually self-chosen predicament of being a research subject. These dilemmas are not resolved by simple linear arithmetic, that is, subjects do not add up what they want and what the researcher wants and then divide by two to make their decision. As a result, it is dubious whether subjects' annoying propensities to construct their own solutions are well handled by various attempts at "correction" used with personality scales or by statistical controls, or even by researchers' ever more artful and careful deceptions of intent. If the subject is a compliant fellow, or if he cannily takes the path of least resistance, he may try the best he can to confirm the researcher's hypotheses. If he is an obstreperous sort, he may go underground and work more devious and hostile kinds of sabotage. Whatever he decides, he did it, so it is authentically him. The experimenter's problem is to reckon with meanings of the subject's actions.

The problem of the "dishonest" and "unreliable" subject has plagued psychological research for some time, but it is usually regarded as arising from inept designs and as resulting in error variance. The methodological remedies were first to take greater pains to deceive subjects and later to devise ever more complicated forms of "blinding" both subjects and researchers when the sensitive compliance of subjects to researchers' hypotheses was recognized. The present state of affairs seems to be one of confusion, particularly among social psychologists, whose research usually requires naive or "empty" subjects who are confronted with some kind of social coercion. From the constructivist view there is no basis for regarding the subject's resolution of his subject status as arising from inept designs (although these surely exist) or as troublesome or as an artifact, as for instance the volume *Artifact in behavioral research* (Rosenthal & Rosnow, 1969), would have it. How the subject resolves being a subject is not artifactual from his point of view—his dilemma is a very real one. Moreover his final choice will often be typical of his usual methods of problem solving. Still, the subject's constructions are artifactual from the standpoint of the researcher who does not want to study problem solving and who would rather observe behavior that represents the pure outcome of his experimental manipulation or of the stimulus questions he asks. People will never regard the experience of being a research subject as trivial (nor do psychologists, when the tables are turned); consequently, they need to decide what their stance will be. An unobtrusive study of subjects (for instance, a study of bystanders in a subway who witness a researcher's accomplice feigning a drunken stupor) does not provide the investigator with information about the subjects' decision making processes; he can only know what the outcome appeared to be. He can only suppose that the instigating situation was assimilated by all prospective subjects in a standardized way. Nevertheless, in unobtrusive studies the interpretations of results usually lean heavily or entirely on suppositions about subjects' decision processes.

As an example several amusing errors in unobtrusive counts of behaviorial outcome occurred during a study of student activists conducted by Brewster Smith, Jeanne Block, and myself in the 1960s with Berkeley students. The behavioral outcome that we counted was whether or not students were arrested in the administration building after a sit-in that began one afternoon (we did nothing to promote this research opportunity). Several nonarrested students went out of their way to inform us, hotly, that they should be counted as arrested, because had it not been for mistaken information, they too would have been arrested. They understood that the "cops" were not going to come until the next morning so they spent the night in the computer center or the library getting some work out of the way. The next morning when they tried to get into the building in order to be arrested, the police had already begun the arrests and barred them from entering. Without doubt some of our subjects were also caught in the building and were arrested when they did not intend to be.

From the standpoint of the process formulation, more deviant (defensive) behavior, and less normative (coping) behavior can be predicted from the deceived or factually deprived subjects. People become defensive when they are scrutinized and feel used. According to this line of reasoning, we see that a great deal of psychological research unintentionally investigates the effects of stress stimuli, albeit usually mild in form. As a result, defensive not coping behavior is frequently studied. A close examination of the pages of the *Journal of Personality and Social Psychology* with the present definition of defense in mind may convince the reader that this is not a rare occurrence. A parallel can also be noted in recent conclusions that rats reared and tested in field-free circumstances are considerably more "intelligent" and adaptive than their laboratory-incarcerated relatives. Whatever the subject's reactions, they are not artifactual as far as he is concerned, but are instead bona fide self-expressions, probably typical of him in other contexts where he is an object of another's scrutiny and a creature of another's wishes. When the so-called response sets—acquiescence, yea-saying, nay-saying—are reformulated in terms of the demand characteristics of test taking, they can also be seen to represent well-articulated defenses.

Clearly some subjects move more readily to the deviance of defense than others and some scenes of data collections are more likely than others to instigate defensiveness. In fact, fragmenting in reaction to experimental settings is not unheard of and seems to have occurred with a number of Milgram's (1974) subjects who were pressured into supposedly shocking slow learners.

Rosenberg's (1969) concept of the "evaluation apprehensions" of subjects represents one aspect of the syndrome we are considering here. After various studies and considerations, Rosenberg concluded that the biasing influence of evaluation apprehension can be reduced: (*1*) if the data are collected by someone other than the one who was the original focus of the subject's apprehension (because experimenters often telegraph the results they want), (*2*) when subjects are low in need for approval (intrinsically not needing to comply), (*3*) when the subject is not given the continuous feedback he needs to shape his performance (he is kept from knowing what the experimenter wants), (*4*) when the subject does not perceive the experimenter as having power over him (the demand characteristics of the situation are reduced), and (5) when the alternative responses, which the experimenter cues as positive, all involve equal effort and are of equal clarity (anything the subject does is greeted with approval). Note, however, that Rosenberg's recommendations do not regard subjects' reactions to researchers' situations as data in themselves, but are instead solely concerned with reducing "bias" in the data.

Related to the present view of the subject as an active fellow is Rosenberg's discussion of subjects who covertly decide to challenge the experimenter and "screw up the works," which, we can see, can be done as effectively by complying as by not complying. All that is required for a subject to "screw up the scientific works" is that he not be "himself." To accomplish such aims, people employ different ego processes, ones they probably prefer to use in problematic situations. The process view suggests that the subject, when he is taken as an example of a generalized human being producing normative responses, cannot be truly observed unless the context makes it possible for him to cope (1) because it is relatively trivial and benign (2) it permits him response options, or (3) it is so inimical to his self-definition that he resigns from the study, just as Milgram's disobedient subjects did.

The vagaries of human cooperation and verisimilitude are salient aspects of the workaday world and of economic survival for psychologists who do psychotherapy. Researchers are threatened much less than psychotherapists if a few of their subjects quit or become uncooperative; these deviant individuals need not affect the results since they cannot be included in the final analyses of data and no income is lost. Despite the relatively loving care of therapists and the individual attention accorded, patients often do not entirely "level" or unambivalently cooperate with their therapist for months on end, and when they finally do, they are then well on their way to a cure. To admit fully to one's therapist is to admit fully to one's self, a step that frees the patient's processes of problem resolution.

If the reader were to take all parts of this argument as true, he might very well be wondering how research can be conducted at all. From the perspective of ego processes, the answer is clear. When the investigation deals with human subjects, their persistent constructions must necessarily be part of the research design and affect the collection and analysis of data and the interpretation of results. Findings can almost never be taken at face value or as direct, pristine evidence of the subject's status. They must rather be regarded as what the generalized subject decided to let us observe. General realities, which are not necessarily predictive of individual subjects' meanings, are found in personal-social investigations. Consequently, data are always (1) what the subject reported, rather than what the subject is, (2) how the subject decided he should be seen rather than who he is, (3) how the subject perceived his world rather than what his world is. (Moreover, if we observe his world, it will be what his world seems to us to be rather than what his world is.) Following this line of reasoning further, we can see that most kinds of deception—consideration of ethical issues aside—only further bias our results since we observe deviant functioning—unless, of course, we intended to study nonnormative actions.

SITUATIONAL CONTEXTS

The above discussion was primarily focused on observations of subjects' processes within the research dyad; we now consider, more directly, the nature of situations designed by experimenters—the test taking scenarios, the formatting of protocols (inkblots to yes—no), and the laboratory experiments—and their peculiar demand characteristics. Some time ago it was recognized that one of the easiest things a subject does is check "no" if he is faced with a series of direct questions and wants to defend himself from the psychometrician's penetration; consequently, inventories were redesigned to word some pathology-revealing questions backwards to catch the unwary respondent. Later, other forms of correction were introduced by the Lie, F, and K scales of the Minnesota Multiphasic Personality Inventory (MMPI) and by the Good Impression and Communality scales of the California Psychological Inventory (CPI). At the time that the K scale was constructed, it represented a technical breakthrough, since it was designed to correct for tendencies to both "fake good" and "fake bad." However, from a view of subjects' processing, we have come to see that these various test-taking attitudes represent typical defensive maneuvers, made by less than self-revealing "subjects" to situations like taking tests. In other words, the corrections represent processes that have meaning in and of themselves because subjects bring them into play to protect their integrity.

The interrelationships of the correction scales and a series of preliminary defense and coping scales previously developed (Haan, 1965) are shown in Table III. The MMPI Lie scale is positively associated with denial and repression and negatively with coping intellectuality and the intraceptive functions of empathy and ego regression. High K scores are similarly associated with denial but also reflect a more deliberate, thinking self-presentation by their lower but still positive associations with coping intellectuality, concentration, and suppression. The faking good aspect of the K scales is related to doubt, projection, regression, and displacement. In the context of these relationships of F scale appears much as it has been described in the MMPI literature: People with high F scores do not concentrate (probably on the task of test taking), do not suppress their feelings, do not work to deny their pathology, and so on. Social desirability has many of the same relationships as the K scale. Making a good impression also has the same pattern of relationships as the K scale, but congruent with Gough's (1957) intent of designing a test of personal soundness is its much stronger relationship with coping concentration and suppression. Perhaps the good impression that can be achieved by answering the CPI items is a less defended and more successful self-description.

Experimental situations are usually not repeated enought times that corrections can be standardized. However, there is every reason to think that the laboratory situation should pull for equal, if not more defensive, strategies. Perhaps the most documented account so far of laboratory subjects' defensiveness and fragmentation in reaction to inexorable situations is now available in Milgram's book (1974), *Obedience to authority*, which is an excellent example of how subjects' ego

Table III
Relationships between Test Correction and Coping and Defense Scales

	MMPI				CPI	
	Lie	K	F	Social desirability	Good impression	Communality
Defense						
Intellectualizing	—	—	$-.23^c$	—	—	—
Doubt	—	$-.48^a$	$.41^a$	$-.69^a$	$-.27^b$	—
Denial	$.44^a$	$.50^a$	$-.47^a$	$.52^a$	$.34^a$	$.21^c$
Projection	—	$-.32^b$	—	$-.29^b$	—	—
Regression	—	$-.29^b$	$.39^a$	$-.37^a$	$-.20^c$	—
Displacement	—	$-.24^c$	$.34^b$	$-.51^a$	—	—
Repression	$.51^a$	—	—	—	$.36^a$	—
Coping scales						
Objectivity	—	—	—	$.18^c$	—	—
Intellectuality	$-.42^a$	$.22^c$	—	$.37^a$	—	—
Concentration	—	$.29^b$	$-.55^a$	$.45^a$	$.59^a$	—
Empathy	$-.39^a$	—	—	—	—	—
Regression-ego	$-.22^c$	—	—	—	—	—
Suppression	—	$.30^b$	$-.43^a$	$.51^a$	$.61^a$	—

Note: $N - 85$ for MMPI scales and 90 for CPI; men and women are combined.
$^a p \leqslant .001$
$^b p \leqslant .01$
$^c p \leqslant .05$

processes can muddy a problem that an experimenter intended to study! From the various transcripts which Milgram provides, it is clear that his subjects were severely stressed by the experimenter's obdurate persistence and lack of responsiveness and were therefore "not themselves"; there are gross instances of projection of responsibility ("You take the responsibility and I'll go on"), isolation between thoughts and feelings (proceeding with the task while disintegrating with revulsion), depersonalization ("I didn't really know what I was doing"), rationalization ("I'm not like this in real life"), regression ("I just gave up"), reaction formation ("I'm really soft hearted"), and so on. Like most psychologists, Milgram's greater interest in pathology leads him to tell us little about the subjects who disobeyed him. He does mention that they often seemed to feel a great calm following their decision to defy the experimenter. His limited analysis of individual differences indicates that the disobedient assigned greater quantitative responsibility to themselves and less to the victim than did the obedient subjects. Since the subjects were the ones who were literally at the switch, it was accurate, and therefore coping, for them to decide that they were responsible, and it also follows that they would be calm after they had coped with this situation, which was personally violating for all subjects. (Milgram does not say he found any happy sadists.) It is a pity that Milgram did not concern himself more with the attributes of his disobedient subjects, but their existence tells us again that the demand characteristics of experiments, however monolithic and stressful, are not processed and uniformly resolved by all subjects.

Milgram's work seems to tell us more about people's reactions to severe stress than it does about the conditions of people's relationships and obedience to petty authority. Milgram found out what we already know: that many stressed people become chaotic in their thinking and actions and thereupon deviate from their more usual modes of problem resolution. There is nothing in the convention of ordinary people's moral thinking that condones hurting others for insufficient reasons; Milgram's descriptions make it seem doubtful that his subjects were given sufficient time to assimilate the conditions of their plight and their relation to that moral principle so as to arrive at an ego resolution that would have represented their typical reaction to authority. We can note that in Hitler's Germany comparatively few people were actually required to "pull the switch" as they were in Milgram's study. What we need to know more about are the conditions, both internal and external, that make it likely that people will deviate and think poorly. These subjects' deteriorated reactions may not have been specific to their reactions to authority.

A person's ego processing can, theoretically, be observed in any situation, but obviously some situations are better than others because ego processing or certain ego processes become more salient (e.g., more representative, articulated, vivid, or complete). The organization of ego processes brought into play at any one time not only relates to the person's propensities, it is also responsive to what it is he must handle. Situations of high relevance to him may energize coping, but if the press is too intense, he may become overburdened and defensively maneuver, or temporarily fragment and leave the field, in a manner of speaking. Moreover, some situations may be especially malignant in their implications to him, although not necessarily so for other people. For instance, there was some evidence from a study of Berkeley students (Haan, 1975) who had witnessed or participated in an incident of civil disobedience, that moral reasoning about the event deteriorated especially among those who were ambivalent about disobeying authority (not among those who were compliant to authority).

Some situations preclude the use of some kinds of ego processes. For instance, circumstances that press for means—ends action are not likely to be occasions for intraceptive processing. Answering personality inventories is likely to be one of these. Work concerned with the construction of ego scales from the item pool of the CPI (Haan, 1965) showed that the intraceptive coping processes recruited fewer and more weakly discriminating items than did the cognitive or affective areas. (However, the work described by Joffe and Naditch in Chapter 13 did not run into the same difficulty.) Although the CPI item pool could be particularly deficient in such items, it is even more likely that it is next to impossible to construct personality inventory items that represent the coping suspension of self-control and disbelief and the quiescent but active openness to experiencing that characterize intraceptiveness. Although the situation of answering yes or no to 500 or more inventory questions is not an opportunity for intraceptive experiencing, the situation of finding precepts in inkblots (Haan, 1964b) seems to be. The assimilatory activity of intraceptiveness is usually concluded when requirements for means–ends processing come to the fore.

Still other kinds of situations require different patterns of ego processes. If subjects are engaged in an objective and dispassionate discussion—for instance, in interviews that are done to collect demographic data, they are not likely to have much need to regulate their affective reactions (except as some subjects' idiosyncratic and not entirely assimilated memories—their childhood social-economic status, for example—may cause them to reaccommodate to past events of pain or joy). Situations where people must act, and thereby publicly actualize themselves, are more likely to require affective regulation. Much research so far done with this ego model has been based on people's ego processing in interviews that call for relatively detached reporting about one's self, rather than acting for one's self. One exception is the work by Hunter and Goodstein (1967) and Margolis (previously Hunter) (1970). These investigators designed four role-playing situations wherein student subjects were called before a "dean," who had either correct or incorrect information about them and who intended to praise or punish the students for superior or inferior performance. Margolis reports that the use of various processes was highly specific to each of the four role-playing situations. This is, of course, the point that needs to be made: Different situations require different ego patterns that usually emerge, not because the situation determines the person, as the social learning theorists assume, but because the person cognizes the situation and in interacting with it, brings specific patterns from his ego repertoire into play.

My own recent study of ego processing and action, which is reported in Chapter 7, shows the importance of affective regulations when friendship groups of teenagers confronted each others' differing points of view in games and simulations of moral dilemmas. The regulation of affective reactions was required along with empathizing and tolerating the complexity of others' view, all within a cognitive framework. If people are regarded as open systems, they can be expected to be responsive to their circumstances and interactive with them; at the same time, each has his own preferred response options.

Another attribute of situations that affects ego processing of subjects is the press of time. For instance, Folkins (1970) led male university students, who were paid volunteers, to think they would be shocked after certain intervals of time had passed, which varied for different subjects from 5 to 1800 (20 min) sec. Immediately after it became clear to the subjects that they were not to be shocked at all, Folkins asked them a few questions concerning their thoughts about the experimental situation itself, the most important being whether they had thought of quitting the experiment and if so, why they had not. Ego ratings were made of their responses. Reports that they had considered quitting characterized the preponderantly coping subjects, while those who defended or fragmented often reported that they entertained no such idea. Coping evaluations of the experimental situation characterized those subjects who were required to wait the shortest time (5 sec) and those who waited moderately long times (180–300 sec). Fragmenting evaluations were made by those who had had moderately short times (30–60 sec) to process the situation. The 20-min interval brought approximately equal coping and fragmentary reactions—most thought this lengthy wait was particularly harsh as well as senseless, since they were paid to sit and do nothing. The preponderantly defensive subjects were not distinguished by the intervals they waited. However, there were significant negative correlations between their self-reported stress and the physiological indices. Thus, the time allowed by the structure of the situation itself markedly affected the kind of ego processes that were used except for those subjects who defended themselves, irrespective of their experiences.

SUMMARY

The line of thought advanced in this section is akin, but not identical, to recent preoccupations, particularly among social psychologists, about the social nature of experimentation and research itself. However, the reactions of subjects were not regarded here as extra and unwanted, but rather as arising from the constructivist nature of the "natural" processing of people themselves. Consequently researchers can only approximate what their subjects' meanings are. When this two-sided constructivist epistemology—the subjects' and the experimenters'—is recognized, subjects' biasing of results and the so-called artifacts in research can be viewed differently: They are hardly annoyances but are instead what personal–social psychology is about. For all these reasons there are few real "discoveries" in the social sciences—only surprises that we welcome, sometimes, like long lost friends. The ethical arguments against the deception of subjects (see for instance Kelman, 1968) are buttressed here by the practical consideration that deceived subjects are likely not "themselves," but are stressed, wary, and deviantly defensive. The strong meanings of subjects' situational interactions and transactions is necessary in order to encompass the social nature of experiments and to understand that the subjects are wary and that therefore they assimilate situations that pull, preclude, and order different arrays of ego processes and construct their own accommodations without being creatures of the occasion.

Partial, but I think faulty, understanding of these circumstances has convinced Mischel (1968) and others that there is no consistency in personhood and that all is situationally determined. In partial rebuttal Bem and Allen (1974) recently demonstrated that some people are trait-consistent across situations and some are not. This interpretation is also incomplete. From the process view it can be said: (*1*) some consistent subjects will be so because they are chronically defensive or because they prefer coping processes such as logical analysis and substitution that are not typified by interpersonal responsiveness; (*2*) it would not be difficult to find a situation, probably a stressful one, where the consistent subjects would not be consistent; (*3*) some inconsistent subjects will be characterized by a different array of defensive processes (for instance, projectiveness, displacement) from those who are consistent; some will be coping but highly differentiated in their reactions to context and some will be in transitional states, a likely possibility with Bem and Allen's subjects, who were undergraduates in an introductory psychology class.

Methodology of Studying Processes

PROBLEMS OF MEASUREMENT

Whether ego processes manifest themselves and are therefore usefully operationalized as (1) quantitative, continuous scores, representing strengths or saliencies, (2) relational attributes, or (3) merely as a present or absent is a first consideration of measurement. Since arguments have already been made against the widely accepted idea that ego develops by stages (as Loevinger & Erikson propose), there is no expectancy that ego functions can be discerned by a fourth kind of measurement, benchmarks that signal the presence of a particular stage.

Moreover in rejecting the milestone, stage conceptualization, the additional supposition that ego processes occupy the predominant role within the person's hierarchy is also discarded, as are the kind of measurements made to discern stage attainments. Both Kohlberg and Loevinger have developed measurement methods that sift through complex samples of subjects' productions—reasoning about moral dilemmas and sentence completion items—to find benchmarks that signal by their frequency or saliency the presence or absence of a stage. In contrast, ego processes are seen as handmaidens of the person's intent to maintain the internal organization of the self. Consequently, ego processes are regarded as always present at least in some simple or complex and latent or actualized form. Consequently, ego processes should have important relational properties: (1) among themselves, (2) to cognitive and moral structures, (3) to affect, (4) to social structures, (5) to other people's ego processes, and so forth. For ego process research, the central problem is the determination of the characteristic patterns of these interregulations and organizations; later chapters present work directed toward this end.

Still, the supposition that different ego processes may be used with particular persistency and vigor—special saliencies or strengths—by different people and by people of different ages seems to be a tenable description of their measurable properties and suggests the practicality of treating processes as quantitative, continuous scores.

Ego processes occur, it is argued, in the contexts of many contents; for instance, we can observe sublimation of anger and of unrequited love or a person's empathy with another who is experiencing both these feelings. Observation of ego processes is not always easily done, because our attention in everyday life is usually drawn more to the contents of people's actions. We tend to scrutinize the forms of their actions only when these are unusually inefficient, blundering, and bizarre or especially efficient, creative, penetrating and apropos. Ordinary processing is usually "silent." However, it should be noted that the naive observer became increasingly apt at identifying defenses after the Freudian tutelage that people's self-deceptiveness is omnipresent.

People themselves are not very accurate when it comes to describing the processes they use. The experience of psychotherapy is intended to help patients become more self-conscious in this regard. But process research must somehow discern the quiet, but not unconscious, workings of ego actions which are complex acts of human creation. The most direct and accurate, though still approximate way of measuring ego actions is by the use of the mind of a trained human observer, who produces some kind of calibrated description of the subject. Arguments were previously made that the human subject is invariably uncooperative, even when he is "cooperative," because he has his own agenda, so we must address the question of how the observer accommodates the subject's dissemblance. (There is probably no more convincing experience of a human being's capabilities for dissembling while attempting to cooperate than working with a motivated, fee-paying psychotherapy patient for months and then have him obliquely refer to some critical fact that he is convinced he told you long ago.) Clearly the dispassionate, professional observer of human beings will be no more able than anyone else to discern the contents of subjects' dissembling, but the actions of negation and dissemblance will take the various, reasonably clear forms represented by the defensive processes and can usually be observed with reasonable reliability (see Chapter 12 for a review of observer reliabilities).

Another, less direct means of measurement is represented by personality questionnaires, and specifically by the ego scales developed from the items of the CPI and MMPI (see Haan, 1965, and subsequent improvements of this work described in Chapter 13 by Paul Joffe and Murray Naditch). We need to consider how the subject's status as a subject affects these measures, since an earlier argument insisted that response sets interfered with knowing the truth of the subject's status. The difference is that the ego scales do not rest on the claim that the content of the subject's status—his diagnosis, his character, his traits—can be directly known. Instead a more modest assertion is made that there should be a parallelism between the ways the subject deploys his ego processes in responding to the situation of test taking and the ways he deploys them generally and that various discriminating items present contents that can be rejected or endorsed by the subject. Consequently, we would expect denying people to deny experiencing unpleasant feelings or thoughts represented by some items, repressive subjects to disagree with items that suggest unpleasant impulse, most defensive subjects to endorse conventionally acceptable, socially desirable items, and so forth. (The relationships reported on p. 90 have already given evidence in this regard, and studies by Alker, 1966, 1968, 1971 are of particular interest.)

INSTRUMENTS OF MEASUREMENTS

Two methods of rating have been used so far with this model of ego processes: normative ratings and Q sorting; both have their uses and their limitations. (The rater's manual, record form, and listing of Q sort items are shown in Appendixes A and B.) The rater needs to have some frame of quantitative reference, and there are several that he can hold in his mind: normative groups—like all other people, all other people of the same age or sex, all other people he has known of the same population (like a psychiatric patient population)—or from the ipsative frame, all other ego processes of the particular subject himself. Actually, the instructions for normative evaluations included in the rating manual shown in Appendix A draw a compromise between the "normative" reference group and the ipsative frame of the subject as his own reference. The suggestion is made that the 30 ratings of coping, defense, and fragmentation provide the opportunity to make an "ego map" of the subject. Following this instruction, the rater is urged to recognize that most subjects will have some saliently preferred and some less frequently and intensely used processes in each of the domains—cognitive, attentional, intraceptive, and affective. The instructions are meant to pull the rater—observer toward the idea that all people must handle problems of living, so that he addresses the questions posed by the rating task: What kinds of patternings does the subject use to process his inevitably cognitive, attentional, intraceptive, and affective problems? The 30 processes are of course abstract, which they must be to achieve general applicability; consequently raters need to be relatively sophisticated about ego functioning.

The generality of the normative ratings contrasts with the specificity of the Q sort items. Three different items representing various facets or manifestations of each of the coping and defense processes were constituted. (Fragmentations have not been included in this Q sort because their comparative infrequency in nonpsychotic samples would markedly imbalance the Q sort's forced distribution.) Any Q sort directly represents a hierarchy of the attributes ordered therein (the procedure is essentially a rank ordering of a single person's attributes). Here the ego sort can be regarded as an ego map because its ipsative framework generates a hierarchy of the person's preferred ego processes (within the limits of the available items, which in themselves represent a limited array of processes).

The method of Q sorting has advantages: It is reasonable to compare the Q sorts of samples with vastly different backgrounds, a procedure that is highly suspect with normative ratings or standardized personality scales. For instance, adults can be compared with children, and blacks with whites without unduly violating the varying contents in the life situations of each. Comparisons between different age and cultural groups reflect the *relatively* different saliencies of ego processes within each group's internal ordering. A mean difference indicates that a particular ego process occupies a more important role in one group's ego hierarchy than it does in another's. Thus the supposition that groups differ in absolute strengths, which at best is a tenuous assumption with all forms of personality measurement, does not need to be made.

It was feasible to generate 3 different items for each ego process, making a total of 60, because the observer—sorter's task in Q sorting is less demanding than it is with rating. The normative frame requires the rater to evaluate each item's position with respect to its weight in some larger and uncertain group of people. In Q sorting, the evaluator is only required to make precise judgments after he has already decided that certain items are near or adjacent to each other within the subject's hierarchy.

Both ratings and Q sorting can be applied to any sample of a person's actions that is reasonably full or involves matters of some importance to him. Clearly, the entire array of ego ratings or the entire set of Q items would not be needed, nor would it be sensible to apply them if the situation of observation is restricted or limits the subject's response options in important ways. In these instances, only certain ego processes can be expected to appear. Both rating and Q sorting are time consuming and expensive ways of doing research, and for that reason some people doing large-scale survey research have preferred to use the ego scales based on personality inventories. No further comment will be made about the ego scales here since Naditch and Joffe discuss them fully in Chapter 13.

Areas of Application

Because the ego model is essentially a linking and synthesizing conceptualization—being based on the assumption that processes organize other aspects of the person and provide his immediate means of relating to his context—the number of different kinds of examinations that would test one or more aspects is great. The ego processes' work in itself and their relation to other aspects of self and situation are all of interest. Moreover, validation work need not be limited to investigations that actually use this particular model of processes, since it merely captures several possible processes and uses labels commonly associated with ideas of coping, defending, and fragmenting. Other processes undoubtedly exist and other labels might very well be more useful (however, to preserve the advantage of the process formulation, proposed ego functions should all be of the same conceptual class and not mix affects, symptoms, drives, and processes, as does the Bellak–Hurvich [1969] model of ego, for instance).

The fundamental distinction to be tested is whether coping, defense, and fragmentation form a hierarchy of utility. If a degree of "truth" underlies this supposition, its manifestations should also be discernible in other investigators' work and in other detailed accounts of the human condition. Several such reinterpretations of previous reports were suggested earlier in this chapter—for the Milgram studies and more generally for the social nature of experiments and research itself.

Minimally, we should expect processes to be related to the intrapersonal realms of development, the dynamic event (microgenesis and macrogenesis), pathological and normative functioning, and to the social contextual areas of primary relations with intimate others and secondary relations within less personal collectivities. Typical patterns of coping, defense, and fragmentation should characterize functioning within each of these areas. The broad question is whether the process conceptualization makes it possible to understand more fully and sensitively the fundamental plans and enterprises of people.

The process conceptualization is not new to psychological investigation, but it is likely that the special contribution of the present work is the serious and full adoption of the conceptualization. The effects of this are felt not only in the conduct of research, but also in understanding results.

The first effect is full recognition that psychological research of human subjects is almost always approximate, given their fluidity (usually regarded as instability). We come to fully appreciate that data must be regarded as representations of what subjects want us to know rather than as concrete, actual representations of facts. It is a testimony to researchers' inventiveness and subjects' altruism that we know as much as we do.

The second impact is the recognition that sequences of actions through time-limited happenings or developmental stages are more likely to model the meanings of processes than are measures taken at a single point in time.

The third is to grow enamored of the phenomenon of change at the same time that we search for the transformations that people bring about in the midst of their conserving of themselves.

The fourth is more than an homage to sociologists and interdisciplinary study; it is the sober understanding that contexts are fundamental, since we cannot understand people or their processes without knowing the meanings they impart and receive from their everyday milieus and from our research contexts.

Fifth, as we underscore the importance of subjects' meaning we see the scientists' as well, and we are forced to admit the approximate quality of our own constructions and appreciate all the more Nagel's analogy, which was well worked over in the chapter concerned with immanent values in research: We are all mariners who must reconstruct our boats, plank by plank, while we remain at sea.

An ideal research design to investigate the implications and worth of this ego model would include the following elements: processes, some kind or kinds of structures (cognitive, moral, social), representations of the relevant social context, and some assessment of the affective reactions of the subjects. Optimally, a temporal sequence of events would be observed; this should include the subjects' relevant history, the cooccurrence and integration of processes, structures, context, and finally the outcomes in the subjects' actions. Finally, to optimize the possibilities of observing coping, the subjects need response options (unless the intent is to stress). Given the complexity of this hypothetical design and its options for subjects to exercise their inventiveness, analytic procedures would have to be multivariant and probabilistic. Clearly these kinds of designs are expensive, time consuming, and complex, and psychology is ill prepared when it comes to measuring contexts as well as structures that are not cognitive. Some of the studies reported in subsequent chapters move toward matching such stipulations, but a sizable number do not.

The chapters that are still to come represent efforts to explore, examine, and in some cases to test with new data, the implications of the ego process model for several important areas of life functioning.

The next chapter, "Configurations of Ego Processes and Cognitive and Moral Structures," will consider a main aspect of the process model, the assumption that ego patterns support various structures. We would expect (1) the presented form of structures to be less differentiated and integrated than they might optimally be when intrasubjective consistency is maintained by defensive strategies at the expense of intersubjective logic and reality, and (2) the presented form of structures to be more differentiated and integrated when coping responses permit the response chain to adhere to intersubjective logic and reality.

The subsequent chapter, "The Development of the Ego Processes," will be much concerned with examining the likelihood of the supposition that ego defined as processes does not develop by stages. A part of the presentation will be an attempt to show that the adequacy of ego processes has more to do with situational sufficiencies of people at various points in their lives than with their structural stages of development.

Chapter 9, "Stress and Ego Processing," will argue that the burgeoning field of stress research cannot afford, for the sake of its own clarity and the accuracy of its representations, to do without some social and psychological formulation of successfully handled stress; here, coping, as it has been defined in this model, will be presumed to represent such a formulation. A definition of psychological distress will be presented that features a threatened state of disorganization which frequently leads to the deviance of defensiveness and fragmentation. Situations of stress will be considered in various ways as synchronic and diachronic events.

Chapter 10, "The Family, Ego Processes, and Child Rearing," explores the implications of ego processing within the most important, intimate, small group that people experience, with particular regard for the role of the family in transmitting or providing the context for children's development of preferred ego processing. Critical to the constructivist basis of this model will be the question of whether offspring's processes tend to be identical, reciprocal, complementary, or independent of their parents' functions. This consideration will ultimately challenge the common wisdom that parents are successful in socializing their children in their own image.

After evaluations of the empirical findings are made, conclusions are drawn, and suggestions made as to where future research might go in Chapter 11, two additional chapters by former associates will follow. Richard Morrissey considers findings now available concerning this model of coping and defense and critically reviews the results for methodological adequacy and substantive claim. Murray Naditch and Paul Joffe report their recent work in developing a series of ego scales, which considerably improves on a previous effort (Haan, 1965).

7. Configurations of Ego Processes and Cognitive and Moral Structures

Coordination of Processes and Structures

BASIC PROPOSITIONS

The description of the interregulation between structures and ego processes set forth in this chapter is primarily concerned with the arrangement of different intrapsychic meaning systems. However, it should be noted that self-regulation is not limited to the intrapsyche because ego processes articulate not only between different structures but also between structures and the fluctuating circumstances of situations. Nevertheless, the discourse and the research described in this chapter does not take extensive note of situations. One reason for this exclusivity is that most structuralists have so far treated the person more as an entity than an "ecosystem" (Wilden, 1975), despite their frequently stated recognition that structural development proceeds only through intrapsychic and ecological interactions. However we know very little about such matters since social, moral, and interpersonal structures have so far not been well identified although several recent efforts in this direction are represented in the work of Swanson (1974), Turiel (1975), and, of course, in the burgeoning work stimulated by the cognitive theory of moral development, which will be considered later in the chapter.

Argument in earlier chapters asserted that personality qua personality cannot be structural because it is commonly understood to be fluid, profligate, reversible, and malleable (in other words, it has political qualities), while structures are commonly understood to incorporate the properties of solidity, conservation, efficiency, and irreversibility. Structures represent stable, organized principles of deciding and knowing, while personality, it was argued, is composed of strategies that deal with the vagaries and the contingencies of living and inevitably include not only affects but also contents. True enough, man is preeminently a thinking being, but his thought cannot be singularly reified (or defied) since he is also a feeling being who is sometimes even foolish. Not all his concerns and acts can be captured in an account of his pristine, linear logic in its varying stages of evolution. Thus, the thrust of this present argument suggests:

1. Even though structures must include within themselves their logical manifestations as a correspondent function (e.g., the child who understands class inclusion and exclusion will so classify objects when he is faced with such a task), the structure's function is very often complicated by the functions of other structures, by attractive and unattractive contents, and by the ego functions which the person uses opportunely to retain or attain a modicum of self-consistency and situational sensibility. In fact, this "creative chaos" must be centrally involved in producing the disequilibrium that leads to the discovery of new structures. Maruyama (1968) argues that morphogenic systems, which change their structure and organization in the face of disturbance, may have longer-term stability than systems that obstinately maintain their structure in the face of disturbance. There is ample research that indicates structures are not easily changed (see Kuhn, 1974), and clinically, we know processing is fluid, an observation that will be empirically examined in the next chapter.

2. The "affective" schemata, which Piaget frequently refers to in his writings, can be regarded as schemas only to the extent that they are structured in some degree by cognition, since feelings themselves are unarticulated and without substance until they are cognized (in fact different feelings are not easily distinguished one from another by their physiological patterns).

3. No cognition is without its feeling component so that formulations of internal organization must consider what kind of feelings—a cognitive formulation— and what role they play in the person's construction of his action.

4. The structure's functions and the ego functions are isomorphic (a) when the situation is manageable, (b) when people's total intrapsychic constructions are efficient, and (c) when differing structural formulations are compatible and can be merged to achieve an integrated intersubjective solution. In these instances we say the person copes.

5. The structures' functions and the ego functions are not isomorphic (a) when situations are not easily manageable (by any one, or by a particular person at a particular developmental level), (b) when the person's total intrapsychic constructions are inefficient because they are overridden by his temporary or persisting needs to preserve intrasubjective consistency, and (c) when various structural formulations are incompatible and lead to contradictory solutions, a frequent occurrence when the person is developmentally transitional. In these instances we can say that the person defends or fragments. However in some instances he moves

to acquire new, more differentiated and efficient, structural understandings, and then we say he copes, diachronically.

6. Ego processes cannot be deified by regarding their role as larger than that of coordinating within the self and between the self and situation. To assume more is "there" that is "ego," and that it can be described by the science of personology, is to attempt to turn science into biography or make it a matter of belief. To assume that there is less "there" is to miss the essence of the constructivist, organizational properties of personality.

ELABORATION OF THE BASIC PROPOSITIONS

Altogether, then, to understand the configurations of ego processes and structures would be to solve the riddle of intrapsychic interregulation, an achievement that is still some way down the road. The present proposal is based on the assertion that processes often adulterate the presentation of structures—simply another way of stating the classical and central problem of psychological measurement: Disparities frequently exist between capacity and performance. Disparities occur even when the person is coping because the various structures' functions that are relevant to the particular situation, must still be coordinated with each other—we cannot plausibly assume that the person or his experience is seamless! Defensive needs and processes override structural capacity and thereby create even more striking discrepancies between capacity and performance. In these instances, the person is temporarily, or even persistently, not "himself" in the sense of not exhibiting his true capability—the chronic state of neurotics.

Structures are "contingent idealizations," to use Rudner's (1966) term, which denotes a theoretical principle that cannot be directly tested but has a chance of being "true" if it serves to order other factual, testable understandings. Only the functional or processual manifestations and ramifications of structures can be evaluated for their truth and for their consistency with the definition of the structure. From this standpoint and from the argumentation presented so far in this volume, most investigators of cognitive or moral functioning and development are not likely to be observing pure examples of the structures' functions. Unfortunately the myth of the unambivalently cooperative subject who truly produces, despite himself, only what the experimenter wants has become as necessary a solution for the cognitive structuralists' work as it has been all along for the learning theorists. The belief in the subjects' verity springs, of course, from the lack of a full understanding of how environments are structured and how people in environments interact with environmental structures. As a result, the research subject is objectified. There are strong reasons to agree with Steiner (1974) that subjects in experimental situations "prestructure" their responses. However, "prestructure" is not the correct word from my point of view, since it implies that subjects respond in a linear fashion by employing their own structures prior to using those that interest the experimenter. Subjects more likely *construct* their own version of the situation at all times to conserve integrity with all appropriate resources, including appropriate and "extraneous" structures, affect, and ego processes. Investigators' preferences as to the size of the unit they want to study undoubtedly influences their views of the reality we are trying to understand. Clearly many cognitive structuralists want to observe only the structure's function and are not interested in their subjects' constructions. They choose thereby to regard manifestations of nontarget structures or of ego processing as error variance. The unit of study chosen here is larger, and the intent is to account for as much of the "error variance" as possible.

The effects of context are relevant here in a special way since it is clear that longer or more complex situational interchanges have increasingly greater likelihood of producing "noise," accompanied by ever more complicated ego processing, which then leads to "improbable order" (or structural inefficiency or negative entrophy, as Wilden [1975] has suggested). However, "improbable order" may often be efficient synchronically and diachronically from the subject's point of view, as well objectively so from the standpoint of his structural progress. In fact, we should expect that noise is probably usual in situations of interpersonal exchange, given the fact that people are much less predictable than physical objects, for example, the conservation of physical matter occurs monotonously and without exception in this world but people do not always do what they say they will. Moreover, our inability to predict the course of interpersonal events accurately and efficiently readily leads to defensive reactions. For these reasons the search for structural purities is defeated; those researchers who seek uncontaminated evidence of cognitive and moral structures must make contact with their subjects, thus the research occasion is made an interpersonal event, an idea that was extensively examined in the last chapter. Clearly, the comparative chaos of the interpersonal event is one of the reasons that we do not yet know much about social structures.

Kohlberg (see 1969, for a summarization) and other moral–cognitive theorists have assumed that moral structures exist in addition to cognitive structures, but they have not made it entirely clear just what these might be. Nevertheless, the character of people's actions when they make moral decisions is compelling evidence that moral reasoning is a search for the relevant "best" principles, rules, or standards; in other words, structures are involved. Of all possible candidates for social structures, the subcategory of moral structures seem the most likely to be first identified and understood, given the compelling necessities of moral regulations and understandings within interdependent human collectivities. In the present view ego processing will have to be part of any account of structural regulation and development.

One other consideration, which is examined more fully in the next chapter, needs to be mentioned before we turn to an examination of empirical findings. If ego processes work to coordinate (or miscoordinate) structures and/or occasionally override structural capacity with more opportune constructions, then ego functions must have longer-term, developmental implications. In general, the persistent use of the coping functions should support structural development, while the persistent use of defensive and fragmenting functions should impede or retard structural development. An additional implication is that the persistent use of one of the ego modes of coping, defense, or fragmentation follows on long-term interactions with people and ecologies that are variously supportive or nonsupportive of coping or defense or fragmenting. Solid evidence for these assertions would have to be secured from longitudinal study of the development of both structures and ego processes. Such information is not now available. However, there are two ways that indirect evidence can be marshaled. The first is by the means of short-term intervention or training studies that intend to accelerate structural development. These investigations are based on the assumption that microgenesis has the same characteristics of macrogenesis. According to the present view, these curricula should be successful to the extent that they simultaneously instigate both structural disequilibrium and ego processing that is, on balance, coping; they should be unsuccessful to the extent that they fail to produce structural disequilibrium—the necessary precondition—or they produce it, but evoke at the same time defensive or fragmenting functions. Results from one such investigation will be considered later in this chapter. The second inferential means of understanding the long-term relationship between ego processing and structural development is to secure findings that coping people have developed greater structural capacity than those who are defensive, when other situational factors that should support coping, like a favorable socioeconomic status (SES), are controlled. The essential idea underlying this supposition is that coping describes an open system that permits new information to be entertained and acted upon—assimilated as well as accommodated—while defensiveness or fragmenting describes a closed system that refuses intersubjective inputs that are necessary for developmental differentiation.

Background of Previous Empirical Work

That personality should affect thought, for better or worse, is by no means a fresh idea. Aristotle found it necessary to make provision in his formulations for the occasions when the temperate, rational, moral Greek citizen was not "himself." The supposition is so commonplace to clinicians that they give no thought to the probability of its truth or falsity. Nevertheless, as noted in Chapter 4, Piaget (1973) and Langer (1973) have argued that affectivity does not modify structures; we have found a way to respect that stipulation by viewing the person as a much more adaptable system: He is not always himself and affectivity does not *cause* structural deterioration, but it obviously accompanies it as people progress through stages (see Turiel, 1974, for a detailed description of adolescents undergoing moral stage transition; however this account is drawn in terms different from the present ones). There are several reasons why we are not yet satisfied with our understandings of the relationships between affect and thought. There is still a need to know exactly how personality does affect thought—the occasions, the nature of the impeding or facilitating impingements, and the recovery rates. In other words, the critical questions are in exactly what manner and with what results does personality affect thought? There is also the question, infrequently asked and likely developmental in nature: How does thought affect personality?

We will briefly review recent studies that are concerned with the varying conceptions of ego or of ego processing and structures. These are not great in number when studies of IQ and personality are excluded, and most are concerned with moral structures. The difficulty with considering IQ in this context is that it is a potpourri of structures, learned contents, self-confidence in testing situations, and willingness to comply with the tester; however, we will consider the patterns of relationships between the ego processes and IQ in conjunction with cognitive and moral structures later in this chapter. The studies concerning structures and processes that are now available cannot be said to arise from any systematic formulation about the interregulation of personality and structures, with the partial exception of those that consider role taking and morality. However, even here the formulations of morality—rather than those of general processing—organize the research questions and result in some oversights.

There is good reason to assume that moral structures should become increasingly differentiated and informed by the person's ability to take other people's positions in morally uncertain situations since morality is a negotiation that arises from human interdependency. However, as Selman and Damon (1975) and Moir (1974) have pointed out role taking in itself is morally neutral. It is represented in the present ego model by the processes of both empathy and projection, an arrangement that leads one to the recognition that cannily fathoming another's position can serve Machivellian as well as moral purposes (as Christie & Geis, 1970, have shown). At any rate several studies of children, who are also capable of manipulation (Moir, 1974; Selman, 1971; Selman & Damon, 1975), have shown positive associations between the developments of role taking abilities and moral judgment. Selman and Damon claim a logical priority for role taking, but they do not make clear why both capacities cannot develop simultaneously since each, recursively, implies the other.

Podd (1972) and Weisbroth (1970) have concerned themselves in studying young adults with the relationship of moral level to several personality concepts derived from psychoanalytic theory. Making a complex assessment of his subjects' state of identity formation, Podd found that those who achieved an identity were of a higher moral stage than those who were still diffused. The subjects in moratorium, who had made no commitment to an identity and who were experiencing a crisis, were the most variable in the moral stages they used. Weisbroth found a positive relationship between moral level and males' identification with both their parents and between females' moral level and their identification with their fathers (most of these subjects were graduate students or professional people). Campagna and Harter (1975) found highly significant differences between the moral levels of normal and sociopathic boys, in favor of the former group, even though the groups were matched for mental age and IQ.

Several studies have successfully related personality attributes to moral structural development in experimental settings. In an Asch-type situation, Saltzstein, Diamond, and Belenky (1972) found that conformity to erroneous perceptual judgments, manipulated to appear as the judgment of the group, particularly typified seventh grade students who used Stage 3 (interpersonal concordance) reasoning. Anchor and Cross (1974) found strong, monotonic negative relations between moral levels and the use of a "zap" option in two-person Prisoner's Dilemma games with college students and psychiatric patients. The zap option could only be viewed as a gratuitous aggression triggered by the stress of Prisoner's Dilemma, since it did not benefit the subjects who exerted it. Arbuthnot (1973) reports he found a relationship between field independence and moral judgment and that his field dependent subjects changed their moral thinking, though only temporarily, to comply with the position of the characters they assumed in role playing situations. Several attempts to relate moral judgment to internal locus of control have not been successful (Alker & Poppen, 1973; Arbuthnot, 1975).

Haan, Smith, and Block (1968) reported a large array of distinctive personality characteristics and perceptions of parents characterized undergraduates of different moral stages. In general, principled students described themselves as autonomous and appeared to be particularly candid, even self-critical, in describing themselves. The conventionally moral described themselves as conventional, ambitious, and not rebellious. The preconventional men and woman (who may have actually been transitional between conventional and principled thinking) were more variable, but both sexes saw themselves as rebellious. Haan (1975) followed this study with another that examined the losses, gains, or equalities in Berkeley students' moral reasoning about an actual situation of campus civil disobedience—the Free Speech Movement crisis—compared to the levels of reasoning they used for the hypothetical standard Kohlberg dilemmas. Two-thirds of the students used a different stage for the actual situation (46% higher and 20% lower) than they had for the stories presenting hypothetical dilemmas. Relevant to the present context were the analyses of personal–social data (controlled for level of hypothetical thinking and political position), which suggested that the men whose moral thinking deteriorated denied social complexities and human conflicts and that the women probably became regressive in situations of conflict. Both groups seemed ill-prepared to deal with the complexities and authority conflict of civil disobedience. The students, whose thinking equalled or exceeded their hypothetically based levels, produced personal constructions that were consistent with their moral patterns. The stage-stable students seemed organized, judicious, and settled, while the students who gained described themselves as situationally and interpersonally reactive. These findings are consistent with the basic formulations of structural-ego process inter-regulation developed here (in fact, these earlier findings helped to clarify my thinking about the relationships between structures and processes). I suggested, ex post facto, that deterioration in thinking about the situation of civil disobedience did not actually represent a structural loss but was rather an instance where these subjects were not "themselves" because they had to choose intrasubjective compartmentalization to prevent disintegration in this situation of stress. As a result, their defenses took priority and their moral thinking became less differentiated and integrated.

The only study so far reported that has directly considered processes and moral stages (Haan, Stroud, & Holstein, 1973) found positive monotonic relationships between moral stages and several coping processes in a study of hippies. The processes were rated in extensive psychiatric interviews. Those most strongly associated with increasing moral stages included the cognitive functions of objectivity, intellectuality, and logical analysis as well as concentration. The intraceptive coping functions were also positively, but less strongly, associated with moral levels, while all the defensive functions were independent of moral level in this unusual sample.

No comparable group of reports exists that studies the relationships between cognitive structures and personality. However, the general importance of personality factors in cognitive functioning has recently been underscored in an impressive report by Handel (1975). He replicated with an Israeli sample of 950 the findings based on thousands of American youngsters, originally reported by Coleman, Hobson, McPartland, Mood, Weinfeld, and York (1966). He found that locus of control, self-concept, and aspirations accounted for more variance in cognitive achievement than did a variety of socioeconomic background variables or the quality of the schools the subjects attended. The cognitive measures used in both studies do represent the mix, of course, of contents and structures found in traditional tests.

As our knowledge of moral structure and personality stands now, we can say that role taking, identity formation, identification with parents, conformity, sociopathy, unwarranted aggression, field independence, autonomy, cognitive and intraceptive coping seem to be related to moral development in ways that we would expect. We also see from one study (Haan, 1975) that the use, on critical occasions, of some stage other than the one employed for hypothetical dilemmas has understandable relations with characteristics that can be regarded as ego processes. Although this array of results attests to the general impingements of personality attributes on the levels of morality produced, it does not actually advance our detailed understandings very far. These results do not tell us, for instance, (1) where structures leave off and where personality or ego processing starts or (2) how these two supposedly different aspects of people are interregulated, or (3) under what kind of circumstances social-emotive pressures take precedence, or when structural understandings overrule and people decide moral issues on the grounds of logical principles that lead without wavering or defection to equivalent moral action.

The Cognitivists' View of Personality and Structures

The greater number of developmental theorists who are now investigating morality are doing so from the cognitive point of view, a choice that represents at maximum a fundamental supposition that moral decision is *nothing more* than thoughtful, rational decision, and at minimum that thought is the most critical element in moral decision. The present position coincides with the latter, but only when moral decision is successful (i.e., coping and therefore accurately representing the stage of moral development). When it is not successful (not accurate) reflective rationality will not be its hallmark. Only a few studies have considered the relationship between moral decision and its eventual fruition or lack of fruition in action. This lacuna betrays the cognitivists' supposition that people follow their best thought (they perform to capacity); in other words, people are always true to themselves. Thus, a fundamental chain of assumptions is made that capacity equals performance, thought equals action, and moral action is nothing *more* than moral thought in action. This series of propositions is compatible with cognitive theory's view of the person as more a bound system than an ecosystem. Moreover, the kind of cognition assumed to be involved, and so far the only kind studied, is that of linear, logical operations. There are other kinds of cognitive reflections, represented in the ego model by tolerance of ambiguity, ego regression, and empathy. All of these processes represent ego strategies that hold the demands of intersubjective, instrumental logic at bay while patterns of intrasubjective experience are evaluated and reassimilated.

Moral–cognitive theorists, including Kohlberg, have not carefully examined the values underlying their systems and instead refer to moral philosophical systems, usually Rawls' (1971), as if they derived empirical support from such friendships. However, there is no surety that cognitive–moral theory is the psychological wing of the Rawlsian system, which appears to be ultimately based more on an experiential model than solely on a logical deductive one. Rawls uses an artificial expository device that starts out the process of choosing moral principles by positing an "original position," wherein all men are initially behind a "veil of ignorance" that prevents them from knowing where their own personal good might eventually lie. In these circumstances, Rawls argues, men would choose out of necessity the moral principle of equalizing all supplies among all men. (Later some may receive more, but only if their doing so will benefit the entire group, particularly those who are the least advantaged; otherwise the disadvantaged would never agree to the differential in the first place.) For a person to ask for more than his share is unreasonable since he should be able to see that such a demand is unworkable because others would not agree to the inequality. Moreover, no one would subscribe to the inequality because he would have no way of knowing in advance whether or not he might be one of those who would ultimately have less. To ask for less, Rawls notes, is irrational in terms of securing one's own good, which he assumes all men naturally want. Parenthetically, a psychological point needs to be made here: People are not always clear in real life about what their own good is, either in the long-term sense of their general welfare, or in the short-term sense of securing their legitimate share.

Nowhere in the cognitivists' formulations can one find direct expression of such ideas. However, Rawls' formulation is, as he notes, a philosophical system of economic or distributive morality, and it is not really intended to be an account of the empirical, everyday problems of moral agents or of their subsequent actions, which is the foremost empirical problem for psychology. Still, there is value in considering the implications of his ideas. Real people, who actually choose to place themselves in something like an original position, would have to coordinate much more than its hard-core, logical deductions. It would appear at minimum that they would need (*1*) a grasp of intersubjective human interrelatedness—in the deepest sense of understanding their own embedment in that network—and (*2*) an intrasubjective understanding that their own good is inextricably enmeshed in it. These two stipulations involve much more than role taking. For instance, understanding one's own needs, rights, and limitations—one's self as a moral object among other moral objects—is also involved. When the conditions of the original position are stated this way, accurately seeing one's self and accurately seeing one's self in the context of others becomes critical. Moreover, it becomes clear that morality cannot solely be a problem in linear, logical operations, even though we cannot at present state clearly or well what else might be involved since we have not identified the deep structures that enable people to organize their understandings of human embedment.

The developmental theorists' disproportionate and overly enthusiastic interest in logical structures has arisen as an understandable antidote to the psychoanalytic and classical behavioristic positions, which insisted that men's morality is emotive. From these points of view, moral thought is only the window dressing of moral behavior, since a man does right or wrong because he possesses automatized, characterological habits he acquired early in life through various forms of conditioning.

The present expectancy, which is certainly not a fully developed position, is that morality rests on much more than the premise that men acquire formal obligations to each other which they should logically fulfill. It adds the recognition that man's social embedment is a two-way street which entails various kinds of *implicit, informal,* interpersonal obligations inherent in all face-to-face primary relationships or are, at any rate, most clearly seen there. The complexity of these less predictable and less objective but probably more powerful human commitments implies intricate forms of processing and more subtle, resolving actions than can be expected solely from the functioning of the logical structure's function.

Having drawn a formulation of the interregulation of process and structure, summarized previous work concerned mostly with moral structures and personality, and criticized the cognitivists' limited formulations, we can turn our attention to new analyses that attempt, within the limitations of available data, to test some of the propositions set forth.

Empirical Analyses

INTRAPSYCHIC PATTERNS OF STRUCTURES, IQ, AND EGO PROCESSES

The Supposition That Cognitive Development Limits and Regulates Moral Development

Two studies (Kuhn *et al.,* in press; Tomlinson–Keasey & Keasey, 1974) have suggested that cognitive level is the necessary but insufficient condition of moral development; thus, cognitive level has come to be regarded as the ultimate limiting factor in moral development. This contention has serious consequences for the definition of morality and moral development since it implies, at the very least, that differentiated and comprehensive principled moral decisions lie within the capability only of those who are advanced in logical development, specifically those who have attained the stage of formal operations. A further implication is that morality must be defined, foremost, as a logical operation in the Piagetian sense. Clearly these findings, whether or not they are true, have immediate political consequences since they mean that people who are unsophisticated in formal operations cannot become morally "mature." However, we can and will make several critical observations about these findings in this section.

Both studies included young subjects ranging in age from 10 to 30 years whom we can reasonably assume were still developmentally viable, both morally and cognitively. The Keaseys' work was not longitudinal, while the Kuhn study included one longitudinally studied sample of 58 children from 10- to 12-years old who had complete data, that is, scores for Piagetian tasks of logical operations and the Kohlberg moral dilemmas. These subjects were tested a second time after a 9-month interval. However, the results were not remarkable. Table IV summarizes the findings and shows that moral and cognitive change, at least after a 9-month period, appears to be almost randomly distributed. As the authors comment, there was a failure "to confirm the possibility that change in the two domains are related in a simple dynamic fashion" (Kuhn *et al.,* in press, p. 58). Thus, the widely accepted interpretation that cognitive development is the necessary precondition of moral level is inferred from the cross-sectional evidence reported in these studies rather than from the longitudinal observations. Moreover, as we noted before, no thorough logical—analytical exegesis of the Kohlberg system has been done, and so we are not prepared to trace parallel or isomorphic stage transformations jointly made by logical operations and moral reasoning.

The cross-age results of these studies could be, for instance, a coincidence in nature or it might be that both developments are due to some other *common* developmental factor, like general social maturing. But, more importantly, both studies relied on the array of moral structures—represented in the Kohlberg system—which so far have not been positively identified. We have no real assurance that this is the complete array, and, as I will argue later, it may be that other kinds

Table IV
Longitudinal Logical-Moral Patterns of No Change, Decrease,
or Increase in 10- to 12-Year Olds

	Moral		
Logical	*No change or decrease*	*Increase*	*Totals*
No change	17	16	33
Increase	12	13	25
Totals	29	29	58

of moral structures, less formal but more interpersonal in nature exist and are used by many people. Formal, "constitutional" means of moral regulation do not assure justice for people who cannot assess these means of protection; consequently there is no reason for such people to develop such structures. The lives of other people have more thoroughly acquainted them with other means of social regulation. For instance, more communal than codified forms can be found within this society, particularly in black culture (Stack, 1974) and in other non-Western societies.

Although the moral literature is not altogether clear—since it is not certain how many investigatory designs have actually included the blinding of protocols as to sex identity—there is a finding from two large samples in which the protocols were blinded that from early adolescence on, females tend to be less mature morally than men (Haan *et al.,* 1968; Haan, Langer, & Kohlberg, 1976). This result threatens the assumption that moral structures are universally found since it implies a radically lesser morality for women who have had roughly the same opportunities as men (all university students in the first study, wives of the men in the second) or it implies women are morally damaged for some reason or another. However, these findings are unconvincing on common sense grounds, and we will consider alternative explanations shortly, but for the time being we need to see how this finding affects the contention that cognitive level is the precondition of moral development. No attempt was made in either the Kuhn *et al.* or Keaseys' studies to control for sex differences or for conditions that generally advantage subjects' handling of sophisticated, intellectual material (e.g., social class and content learning); consequently we do not know whether the findings that cognitive development is a necessary but insufficient precondition of moral development is sufficiently universal that it holds across white samples of different sex and varying advantage and commitments to formal morality in this society, let alone across minority group samples or people in other societies.

If the logical—moral connection actually obtains (and it should be optimized when morality is defined in the formal terms favored by the Kohlberg system), it would probably be most reliably observed with a mature sample. One could presume that opportunities for developing both social—moral wisdom and cognitive differentiation are near to being equalized by adulthood since the cognitive is clearly emphasized in children's experiences and schooling at the expense of the social or moral in our society. Thus, the previously reported findings might be an artifact of differential timing in the occurrence of environmental possibilities.

The Kuhn *et al.* study included a subsample of 47-year-old adults, the subjects and spouses of the Oakland Growth Study (OGS) who constitute one of the longitudinal cohorts of the Institute of Human Development at Berkeley. These data for this group were studied more intensively and reanalyzed to examine the formulations set forth in this chapter. Approximately 100 of these subjects (with the sexes approximately equally divided and the numbers varying somewhat depending on the analysis) had most of the data required for these analyses: Wechsler Adult Intelligence Scale IQ, Hollingshead Indices of social class, scores for the Piaget correlational task (see Inhelder & Piaget, 1958), moral stage scores derived from interviewing with the Kohlberg stories and scoring system, and ego scores of coping and defense. The Piagetian pendulum task of propositional logic was also analyzed in the Kuhn *et al.* study, but it is not included here since preliminary analyses with the ego processes suggested that the women in the sample, who were mostly housewives, were especially defensive (thus not true to themselves) when they faced this task.

Details of scoring the correlation problem and moral reasoning are reported in the Kuhn *et al.* article. For the purposes of this work the various stages of cognitive development were converted to a nine-step continuum: preoperational substages A and B; concrete operational substage A and B; two mixtures of concrete and formal and formal/concrete; formal operational substages A, A/B, and B. The moral stages were converted to an eight-step continuum in the following manner: moral stages 2, 3, 3+, 4, 4+, 5, 5+, and 6.

The ego scores were the composite of at least two ratings based on 2- to 4-hour interviews directed toward life reviews and evaluations of present status. These interviews were conducted and the tests administered during a routine follow-up of this sample several years ago. The ratings had acceptable reliability ranging from .48 to .88 with means of .71 for men and .68 for women (see Haan, 1974c for details).

The thrust of the original findings is shown in Table V, where we can see that most principled people (27 out of 30 or 90%) reason at formal levels. However most people at the formal level do not use principled thinking (50 out of 77 or 65%). This observation was the prime support for the original contention that a developmental decalage exists between logical and moral levels with cognitive development being the necessary precondition. We are faced here, however, with two facts that were not fully considered in the original study.

1. These 50-year-old people cannot be developmentally viable in the structural sense, so it is meaningless to speak of this pattern of findings as representing developmental potentiality since 65% of the people *had not* actualized their moral possibilities. It may be nearer to being correct to think more simply that the moral task may be, for some unknown reason, "harder" than the cognitive for particular

Table V
Relationship of Cognitive and Moral Stages in Oakland Growth Study Adults

	Moral Stages			
Cognitive stages	Preconventional	Conventional	Principled conv/principled	Total
Preoperational	0	7 (4F,3M)	1 (1F)	8
Concrete (including minor formal)	0	21 (15F,6M)	2 (2M)	23
Formal	1 (1F)	49 (29F,20M)	27 (6F,21M)	77
Totals	1	77	30	108

samples. Moreover, although there is an accepted logical progression with cognitive evolution, it is not as clear that moral evolution comes about in exactly the same fashion. But whatever the case, it would not be sensible to assume that these 50-year-olds are still evolving morally in the structural sense, nor can we assume, I think, that they have "regressed" morally. We probably need to look at these observations more broadly and as a reflection of consolidated intrapsychic arrangements. In this event the findings suggest, very simply, that being able to reason in formal terms certainly does not insure that one will be morally principled as it is presently defined in the Kohlberg system.

2. We can note that most of the subjects who are logically formal and morally principled are men (21 out of 27 or 78%), while the subjects who were counted in support of the developmental moral lag are mostly women (30 out of 50 or 60%). This pattern obviously raises a question about the original interpretation. Stated another way, 83% of the women who reason formally are not morally principled compared to only 49% of the men. Calculations from Table 2 in the Keasey study show that 83% of their formal subjects (who were all women) did not reason in principled terms. Plainly the necessary but sufficient interpretation cannot represent a generalized "truth" of universal structural development if the pattern of results is drastically different for the sexes unless one is willing to assume as many have for centuries—including Freud—that women are morally less mature for some other, hardly explicable reason.

The question is whether structural decalage is a sufficient or correct explication of these patterns. Two other possibilities are to be examined in this chapter: (1) Some people may prefer moral structures that are not well represented in the array of formal, Kohlberg structures; (2) some people may use modes of ego processing that do not support, or that even positively preclude the presentation and possibly the evolution of formal moral reasoning. In other words, the interpretation may be misdrawn: Formal operations may not be a necessary prerequisite of principled moral reasoning when a different array of moral structures is measured. Moreover formal operations are already seen and admitted to be an insufficient base for principled moral reasoning.

Since there are so few women who are both principled and formal ($N = 6$), the comparison of their ego processing with that of the conventional and formal women is not sensible (when it was done it did not produce significant results!). However, the group comparisons for males within the formal level showed that the principled ($Ns = 21$ versus 21) were significantly higher than the conventional for tolerance of ambiguity ($t = 2.18$, $p \leqslant .05$) and empathy ($t = 2.58$, $p \leqslant .01$) and lower for regression ($t = 2.29$, $p \leqslant .05$). Thus principled reasoning in males, given the capability of formal logic, is associated with cognitive freedom, role taking, and the ability to tolerate uncertainty, a finding that may tell us something of what needs to be added to provide the necessary basis for principled reasoning in men. However, when the women are added to the comparisons (making the comparison 27 principled, formal versus 51 conventional, formal subjects) the principled, formal group is more intellectualizing ($t = 2.27$, $p \leqslant .05$), less repressive ($t = 2.03$,

$p \leqslant .05$) and higher for total ego ($t = 2.53$, $p \leqslant .05$), a pattern that suggests that moral reasoning, in the Kohlbergian sense, is importantly based on sheer productivity of ideas. However these analyses still do not directly address the question of why so many people in this mature, developmentally stable sample, did not actualize a sufficient condition and go on to principled reasoning, if the capability is powerful.

To examine these questions further we will turn to other kinds of analyses of the OGS adults that directly consider the interregulation of cognitive and moral structures within the framework of social class and IQ. The latter are included as rough indices of conditions—nonstructural in nature—that provide general, fertile grounds for learning the behavior and jargon that is rewarded in testing situations, an important consideration since the findings just reported suggest that productivity may be an important factor in facilitating responses that are scored at higher moral levels.

An Exploration of Intrapsychic Interregulation

Various multiple regression models were generated for the sexes separately and together to predict the OGS adults' cognitive and moral levels and IQs. The independent variables included various elements that might be relevant to the interregulation of processes and structures: the cognitive and moral measures, SES level, as a general advantage, IQ, as a mixture of content and structures, and, of course, ego processes. The intent of these analyses was to address the problem of intrapsychic regulation in the broadest way possible within the resources of the data, rather than to predetermine which factors might be the critical ones. A variant of path analysis was employed to construct the "maps" shown in Figures 2–4. However the usual causal attributions of path analysis are not implied or made in the arrangement of the calculations and figures. Instead, the models were con-

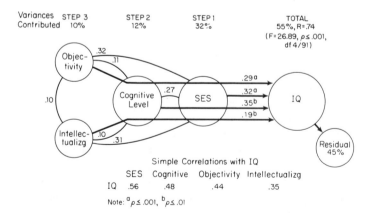

Figure 2. Differential weights contributed to IQ by ego processes after successively controlling for SES and cognitive stages.

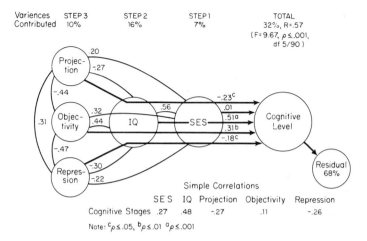

Figure 3. Differential weights contributed to cognitive stages by ego processes after successively controlling for SES and IQ.

structed in accordance with the following rationale: (*1*) SES level is a general advantaging condition, while cognitive, moral, and IQ developments are achievements; consequently structural-process patterns must be shown to exist *across* SES differences if they are to be anything more than replications of general social advantage. Thus, SES was controlled by forcing it to enter all the models as the first step in recruitment; (*2*) IQ is another general advantaging condition (note for instance that its simple correlation with SES is .56) in the sense that people of middle or higher classes have greater opportunity to become familiar with the

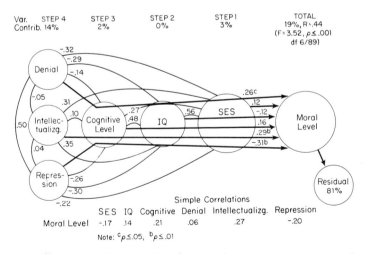

Figure 4. Differential weights contributed to moral stages by ego processes after successively controlling for SES, IQ, and cognitive stages.

contents of answers that are included in many of WAIS subtests; consequently, IQ was forced into the models to predict cognitive and moral levels on the second step; (3) the contention that cognitive level is the necessary but insufficient condition of moral development should result in positive correlations between the two. Only the relationship between their absolute levels was the major focus of the Kuhn *et al.* and Keaseys' studies; consequently, cognitive level was forced into the moral and IQ model on the third step. (4) finally, the ego processes were permitted to enter all models in the stepwise fashion, providing their F ratios $\geqslant 3.00$. Holding the ego processes until the last step of recruitment makes their unique contribution to intrapsychic regulation particularly clear. Moreover this procedure operationalizes the formulation that ego processes follow on and coordinate structural developments and the various contents of social knowledges represented by SES level and IQ. The models presented are for the sexes combined; some differences between the sexes did occur in separate analyses and will be mentioned later. The straight lines in the figures represent the paths of contribution and control, and the adjacent numbers are the Beta weights; the curved lines and their adjacent numbers represent the simple correlations between the various elements.

To build a foundation for understanding the differentially weighted patterns, we will first consider the maximum predictive pattern for IQ, which is the most strongly predicted of the three models, largely because the subjects' SES levels accounts for a substantial amount of the variance, 32%. However, cognitive level does enter the equation and accounts for an additional and unique variance of 12% after SES is controlled. Two ego processes—intellectualizing and objectivity, both cognitive and both likely to support the kind of cool and ambitious production needed to optimize IQ performance—contribute another 10% unique variance. Thus, the regulatory pattern in these mature subjects that predicts high performance on IQ tests includes: most importantly, higher socioeconomic level, smaller unique contributions from cognitive level, and the ego processes of coping objectivity and defensive intellectualizing, which probably work to coordinate and optimize performance in the test situation.

Considering the pattern associated with cognitive level next, we find that SES does not make a significant contribution in this mature sample—a finding that seems to support the claim of universal structural development—but that IQ, even after SES is controlled, does make a sizable contribution (16% of the variance) to cognitive level. (Thus, there is somewhat more of IQ in cognitive level after SES is partialled out than there is of cognitive level in IQ after SES is partialled out.) Moving on, we find three ego processes still account for significant amounts of variance in cognitive performance. Objectivity and the lack of repressiveness and of projectiveness facilitate cognitive performance. A fair amount of inventiveness seems required to solve the correlational problem at the stage of formal operations, and repressive processes probably counter such freedom while projectivity would mean that the task was handled with deliberate wariness and suspicion. Neither of these defensive strategies is suitable for dealing with the uncertainties of this cognitive task, but objective functioning should permit the subject to disengage himself and calculate the required probabilities.

Finally, in considering the model for moral level, we find that none of the preconditions of SES, IQ, or cognitive level make a significant contribution, but their entry still exercises the stipulation that the ego processes must contribute unique and significant variances. Denial and intellectualizing make *positive* contributions to moral level while repressiveness makes a negative one. These findings are, of course, striking on three counts: (*1*) SES and IQ do not predict moral level as they are frequently reported to do with immature samples; (*2*) cognitive level does not make a significant contribution once SES and IQ are controlled; (*3*) two defenses make *positive* contributions to formal moral reasoning *after* all three general preconditions are controlled. When these more general factors are not controlled and simple comparisons are made between the subjects of various moral stages, the analyses produce the same differentiating coping functions—cognitive coping and intraceptive coping—previously found by Haan *et al.* (1973) as characterizing those of a higher moral stage in a hippie sample. However, the pattern resulting after the controls are exerted, which removes the general factor of goodness, suggests that people in this sample who reach the higher levels of formal moral reasoning are verbally productive and nonrepressive but their denying and intellectualizing propensities suggest that they are evidently socially and emotionally illiterate in some degree.

Before we go on to examine the general import of these analyses, we need to note several sex-specific findings. SES makes bigger contributions to men's IQ than to women's, 41% compared to 21%. This pattern is repeated in the contribution of IQ to cognitive level after SES is controlled (11% for men and 4% for women). Thus we can say that men's intellectual achievements are more integrated and tightly organized with their content achievements than women's and appear to merge general content, social advantage, and structural development. Neither of the sex-separated models predicting moral levels were significant.

In summarizing the observations that can be made from the analyses reported in this section, we can note the following most important findings:

1. IQ was the most powerfully predicted (54% of the variance compared to 30% for the cognitive model and 19% for the moral model). However, SES level accounted for the greatest amount of variance in IQ, while SES's contributions to cognitive and moral levels were not significant. This pattern of findings is consistent with the cognitivists' claim that structural development is universal and independent of social advantage and gains added weight since it emerged here with a mature sample whose structural development is probably terminal. The argument was made earlier that early social advantage may accelerate development (or accelerate test-taking wisdom), but still not affect the outcome.

2. A modest portion of variance is shared by IQ and cognitive structures after SES is controlled. This finding is entirely expected since the early pioneers who

designed IQ tests had some idea that intelligence is a constructivist, problem-solving activity.

3. Cognitive level does not make a significant contribution to moral level in this sample—only 2% of the variance after SES and IQ are controlled (in the sex-separated analyses cognitive level contributes only 1% of the variance for men and 4% for women). Thus, the findings from previous studies of Kuhn and her associates and the Keaseys are inconsistent with these analyses, which control for general social advantage, use continuous scores, and solely concern the mature portion of the OGS sample.

4. Ego processes still contribute significant, although not absolutely high, amounts of variance to all three achievement measures after the content and structural factors are controlled. The interpretations were couched in terms of the ego processes' effects on people's performance in varying kinds of test-taking situations (an argument was made in the last chapter that the social nature of research is not controllable and that it constitutes an irreducible reality of studying people). Both IQ and moral performance was improved by the subjects' degree of intellectualizing, a finding that suggests that a defensive production of verbalization increases the performance of these two achievements. Performance in both the intellective tasks—IQ and cognitive—improved with the subjects' coping objectivity. Both the structural tasks, which require a degree of self-initiated productivity, are diminished by the subjects' repressiveness. Projectivity relates to lower cognitive performance probably because the test-sophisticated OGS subjects had never before faced a task like the correlational problem. The projective subjects likely became suspicious and cagey when so much of their intellective activity had to be disclosed (see Alker, 1971 for similar findings). The positive contribution of denial to moral level was an unexpected finding; nevertheless, I suggest it may make sense. Reasoning about the hypothetical Kohlberg dilemmas at a level that is scored high may actually be facilitated by a degree of obliviousness or, at any rate, aloofness from the details of human suffering and the complexities of human interchange. Only Stage 3 reasoning allows much concern to be given to these matters. However, full development of these suppositions about formal moral reasoning is made in detail in the next section, which will report a comparative study of formal and interpersonal morality as both are coordinated by ego processes.

Altogether these analyses appear to support the contention derived from the ego model that the structures' functions are not often purely presented and that ego processes are importantly involved in these intellective performances. Moreover the ego processes that made significant contributions were not always the cognitive coping processes, those closest to being the unadulterated presentation of structures. Even though the two structural measures were not importantly affected by the degree of general social advantage, the modes of ego processing did appear to facilitate or impede intersubjective performance (the degree of repressiveness), but in other instances the ego processes appear to be reflecting the intrasubjective necessities incited by the task—denial for moral reasoning and projectivity for the cognitive task. Moreover, cognitive level did not appear as an important precondition of moral level in this developmentally terminated sample.

A Study of the Ego Processing of Interpersonal and Formal Moral Reasoning

Since the formulation of ego processing extended and elaborated understandings of the structural data in the study just described, and since it seemed, as well, to offer an explanation for the Berkeley students' shifts in moral judgments which occurred when they reasoned about an actual situation of civil disobedience, another project was undertaken to address the following core considerations more directly: (1) Perhaps the definition of morality and its scoring in the Kohlberg system represent an insufficient array of moral structures, which, indeed, may be especially used and used more adequately by people who deal with moral dilemmas in highly formal, detached, even intellectualizing and denying ways that neglect the deeper, interpersonally moral aspects of their human embedment; (2) it appeared from the Berkeley student study that moral reasoning fluctuates in different actual situations and that these shifts are coordinated by ego processes that are variously appropriate to the person's intrapsychic and extrapsychic circumstances. However this interpretation was made ex post facto, and the coordinative functions of ego processing needed to be directly examined.

The sample—white and black adolescents ranging in age from 12 to 17—was studied in situations that were only mildly stressful, however they were designed to facilitate moral development (a matter that will not be considered here). Six racially homogeneous friendship groups, usually 10 teenagers, half boys and half girls, who were all of low or high SES level were first pretested to obtain an assessment of their formal and interpersonal moral reasoning; second they were engaged in five group sessions of games or simulations that posed moral conflicts. The group sessions each lasted for approximately 3 hours; third, they were tested again within several weeks of the sessions' termination. To insure independence of evaluations, interviewers did not observe group sessions, interviewers who did the pretesting of an adolescent did not posttest him, and reliability scoring of the moral responses were done with the adolescent's sex, race, and SES level removed from the protocol.

The group sessions were observed and evaluated for three different aspects: (1) the entire group's structure, functioning, and feeling tone by sociology graduate students who expressed their evaluations in a Q sort that was developed for this purpose; (2) the individual teenagers' ego processing by clinical psychology graduate students who expressed their evaluations with the Q sort of Ego Processes (see Appendix B); (3) the individual teenagers' level of moral reasoning and action by developmental graduate students who recorded all such statements and scored the statements after the sessions were over.

Opportunities for both formal and interpersonal moral reasoning were represented in the interviews by four of Kohlberg's moral stories and four additional interpersonal stories, especially designed for this study. Scoring of all stories and group sessions was based on either the formal or interpersonal system or on both, depending on the teenager's response. The Kohlberg stages are well known and need no explanation here. The definitions of the various levels of interpersonal morality are shown in Table VI; it would be ill advised to call these levels "stages" at this time since we have no evidence about their homogeneity, sequentiality, or whether they are age graded. The reader will note in the table, however, that sequentiality is implied and it has two bases: first, an evolution of increasing complexity and depth in understanding interpersonal moral balances and exchange is outlined, and second, it is obvious that the definitions owe a great deal, to the Kohlberg sequence.

However, the important distinction is that the key concept of the interpersonal system is that of the fluctuating, immediate, and intimate moral balance that is particularly operative in face to face relationships. The moral balance involves grasping one's own and another's pecularities and one's own implicit and nonformal obligations to him because of his mutual expectancies of you and yours of him. This kind of reasoning has been almost entirely relegated by the Kohlberg scoring scheme to Stage 3, called Good Boy or Good Girl morality or Interpersonal Concordance. In the present study, correlations between formal and interpersonal morality were .50 for the first interview and .35 for the second. Relationships between the two kinds of moral levels fluctuated in the game situations from .68 to .19.

Instead of making a full report of the results from this recently completed project, we will focus only on those aspects that consider the differences between the ego regulation of formal as contrasted with interpersonal morality and this discrepancy within the contexts of the varying situations of interviewing and two of the five group situations. The first game which we will examine here, called Neo PD (designed for the project by Mark Pilisuk, University of California, Berkeley), is a version of Prisoner's Dilemma. The teenagers were divided into two subgroups who could, by the color of cards their groups turned up, decide to cooperate or compete with each other to receive pennies. Cooperation meant each group would receive moderate payoffs, whereas competition produced an alternation of losses and gains between the subgroups. All decisions were to be made by each subgroup as a whole, and after the third block of five trials each, it was suggested that the groups negotiate with each other. According to the sociologists' evaluations, Neo PD resulted in the teenagers' becoming competitive and distrustful, and tending to pressure their fellow group members, resulting in a loss of group solidarity. The second group experience is a simulation called Humanus by its authors (Twelker & Layden, 1973). In the beginning the teenagers were informed by an audiotaped voice, who says he is a computer called Humanus, that they are the last surviving group of people on earth following, presumably, a nuclear disaster. Humanus poses a number of problems to the group for resolution: Which 10 items would they want to have with them, how will they regulate their new society, whether or not they will let a survivor in, and so forth. This experience, according to the sociologists,

Table VI
A "Level" Conceptualization of Interpersonal Morality

Level (1)

The young child has no separate view of himself (Piaget's adualism) and there is therefore merged with his caretakers. Consequently he can have no idea of moral *exchange* but instead attempts to restore the moral balance by fitting in and acting out his caretakers' wishes. He may punish his caretakers by refusing or thwarting their expectancies of an interpersonal exchange with him.

Level (2)

As the child acquires a sense of self as separate from others, he can view himself as both subject and an object. But his ideas of moral exchange are defined, essentially, by using himself as the example; consequently he expects as much bad faith from others as he himself holds towards them, particularly toward others who thwart his wishes. He expects others will demand their just deserts, irrespective of their circumstances, just as he does for himself. In other words, he feels justified in fulfilling his own wishes because he believes others do the same. He expects good faith from others when he holds good faith, and is deeply hurt and angered if the exchange is not completed. This concrete formulation of exchange constitutes his definition of the moral balance. He gambles that others' intentions will be the same as his, that is, that they think like he does. They will regard him morally when they want something, as he does when he wants moral consideration. He reasons in terms of the concrete moral situation, sees his own particularly individuality, but projects his individuality on others. Everybody wants the same things he does. His punishment of others when they fail him morally is also concrete, tit for tat, an eye for an eye.

Level (3)

The child is now embedded in moral-social interchanges; he sees himself as a part of the human collectivity, as a member of the class of human beings who must out of necessity and human goodness act morally toward each other. (The cognitive capability of reasoning by groupings and class inclusions is probably important to moving to Level 3). His formulation of himself is that of a good, cooperating human being, and he regards himself as a good person among other good people. His conceptualization of the moral balance is simplistic and overinclusive: It is a harmonious grouping, and he needs to maintain it to be a person among people. He gambles naively that peoples' moral exchanges are in good faith. Instances of bad faith trouble him since they point to exceptional cases that he cannot yet fit into his classification. His formulation of moral exchange is still in kind, concrete, and nontransitive. He does not fully appreciate the exceptions that spring from others' individuality, nor does he see his own individuality objectively or in sufficient detail to recognize that he himself can and sometimes does fall from moral grace. As a result he cannot view himself morally as a complete object involved in exchange from others (e.g., he cannot take Rawl's original position) nor admit the necessities of canny self protection. Both these formulations would open up exceptions to his definition of morality, a matter which he is not yet ready to entertain or differentiate.

---

continued

Table VI—Continued

Level (4)

The child now has an objective, transitive sense of himself as a moral object among other moral objects, so he believes that he and all others must be subjected to the same requirements of moral exchange. Thus he expects all have the same duties and all should enjoy the same rights. The scales are off his eyes, and he is able to see the exceptions—moral exchanges are not always in good faith. However, he is overly impressed with that fact and strenuously supports the necessities of maintaining clear and proper moral balances. He breaks "the set" of specific situations and postulates that general rules and codifications should regulate human moral exchange; consequently, from his point of view, it is only an invitation to trouble for a society to take chances that others' moral intentions are good. Clarity, not sensitivity of exchange, is supported. He recognizes aspects of others' individuality, but his central idea that rule-following should regulate moral exchange means that individualities only confuse moral matters. His friendships are likely to be legalistic. To support his idea of rule-following, he favors clear punishments for violators and requires that he himself must conform to the codifications that he is now able to posit.

Level (5)

(Here the Level 3 naive assumptions of people's good faith and the Level 4 assumptions that rules are necessary to protect the self and others from people's bad faith are recycled and transformed, and then both are integrated into a new structure, which is more differentiated, sensitive, and flexible than either was before.) He now regards himself as a moral object among other objects in a thoroughgoing sense—seeing both himself and others in particular individuality and reversing his own position to see himself as others see him. In other words, he has a sense of detachment and humor about himself. In so doing, he recognizes the delicacy and complexity of the moral balance, and most importantly, that *he,* as well as others frequently contribute to imbalances. Consequently, he is ready to forgive violations and sees that the restoration and maintenance of the moral balance is everybody's business all the time. He breaks the set of the immediate situation and considers the qualities of ideal interpersonal morality in terms of moral reciprocity. He expects a diffused, flexible loyalty rather than rule observance from intimates. He expects there are explanations why loyalty cannot always be forthcoming. He recognizes the chronic insufficiency of any stated principle without needing to forego his principles—instances of bad faith and good faith are to be expected and understood, as well as foreborne and forgiven. He knows, nevertheless, that one cannot afford to quit gambling on the possibility that others' moral intentions are more often good than otherwise, because there is, ultimately, no other meaningful solution for people as social beings. He recognizes that the individual person must take initiative and assume responsibility for differentiating the instances of good faith from those of bad faith and he believes that not all matters of interpersonal morality can be "legislated."

---

produced group solidarity, attempts to maintain consensus, domination by one or two personalities, and so on.

The items of the Q sort of Ego Processes were submitted to a factor analysis with a principal components solution followed by a equimax rotation which produced 14 factors. No reliability measure was available for the ego Q sorts so the factoring was done to compensate for that lack; scoring reliability of moral levels for the interviewing was .73 and .83 at pretest and .80 and .80 at posttest for formal and interpersonal morality, respectively. Moral level scores were converted to moral maturity scores (MMS) by weighting the major mode of reasoning by 2 and the minor by 1. The ego factors were entered into stepwise multiple regression models (if their F ratios $\geqslant 3.00$) to predict the moral levels used in Neo PD, Humanus, and the interview situations, after SES level, sex, and race were controlled. The ego scores derived for particular games were used to predict the overall moral level for that game, while the average of each teenager's ego scores for all games (as a best estimate of his usual status) were used to predict the moral scores for the interviews.

Figure 5 shows the average formal and interpersonal moral maturity scores for the interview and group situations for all subjects ($N = 56$) who had complete data. Moral thinking clearly fluctuated in the game situations for both forms of thinking, but formal reasoning fluctuated more than interpersonal reasoning. This differential pattern was maintained in varying degrees across the different segments of the total sample, that is, the older, younger, upper SES, lower SES, male, female, black, and white adolescents. With these observations in hand, the question could then be asked as to whether distinctive patterns of ego processing were associated with moral reasoning in these different kinds of settings.

Turning to Table VII, we can see that the multiple regression models generally account for higher amounts of variance in formal reasoning than they do for interpersonal reasoning in both the game and the interview situations. In other words, the production of formal reasoning seems to be more easily thwarted or accelerated by the nature of situations, and thus less of the structures' functions

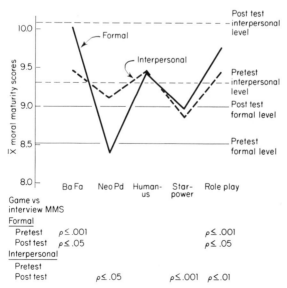

Figure 5. Average moral maturity scores for different group sessions compared to interview scores (all subjects).

Table VII
Interregulation of Ego Processes and Moral Levels in Interviews and Group Sessions (SES, Sex, and Race Controlled)

Interpersonal Reasoning

	F Ratio	β	% Var.	Simple r
Pretest				
SES	.63	-.12	0	.05
Sex	.32	-.08	0	-.01
Race	8.07[b]	-.44	9	-.29
Interpersonal accurate	4.76[c]	.32	8	.16
Model	2.51[c]	4/48	17	.42
Neo PD				
SES	.86	.06	5	.22
Sex	.22	.08	0	.08
Race	.21	.01	0	-.06
Cognitive coping	6.49[b]	.45	18	.47
Model	2.34[c]	4/32	24	49

Formal Reasoning

	F Ratio	β	% Var.	Simple r
Pretest				
SES	3.70[c]	.28	9	.26
Sex	.41	.03	2	.18
Race	2.13	-.21	0	-.16
Interpersonal accurate	8.30[b]	.40	12	.35
Displacement	3.03	.24	5	.14
Model	3.67[b]	5/47	28	.53
Neo PD				
SES	1.29	-.16	0	.04
Sex	.54	-.03	1	.09
Race	.92	-.13	0	.05
Doubt	14.86[a]	.47	24	.45
Cognitive coping	16.51[a]	.51	18	.45
Interpersonal accurate	15.31[a]	.50	18	.41
Denial-repression	3.57[c]	-.25	5	-.20
Model	6.80[a]	7/25	66	.01

Humanus

SES	6.81[b]	.43	6	.24
Sex	.80	.00	1	.13
Race	4.40[c]	.35	7	.14
Empathy	4.43[c]	.33	9	.25
Model	2.75[c]	4/36	23	.48

Posttest

SES	.37	.08	4	20
Sex	.31	.07	5	.22
Race	2.53	.25	0	.11
Objectivity	7.12[b]	.36	10	.32
Interpersonal accurate	4.76[c]	.30	8	.29
Suppression	4.03[c]	−.25	6	−.26
Model	3.76[b]	6/46	33	.57

Humanus

SES	11.35[b]	.54	14	.38
Sex	.36	−.09	0	.03
Race	2.93	.27	4	.01
Empathy	4.67[c]	.32	9	.22
Model	3.45[b]	4/36	28	.53

Posttest

SES	.52	.12	3	.17
Sex	1.65	.17	4	.20
Race	3.05	−.28	0	.08
Objectivity	5.40[c]	.33	10	.33
Cognitive coping	4.54[c]	.33	7	.29
Model	2.97[c]	5/47	24	.49

NOTE: [a] $p \leq .001$, [b] $p \leq .01$, [c] $p \leq .05$. Sex: 1 = Males, 2 = females; 1 = whites, 2 = blacks. SES scale is Hollingshead's with the sign reversed so + scores signify higher SES status.

and more of ego processing is brought into play. This observation is consistent with the comparatively greater fluctuations of formal morality shown in the graph and would suggest, if further verified with other samples, that formal reasoning is a less-durable reflection of people's moral status than is interpersonal reasoning. Alternatively, this pattern might be particularly characteristic of adolescents. The second observation is that, in general, different patterns of ego processes coordinate moral levels in different situations. However, interpersonal accuracy (factor loadings include positively, Item #34: gives accurate reasons why interpersonal events arose, and negatively, Item #48: has a tentative attitude toward others) makes a significant contribution to moral level in four out of eight analyses. We need to bear in mind that pretesting is a different situation from posttesting; not only were the moral stories different, but, more importantly, by posttesting the adolescents had a different relationship to the project.

At pretest, formal levels are positively associated with SES and interpersonal levels with race (white). In the beginning the more confident and upper SES white teenagers were undoubtedly more test wise since both trends reverse themselves by posttest. (Despite our efforts to secure equal SES levels between black and white subjects, the disparities in occupational opportunities despite the same living locale resulted in a correlation between race and SES levels of $-.44$, $p \leqslant .01$, where 1 = white and 2 = black.) After the advantages of being test-sophisticated are controlled, the ego factor scores for interpersonal accuracy made a significant contribution to both interpersonal and formal reasoning. Note that displacement makes a small and not quite significant contribution to formal moral reasoning, suggesting that some defensive, externalizing aggressivity supported the production of higher-stage reasoning during this first experience that these adolescents had with the project.

Moral levels in the conflictual Neo PD game, which resulted in a sharp drop in formal reasoning, are not affected by any of the demographic variables. Apparently the impact of this game overrode such factors. However, the factor of cognitive coping (high loadings for logical analysis, ego regression, and intellectuality) contributes 18% of the variance to both kinds of reasoning, but formal morality is also predicted by strong contributions from doubt (24%), interpersonal accuracy (18%), and a smaller and negative amount (5%) from denial-repression. Thus the pressure of Neo PD required that the adolescents mobilize a combination of coping and defensive strategies to produce formal moral reasoning. If a participant in Neo PD jumps to the conclusion that the situation is best handled by attempts to defeat the other subgroup—rather than work with them so that both groups can achieve moderate benefits—he locks himself into a point of view that repeatedly proves to be malfunctional. The defensively doubting youngster would be less trapped by this situation. Despite the heat of this situation, interpersonal morality dropped only slightly and was coordinated by cognitive coping.

The simulation Humanus does not structure a situation of conflict in action, but rather a more moderate one of occasional ideological disputes. We find that the upper-status adolescents did significantly better with formal morality while the black adolescents did significantly better with interpersonal reasoning in this situation. (One striking finding was a perfect correlation between race and the decision to let another survivor enter the cell. After argumentation, all black groups decided to let him in, while all white groups decided to keep him out. It needs to be pointed out that the white youngsters, particularly the girls, did not feel comfortable with their decisions, but having made them they found all manner of "moral" reasons to justify their position.) After these demographic variations are controlled, empathy significantly contributes to the production of both kinds of morality.

The final posttesting experience for the youngsters (a second delayed posttest has not been completed at the time of this writing) produced quite a different picture of ego regulation. Neither kind of morality is significantly predicted by the demographic variables. Interpersonal morality is positively supported by objectivity, interpersonal accuracy, and a *lack* of suppression, while formal morality is supported by objectivity and cognitive coping. The contrast between these two patterns is consistent with expectations: Formal morality is preeminently an intellectual calculation, while interpersonal morality inculcates cognitive, interpersonal, and affective-cognitive schema.

The purpose of making a partial report here of this investigation was to examine two questions: (1) whether different moral situations require different kinds of ego support, and (2) whether moral reasoning fluctuates in different situations and thereby requires different patterns of ego support. Both suppositions seem to be borne out by the results.

Conclusion

The intent of this chapter was to outline and investigate some of the considerations necessarily involved in understanding the coordination of ego processing and structures. I argued in the beginning that structures are not often purely presented because their functions are complicated by the person's need for self and situational sensibility, a personal concern that extends beyond the structures or at any rate beyond what we now understand to be their scope. The results for the adolescent project, showing that the presentations of moral structures fluctuated with varying situations and were concomitantly processed by varying patterns of coping and defense, support that view. We also found with the 47-year-old OGS subjects that ego processing still made unique and significant contributions after other advantaging and achievement measures were controlled. In fact, the very social nature of the experience of being tested seemed a likely enough inducement for the ego processes to enter the interregulatory equation of the moment. Moreover, we saw that achievement was not always or necessarily processed by coping functions. The defensive processes were also sometimes involved. If testing itself can interfere with the production of pure structures, there is good basis for thinking that real life produces the same effects, at least as frequently.

Finally, an extensive case was built, using the Kohlberg definition of morality as the example, to argue the point that structures are not readily identified by their presumed manifestations and that what we take to be a manifestation of structures may instead be a conglomeration of structures and processes, some defensive in nature. If this line of reasoning is valid, it would follow that we cannot know about structures of any kind without also knowing the conditions of their coordination and presentation by ego processes.

8. The Development of Ego Processes

The Structures' Empowerment of Ego Process Development

A complete accounting of the development of ego processes would necessarily include a description of the cognitive and social structural developments that empower ego development. Unfortunately the data and the analyses to test this key assumption do not presently exist. As a consequence, the empirical work reported in this chapter concerns the longitudinal description of ego functioning alone. Nevertheless, we are left with a number of interesting propositions to consider. Before turning to this longitudinal analysis of ego processing, however, I want first to propose an investigatory program for mapping the conjoint evolution of the cognitive structures and ego processes. This diachronic admixture implies, in turn, the supposition that the newly evolved ego processes then permit the structures to be presented in action. Table VIII displays the apparent commonalities between the various cognitive structures and properties as they are understood by developmentalists and the ego processes as they are understood by personologists and clinicians. It would be tedious to consider each of these connections, especially in view of the fact that the proposal is not yet supported by empirical data. There are, however, a number of general comments that are worth making:

1. The intrapsychic situation of a "equilibrated moment" (whether structurally equilibrated and processed by coping functions or falsely equilibrated by means of defensive or fragmented functions) is presented in the table, but implied in each instance is the supposition that the cognitive capability precedes or at least coincides with the appearance of the mature form of each ego process. For instance, in the case of coping objectivity, the minimally required structural

Table VIII
Various Cognitive Structures and Properties Arranged According to the Modalities of Ego Processes

Generic processes	Possible cognitive structures and characteristics	Coping	Defense	Fragmentation
		COGNITIVE FUNCTIONS		
		Objectivity	*Isolation*	*Tangentiality concretisms*
	Classification; logic of relations; variable exclusion	Weighs and orders inputs	Separates inputs; classifies intrasubjectively	Illogical relations; reifies seriation
		Intellectuality	*Intellectualization*	*Word salads and neologisms*
Detachment	Propositions and formal logic	Classifications of classifications checked against evidence	Classifys and propositionalizes without checking evidence	Construction of private symbols, propositions
		Logical analysis	*Rationalization*	*Confabulation*
Means–end symbolization	Seriation; causality	Coordination of means relevant to intersubjective ends	Intrasubjective coordination of means relevant to intrasubjective ends	Coordination of means relevant to privatistic ends
		INTRACEPTIVE-FUNCTIONS		
		Tolerance of ambiguity	*Doubt*	*Immobilized*
Delayed response	Disequilibrium	Disequilibrium tolerated	Disequilibrium prolonged	Disequilibrium reified
		Empathy	*Projection*	*Delusional*
Sensitivity	Decentration and reciprocity	Intersubjective construction of others' constructions	Intrasubjective construction of others' constructions	Privatistic construction of others' constructions

	Repression-ego	*Regression*	*Decompensation*
Time reversion Temporal reversibility and self conservation	Relinquishes the immediate and returns to the beginning	Relinquishes the immediate and chooses intrasubjective advantage	Returns to privatistic state

ATTENTION-FOCUSING FUNCTION

	Concentration	*Denial*	*Fixation*
Selective awareness Coordination of intents	Temporarily sets aside contrary observations	Negates contrary observations	Fixes on one intent

AFFECTIVE-IMPULSE REGULATIONS

	Sublimation	*Displacement*	*Preoccupation*
Diversion Alteration of affective-cognitive schemas via correlative means	Intersubjective expression via correlative affective-cognitive schemata	Intrasubjective expression via correlative affective-cognitive schemas	Expression via privatistic affective schemas

	Substitution	*Reaction formation*	*Alteration*
Transformation Inversion of affective-cognitive schemata via negation	Intersubjective expression via inverted affective-cognitive schemata	Intrasubjective expression via inverted affective-cognitive schemata	Vacillation between intra-subjective and inter-subjective oppository schemata

	Suppression	*Repression*	*Depersonalization*
Restraint Conservation of affective-cognitive schemata	Temporary accommodation of affective-cognitive schemata via cognitive constructions	Retention of affective-action schemata but repression of cognitive elements	De-differentiation of self from own schemata

capability is clearly concrete operations. As Piaget has noted, decentration permits the appearance of operational thought since the latter liberates the child from the egocentricity of his own point of view and gives him appreciation and use of intersubjective thought (in ego terms, this juncture permits him to become objective in the social meaning of the word).

2. Perhaps the most unusual feature of the arrangement is the relationships it suggests between the defensive and fragmenting processes and the cognitive structures and properties. Obviously, achieved—even mature—structural capability can be thought to participate in poor thinking without its being necessary to posit that the structure itself is destroyed. In other words, regression and decompensation can be personal social solutions and not necessarily, except in extreme cases, nominal deteriorations. Most clinical theories have tacitly assumed that some kind of loss actually occurs. Under the theory proposed here, it is thought instead that a structure can be erroneously used when its function is overridden by ego functions that are defensive and fragmenting. For instance, in the present proposal, isolation is a matter of overclassification, intellectualization is a matter of artificially propositionalizing, and rationalization is a matter of searching for self-justifying causes. In each instance allegiance to intersubjectivity is sacrificed in some way or in some degree. This feature of the relation between structures and ego processes rests on two assumptions that are redrawn in the present formulation: (a) Regression or primitivization is not a permanent deterioration except in organic psychoses. The ways that adults regress, and the states that they assume when they are regressed or decompensated, are not the same as young childrens'. Even the grossly psychotic person is capable of more finesse—a method to his madness—than the young child; (b) the word "intrasubjective" is differentiated from "egocentricity" to make an important distinction: never to have known another's point of view (egocentricity) is a radically different condition than to have understood another but to have relinquished that knowledge in favor of one's own intrasubjective reality when one's self-consistency is threatened.

3. Not unexpectedly, we can see in the table that the cognitive ego processes are most clearly and directly implied by the logical structures. The intraceptive functions seem less directly related to the structures per se and instead seem to be concomitants of the broader descriptive properties of structural development, such as disequilibrium, reciprocity, and decentration. Deficiencies in our understanding how structures relate to intraceptive processing occur because we know little about either intrapersonal or interpersonal structures. During intraceptive functioning, whether it is coping or defense, the self is assimilated as an object and viewed with some detachment although not in an intersubjective, instrumental way. The intraceptive functions are particular to dealing with one's self and one's self in relation to the unpredictability of others. Clearly we do not understand these aspects of self-functioning very well because we have not yet found a way to identify the fundamental elements of intraceptive processing and have instead used nominal surface words like fantasy, reverie, role taking, and so on. We understand how human communication prompts the child to become logical, but why should he

work to maintain a modicuum of self-consistency? Or is his logical development so compelling that it pulls all else in its wake? It seems unlikely that this answer—favored by Piagetians—conclusively solves all problems. Clearly we need to know more about peoples' social constructions and self-constructions, their attachments, and their human embedment.

4. The affective regulations are imbued with the following kinds of cognitive participations: Diversion of feelings involves correlated activities that belong to the same affective-cognitive group, a kind of asymmetrical emotional lag (hitting a handball instead of the departmental chairman); transformation involves the negation of affective-cognitive schemata in a symmetrical bipolarity (bad to good, impatient to patient); restraint in expressing affective-cognitive schemata involves a differentiation between the self's feelings and the self recognizing the nature of the immediate situation. We are well acquainted with these phenomena clinically, but we do not yet understand how structural development participates in the increasing refinement of emotional regulations, although we know that the latter do become more sophisticated. Stress research has shown that people's thoughts markedly affect their emotive reactions (see Chapter 9 in this regard). Moreover, the toddler immediately acts out his feelings; he does not divert, transform, or restrain them—all these processes seem to require at least rudimentary classificatory abilities that appropriately sort and differentiate feelings from situations or correlative or oppositive affective schemata in relationship to situations.

The arrangement in Table VIII is meant as a heuristic device and some areas of its indicated interrelationships are more convincing than others. The overall intent is to illustrate the possible integral qualities of structures and ego processes in both synchronic and diachronic interregulation.

The Question of a Developmental Taxonomy

A DESIGN FOR LONGITUDINAL DESCRIPTION

Turning now to consider the longitudinal patterns of the ego processes—apart from their relationships to structural developments—I propose that there are four major kinds of empirically based descriptions that can be made from the diachronic, historical point of view: (1) the person's sameness; (2) his change; (3) the organization and reorganization of his ego processes; and (4) his convergence or divergences at different points in time with other people of the same age.

Sameness is a matter of essential conservation of the self, while continuity, a subcategory of sameness, is the conservation of the main themes or threads of self within a framework of change, transformation, or reorganization of self. Both occur within the passing, shifting scenes of the social milieus. Sameness without change can only be brittle and maladaptive, while change without sameness may be personal nothingness. Thus development is a dialectic between twin necessities of conserving and of changing the self. One kind of traumatic experience is to discover that one has, in a negative way, not been one's self, for example, one has committed a "sin" or a "stupidity" that is foreign to one's self. To discover that one, in a positive way, is not one's self, is to entertain the notion that one is *more* than one's self, an experience that is often greated at first with caution instead of wholehearted delight, until further confirmation of the new self occurs.

As for sameness in ego processing, it is, first, the conservation of the preferred hierarchical repertoire of ego problem-solving strategies, and, second, a general inclination toward operating in normative and/or stressed circumstances in one of the three modes of coping, defense, or fragmentation. The formulation of ego processing has resulted in the stipulation that within a "normal" range of social experiences people are truer to themselves when they are coping and less themselves when they are defensive or fragmenting because both of the latter strategies are more situational or epoch-reactive. Thus it follows that coping should have greater temporal stability than defensiveness in structurally mature people who have experienced an ordinary range of social experiences. Fragmentation will not be considered here, but it is well known that the psychotic condition is a persisting one for at least two reasons: (*1*) it is probably physiologically supported in an important way; (*2*) socially it carries the seeds of a self-fulfilling prophecy—if one presents oneself as psychotic, society angrily treats one as a psychotic since the solution signals that social commitment and responsibility in human commerce are being rejected. The fragmenting processes present a definitively different set of problems that I will not consider here because of the lack of available data.

The two words that connote the general notion of self conservation—sameness and continuity—do not refer to identical developmental phenomena. Sameness indicates that the person's processes are not altered in any way. However, continuity relaxes the criterion of identicality somewhat and suggests that intrapsychic sameness is being preserved within a framework that becomes transposed, that is, the melody is the same but it is played in a different key. According to this analysis, the word "discontinuity" implies a break in sameness and leaves open the possibility that the former state will be reattained, in other words, a latent preservation of sameness is possible. Thus, continuity seems to indicate phenomena that are transposed while discontinuity seems to indicate phenomena that are interrupted. The Piagetians use the word "transformation" to mean much the same as "transposition," but the forcefulness of the word transformation seems to make it more appropriate for the dramatic empowerments brought about by structural shifts.

To illustrate the differences between these conceptualizations and to anticipate at the same time the actual statistics that will be used to describe ego processing across time, we can operationalize these phenomena as follows: Sameness would be indicated by (*1*) a high or significant correlation between time periods and (*2*) no, or an insignificant, absolute difference between the same periods. Continuity (as differentiated from sameness) should be indicated by (*1*) a high or significant correlation between the periods; and (*2*) a significant absolute difference between the same time periods. (Discontinuity would be indicated by a high or significant correlation and a significant absolute difference between periods 1 and 3 but insignificant findings in both regards between periods 1 to 2 and 2 to 3; however there are insufficient data to evaluate this trend.) Change should be indicated by zero order correlations between time periods but significant absolute differences. According to these definitions, change and sameness are the more general phenomena while continuity and discontinuity are more particular categories.

Thus, the interplay of change and sameness defines a dialectic—the person's change is limited by his need to maintain a degree of self-conservation, and his sameness is limited by his wishes or his necessities to develop and to change in interaction with shifting social milieus. Three different factors encourage the person's change: his intrapsychic structural development, contextual changes in his life, and the elaboration of his content knowledge. It is contended that structural development is primarily responsible for the appearance of new ego processes. Interaction with context is responsible for both the elaboration of content and the organization of the preferred hierarchical repertoire of ego processes (all constitutional propensities being equal). Whether or not change results in enhanced coping or intensified defensiveness depends, of course, on the nature of the context and one's relationship to it.

The organization of psychic elements both includes and is determined by self-conservation, adaptation, and the relationship of both of these to the person's social ecology. The life span successively presents various standardized milieus: being succored as a baby, being expected to walk, being required to become sanitary in one's toileting, being expected to talk, going to school, becoming work productive, marrying, procreating, retiring, dying. Each of these tasks, and many more that represent either culturally specific contents or the universal deep structures of social living (of which we now have little or no knowledge), encourage and require that the person organize his accommodations. He, himself, requires organization of his assimilations. If his context does not require organized accommodation and he is left to his own assimilative activity, he can only become, as noted earlier, a very odd fellow who has no commitment other than to himself—he is his own baby. The organizations of ego are identical to the hierarchical repertoire of preferred processes. Thus, immediate life tasks are met with organized mobilizations of ego processes that take on either a coping, defensive, or fragmenting cast depending on the intrapsychic and extrapsychic circumstances. An example, which will be close to home for many readers, is the organized pattern of defensive intellectualization, affective restraint, doubt, coping concentration and objectivity of the mature person who must organize himself to be a good graduate student or to be an assistant professor, both struggling for formal and tenured membership in the fraternity of certified working people. Once these life situations have passed, other kinds of organizations—less intellectualizing, more intellectuality, less doubt and more tolerance of uncertainty, but hopefully continued concentration and objectivity and more ego regression—would be viable. The questions of diachronic organization and reorganization concern: What taxonomies of preferred ego processes express currently attained structural developments and whether they deal, at any one time, with social-contextual demands. We should expect, then, not only close connections between structural developments and ego reorganizations, but also between changes in life situations and ego reorganizations. Following previous indications of statistics that describe this phenomena, we can note here that various methods of clustering people (O or Q factoring) construct pictures of organizations. When these procedures are successively repeated for different time periods, diachronic organization and reorganization can be observed by the changing nature of the clusters and individual peoples' shifts in cluster membership.

The movement of an entire sample toward homogeneity or heterogeneity in some attribute or process is not directly relevant to the individual person's course of development, since the individual makes, at all times, what he can out of his own personal—social circumstances. Nevertheless, study of an entire sample will yield observations that indicate that at certain periods during the life span people of the same age group will become more alike or very different—they will converge or diverge in their preference for certain processes or certain organizations. These phenomena are essentially ones of the timing of new experiences and they signal: (1) common experiences of structural stage transitions that lead initially to divergence or stage consolidations that lead later to convergence; (2) periods of common environmental demands that result in similar assimilations and accommodations that lead to sample convergence; (3) uncommon life circumstances that lead to sample divergence. An example is the initially divergent reactions of children entering school, later followed by the unhappy standardized outcome—most children come to dislike school. The statistical means of observation is direct: The difference between variances at two time periods tracks a process' convergences or divergences.

OTHER VIEWS OF THE TAXONOMY OF DEVELOPMENT

The volume *Life span developmental psychology: research and theory* (Goulet & Baltes, 1970) contains divergent opinions as to the fundamental questions of development and, concomitantly, contrasting recommendations as to how the life course should be investigated. Goulet and Baltes (1970) argue that the functional relationship between time and attributes can be found by identifying those situational antecedents that are the cause of the consequent attribute. Having accepted that premise, Goulet and Baltes suggest that one should go on to discover who is changing, what is changing, and when and why changes occur. Clearly this paradigm represents a behavioristic position, applied here to developmental questions. Taking a different and organismic tack, Wohlwill (1970) argues that age (or time) itself is not an independent variable and that the important questions concern the discovery and description of the basic developmental functions themselves. If these fundamental functions were to be identified, we would already know much about their form, temporal pattern, direction, rate, maxima, minima, and terminal level, the characteristics that Wohlwill designates as important. Corollary to this view is Wohlwill's belief that the true dimensions of development should, within normal ranges, "rise above" the vast and differing details of different peoples' situations; this expectancy gives priority to the idea that the growing and interacting person makes the determinative contribution to his status.

Goulet and Baltes' view, logically and necessarily, requires traditional antecedent consequence designs applied across a large number of diverse situations and has led to great interest in extrapsychic social causality. Their view, I argue, is essentially a nondevelopmental consideration of the secular trend as cause (Nesselroade & Baltes, 1974). Secular trends are food for a developmental course, but they are not developments in themselves. Instead, they are a kind of error variance, as far as the main questions of developmental research are concerned. The secular trends identified by researchers so far have to be more shifts in content than anything else, because we lack sufficient understanding of the potentially relevant, deep social structures, which can only shift imperceptibly from one historical epoch to another. This is not to say that the immediate personal–social experiences of people are not critical to the development of the individual, but these are not what is meant by secular trends.

When development is considered in the light of Goulet and Baltes' and Wohlwill's points of view, it must be immediately admitted that neither approach can be fully incorporated by research designs that focus on personality. Unlike their fellows who investigate cognitive or intellectual development, personologists have achieved neither reasonable consensus as to the identity of the critical personality variables nor adequate ways of measuring personality variables or functions that might be the candidates for temporal roles. Partial exceptions include psychological differentiation (Witkin, Goodenough, & Karp, 1967) and the fact that some evidence suggests that the ego, as measured by the Loevinger sentence completion test, "develops" (Loevinger et al., 1970). However we do not know the kind of developmental detail that Goulet and Baltes or Wohlwill recommend that we should. The maxima, minima, and direction of personality development is an unsolved substantive question—when does the personality begin? When has it reached its terminal development? When is it optimum? Some time ago Bloom (1964) proposed measuring personality maxima and minima by percent of mature growth obtained at any one time. This recommendation was impossible to follow since no one was clear about what aspects of personality should reach mature growth or even what mature growth is. Moreover, some investigators would reject Bloom's underlying assumption that personality development is quantitative and accumulative.

When the research problems of personality development are stated in these ways, it seems clear that common thrusts must be shown to exist across diverse life situations, that is, these thrusts must be developmental rather than situational unless it can be established or assumed that certain situations invariably present themselves at particular points in the life course. However, Nesselroade and Baltes'

(1974) paper indicates very little interest in the details or in fundamental aspects of routinely occurring situations, beyond their noting the chronological years of their data collections.

The specification of situational antecedent as causal of consequent attribute is not the strong suit of long-term study (since people live their lives in diverse ways), even if it were conceptually preferred. However long-term naturalistic study does lend itself to systematic descriptions of changes in intraindividual repertoires and in organizations in the face of situational diversity. Thus, the analyses to be presented, by necessity as well as by choice, are more compatible with Wohlwill's recommendation. However, we cannot obtain information concerning minima, maxima, rate, and terminal level, since the present work is a study of personality. If it had been possible to include the parallel structural developments, which I argue enable the development and differentiation of ego processes, we might know more about absolute minima, maxima, rate, and terminal levels. However, questions concerning the components of change, their form, and their direction can be addressed. Despite the fact that ego processes do not represent developmental functions in themselves, the hope is that more general developmental functions may be at least tentatively inferred from the organizational form and the directions of movement the ego processes take.

Empirical Description of the Development of Ego Processing

METHODS

Data and Subjects

These questions concerning the development of ego processing were studied by using data for four longitudinal samples at Berkeley's Institute of Human Development: (1) The Oakland Growth Study (OGS) men and women for two time periods, at age 37 and again at age 47; (2) The Berkeley Guidance and Control Study (GCS) men and women—the Guidance subsample—at late childhood, that is, age 9½–11½, and both the Guidance and Control subsamples at age 30 and at age 40. As was explained in the last chapter, ego ratings were done for the subjects when they were adults by at least two clinicians and were based on extensive interviewing that ranged for various samples and times of data collection from 3 to 12 hours. The childhood ego ratings, which exist for only the Guidance subsample, were based on several shorter interviews that usually occurred, however, every 6 months during childhood; various other materials were included in the basic case assembly, for example, Rorschachs, TATS, sociometric ratings, IQ tests, and so on. The vehicle for these ratings, also done by expert clinicians who work with children, was the Q sort of Ego processes (see Appendix B). Q reliability based on at least two judges' evaluations for each case ranged from .45 to .78 with a mean, calculated by the r to z transformation, of .67. Reasonable levels of reliability were insured for both the adult and childhood periods by the addition of more judges if the initial level of agreement between the first two evaluations was insufficient (Q correlation $< .45$). All judges worked independently of each other and of any other information about the subject.

In order to align the 60 Q-sort items with the 20 coping and defense ratings for the adult periods, the three Q-sort items representing each of the 20 processes were composited. (Previous work showed that the various trios of items representing the same processes were generally highly intercorrelated.) All raw scores for the adult and childhood periods were converted to standard scores with means of 50 and standard deviations of 10 to correct for possible shifts in the judges' frames of reference and for the metric difference between the 5-step ratings and the 9-step Q sort ratings.

All available subjects who had data in common for at least two time periods were used for each analysis. This decision optimizes the stability of the results by basing them on larger Ns, (all Ns are shown in Table IX) but it still has difficulties because the various analyses do not include the same, identical subjects. This is especially marked for the GCS males. Their N for early childhood was 22, but it became 41 for the two adults periods, a pattern of change that also characterizes the GCS women. This fact is particularly bothersome with the male GCS sample because it contains a number of highly unusual individuals whose effects are particularly felt when the N becomes small (see Haan and Day, 1974, for previous longitudinal work with other data from these same samples that shows the frequent failure of the GCS men to conform to trends that were common for three other samples). The results for the GCS males are reported here, but they should be regarded with some skepticism.

Forms of Analyses

Pearsonian correlations between time periods were calculated as the indices of sameness. Sign tests, which were based on the proportion of subjects increasing their standing on each of the variables from first to second time periods, were the indices of change. This nonparametric measure was used because the standardization of scores to a mean of 50 meant that a paired subjects t test would not reveal differences that might truly exist. If significant levels of association *and* change between the time period for a particular process occurred, then the process was counted as an instance of continuity. F ratios for the variances for two time periods were the indices of sample convergence and divergence. Modal organizations of ego processes were determined by submitting the data for each sample at each time period to separate Q factor analyses, using principal components solution and varimax rotations on the tilted matrices, to obtain person clusters with factor scores for each of the ego processes.

Table IX
Longitudinal Patterns of Sameness, Continuity, and Heterogeneity in Four Samples

	GCS Women						GCS Men					
	Child to 30 Years (N = 23)			30 to 40 Years (N = 62)			Child to 30 Years (N = 22)			30 to 40 Years (N = 41)		
	r	Sign test (p level)	F Ratio (p level)	r	Sign test (p level)	F ratio (p level)	r	Sign test (p level)	F ratio (p level)	r	Sign test (p level)	F ratio (p level)
Cognitive processes												
Objectivity	$.43^c$	.02/2	.05/1	.18			.33		.01/1	.20		.05/2
Isolation	.13			.15			$.45^c$		.01/1	$-.44^b$		.05/2
Intellectuality	$.56^b$		.02/2	$.45^a$	.02/2		.21		.01/1	$.39^b$		.02/2
Intellectualizing	.19			$.38^b$			$.54^b$		.05/1	$.31^c$	.004/2	
Logical analysis	$.37^c$			$.47^a$	04/1	.001/1	.31	.04/2		.23		
Rationalization	$.54^b$	.008/1	.01/1	$.38^b$			.09		.001/1	.14		
Intraceptive processes												
Tolerance of ambiguity	.29			.17			.13			.13	.001/2	
Doubt	-.15			10	.05/1		-.07		.01/1	.14	.02/2	
Empathy	.35			.12	.05/1		$.66^a$		.01/1	.17	.04/1	
Projection	$.55^b$		.01/1	.11			.29		.01/1	-.07		
Regression-ego	$.49^c$		.01/1	$.29^c$	.04/2		-.03		.01/1	.22		
Repression	.28			.08	.01/1		-.23		.01/1	.23		
Attention-focusing process												
Concentration	$.41^c$		.01/1	$.33^b$			.07	.04/1	.01/1	$.52^a$	.001/2	
Denial	.34	.02/1	.05/1	.23			.14		.01/1	.08	.02/2	.02/2
Affective regulations												
Sublimation	$.42^c$	01/1		-.12			.12		.001/1	.16	.02/1	
Displacement	.15			.19		.01/1	.35		.01/1	.19	.04/2	

continued

Summary measures

	r	Sign test (p level)	F ratio (p level)	r	Sign test (p level)	F ratio (p level)	r	Sign test (p level)	F ratio (p level)	r	Sign test (p level)	F ratio (p level)
Substitution	.44[c]			.19		.01/1	.06			.38[b]	.04/2	.01/1
Reaction formation	.36		.02/1	.15		.03/1	−.12			.08	.02/2	.01/1
Suppression	.46[c]		.02/1	.05			.13			.03		.02/1
Repression	.22		.05/1	.22			.24			.16		.01/1
$\bar{x}$coping	.42			.23			.20			.24		
$\bar{x}$ defense	.28			.19			.17			.08		
Total coping	.53[b]			.31[c]		.05/1	.35			.26		.01/1
Total defense	.53[b]		.02/1	.14			.31			−.08	.02/1	.01/1

	OGS Women 37 to 47 Years (N = 41)			OGS Men 37 to 47 Years (N = 40)		
	r	Sign test (p level)	F ratio (p level)	r	Sign test (p level)	F ratio (p level)
Cognitive processes						
Objectivity	.54[a]			.56[a]		
Isolation	.28	.05/2		−.10	.05/2	
Intellectuality	.48[b]			.55[a]		
Intellectualizing	.00			.42[b]	.002/2	
Logical analysis	.44[b]			.61[a]	.03/2	
Rationalization	.01			.44[b]		
Intraceptive processes						
Tolerance of ambiguity	.17			.46[b]		
Doubt	.47[b]			.26		
Empathy	.16			.65[a]		
Projection	.32[c]			.48[b]		.01/1
Regression-ego	.16			.34[c]		
Repression	.53[a]		.04/2	.31		

continued

Table IX—Continued

	OGS Women 37 to 47 Years (N = 41)			OGS Men 37 to 47 Years (N = 40)		
	r	Sign test (p level)	F ratio (p level)	r	Sign test (p level)	F ratio (p level)
Attention-focusing processes						
Concentration	.12			$.32^c$		
Denial	.08			$.53^a$		
Affective regulations						
Sublimation	$.65^a$			$.48^b$		
Displacement	$.37^c$			$.33^c$	.03/2	
Substitution	.21			.24	.04/2	
Reaction formation	.08		.02/1	$.46^b$	.03/2	
Suppression	.09			.11		
Repression	.07			$.36^c$		
$\bar{x}$ coping	.32			.45		
$\bar{x}$ defense	.23			.36		
Summary measures						
Total coping	$.52^a$		.02/2	$.61^a$		
Total defense	$.33^c$			$.44^b$		

Note: numbers following *p* level for Sign and *F* tests indicate whether the first or second time period was bigger.
$^a p \leqslant .001.$
$^b p \leqslant .01.$
$^c p \leqslant .05.$

RESULTS FOR SAMENESS, CONTINUITY, AND CHANGE

From the ego process point of view, results for stability or change that are sample-specific require further analysis in terms of the special life experiences of any one group and thus cannot be regarded, in themselves, as necessarily indicative of developmental trends. Consequently, before any trend in ego processing is discussed it must meet the following stipulations: (1) at least three of the six cross-time analyses must show the same developmental trend of the same import unless (2) two samples have the same trend for the same general time interval, for example, the two GCS samples for childhood to 30 years or any two of the samples for the adult intervals. This stipulation, practically speaking, reduces the number but strengthens the results we will consider. Should the reader want to attend to the findings in great specificity, he can do so by turning to Table IX.

Before we turn to the examination of results, we need to draw a sketch of the varying intrapsychic and extrapsychic contexts presented from ages 9½ to 47 years for the development of the ego processes. It is a pity, of course, that data are not available for the socially turbulent and structurally disequilibrated period of the adolescent's transition from concrete to formal, logical operations. In any event, we can reasonably expect that the GCS subjects were structurally at the stage of concrete operations during the childhood period and that the life span studied here carried most of these subjects into the stage of formal operations (see a reanalysis of the results of previous study (Kuhn *et al.*, in press) described in the last chapter for evidence that most OGS subjects do obtain the stage of formal operations). Socially, they will have moved from being schoolchildren to being economically independent, married, parents, and, in the case of some OGS subjects, to being grandparents and even retired persons. Clearly these social changes, as well as structural changes, contribute to and interfere with our capacity to discern trends in ego development.

First we can note in Table IX that the $\bar{X}$ correlation for the coping processes are always higher than for and defense in all six analyses. This trend supports the expectancy that coping, the normative form of functioning, has greater temporal sameness than defense, the more situationally specific kind of ego action. The absolute differences between the coping and defense $\bar{X}$s are not great, but they consistently favor the greater stability of coping.

Next, considering the processes that can be classified as being temporally the same, we find that nine of them meet the replicatory criterion; most occur for the shorter and probably less-changeable adult interval. Only three are defensive processes—rationalization, projection, and total defense—while the remainder are coping processes. Not unexpectedly, the cognitive processes of objectivity, intellectuality, and defensive rationalization meet the sameness criteria, as does concentration. Thus "cognitive style" and task orientation are relatively stable across time. The general tendency to regulate affective expressions via sublimation is in the sameness category, along with ego regression and total coping.

Turning now to the category of continuity (a significant correlation and significant change), we find that three processes meet the criteria—all during the adult intervals and all increasing with increasing age. GCS females and OGS males increase their use of logical analysis, while both male samples become more intellectualizing and displacing. These mixed sample findings occur despite the 7-year age difference between the GCS and OGS samples. Apparently the middle years, from 30 to 47, are times of increasing cognitive investment, both coping and defensive, as well as times of greater willingness to take one's feelings out on others.

Only one process meets the replicatory requirements for change (zero order correlations but a significant sample change). Both GCS samples draw away from using denial, the most primitive of defenses, between childhood and age 30. There are many other instances, of course, where a single sample changes.

Another group of processes of mixed classification need comment. Four intraceptive processes—doubt, tolerance of ambiguity, empathy, and regression—and two affective regulations—substitution and suppression—could be allocated to the sameness category for one adult sample but to the continuity category for another. The thurst of the movement was toward a greater number of samples preferring to use the processes of doubt, tolerance of ambiguity, empathy, regression, and suppression, and becoming less likely to use substitution. These findings imply that people can afford to be more intraceptive during the later adult years and that they are better able to moderate their affective expression, finding less necessity for resorting to transforming their negative feelings to their positive counterparts.

Two additional processes were essentially adevelopmental: isolation and repression. The fact that isolation tended to have lower reliability ratings at some periods may explain its lack of replication, but finding that repression shows neither sameness or continuity across time is particularly important since psychoanalytic theory suggests great stability for this defense, but its fate in this longitudinal analysis suggests that repression may be highly reactive to individual people's changing situations.

To summarize, the general developmental thrusts indicate greater stability for coping than for defense and greater stability for task orientation and for the cognitive processes than for other sectors of ego. The simplest, most undifferentiated, defense, denial, decreases for both GCS samples between childhood and age 30. During the adult interval, orderly increases occurred in logical analysis and the males became more displacing and intellectualizing. Mixed results for intraceptiveness occurred and the subjects had less need of transforming their feelings to the opposite expression. Repression and isolation were the only processes that appeared to be adevelopmental in these analyses.

RESULTS CONCERNING SAMPLE CONVERGENCE AND DIVERGENCE OVER TIME

Keeping the caveat in mind concerning the GCS men (particularly for the childhood-to-30-year period where all their processes but two had significantly greater variances), we can find that both GCS samples became more homogeneous in a number of ways from childhood to 30 years. As children, they differed one from another in the saliency of their coping objectivity, concentration, sublimation, and suppression as well as in their defensive rationalizing, denial, repression, and total defensiveness. By age 30, they had become more alike in all these respects. The replications that include the adult intervals show that the three samples diverged between the two adult follow-ups for isolation and that three converged for projection and repression.

The general thrust of the trends toward convergence or divergence suggests, then, that childhood is a time of great individual differences. By age 30, people have become more alike in their coping capacities—their objectivity and ability to concentrate as well as their ability to handle their feelings in coping ways. These convergences may have occurred because all had achieved a modicum of structural maturity. Some defensive forms—particularly the more undifferentiated ones—also became more standardized from childhood to age 30. In general, the defenses show a greater variability—26 significant differences across all ages and samples as compared to 16 differences for coping. This finding again emphasizes the likelihood that defenses are situationally reactive. Heterogeneity more frequently characterizes the earlier period in all sample comparisons than it does the later period (46 times as compared to 6). Thus development is toward greater homogeneity. Between the two adult periods, isolation diverges, a phenomena that probably can only occur if cognitive development is advanced while projectiveness and regressiveness converge; both of these processes are likely to be particularly maladaptive to the adult in his workaday world.

ORGANIZATIONS OF EGO PROCESSES AT DIFFERENT TIME PERIODS

The standard scores for the ego ratings were submitted separately for each sample and each time period to principal components solutions to attain five factors, followed by varimax rotations. The intent was to achieve a reasonably simple picture of the main ego organizations at various times in the life span. This procedure was not undertaken to find the "basic" structure of the ego data, but was regarded, more informally, as a means of grouping people according to common ego organizations, so whatever variations occurred at different points in the life span could be discerned. One could say that this was a "clinical" use of factor analysis.

This procedure produced, however, more results than it is sensible to consider here. Consequently we will attend only to the first factor, which in all cases is the largest and therefore represents the modal person clustering for each sample at that time period. These modal groups accounted for 24% to 49% of the variances in different matrices. The first cluster for all solutions have considerable similarity. All were primarily coping and were specifically, that version called controlled or regulative coping, previously found in several factor analyses of ego variables (see Haan, 1963, and the Joffe–Naditch factor analysis in Chapter 13 of this volume.) The similarity among these modal organizations are indicated by their inter Q correlations which ranged from .20 to .96 with a mean of .67. When the GCS males' correlations are removed, the range is .32 to .96 and the mean is .77. The percentage of persons within each sample who were members of the first modal cluster for different time periods (factor loadings ⩾ .40) ranged 80% for the OGS females, 67% for the OGS males, 44% and 56% for the GCS females and 20% and 25% for the aberrant GCS males. Thus there is some stability in the ego organizations these subjects used across time but obviously considerable latitude for adopting new solutions when intrapsychic or extrapsychic conditions make it advantageous or necessary to do so.

Turning first to the GCS females shown in Figure 6, we can see that even though the general nature of their coping solutions for three time periods are similar, the childhood organization is in marked contrast to the two adult organizations. This difference is expected on two counts: (1) The number of years between childhood and the adult years is greater then between the two adult periods and (2) structural development probably requires that childhood ego organizations have quite different characteristics than adult ones. The girls' solution saliently features the coping processes of logical analysis, ego regression and sublimation and compared to the adults' solution, the undifferentiated but not socially threatening defenses of rationlizing and regressing, methods which these 9¾- to 11-year-old coping girls probably resorted to when they were under pressure. They deviated from the adults in their comparatively low level of tolerance for ambiguity. Another consistent difference between the children's and the adults' solution lies in their varying methods of regulating affect. The girls sublimate, but they are unlikely to transform or restrain their feelings, in either a coping or a defensive fashion. Altogether we can say that the girls' childhood organization describes a relatively expressive,

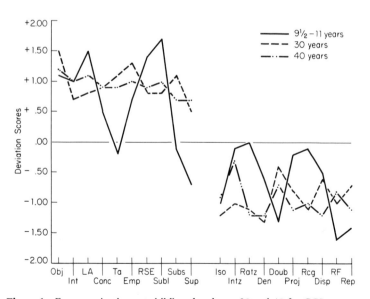

Figure 6. Ego organizations at childhood and ages 30 and 40 for GCS women.

logical, but intolerant person who is not definitively socialized and who, more readily than her adult counterparts, rationalizes and regresses.

Although there is a high degree of similarity between the GCS women's coping organizations at 30 and 40 years, two differences stand out: the earlier solution gives greater prominence to displacement while the later one accords greater importance to intellectualizing. Thus these 30-year-old women tended to act out their feelings, a defense that may be more socially tolerated from 30-year-olds than from children. By the time they are 40 this process is not as likely to be used. Instead, threat and challenge are made more remote by intellectualization.

Considering next the childhood organizations for the GCS males shown in Figure 7 and keeping in mind that the results for this sample need to be regarded with caution, we find their methods of regulating affect during the childhood period were quite different from the girls': They were substituting, suppressive, and were noteworthy for their level of reaction formation. Thus while the coping girls appear relatively free in self-expression, the coping boys appear defensive but well socialized. Although this organization does seem to be consistent with the conventional view of well-functioning 9- to 11-year-old boys—they have become little "men"—it does not award great importance to the cognitive coping functions, as did the girls' organization.

The organization for the GCS men at 30 years is the least cognitively coping, the most sublimating suppressive, and denying, an organizational pattern that is not consistent with their childhood solution. Between the time that the data were collected for the 30- and 40-year-old follow-up, a number of these men were divorced from their wives. These eminent experiences may have already affected

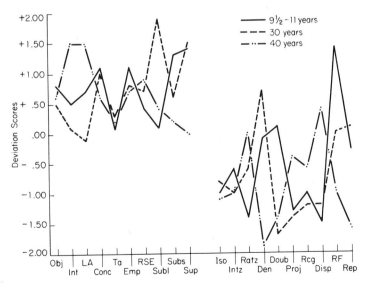

Figure 7. Ego organizations at childhood and ages 30 and 40 for GCS men.

their solutions at age 30 because their modal organization by age 40 gives highest prominence to cognitive coping while all the means of regulating affect have diminished in importance except for displacement, which has considerably increased. Moreover, the 40-year-old organization is less denying than the 30-year one.

The two adult organizations for the OGS females are shown in Figure 8. Although they are very similar to each other, the earlier solution is less intraceptive since it does not feature a great deal of empathy or ego regression and, consistent with this restrictiveness, is the greater prominence accorded to defensive intellectualizing and reaction formation. The striking feature of the two solutions for both the women's samples at the time of the last follow-up is the indication that their organization was highly integrated—almost all coping processes are equally salient.

The two OGS men's organizations, shown in Figure 9, vary from each other in the saliency of the 47-year-olds' cognitive coping compared to the 37-year-olds' greater investment in affective regulation and ego regression. In the defensive sector all processes are absolutely low except for both solutions' comparatively salient repression.

In summarizing these descriptions of temporal variations in ego organizations (and disregarding the GCS males' anomalies), we appear to have found at least two different series of ego organization, one for the coping males and the other for the coping females. It seems that at childhood the girls did not react to pressures to socialize their affective reactions and perhaps for this reason were freer to cope cognitively. As girls they succumbed, more readily than they did as adults, to using the socially nonthreatening but simplistic defenses of regression and rationalizing.

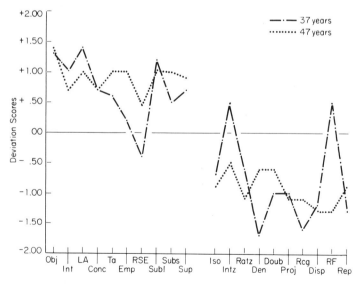

Figure 8. Ego organizations at ages 37 and 47 for OGS females.

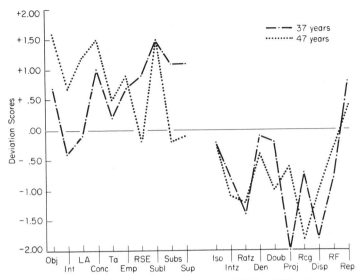

Figure 9. Ego organizations at ages 37 and 47 for OGS males.

Their solution at age 30 compared to the one for age 40 is only more displacing; however, by age 40 for GCS and age 37 for the OGS, intellectualizing had become a salient part of these women's repertoires. The most striking aspect of the females' age-organizational differences is the clear trend, observed for both groups, toward their coping processes (less definitely their defensive processes) becoming more of a piece—more integrated—with increasing age.

At childhood these coping males seem to have already absorbed and used, both defensively and copingly, the more socialized forms of regulating their impulses—restraint and transformation. Compared to their investments in other processes, neither of the male groups actually place much weight on coping cognitively or intraceptively until the last time they were observed. The comparatively chaotic course of the GCS men made it difficult to achieve replication between the male samples, but one observation is clear: Neither group achieved the integration of coping functions that typified the women at the time of last observation.

CHANGES IN FAMILY MEMBERSHIP AND EGO PROCESSING

Before we terminate this chapter, the results of a set of analyses need to be reported that illustrate how changes in the contexts of intimate living affect ego processing. Such findings are essentially adevelopmental and could just as well have been in the chapter on stress. Still, they will be discussed here since they illustrate why developmental trends are almost never purely observed.

A count was made of changes in the membership of a subject's primary family at various times in his life span. Up to age 18, the changes which were counted as primary were: the death of a parent or a sib, separation, divorce, or desertion of a parent, remarriage of a parent, the subject's own marriage, divorce, or annullment. After the age of 18 the changes counted were: subject's own marriage, divorce, or annullment, remarriage, or the death of his spouse or offspring. Thus, primary changes were defined as shifts in the members who peopled the subjects' intimate living context. Chapter 10, concerned with ego processing and the family group, develops a full rationale for why ego processing should be affected by these kinds of changes. However, we can briefly say here that family living occupies a great deal of people's emotionally important time and that a family group can be regarded as an integral body to which each member contributes a unique kind of processing that is needed by the whole. Thus the loss or the addition of a member makes it necessary that the whole family and each individual member reorganize methods of problem solving at least to some degree.

Readers acquainted with stress research will notice that there is a relationship between the present formulation and the Holmes and Rahe (1967) conceptualization that all life change requires readjustment and is therefore stressful. However, no argument is made here that the changes entailed are necessarily "bad" since the change in ego processing may actually be toward coping in a new intersubjectively expanded or intrasubjectively deepened way.

The ego processes for the OGS and GCS subjects at the two adult intervals were regressed on the number of family changes during five different time periods and for the total number of changes during the segment of the life span studied (essentially birth to 40 years for GCS and to 47 years for OGS). Turning to Table X, we can see a summary of the results of these analyses. SES was forced to enter each equation first so that subsequent effects were controlled in this regard. SES itself made significant and, as it turned out, negative ($p \leqslant .05$) contributions in only two analyses: the OGS womens' and men's ego processing at age 37. We can say, then, that lower-status OGS subjects were likely to experience family changes between the ages of 30 and 42.

Considering the effects of family changes for each period consecutively, we find that changes from birth to 12 years had mixed effects on the subjects' coping and defense at both adult periods. No cognitive processes are involved, but both intraceptive and affective regulations are. Two samples, OGS men at age 37 and GCS women at 40 years, are more tolerant of ambiguity, and OGS men are more suppressive and less substituting at age 47. However, OGS women at age 47 and GCS men at age 30 who have experienced these changes are more displacing and these women are less sublimating. The GCS men's acting out is further elaborated by negative contributions from reaction formation and doubt. The general thrust, then, is the OGS men and GCS women who experienced changes are the better, intraceptively, for having had these experiences, while the two other samples have difficulties in regulating their feelings and tend to externalize them.

Changes during the 13- to 18-year period only have effects on the females' ego processes and only for the earlier adult period. Other reports (Haan & Day, 1974; Livson & Peskin, 1967; Peskin, 1972) have shown that the adolescent period for these females was a time of particular turbulence and rapid change. Consequently they might have been particularly vulnerable, or at any rate, reactive to family changes during at this time. However, in both samples, the women who had experienced family changes during adolescence were more empathic at the time of the first adult follow-up, but beyond this one observation their solutions diverge. The GCS women were more intellectual and displacing; The OGS women handled their affective problems with reaction formations and they were not likely to sublimate.

Changes during the 19 to 29 span have effects only for the OGS males and GCS females. The men who experienced changes during this period are again tolerant of ambiguity at 37 and at age 47 they are more isolating and empathic. The GCS women who experienced changes again opt for the more cognitive solutions: At age 30 they are both defensively rationalizing, and more objective.

Changes during the span from 30 to 42 years immediately precede or coincide with the first adult follow-up for OGS and antedate the second follow-up, while this age span covers both follow-ups for GCS. At age 37, the OGS women who experienced changes became less substituting, while the OGS men were more empathic. However, by age 47, the men are isolating and suppressive, a pattern which suggests that they controlled their affective reactions and became more concerned for others after they had experienced family disruption. The GCS women again move toward an intellectual solution for their concerns: At age 30 they are more defensively rationalizing but still intellectual. At age 40 they remain more intellectual, but now also cope with logical analysis as well as defend by intellectualizing. However this purely thinking solution is tempered by their salient tolerance of ambiguity. The effects on the GCS men also seem to be intellectual: They are noteworthy for their objectivity.

No indices of changes were available, of course, for the GCS samples between 43 and 47 years because this period is beyond the time of the last follow-up. We find, however, that the OGS women who had experienced changes during this time were more empathic but less tolerant of ambiguity.

Finally we consider the overall effects of these changes throughout the life span. The effects on OGS women only appear for age 37, when they are noteworthy for their poor suppression. OGS men are more tolerant of ambiguity at age 37, but more isolating and repressive at age 47. Effects on the GCS women are seen only at age 40, when they too are more tolerant of ambiguity, intellectual, and decidedly not denying. The GCS men, as they so often have, upset the trend for tolerance of ambiguity by appearing to be less so at age 40 if they have experienced many changes, but they have clear investments in affective regulation: They are not repressive, but do employ *both* of the possible methods of transforming their feelings; coping substitution and defensive reaction formations are both positively related to the number of family changes.

The general thrust of these findings suggests that even though change in the family composition is undoubtedly a cause of readjustment, it is not always deleterious. In fact, tolerance of ambiguity and empathy—both processes that are

Table X

Relationships of Primary Changes in the Family with Ego Processing at Two Adult Periods with SES Controlled (Significant Components from Multiple Regression Models)

	Age periods of family changes					
	0–12 years	13–18 years	19–29 years	30–42 years	43–47 years (OGS only)	0–47 (OGS) 0–40 (GCS)
OGS Women						
37 years	Model ns Sublimation −[c]	Empathy +[b] Sublimation −[b] Reaction formation +[c]	Model ns	SES −[c] Substitution −[b]	Model ns	Suppression −[c]
47 years	Displacement +[b]	Model ns	Model ns	Model ns	Tolerance of ambiguity −[b] Empathy +[c]	Model ns
OGS Men						
37 years	Tolerance of ambiguity +[b]	Model ns	Tolerance of ambiguity +[b]	SES −[c] Empathy +[c] Isolation +[c] Suppression +[c]	Model ns	Tolerance of ambiguity +[b]
47 years	Suppression +[a] Substitution −[c]		Isolation +[a] Empathy +[c]		Model ns	Isolation +[b] Repression +[b]

GSC Women						
30 years	Model ns	**Displacement +b** Empathy +b Intellectuality +c	**Rationalization +b** Objectivity +c	**Rationalization +b** Intellectuality +c	—	**Model ns** **Model ns**
40 years	Tolerance of ambiguity +a	Model ns	Model ns	Tolerance of ambiguity +a Intellectuality +a Logical analysis +b Tolerance of ambiguity +b Intellectualization +b	—	Tolerance of ambiguity +a Intellectuality +a Denial –c
GCS Men						
30 years	Reaction formation –b Displacement +b Doubt –b	Model ns	Model ns	Model ns	—	Model ns
40 years	Model ns	Model ns	Model ns	Objectivity +b	—	Tolerance of ambiguity na Repression –b Sublimation +c Reaction formation +c

$a_p \leq .001.$
$b_p \leq .01.$
$c_p \leq .05.$
Signs of + or – indicate direction of the relationship.

153

particularly suited for dealing with the complexities and uncertainties of intimate interpersonal relations—are frequently associated with changes in family membership. The various patterns suggest other facets of ego adaptation. Both OGS men and GCS women (who are usually regarded as the most intellectual of the longitudinal samples; see Haan and Day, 1974) are salient for their cognitive reactions, both coping and defensive. Consistent for all the groups, but especially OGS women and GCS men, is their especially strenuous efforts to deal with the regulation of affective expressions.

Conclusion

A variety of results were related in this chapter. It should be recognized that their numerosity is due to the necessarily once-removed, descriptive quality of this account of ego processing over time. Since the laws of ego development are not known, there was no means of parsimoniously structuring the findings or their interpretations. Structural developmental data did not exist, and only one measure of contextual chance was available. Perhaps the complexity of human change over time is most appreciated at the present time by longitudinal researchers who find they can only submit to their subjects' inventiveness and the "noise" of their social contexts. Nevertheless, several general achievements were made and some benchmarks were established at least for these four samples.

Not the least among these was the fact that the ego processing of 9½- to 11-year-old children was measured and shown to have sensible relations to that of adults', a sizable portion of the adults being the children themselves grown-up. Few personality measures are shown to have sufficient generality to describe people ranging in age from 9½ to 47 years.

These analyses were approached with one clear hypothesis: Coping should be more temporally stable than defensiveness because the latter is situationally reactive while coping involves the dialectic of conserving the self within a framework of change. This hypothesis was handily supported (coping had consistently higher indices of sameness). The situational reactiveness of defensiveness was supported also by its consistently greater variable within samples across time, but variability in all ego processing is reduced over time, and the older age groups, particularly the older women, have more integrated organizations of ego processing, especially with respect to their coping processes. Undoubtedly the latter results occurred for women because this ego model includes intraceptive and affective regulations as well as the more traditional, instrumental forms of ego functions. The intrasample correlations for the females' coping organizations between various time periods had a mean, calculated by the r to z transformation, of .82 but of only .53 for the men. When the GCS males were removed from those calculations it was still only .64 for the OGS males.

Since we have observed that coping is, longitudinally, more stable than defense, it is less variable within samples at any one point in time, its variability is further reduced over time, and various coping functions come to be part of repertoires that are more integrated, I suggest, with some hesitation, that a diachronic description of coping might, in itself, identify a broad and general developmental function of personality the kind that Wohlwill (1970) suggests we should consider. We have found a tentative developmental form and a direction, but there can clearly be no minimum or maximum of coping—only a beginning at birth and an ending at death. Although we could not adequately deal here with the idea of rate since the data were mostly ratings tied to the framework of normative age groups, it could be done. If the Q sort of ego processes had been available for all age groups, we could have approached the question of rate at least in terms of the directional shifts in the rank ordering of ego processes within individuals. Nonetheless, we did observe different saliencies appearing with each new life epoch. Even though the boys and girls were very different from each other at early childhood, neither sample used isolation to any great extent but both were more denying than they were later. The GSC women became more displacing at age 30. At approximately age 40 the women of both samples became more intellectualizing, and at age 47 both OGS samples came to prefer denial more than they had. However, cognitive style, task orientation (concentration), sublimation and ego regression were often the same over the time span studied here while other kinds of intraceptiveness and affective regulations, such as substitution and suppressiveness appeared to be mercurial.

Finally we noted the effects of changes in family composition at different time spans on the subjects' ego processing at the two adult periods. The results followed Holmes and Rahe's (1967) ideas that life changes require readjustment, since effects of family changes were observed. However, these effects were by no means wholly negative in their meanings. There are frequent instances where enhanced coping intraceptiveness was associated with family changes, but some groups did have chronic problems in affective regulations and some appeared to be propelled into using cognitive strategies, both defensive and coping. Since many of the changes that occurred were not the responsibility of the subjects themselves, we can conclude from this one study of the effects of social context on ego processing that the environment often interferes with observing development in its pure form.

9. Stress and Ego Processing

Stress seems to be the label we now increasingly apply to the areas of research that have been traditionally identified as emotion, motivation, anxiety, frustration, aggression, and so on—all topics that lay at the heart of psychology's attempts to achieve dynamic models of man. Now, through a slow drift of ideas that give greater importance to interaction and transaction than to reaction, stress research seems to be incorporating and redefining a number of foci with the result that subject matter boundaries are being redrawn. Although there are unmistakable reasons of social conscience for the personologists' interest in stress, this refocusing probably represents an ontological shift toward viewing men in interaction with their world and an epistemological shift toward recognizing that the personologists' knowledge, far from being nominal, is constructed from their understandings of the urgencies and poignancies of life. For such a revolution to get well underway, however, we will first have to conclude that stress is a concomitant of life—in other words, not an unusual occurrence—and that intense or dramatic stress does not require formulations *qualitatively* different from everyday, garden varieties of pressure. This latter point will be elaborated as one of the main arguments in this chapter. Whatever the professionals' substantive or conscientious reasons, interest has also burgeoned because society's money providers are eager to fund research concerned with a variety of stress problems in all areas of health, aging, death, social change, social isolation, personal crises, the normal life span, overcrowding, family violence, and much more. Whether we are more stressed nowadays, or merely more aware that we are, is by no means clear. Consider, for instance, Dickens' documentation of stress in *David Copperfield*.

To attempt a summarization of the mass of recent findings emerging from the conglomerate of stress-relevant studies would be foolhardy, most particularly because they do not now form a coherent body of knowledge, nor is there

ommanding formulation that directs their evaluation and coordination. Several
ecent and impressive efforts to suggest modest structures and theories that would
ntegrate observations and guide future investigation have been made by Lazarus *et
l.* (1974), Mechanic (1974a), Janis (1974), French, Rodgers, and Cobb (1974), and
Veick (1970). This chapter has a related intent, and that is to make another modest
uggestion as to how a thorough application of the ego model of coping, defense,
nd fragmentation might serve to order the central concepts of stress and explicate
arious findings. At various times in the discussion the present formulation is
ompared with the others previously proposed, and the results of several different
tudies that have used the ego model will be reported.

The Difficulties of Stress Research

SOCIAL VALUATION OF STRESS MANAGEMENT

The stimulus (stress that leads to the person's distress) is a knotty matter in
tself, but involves, in essence, questions of what is bad, neutral, or good for people.
Avoidance of these implicit and detailed suppositions of value typically leads into a
losed loop in thinking about stress. To wit, within the positivist framework of
nost stress research, physiologically oriented or not, the man who defends himself
gainst stress and shows little arousal is the strong man, invulnerable by virtue of his
ack of arousal. When less quantitative and psychological rather than physiological
ndices of stress arousal are used, the adequacy or inadequacy of responses is often
nore obvious—at least to naive observers—since then the strong man appears
bblivious of his impending doom In contrast, the person who is aroused, who
ttempts to deal with the situation (and who may possibly fail, if his social or
conomic situation is irreparable), is counted as being stress-vulnerable.

There is no way to escape this researcher-manufactured conundrum without
pening up the loop and considering the social-personal conditions of being human
nd the ways in which our own social embedment affects our investigatory
ecisions as to (*1*) what evidence is, (*2*) what stress means, and (*3*) what a "good"
vay to handle stress might be. Mechanic (1974b) touched on this problem when he
ecently reminded us of Dubos' thought that being human entails the capacity to
eel distress and to become diseased. In a way, stress research seems to have
nwittingly designed a scientific "Catch 22" situation. If you do not admit that
ou can be killed in a war, you are strong and courageous, but you are also a fool.

Thus stress research has rediscovered the same core problems that have plagued
past personality research based on positivist strategies. The unwillingness to depend
or a time on common sense leads to unlikely and convoluted solutions and
ltimately to an infinite regress toward microresolutions. Acknowledging that men
xperience stress in social-psychological ways entails the adoption of a constructiv-
st epistemology. Only then can we understand the meanings of subjects' interac-

tions and commerces with their environments as being stressed, not stressed, or ;
successfully or unsuccessfully resolving stress. Just as we cannot, on ration
grounds, avoid considering that some social arrangements are better for son
people than others, or that some organizations of personality are better than other
we cannot avoid recognizing that some resolutions of stress are more socially ar
personally satisfactory for all concerned than are others. Strictly speaking, we a:
not permitted to say that the man who effectively turns his back on the inte
personal and social chaos surrounding him and thereby evidences little arousal
impervious to stress. Instead, he has made one kind of solution to stress that mu
inevitably have social and personal valuation and consequences. If his lack c
arousal is based on his avoiding the recognition that his child has leukemia and
consequent need for medical attention, we may need to inhibit our Judeo-Christia
propensity to "blame" him in the construction of our research designs and interpr
tations. Greater imagination and differentiation is needed to see that by his ow
necessity he chooses a resolution to stress that involves self-compartmentalizatio
instead of disintegration.

An assessment of social "reality" is needed to open up the closed-loop thinkir
and freshen the conceptualizations of stress research. In recently formulating the
model of adjustment, French and his associates (1974) have argued that a
assessment of both objective and subjective reality is needed. Such a move is not
simple matter since it would open up the Pandora's box of problems discussed i
Chapter 5, "Immanent Value in Personality Theory": What is it that people woul
like to do and what do others think they should do, when they are faced wit
stress? Should they do what others normatively do, should they do the health
thing, should they self-actualize themselves, should they reachieve their own happ
ness, should they reattain stasis, should they cope? In an important way th
chapter is symmetrical to Chapter 5, since the social valuation of often less-tha
adequate acts is the centerpiece. The arguments previously made to support th
value of accurately processing intrasubjective and intersubjective phenomena—i
other words, of coping—need not be repeated here. However, the coping formul;
tion does provide one possible solution to the question of whether stress has bee
managed within a social and psychological context and whether we can possibly sa
it has been successfully or unsuccessfully resolved.

THE QUESTION OF REALITY

The stimulus (objective reality) is a problem in yet another way that we hav
been considering throughout this volume. The beholder constructs the meaning
and relevancies of various stress stimuli within the frame of his own phenomeno
ogy, so one man's responses will suggest that the situation is his cup of tea, whil
another's will suggest that it is his poison. However, pointing to the individualiz;
tions of different people's phenomenologies does not completely convey all of th
ways that subjects' "obscurantisms" interfere with standardizing stimuli in stre:

search. All people, except one, may agree that stress objectively exists, but that he person may negate it and successfully defend himself against any knowledge of , thus appearing not to experience stress, or at least not immediately or directly. ome points of view would argue that he must have a middle knowledge of the ress, being a creature among other social creatures, and that he might "somatize" s knowledge.) The vagaries of stress perception are so common and well under-ood that they are the basis of stock comedy as well as tragedy. The oblivious and witting protagonist is surrounded by impending disaster, while the audience, inking what a bumpkin he is, waits for him to meet his fate. If it is to be funny, owever, we cannot bear that his situation be too disastrous; it must somehow rove to be a "blessing in disguise."

The recognition that some people most of the time, or many people much of the me, construct their own realities caused researchers to dispair about achieving andardized psychological meanings of stress stimuli and responses and to move stead to using molecular, material indices of stress reactions. But the relativity of eoples' constructions need not lead to an epistemological nihilism, for as Quine bserves, "I find the public circumstances of your affirmations and denials agree retty well with those of my own [1969, p. 5]." Undoubtedly the longer and less ertain route to truth that this recognition suggests propelled the rush to use hysiological indices of stress reaction. A pointer reading of a heightened auto-omic reaction seemed a certain basis for deciding whether or not the subject was the presence of stress and whether or not he was distressed. However, it is now ell understood (see McGrath, 1970, p. 69) that the various autonomic reactions re not unidimensional, that various indices do not form a unity called stress eaction, and that strong individual differences in physiological reactivity exist even hen people are within the same benign circumstances.

Most importantly, we do not understand the mechanisms that actually connect hought and physiological reactions—the mind and the body. As Lazarus' various udies well show, the thought does generally influence the physiological reaction; ut the various indices are highly reactive to the demand characteristics of the xperiment and subjects' private formulations. For instance, Maguire, Maclean, and itkin (1973) fully expected their subjects' physiological responses to habituate fter successive presentations of Lazarus' stress film, which depicts subincision rites mong a group of preindustrial people. However, their subjects' skin conductance ailed to adapt. Postexperimental interviews revealed that the subjects had thought o the very end of the experiment that they would be stressed further by still nother and even more horrifying film. Laboratory stress research is no less nvulnerable to subjects' extra or preliminary constructions (and is probably a great eal more, given the experimenter's intent to stress and his frequently strange cenarios) than are the social-psychological experiments and the psychometric ollections of data, a design difficulty discussed at various points earlier in this olume. Stress research has yet to consider thoroughly the social nature of its work, nd some stress experts (for example, Lazarus and Mechanic) are now advocating he naturalistic, and therefore less obtrusive, study of stress.

However, naturalistic research hardly escapes problems. For instance, Mechani (1974b) emphasizes that there is a wide variation in people's health-reportin behaviors. The same symptoms are reported, overreported, or underreported b different but presumably equally healthy populations. Furthermore, Hinkle (1974 observes from his long-term studies of the life experiences and subsequent diseas proneness of large samples of telephone company employees in New York City an his investigations of Hungarian and Chinese refugees that the people who remaine physically the healthiest "seemed to have a shallow attachment to people, goals, o groups" and they often showed "little psychological reaction to events and situa tions which caused profound reactions in other members [pp. 40–41]." Thus th same real life stress stimuli are also perceived and resolved in different fashions b different people, and there is no assurance that "stress-invulnerable" people ar socially committed to alleviating the despair of their families or their fellow beings A homey question may express the difference between peoples' preferences i brands of stress: Is it better to rust out or to burn out?

NEEDED: A PSYCHOLOGY OF STRESS

Thus the endemic problems of personality research reassert themselves on botl sides of the stimulus–response paradigm. People make what they will out of th stimulus, and in responding people accommodate to much more than the stres stimulus. Furthermore, the stimulus and the response cannot serve as the mai headings in an organization of a psychology of stress because they cannot be cleanly severed one from another despite the implications of McGrath's (1970 recent overview. Stress entails particularly complex and sequential interaction between people and situations. If any systematic description is to be achieved, the elements of the interaction model will have to be general in order to describe no only a multitude of situations but the virtuosity of subjects' coping, self-deception and deviousness, since the stakes are high in stress situations. In arguing for the strategy of a general formulation, I go against recent recommendations by Cobt (1974) and Mechanic (1974b), who have urged that priority should be given to the intensive study of single illnesses. I urge instead that a satisfactory general model o the psychology of stress is needed first and that it would go a long way in makin, subsequent research coherent.

Large scale, naturalistic research of stress has been able, almost at will, to establish correlates between noxious social situations and various indices of break down in people, such as psychiatric and physical illness (see for instance the variou papers in Dohrenwend and Dohrenwend, 1974, or in the volume edited by Levi Society, stress, and disease, Volume I, 1971, which includes the papers from the Stockholm Stress Conference). However, correlates between inimical social condi tions and personal damage do not form a basis for a psychology of stress. They only reinvent the wheel. That noxious social arrangements like poverty, starvation constant danger, and incessant social confusion are deleterious and result in chronic insecurity, stress, and frequent personal deterioration or retardation is not only common sense, but is well documented as the sociology of stress. People concerned with the public's health have had intelligible grounds for many centuries to work to prod and disturb national and world consciences in these regards. Mechanic (1974b) reminds us of the fact that the very structures of some institutional arrangements mean that the major stresses experienced by an individual person are not only long term, but are also not amenable to solution by him. Barbara Dohrenwend (1973) empirically demonstrated again that the lower classes and women experience more stressful events—defined on common sense bases—than other groups.

However, the psychology of stress is not as well understood as the effects of social powerlessness: Why do some people when they are faced with stress do far better or far worse than anyone had suspected they would, and why do they do better or worse than they have done before? Why do some kinds of social conditions totally define the actors, and why are other conditions that seem equally monolithic susceptible to being revised by some people? An impressive finding, first reported by Coleman et al. (1966) and now replicated in Israel (Handel, 1975) suggests that the answer is not always completely referable to noxious social conditions. The first study, based on thousands of subjects, showed that black adolescents' achievement was more related to their own sense that they could by their own efforts determine their fate (a matter of coping) than to familial or geographical socioeconomic indices, which, nevertheless, still accounted for substantial amounts of variance. Handel has now replicated that finding with 950 economically advantaged and disadvantaged adolescents in Israel.

What is needed for an adequate model of the psychology of stress is one that is designed to include the active processing of interactions with environments in the strong, not token, meaning of these terms.

Witness, for instance, the nature of the present controversy over Holmes and Rahe's (1967) social readjustment scale or the Subjective Life Change Unit scaling system (Rahe, 1974). Arrays of life change events were scaled and weighted after extensive work with various samples of "judges" who indicated how much and how protracted a readjustment they thought each life event required. The events included the death of a spouse (which was widely thought to require the most change), marriage, divorce, and Christmas to minor law violations. The assumption behind the scaling is that *all* change, whether for the good or the bad, takes its toll. More subtly and profoundly entailed is the ontological view that the person is a passive processor or appraiser of events that occur *to* him and that he is better off if fewer events come within his ken. The scaling, but apparently not the underlying assumptions, has occasioned considerable skepticism. A number of subsequent efforts have set out to show that the details of the scaling are in error. Evidence shows, not surprisingly, that the life events have varying meanings for different populations (see Dohrenwend & Dohrenwend, 1974). Obviously taking on a house mortage does not mean the same to a middle class person as it must to a lower class person (Miller, Bentz, Aponte, & Brogan, 1974); some investigators find it hard to believe that positive life events take a toll; and others argue that the "nonevent"—

that which never occurs but is eagerly anticipated—also requires readjustment. In one study Bruce Dohrenwend (1974) limited the events to (*1*) those that were independent of psychiatric status and (*2*) those that could be independently verified. He found that community leaders had experienced as many prior life change events as psychiatric patients and convicts reported occurred to them prior to their institutionalization. Congruent with the present view is Dohrenwend's focus on events that are in or out of people's control.

What is needed is a psychological model that forms a bridge between the stress and the person's distress, in other words, one that is concerned with how people process objective stress: how they perceive and construct meanings, what value they place on various actions, how they interact with events. Mechanic (1974a), with less-explicit emphasis, would appear to agree with this proposal, since he argues that subjects' complex mastery skills, their activities and plans, and their own choices need to be investigated, particularly within temporal contexts. Janis (1974) has described a five-step model of decision making following the impact of stress, and Lazarus *et al.* (1974) have proposed a model of successive appraisals and reappraisals. All of these have some similarity to the model of ego interaction that will be presented later. However, these formulations describe the subjects' activity as essentially a linear progression, wherein a stimulus acts on a dispositional state to produce a response. Although this activity is frequently called interaction, I argue it is only so in the weak sense of the term and should be called a reaction. In fact, interaction can only be inferred when there is explicit provision for (*1*) an open system in an ecology and (*2*) processes that reverberate from subject to object and vice versa and (*3*) the nature of the second exchange being affected by the first. More simply, "mediation" between stimulus and response is the label that is preferred by most.

The Uses of the Word Coping in Stress Research

To cope means, according to *Webster's third unabridged dictionary*, "to maintain a contest or combat, usually on equal terms or even with success, . . . or to face, encounter, . . . or overcome problems and difficulties;" thus the accepted definition does not particularly feature the idea that people cope only with stress. Instead the connotation of managing problems and difficulties *usually on equal terms* is primary. Nevertheless, the word has been used in divergent ways by various stress researchers, and the various definitions reflect conceptual differences. The reluctance to admit criteria based on the common sense of socially constructed reality has led to these several "scientific" meanings of the word *coping*. Moreover, the logically inelegant, psychoanalytically based formulation that defenses can and should be successful has added to the confusion, so that coping is sometimes regarded as a subcategory of defense.

In contrast, others regard defense as a form of coping. For instance, Lazarus, in his book (1966) and in various papers with different colleagues (for instance, Cohen & Lazarus, 1973; Lazarus *et al.*, 1974), identifies coping as specific to stress and a encompassing any problem solving or mastery effort, including both realistic forms and the most pathological processes. A distinction is made, nevertheless, between rational and irrational efforts as well as between realistic problem solving and primitive defenses, and these differences are noted as being "two sides of the same coin [Lazarus *et al.*, 1974, p. 250]." I argue that these two sides (actually, if fragmentation were to be included, there are three sides) represents a vital distinction that needs to be explicitly recognized and maintained in theory and research as it clearly is in common parlance.

Despite the different meanings, there is nothing in the definition of coping that implies self-deception or deception of others, nor can the realistic, intersubjective-adhering efforts be called defensive without bowlderizing the classical definition and orthogenesis of defense. Again we need to emphasize the intersubjective reality is not exclusively someone else's reality, but includes as well the part of the self that is consensually validated in experiences with others. A man who does not include intersubjective reality within his intrasubjective reality does not know and cannot understand himself and in time becomes an odd creature who cannot cope with the stress he generates for himself with his own thoughts.

Not to take the distinction between successful and unsuccessful management of stress seriously leads to other confusions and implausible suppositions. Weick (1970) comments that Lazarus' (1966, p. 175) contention that people are better able to cope with threat if they locate the agent of harm outside themselves represents a "rather specious mode of control." Weick goes on to argue that such externalizations (displacements and/or projections in the present system) are unlikely to result in the person's reevaluating and modifying his own resources. Lazarus (1976) counters that he only asserts that such externalizations make people feel better since it gives them an illusory sense of control. It would appear simpler to decide at the outset that displacements and projections carry the seed of self-defeat, whether or not they make people feel better. Externalization of these kinds can only be, at best, a temporary solution because others and situations invariably need to correct the accusation.

Mechanic (1974b) moves somewhat closer to the present view by equating coping with instrumental skills. However, stress cannot always be handled by means—end processes. Sometimes all one can do is to wait the problem out by tolerating a degree of ambiguity, by withdrawing via ego regression, by empathizing with another's pain, by suppressing one's feelings, by sublimating one's reactions in work, by substituting what must be for what one wants, and by turning one's concentration to other things that must be done immediately. The intraceptive means of coping with stress are probably preferred by those people whose life experiences does not permit payoff from instrumental solution, for example, women and blacks. Clearly some stress situations, such as impending death, cannot be readily resolved instrumentally by anyone except by suicide, which is a course some take, undoubtedly for instrumental reasons.

Mechanic (1974b) again suggests the present distinction between coping and defense when he observes that the stronger a person's coping skills are, the less need he will have for defensive manipulation. But then, perplexingly to his reader, he goes on to say that the primary function of defense is the facilitation of the coping process. In another context Mechanic proposes that coping should be regarded as a process that deals with extrapsychic phenomena while the defenses deal with intrapsychic phenomena. This same distinction was made much earlier by Anna Freud (1937). She expected, following the classical line of thought, that defenses constituted the whole of the ego's work, which in itself was solely intrapsychic. Still, she wondered whether a counterpart to the ego's defensiveness existed in its attempt to deal with external danger by active intervention. Unfortunately she terminated this interesting line of thought, which carried the potential for discomforting psychoanalytic theory, by summarily noting "upon this last side of the ego activities I cannot enlarge here [p. 191]." Mechanic's suggestion for clarifying the intrapsychic and extrapsychic distinction between coping and defense seems regressive, since it would turn formulations of stress processing back to the view of the person as a closed system rather than an open interactive one and would necessitate the supposition that people perform qualitatively different operations in managing internal and external phenomenon. This is unlikely, given all we now know about the development of thought as action.

Like Lazarus, White (1974) suggests that coping is merely adaptation under very difficult conditions. He seems to posit a mild to severe continuum of stress stimuli, which is successively associated with qualitatively different kinds of response. This stipulation merely changes the sector wherein the word is to be applied, but at the same time the switch changes the conceptualization. Furthermore, it is not all clear, nor does it seem likely in a process or structural sense, that people radically alter themselves and do qualitatively different things when they are faced with situations of mild stress as opposed to what they do when they are confronted with ones of moderate or even severe stress. Moreover, White's conceptualization makes the stimulus the basis for deciding when we are in the presence of coping and when it is adaptation that we see.

We have already considered the traps involved in attempting to approach the psychology of stress solely through the stimulus. One man's poison is another's cup of tea. Undoubtedly the effect of investigating stress instead of frustration, aggression, or emotion is to put research in closer contact with the meanings of real-life situations and the ways in which people process and interact with their environments. But this shift entails an ontological move toward viewing people and their actions as open systems, resulting in a heightened concern with how people affect and construct their situations when they have the options to do so. A nominal, behavioral language is insufficient for this task and a processual or general systems language is needed. At present much of the discourse about stress uses a potpourri of language appropriate to both behavioral and meaning systems. The argument here is that conceptual clarity can only be achieved by a thoroughgoing adoption of the language of meaning systems. Although we have considered the uses of the word *coping* here that diverge from the present use, there is agreement among all that coping means doing something about a problematic situation. The added emphasis here is to insist that the person's accuracy is the hallmark of coping, whether or not he is actually situationally successful, and that it makes no sense to toss aside the consensus we have already achieved about defensiveness, that is, it is some negation of reality or integrity. Having this toehold on the problem, why not make the next move and formulate a generic method of dealing with stress that is based on an accurate assessment and management of the stress situation, irrespective of its success.

Empirically Based Understandings about the Processing of Stress

As we survey the general findings that describe psychological reactions to stress, we find a sizable number can be encompassed by a process formulation. The task here of relating these findings will be made easier by grouping them according to whether their focus is the assimilatory or the accommodatory aspect of the ego processes. Evidently people (and in some instances animals) react with response decrements if their assimilation is impaired because (1) they did not anticipate the onset of stress, (2) they had expected something different or better, (3) the conditions of the situation are ambiguous, (4) they thought they would be stressed, (5) they regarded the situation as being similar to ones that they had previously been unable to handle, (6) they were already in a depleted state at the onset of stress, or (7) the situation deprived them of necessary information. People also react with response decrement when they are unable to accommodate because (1) they can do little or nothing to change or control the stress, (2) the stress is prolonged, (3) it is intense, (4) different stress experiences come immediately one upon another, or (5) they have had little previous experience in dealing with this brand of stress (see McGrath, 1970, for a summary of most of these findings).

A U-shaped curve has been proposed, most vigorously by Janis (1974), to demonstrate graphically that the subject's arousal and productivity is a function of the sheer intensity of the stimulus. Moderate stimulus intensity produces maximum productivity, while too little or too much results in the subject's lack of arousal and/or incompetent productivity. The orderly elegance of the inverted U-curve points to an "optimal" middle zone of stimulus intensity, and thus suggests on the one hand that the "good" response results from moderate stimulation, and on the other hand that the optimal man neither overresponds nor underresponds. The optimal man has, following Janis' (1974) formulation, the "appropriate" amount of vigilance. The U-shaped relationship seems to be a reasonable expression of one effect of general stimulus intensity that might apply to some situations of stress. Clearly, all other matters being equal, a very weak stimulus should often result in very little response, a moderate one, in an efficient response, while a very strong, intolerable stimulus may very well disorganize the response. In other words, isomorphism between stimulus and response seems on its face to be a reasonable supposition.

This equation, however, is based on positivist ideas of arousal rather than on constructivist ideas of deploying attention, assimilating the stimulus, interpreting meanings, and accommodating. The contrast between these two differing constructions needs to be made clear. Undoubtedly the inverted U-shaped curve holds if the organism is viewed as a mechanical processing apparatus that can be underloaded, overloaded, or loaded in a way appropriate to its capacity, and these situations may sometimes obtain with stimulus intensity, density (as a rate of impact), or complexity (as too many or too contradictory or too disparate). Moreover, on the response side of the equation, there is no difficulty in seeing how too little or too much responding might be "nonoptimal" and how just the *right* amount of response is needed. Still, it is clear that when a single, very weak, and simple stimulus has ominous implications in the mind of the person, the stimulus' relationship to the response will not be represented by the U-shaped curve. Moreover, people sometimes rise to occasions and do far better than they or others have ever done before (to paraphrase Sidney Carton in *A tale of two cities*). In other words, a constructivist viewpoint suggests that meaning, not amount, is the critical factor.

When reinterpreted from the constructivist view, some findings, primarily those of Janis (1965, 1974), point to another clearer and more probable meaning of the U-shaped curve. Janis reports that the adequacy of postoperational recovery is predicted by the degree of preoperational anxiety. After surgery, the least anxious tend to be the most angry and resentful, the most anxious do not adjust well, and the moderately anxious recover well. However, the present view suggests this formulation should not hinge on the degree but rather on the *kind* of processes the patients use within the meaningful situation of their being preoperational or postoperational. Various processes represent different constructions—different assimilations and accommodations—of stress and as a consequence have different poststress sequelae as well. Blanket denial that major surgery will be frightening, painful, and inconvenient can only result in anger and resentment once the actual experience is over. To displace and project preoperationally can readily find support and confirmation in the assault of the surgery itself and in the typical postoperational lack of great concern shown by surgeons and hospital personnel when the procedure is successful and the patient is recovering well from the medical point of view. Moreover, medical people must positively resist and therefore may anger the regressive patient. Janis' (1965) interpretation is especially flawed in its treatment of the moderately anxious group who seek out realistic information about the experience they are to undergo. In my view, they are not halfway anxious or halfway between denying on the one hand and regressing, displacing, and projecting on the other, but many may well be coping. Their anxiety prior to major surgery would seem to be a realistic appraisal, and once the trauma is over and if it went well in realistic terms (the surgeon says he was able to correct the problem in a definitive way), they have every reason to recover rapidly and put the experience behind them. The failure to understand the likely status of the people in this middle group has confused analyses. For instance, Cohen and Lazarus (1973) formed three groups of presurgical patients on the basis of interviews and tests: those who were avoiding, those who were vigilant, and a middle group made up of those who were *both* avoiding and vigilant. Although it is plausible to think that a few people may alternate between avoidance and vigilance, it is not clear how a person could do both at one and the same time. Cohen and Lazarus found that the avoiding group recovered more rapidly than the middle group.

We turn now to consider how the ego process model might be used to order the array of stress findings and what kind of programs for further research it might suggest. The first task will be to describe a psychology of how people process stress, irrespective of content, and to do so in sufficiently general terms to encompass the stress effects of deprivation, overload, intensity, extensity, and complexity, and to make the description applicable to acute, chronic, and developmental stress phenomena.

The Ego Process Model and Stress

Leo Rosten has said it well: "Destiny came down to an island, centuries ago, and summoned three of the inhabitants before him. 'What would you do,' asked Destiny, 'if I told you that tommorrow this island will be completely inundated by an immense tidal wave?' The first man, who was a cynic, said, 'Why, I would eat, drink, carouse, and make love all night long!' The second man, who was a mystic, said, 'I would go to the sacred grove with my loved ones and make sacrifices to the gods and pray without ceasing.' And the third man, who loved reason, thought for a while, confused and troubled, and said, 'Why, I would assemble our wisest men and begin at once to study how to live under water' [*Captain Newman, M.D.*, Rosten, 1956, p. 272]."

GENERAL DESCRIPTION AND THE ROLE OF EMOTION

A necessary but insufficient element in the definition of stress is noxious emotion, feelings that people prefer not to experience. But critical in this proposal is the observation that if people develop a plan, execute it, and handle the stress to their own satisfaction, they will have managed their feelings, will usually feel strengthened, and will later relate their experience to others with relish. People clearly enjoy talking about their operations, childbirth, war experiences, car accidents, and so forth. Lazarus (1973) has recently drawn a distinction between the stimuli of a threat and a challenge, but this dichotomy disappears in the present formulation. A threat turns into a challenge if the person copes by developing and successfully executing a plan; a challenge turns into a threat if a person's need for intrasubjective security takes priority over his intersubjective embedment. Selye's (1974) recent distinction between harmful and constructive stress can also be understood in this way, as essentially defined by the meanings of the stimuli within the phenomenology of the distressed. However Lazarus' (1973) recent exposition seems to agree, basically, with the present one, since he also emphasizes that a successful coping plan reduces negative emotion. Thus, at least in retrospect, people actually like some kinds of stress, and we have seen in recent years how some well-cared-for, middle class youths attempt to mature and strengthen themselves by inviting the stress of poverty. If the person is unable to formulate or execute a reasonable plan, he will not have managed the stress, and this evaluation will not only be objectively observable but also subjectively experienced, even if not self-admitted. If the objective stress endures, he will need to manage his bad feelings somehow, so he may turn to defending himself in some fashion or temporarily fragment and thereby actively refuse to take responsibility for his fate.

Examples of unmanaged stress are provided by Folkins' (1970) subjects. After finding out that an announced shock stimulus was not going to occur and being asked why they hadn't called a halt to the proceedings, various subjects said: "I was off in another world which was unrelated to what you were doing;" "I didn't know how to quit (the experiment), the room just closed in;" "I couldn't afford to think about it . . . my defneses were all gone;" "It's like I wasn't here. If somebody was going to find out about you, it's be different—you'd be tense, but with a shock there's nothing to worry about." Watson (1975) has described another phenomenon of more passive resignation which he suggests is akin to depression. In the laboratory very young babies tend not to take the opportunity to control a mobile by turning their heads to activate sensors under their pillows if they have previously experienced a noncontrollable mobile over their cribs at home.

Unpleasant emotions arise, as was argued in Chapter 4, "Conceptualizations of Ego: Processes, Functions, Regulations," when there is a mismatch, unfavorable in its implications, between the person's intrasubjective sense of his own reality and his situational appraisal of intersubjective reality. Thus a dynamic, fluid balance is involved, and when the person recognizes that an outer or inner reality is bad or might prove bad for him, he is at least temporarily out of balance and emotional, but not yet motivational. Whatever the evantual physiological description of emotions, they are psychologically of a different class from cognitions, being more adjectival than structural and substantive. However, we have to recognize that at least some preliminary cognitive evaluation at some level of consciousness is requried for emotion to appear. As Lazarus and his associates (1974) review a number of their own and others' studies, they leave little doubt that physiologically measured stress reactions relate in some not entirely explicated way to the styles of thinking that subjects use or are led by the experimenters to use. Thus we must posit an initial, rapid assimilation of the objective, cognitive elements of the situation that results in some judgment about the likely implications for the beholder—whether these are good or bad for him. All of this activity must occur before the person has made definitive accommodations. The rapidity of assimilation causes some people to assume that emotion is automatic, instantaneous, and unbidden, but this supposition is untenable and not logical. A person cannot be emotional about a situation without first knowing, or having some inkling, of what it means for him.

Cognitions that precede and then identify or label emotions may often be more preconceptual (intuitive) than are later cognitions or ones that represent less imbalancing matters. The education of the child does not consistently or often include the necessity of articulating his emotions; more often, he must only roughly summarize his feelings to communicate to others. Consequently, affective-cognitive schemata unlike cognitive-affective schemata have no great call to become highly differentiated (except, of course, in psychotherapy). Moreover, emotions are often part of nonverbal figurative schemata (the images of peoples' angry expressions, of scenes where one was helpless, or of impending car accidents). Figurative schemata are highly individualized and particularized so that it is impossible to communicate them fully. Therefore they are not required to become highly socialized and standardized. (Instead we attempt to appreciate and communicate their meanings to others through the visual arts and perhaps to ourselves through rehearsals, fantasies, and dreams.) The infirmly or incompletely cognized features of both figurative schema and emotions make coordination with intersubjective realities difficult. Altogether then, even though figurative schemata are *less* cognized, they cannot influence assimilation and accommodation without being at least preconsciously cognized at some level and in some way.

The situations that people decide are bad for them involve a multitude of different kinds of stress stimuli that we need not necessarily consider in attempting to formulate a psychology of stress. The various kinds of stimuli are essentially the contents of stress and anything that an individual person regards as bad for him, in an acute or chronic situation or over a developmental epoch, is grist for the present exposition. Aside from the most dire or life-threatening situations, we can expect great variety in what threatens whom, for example, the vast and fluctuating individual differences in stage fright. Moreover there is no reason to think some people are stress-impervious; undoubtedly every one has his Achilles' heel. Furthermore, imbalances between intrasubjective and intersubjective reality are not unusual occurrences and in a strict, hypothetical sense can be said to occur in some degree and in essentially the same way (1) when any situation requires accommodation or (2) when any situation prolongs assimilation without permitting corrective accommodation (reality testing) to take place (for instance in sensory deprivation experiments). According to this line of reasoning, stress is not qualitatively different from many other life experiences, but is instead only more marked by aversive meanings.

TEMPORAL ACCOMMODATIONS TO STRESS

We need to underscore the fact that the person's cognitive accommodation to stress is likely to require a greater length of time than is his immediate perceptual assimilation of the situation including the immediate sequela of felt emotion. This temporal accommodative phenomenon of "working through" was recognized by Freud as typifying therapeutic patients after they had achieved new self-insights, and Janis (1965) has described a similar reaction, which he calls, "the work of worrying," in subjects who were witnesses to a disastrous gas explosion and in cancer patients. Lazarus and his associates (1974) have also emphasized that time is involved in dealing with stress. All of these observations can be usefully integrated and generalized by the assumption that greater time is needed for accommodation than is usually the case for assimilation. Stress situations may be, and often are in real life, complicated. The various elements, options, and limitations must be sifted through and sorted out to find a workable accommodation, and some people are able or willing to persist longer than others in attempting to find reasonable accommodations. However some stress situations require immediate accommodation and some are actually irresolvable, and the only possible accommodation is that they be endured. During the period when accommodatory efforts are under way, later recognitions and reformulations of the situation may produce even further imbalance and concomitant resurgence of emotion. However if the person develops a definitive and satisfactory intersubjective accommodation—in other words a motive plan—he reachieves an intrasubjective—intersubjective balance and can justifiably be pleased with himself.

INDIVIDUAL PHENOMENOLOGIES AND VARIETIES OF EGO PROCESSING

Some people will find some situations so fraught with their own particular brand of terror that they will opt sooner or later for maintaining their intrasubjective coherence at the expense of intersubjective reality. In these instances they also reachieve a balance, a false equilibration, that rests on the negation of various elements of objective and subjective reality. Thus they chose to compartmentalize rather than to disintegrate. Situations contain peculiar brands of terror either because their contents have historical meaning to the subject or because their structure is impossible for the person to resolve with his own existing resources. The latter is often the case with children. In all these circumstances response decrements occur. Lazarus (1966) calls this phenomenon "a primitivization." However, response decrement is not always a simple matter of defensive regression or fragmentary decompensation, the direct representations of primitivization in the present model. Both these processes tend toward primitivization since they represent a de-differentiation of the person's organization and processing. Alternatively the person may rationalize, intellectualize, deny, project, displace, repress, and isolate, depending on his preferred defenses and the situation.

We can note, parenthetically, that coping with a problem does not necessarily mean that one must be constantly making a frontal, means—end assault on the problem of stress or that one is always preoccupied with it. As I noted above, there are other ways of coping with stress. For instance, time may be taken to reassimilate rather than continuing to accommodate. The conscious setting aside of a recognition of acute stress, for instance impending surgery or death, in order to turn to and concentrate on other necessary matters of life may be a form of coping suppression. People can tolerate the ambiguity, attempt to empathize with the stress-provoking persons or situation, or give up active problem solving and turn instead to "brainstorming" (regression in the service of the ego) in a hunt for new assimilations. Weisman (1972) has described a phenomenon which he calls the "middle knowledge" of one's own death likely involves various patterns of these processes. However, middle knowledge may sometimes typify a state of partial assimilation that is being supported by some mixture of coping and defense processes.

Whenever defenses or fragmentary processes are used to negate situations, the person's possibilities are diminished in some way, for instance his opportunity to die well, with dignity and grace. If this contention can be accepted, it solves one of the conundrums of stress research. Some stress researchers argue with sympathetic fervor that stressed people "need" their defenses when they are faced with trying and devastating situations. Clearly man's consciousness makes him unavoidably aware of more kinds of hell than come into the ken of other living beings. Unlike other beings, he anticipates his own death. Clearly, in all humanity, people need their defenses, if their only other alternative is to fragment or disintegrate. However for stress researchers to move from the knowledge of the frequent need for defenses to designating the negation of information as the empirical response to stress distorts logic itself. A man is a social being who must for his own enhancement and salvation share and correct his knowledge of intersubjective reality even though he may on occasion decide that the common wisdom is wrong. If he "resolves" his situation of stress by negation, it may turn out that it has not been laid to rest. His solution, then, is inevitably faulty in some degree, and if the situation is unavoidable and inexorable, the threat will likely re-present itself. In these instances, his defensiveness—no matter how badly he needs it—can only deprive him of the information necessary to work through and manage his situation. The chronic neurotic accumulates indeterminate resolutions. As a result he experiences stress without intermission. Irresolved matters are always reappearing, and he has a hard time knowing when one stress experience is over or, for that matter, when another has started. The negation of knowledge about new opportunities and new threats during developmental change can likewise be seen to make for unceasing alternations between threat and temptation, and in the end result in developmental retardation.

REPERTOIRES OF EGO PROCESSES AND SITUATIONS

Before we turn to a more detailed consideration of empirical studies and the ego processing of stress, there are several general aspects of the ego model relevant to stress that need to be brought to mind again. As was noted in earlier chapters, it seems reasonable to assume that all the coping, defensive, and fragmentary actions are within the armamentarium of all people and potentially can be brought into play according to the person's interactional needs within different situations, here various stress situations. However, the different processes are clearly not equipotential, since people have histories and therefore preferences as to what has worked for them. Moreover, the deployment of one method, say, logical analysis, may make it unnecessary to use another, say, tolerance of ambiguity. The definitive socialization, represented by strong reaction formations, may make it unnecessary to use repressiveness.

Various situations pull and require different patterns of ego processes. Situations of stress would seem to require, at a minimum: (*1*) Some one or more means of regulating the concomitant affect; (*2*) some focusing of attention; (*3*) and some kind of cognitive processing. However, the strictly cognitive processes may yield diminishing returns in enduring, long-term stress situations after all possibilities and meanings have been examined and no solution but acceptance is feasible. People may turn then to intraceptive processing, which is not directly means—end but represents instead the ways people relate to themselves: (*1*) whether they defensively regress or cope by finding radically new solutions after shifting their internal field; (*2*) whether they tolerate their dilemma, or hang themselves up in endless doubting vacillation; (*3*) whether they project, deciding the enemy is outside, or empathetically reconsider the situation and its people. In other words, they attempt to deal with situations by dealing with themselves.

Some people handle stress less ably than others. The most obvious reason, which was suggested above, is that the nature of the particular situation has special ominous meanings to them, that is, it is similar in structure, content, or affective overtones to past unsuccessfully resolved situations. A second reason may be that the particular situation requires ego capabilities that the person does not easily use or has not developed either because he is a child, he is retarded in some way, or he prefers processes that are inappropriate to the situation. A third reason may be that the person's chronically stressed and habitually defensive condition is only exacerbated by the onset of new stress. Finally, the alleviation of stress often requires the help of others, and some people are without such support systems because they are without intimates or because their cultural subsystem does not value and promote mutual aid.

The potential for coping successfully with severe stress is probably not general, and the effectiveness of response will vary according to the kind of stress, the person's ego repertoire, and whether he can secure support from others. That unmarried people and social isolates have shorter life expectancies is well known. Stack (1974) has described a complex, intimate network of kin support in a black, poverty-level ghetto that enables the stressed person to secure help, cope emotionally, and in some fashion survive economically, despite gross inadequacies in aid from the welfare system. We observed a similar phenomenon with the black teenagers from economically disadvantaged families who participated in the moral dilemmas project described in Chapter 7. When the going was rough and the group disagreed with some number, the black lower class adolescents unlike the whites, soon offered the rejected teenager reacceptance and nurturance. In so doing, the black adolescents preserved the cohesiveness of their group and saved the temporarily ostracized member from being unduly stressed.

If there is a generally stress-resistant person, he clearly would have to be not only rather consistently coping, but also versatile in the deployment and organization of his ego actions. The persistent and exclusive use of only one or two ways of ego processing cannot favor the evolution of motive-plans and the dynamic conservation of intrasubjective—intersubjective balances vis à vis the "noise" of different kinds of situations.

SEVERAL OTHER PROCESS—STRESS FORMULATIONS

Finally, we need to note the relationship between aspects of the present formulation and several special formulations that have sometimes been considered in descriptions of stress processing, namely Brehm's (1966) reactance, Shaver's (1970) defensive attribution, and Festinger's (1964) dissonance reduction. All of these—reactance, dissonance reduction, and defense attribution—are thought to occur in at least trying, if not stressful, situations, and all three can be viewed as forms of defense, since they involve undifferentiated behaviors that are expected to occur *irrespective* of the objective realities of situations. Reactance occurs whenever a person thinks he is being deprived of any actual or potential freedom of preference, option, or whatever. He responds by valuing this lost freedom all the more and tries to resecure it, regardless of whether it is trivial or not, or whether it makes sense for him to do so or not. Reactance thus seems to represent defensive doubt and isolation. Defensive attribution is a means of avoiding blame and is manifested by attributing responsibility for a wrongdoing to someone else, irrespective of where the truth might lie; thus it appears to involve projection and displacement. Dissonance reduction occurs when a person wants to freeze his decision and therefore eliminates or discounts all other counter beliefs as being unworthy, a clear instance of isolation. The fact that these investigators found sufficient empirical evidence to justify the existence of their concepts attests to the actuarial prevalence of defensiveness. All of these maneuvers undoubtedly occur and all seem to be already represented by various classical defenses, reminding one that the more things change, the more they remain the same. The pity is that these new theories are only part descriptions, which treat the defenses, just as psychoanalysis did, as the whole of people's strategies for dealing with stress, a structural arrangement that results in the nondistorting, resolving coping actions being overlooked.

SUMMARY

The general ramifications of using this ego model to understand stress are as follows: First, a shift in foci is entailed from the amount of anxiety aroused to the various ways in which people handle the affect that invariably accompanies the experience of stress. In other words, the ego model gives priority to the processing mind. The sheer, absolute intensity of arousal has often been the target of measurement, but the ego model suggests that the same amounts of affect can occur for different reasons, and that it may have different sequelae depending on how the arousal is handled. (Actually, the operationalizations of anxiety are constructions of our imaginations, since anxiety has no material reality and we now know that the material, physiological indices of anxiety are not the royal road to certainty.) The slippery word anxiety has masked our ignorance; we are not clear about the denotations of anxiety other than its representation as some kind of vague, bad affective reaction.

A second consequence of applying the ego model is the specification and separation of the different processes that people employ in attempting to deal with stress. The usual classifications label all methods that negate the stimulus by refusing its assimilation as denial or sometimes as avoidance, and all methods that recognize and assimilate the stimulus, but then negate its implications by ineffective accommodation, as hypervigilance. We can see, for instance, that isolation and repression also negate the situation, while failures of accommodation are better represented by doubt, displacement, projection, intellectualization, and so on. Essentially, failed assimilation is the work of a closed system, while failed accommodation is the mark of an open system in distress.

Third, the possibility that people do not always cringe before stress has been objectified and made part of the investigatory armamentarium. This possibility accords with common sense and with various empirical observations—for instance, some surviving concentration camp inmates were found to be in reasonably good condition 25 years later, (Antonovsky, Maoz, Dowty, & Wijsenbeck, 1971)—and it also leads to advantageous changes in research designs—the coper is recognized and separated from the nonspecific defender.

Fourth, the addition of the coping criteria means that the "success" of stress management can be evaluated in terms of its psychological, social-personal meanings and not merely by pointing to the extent of physiological arousal. As far as I know, no one has yet demonstrated that readily mobilized physiological arousal vis à vis stress that is not a constant accompaniment of experience necessarily leads to detrimental physiological wear and tear. If this assumption is true, physiological arousal may not be a worthwhile target for personologists to spend much time exploring, although its eventual convergence with physiology means psychology needs to be mindful of physiological findings so as not to violate its behavioral predictions.

Fifth, the possible patternings and sequencings of ego functions suggest a relational rather than a dimensionalizing way of thinking about the handling and resolving of stress. Janis' excellent observations concerning the preoperative reactions of surgical patients have not had the impact they might have had because he was persuaded that personality must be dimensionalized and that the inverted U-shaped curve was a singular continuum of anxiety. His scale assumed (1) little fear (which may rather be seen as failure to assimilate the implications of the forthcoming experience), (2) moderate fear (which may reflect the realistic recognition of the implications of the forthcoming experience, or, more simply, just moderate fear), and (3) intense fear (realistic expectancy of no cure and death, or projection and displacement of anger at the world and the doctor for the diagnosis and the necessity of surgery). Probably, matters are not this simple.

The measurement of the amount of fear and anxiety has reached a dead end, but the inclusion of the processes in the research design suggests that there should be different sequences of processes, prestress and poststress, and that they should be of different value for the patients.

Empirical Studies

SYNCHRONIC STRESS

Most of what has been said up to this point has taken synchronic stress, an aversive event that occurs within a limited period of time, as the implicit frame of reference. Although diachronic stress does not require a different class of explanation, it still warrants consideration in its own right and will be the subject of the next section. However, people do have histories of previous stress experiences that they bring to contemporary events; thus, history is always a part of the synchronic event, but it is the point of the account of diachronic events.

The "Success" of Denial

As we turn to various recent studies of synchronic stress—some that we will consider have used the ego model—we are confronted with the disagreement in terminology and confusions that were described earlier. Table XI briefly summarizes an assortment of studies concerned with the processing of stress that will serve to develop the argument to be made here—another assortment might have done almost as well.

Goldstein and Adams (1967), Cohen and Lazarus (1973), Houston (1971), Steiner (1970), and Katz, Weiner, Gallagher, and Hellman (1970) conducted very different kinds of studies, but report, nevertheless, a common finding: Avoiding or denying stress is *better* than confronting it. Their samples include students, surgical patients, and women with breast tumors. The various student samples were stressed with a threatening film, by the requirement to repeat digits backwards rapidly, and by fellow students' disagreements, while the patients and women were stressed by their medical diagnosis and impending surgery. None of these studies directly or clearly made provision for identifying subjects who might have coped with stress, or, at any rate, coped in the way that the concept has been developed here. Houston (1971) concludes that "the use of denial in a stressful situation is advantageous [p. 292]," but he is mindful that denial has been consistently found to relate to lower SES status (e.g., Miller & Swanson, 1960; Weinstock, 1967b; the

Table XI
Various Process Studies of Stress

Study	Subjects	Ego variables (Measurement)	Stress stimulus/stress response	Results
Goldstein & Adams (1967)	University students, total $N = 32$ who met criteria on ego variables	Low and high anxious Subjects divided into nonspecific defenders or avoiders (difference between neutral and anxiety words on tachistoscopic exposure—avoiders=big difference; nonspecific defenders=little difference)	Movie—"wages of fear," pressing lever to keep movie going; physiological indices	Anxiety failed to predict, but avoiders less physiological reaction and less behavioral reactivity than nonspecific
Cohen & Lazarus (1973)	Surgical patients, $N = 61$	Avoidant, vigilant, or mixed reactions, preoperatively (interviews and tests)	Surgery: postoperative recovery	Recovery: fewer days in hospital and fewer complications
Houston (1971)	Students, $N = 48$	Trait denial (personality inventory) Situational denial (less self-report of arousal than physiological arousal)	Repeating digits backwards; instructions to do or do fast.	Both kinds of denial related to better performance.

Steiner (1974)	Students ($N = 60$ experimental $N = 14$ control)	Defensive conformity, rejection, devaluation, undercall of disagreement, or not salient (various operationalizations)	Accomplice's disagreement about common knowledge or preferences; skin conductance	Defenders lower physiological arousal
Katz *et al.* (1970)	Women with breast tumors, $N = 30$	Affective distress, disruption of functioning, impairment of defensive reserve (interview ratings)	Diagnosis of tumor; hydrocortisone production	Affect, functioning and defense reserve all related to hydrocortisone production; deniers least upset, but delayed seeking help.
Naditch *et al.* (1975)	Army trainees, $N = 547$	Denial, anxiety, locus of control, (personality inventories)	Existing self-reported; depression	Anxiety positively related; denial negatively related.
Naditch (1975)	Young adult psychoactive drug users (65% students), $N = 483$	Inventory responses, number of ego scales (personality inventories)	Drug-taking self-reported aversive drug reactions	Denial & intellectualization negatively related; regression & repression positively related; coping negatively related (LSD only)

correlations between denial and SES for Oakland Growth Study members described in Chapter 7 are −.43 for men and −.30 for women, $ps \leqslant .01$ and .05; the correlations between denial and IQ are −.30 for men and −.36 for women, both $ps \leqslant .01$). Houston suggests a resolution for the conflicting evidence: The consistent use of denial may very well be maladaptive, but it may, nevertheless, be beneficial in stress conditions. Still, the use of denial during an emergency should, logically, have the same end result as its persistent use—a part of intersubjective reality is not admitted and therefore cannot be assimilated. On the basis of the logical grounds previously developed, we can wonder how such a maneuver can be truly beneficial. Undoubtedly impressed with the persistent finding that denial is negatively related to arousal, Lazarus (1973) recently suggested in a paper delivered to an Israeli audience that self-deception may be useful at the outset of stress, since it may give the person time "to get himself going." However, if a person were fully denying, it is not clear how he would know that he should mobilize himself. In the meantime, the damage may already have been done!

Scrutinizing the Katz *et al.* (1971) study of women with tumors more carefully, we note a problem with the supposition that denial is beneficial: Although their denying subjects did produce less hydrocortisone than the others who were more overtly upset, these investigators comment, almost casually and without actual supporting data, that the deniers had waited the longest after noticing the tumor to seek help. Moreover, Cobb, Clark, Carson, and Howe (1954) much earlier reported the same observation for women with breast tumors. Here, where the focus is on the ways in which people construct the meanings of stress, it is evident that denial is a far from successful reaction to stress and can be, in fact, downright self-destructive. Janis (1965) reviews a number of studies by other investigators, which will not be described in detail here, that support the casual observation of Katz and his associates: increased fear preoperatively being associated with good adjustment postoperatively; a history of suppression or repression of feelings being associated with dysfunctional labor during childbirth, denial of fear of air raids characterizing people who later became psychiatric casualties; denial that husbands or sons would be drafted during World War II characterizing wives who became emotionally upset when their husbands or sons were drafted; and Air Force personnel who were very enthusiastic about combat flying and who felt a sense of personal invulnerability during World War II later becoming psychiatric casualties. Although these studies are mostly retrospective in focus, there is a logic to their implications.

Let us turn finally to the two large-scale survey studies summarized in Table XI that were conducted by Naditch, Gargan, and Michael (1975) and by Naditch alone (1975b). Both used ego scales based on personality inventories (Haan, 1965). We see that the first generally replicates the main finding we have been considering: Denying people are not depressed people. However, the second study of aversive reactions, "bad trips" after taking LSD or marijuana, which used both coping and defensive ego scales, has more complex and interesting findings. First Naditch finds that there are more processes than denial that come into play in dealing with the physiological and social situation of drug taking. Both intellectualization and denial were related to fewer aversive reactions than was coping in general. Secondly, succumbing to the effects of psychoactive drugs was associated with two very different processes: regression and repression. Of additional interest is Naditch's finding that regression in the service of the ego—the free and coping exploration of the psyche—was strongly and positively related to marijuana and LSD usage, but not to aversive reactions for either drug. (One would not expect ego regression to be negatively related to aversive reactions because it does not necessarily provide assurance in itself that self-exposing experiences will be accommodated.)

We can conclude from this study, which employed multiple regression techniques to assess the independent contributions of the various processes, that coping, negating by denial, and negating by intellectualizing are three unique ways of "successfully" handling the stress of drugs, while repressive and regressive people are not able to do so. The attributes of the process of regression are consistent with "giving in" to the impact of the drug, while the more rigid attributes of repression suggest a different route—the collapsing of a blanket, brittle defense before the onslaught of the physiological imbalance and social fear (perhaps fulfilling, however, a secret wish of submission).

In another large-scale survey study of drinking behavior ($N = 547$), Naditch (1975d) again found, with multiple regression analyses, that regression was positively related to the extent of drinking. However, unlike aversive drug reactions, repression was negatively associated to drinking, as were two other very different processes—displacement and total coping. When these findings are considered in juxtaposition with those for aversive drug reactions, the aggregate suggests some specificity of processing—to lost one's self in the alcoholic or drug experience is associated with, and perhaps facilitated by, regressive processes. However, the role of repression in the two contexts varies, being positively associated with the ego collapse of a bad trip, but appearing to forestall, probably at the outset, the excessive use of alcohol.

Other Studies of Stress Using the Ego Model

Several other studies of stress, which used processes derived from the coping and defense model, are also informative. Margolis (1970) induced 40 student subjects to role play four different situations wherein the "dean" justifiably or unjustifiably praised or punished them for their conduct. Judges rated the transcript of the students' role playing sessions for total coping or defense and for several individual processes. The investigators report that the reliability of overall ratings was good, while those for the specific processes was moderate or adequate. The individual processes were highly specific to the various role playing situations, a finding which emphasizes the situational specificity with which persons deploy various ego strategies that are in their repertoire. Of further interest to stress research was the finding that significantly more defensive responses were observed in the two situations where the subjects were in a "guilty" position, being falsely praised or justly punished by the dean. This study rests, of course, on the supposition that people's role playing is an extension of their usual predispositions.

Powers and Alker (1968) report a study wherein the demand characteristics of their experiment were manipulated so that observations could be made to see whether students' subsequent mild stress reactions were consistent with their scores on the ego scales of repression and suppression. To mobilize stress reactions, Powers and Alker's subjects were attached to a polygraph, told that they could quit the experiment at any time, and were warned to sit still. There were successively shown 13 sets of the same test words which gradually became more legible and included a number of "taboo" items. Their GSR levels turned out to be entirely independent of the ego processes and the efficiency of their word identification. However, as expected, the *relative* strength of repression over suppression was significantly related to the *relative* failure to identify taboo as compared to neutral words.

In the study by Alker (1971) alone, test-taking suspiciousness was subtly manipulated by varying the order of presentation for a variety of test and laboratory tasks to students in a class in government so as to make the procedures appear logically or illogically part of a study of political attitudes. Defensive projection, measured by the ego scale, was found to be a function of the interaction between the logical and manipulated order of test administration and the students' attitudes toward colonialism (a right to left wing measure). During manipulated administrations, projective and anticolonial students became more vigilant, "overinterpreted" the situation and thus increased their efforts to show that they were *not* suspicious, but they increased their suspiciousness when the administration was in fixed order. Students' willingness or unwillingness to sign a form consenting to the release of information was also consistent with this main interactional trend. Both of these studies point to the finesse and complexity of people's strategies vis à vis the stress of being a subject when the design appears to hide or obfuscate the purposes of the study.

The Folkins (1970) study, described in Chapter 6, needs to be considered again in this context since it exemplifies several kinds of relations between stress and ego processing: coping and fragmentation functions were found to be reactive to lengths of time that different subjects had to wait before discovering that an announced shock was not going to occur. Greater coping (as well as less physiological arousal) characterized subjects whose wait was very short (5 sec) or long (3,5, or 20 min), while defensiveness was independent of the length of waiting. However, defensiveness did have significant and negative relationships with three measures of self-reported, admitted tension, as the ego model would predict. Thus we see again in another context that physiological, self-reported, and social-psychological constructions of stress reactions are not isomorphic. We cannot know what Folkins' subjects were thinking during their wait (they were interviewed afterwards), but it would appear that coping occurred either as an emergency reaction or as an examined accommodation.

The results of a study by Thelen and Varble (1970) concern the differences in coping and defensive patterns, as measured by the ego scales, between two groups of students: those seeking psychotherapy, presumably because they were stressed ($N = 65$), and those enrolled in introductory psychology class who had not had therapeutic contact for the past two years ($N = 112$). Although the data for the sexes were separately analyzed, the preferred ego processes distinguishing the two main groups were the same in almost all instances so we will only consider the replications. The therapy group was significantly higher than the nontherapy group for logical analysis, suggesting that their seeking help was a coping strategy, and more specifically, consistent with their tendency to process problems in means—end terms: They were troubled, therefore psychotherapy was a logical and coping route to take to alleviate their concerns. However they were also more defensive in two ways: higher for displacement and projection—both of these involve externalization and both suggest difficulty in accommodation but not in assimilation (they recognized their situation and were discomforted by it). In contrast, both nontherapy groups regulated their affect by coping suppression and were more coping generally. Very interestingly, the nontherapy groups were also higher for the two ways of focusing attention—defensive denial and coping concentration, an observation that suggests that they were not likely to succumb to the attractive, disequilibrating, nonacademic aspects of college life.

Summary

1. We may conclude from this array of studies that denial and other forms of negation or avoidance, whatever their short-term benefits, are not successful in a social-psychological or a long-term sense. This becomes immediately clear when temporally longer, real-life units of synchronic stress are investigated, as in the real life studies of breast tumors, or when the subject reports his habitual reactions, as in the Naditch studies. Handling stress by denial is a cheap and easy way for the subject to last out a situation of experimental stress, and it protects him from the experimenter's intention to stress, but there is no evidence from the naturalistic studies that denial gives the stressed person time to mobilize himself and then successfully deal with his problem, as Lazarus (1973) suggested.

2. The ego model applied to stress reactions does not yield the usual amorphous and dichotomous results found by personality research that good character traits relate to good responses and bad traits to bad responses (e.g., young drug users were typified by regression in the service of the ego). Moreover, some specificity of processes characteristic of particular syndromes was found by Naditch and his associates (drug users reported aversive reactions and problem drinkers tended to regress, but users were repressive while the drinkers were not).

3. Specificity in processing various situations was also observed (Margolis, Alker, Folkins). These kinds of findings have led Mischel (1968) to conclude that there is no generality of personality, but the interpretation here is different. People are

open systems and necessarily construct with the processes in their repertoire reactions that sensibly recognize and fit different situations.

4. Being a subject in an experiment is a matter of ego processing in itself, and the Powers and Alker study and Alker's alone suggest that the particular ego propensities that subjects bring to experiments will affect their actions in the most devious and substantial ways, even as the data are being collected.

5. We see from the Folkins work that physiological measures, self-reports, and observations by professionals are by no means equivalent, but the process formulation suggests a coherent pattern for their ordering and relationships.

6. Finally, Thelen and Varble's study supports a basic supposition of this chapter: To admit stress is a first step toward coping with it.

DIACHRONIC STRESS

To understand diachronic stress, two separate developmental matters need to be considered: (1) a mark of the young is their comparative inability to conceptualize their experience and thereby develop motive-plans to reestablish intrasubjective–intersubjective balance when it is out of kilter, (2) the various transitional periods in the life span are likely to be stressful for many persons.

Children's Natural Vulnerability to Stress

The newly born infant can hardly be said to experience emotions; he probably has only gross feeling reactions that are not different from good or bad physiological experiences. The infant's physical and mental inability to differentiate what and who he is, as separate from what is done to him, makes him liable to being wholly stressed and thus fragmented by any noxious stimuli, such as illness, hunger, or sudden intense stimuli. Thus he is readily "flooded with affect" since he is without adequate means of developing an accommodatory plan or of even understanding that such exists. Only his caretakers can make the accommodations that he needs.

As he matures and begins to differentiate himself as a separate actor among other actors—by distinguishing between himself and what happens to him—he acquires a repertoire of past situations and evaluations that have been stressful *to* him. Still his means of integrating this knowledge and mobilizing himself to develop motive-plans in order to reestablish balance and manage the stressful situation are limited. According to this line of reasoning, we would expect, as I think we can see, that the most frequent class of early childhood responses to stress is defensive and/or fragmentary (for instance, they cry). This is the reason that parents usually give special attention to the stressed reactions of the very young, but more often expect older children to manage by themselves.

Young children's defenses are marvelously fluid, readily applied, grossly distorting of reality, and do not usually result in the sequelae of continued social difficulty that typifies adults' uses of defenses because children's choices are not regarded by others as being definitive, irreparable, or irreversible. Children's definition of what is bad and stressful for them will have some commonality with all other human beings' evaluations, but will also include experiences that they alone define as stressful. Their formulations of stress adduce schemata that are a disproportionately affective and figurative rather than cognitive. The more affective and the less cognitive the schemata, the more ready are children to assimilate present to past stress by overgeneralizing, and thus they more often defend rather than cope when they are stressed. However, as was elaborated in Chapter 8, "The Development of Ego Processes," the interaction between the interpersonally moral characteristics of social living and children's evolving structural capability results in their ever increasing adherences to veracity, and so stress experiences, too, are processed with increasing accuracy and skill as children become less prone to conserving intrasubjective logic at the expense of intersubjective reality.

The Stress of Stage Transition

With these matters of the young child's natural vulnerability stated, we can turn to various transitions between developmental stages. All movement between structural stages is, by definition, characterized by a degree of stress, because these are times when intrasubjective and intersubjective equations are imbalanced. The child opts for new intrasubjective and intersubjective self-definitions, but he is not always clear or consistent in his bid for others to share and validate his new self-definition. This imbalance, in and of itself, accords with the personal-structural formulation proposed as the basic circumstances of all distress. In Piagetian terms, the stage-transitional child is disequilibrated. He is confused because he is not yet able to integrate new with old assimilations or accommodate to new assimilations, although he tries to do so. We understand the child's experiences at these junctures in moral and cognitive terms rather well, because of the vast array of Piagetian research. Turiel (1974) has empirically described the transitional period from conventional to principled formal moral reasoning, finding that at one moment the adolescent speaks with moral fervor (as a reflection of his intrasubjective state), but at the next, rejects the idea that normative evaluations can or should be made (a rejection of intersubjective reality).

We have no fully developed description of the transitional periods of social development and still have almost everything to learn. Erikson's (1959) account of the adolescent's problem of ego identity, which he treats more in structural terms than he does any of the other stages, is probably the most detailed account of transition available. His formulation emphasizes the dialectic of preserving continuity while integrating change so as to achieve a new systematic organization that must be publicly recognized and interpersonally admitted to be validated by one's own and others' judgments. This description—when Erikson's other insistence that the transition between childhood and adulthood is typified by the contents of achieving intimacy is left aside—is essentially social-structural, and the idea of the intrasubjective—intersubjective balance is implicit but pivotal in the formulation.

The adolescent feels himself to be capable of independence, but not to such a degree that he can honestly impose this achievement on others' definition of him. When he can, he is no longer adolescent, since he has forced the intersubjective reality of the community to balance and accord with his own.

Empirical Studies of Diachronic Stress Using the Ego Model

The empirical work directly concerned with diachronic stress is sparse, although related discussion of it is abundant. Even though we have generally assumed that a degree of stress attends growing up, there has been reluctance to investigate it as a normative phenomenon. Interest has centered instead on the more malignant and less subtle phenomenon of rebellion.

We first consider those problems of stress that are specifically germane to the life span—the normative life "crises," which include transitions between structural stages in children to the probably nonstructural self-redefinitions that occur in older people, say from parenting to childlessness or from working to retirement. Later the long-term sequelae of stress that was experienced earlier will be considered. The ego model has not been applied at all points in the life span nor is there a study now available that directly and precisely concerns the defensiveness and occasional fragmentation that are hypothesized to accompany moves from one structural stage to the next. All that can be presented now is the post hoc supposition that various observations suggest that during stage interregnums peoples' intrasubjective sense of self is neither coordinated nor integrated with intersubjective reality—the essential conditions of synchronic and diachronic stress advanced here. The same imbalance seems to occur in nonstructural periods of self-redefinition. I assume for convenience, since no study or argument yet causes one to assume the contrary, that cognitive and moral structural development is generally concluded by early adulthood. If we knew more about social structural developments, such as the universal ramifications of parenting, we might conclude otherwise. In any event, we must now content ourselves with considering diachronic stress more obliquely than would be desirable, and we will have to focus almost exclusively on the diachronic stress of the adolescent period since this transitional state has been the most extensively, if not intensively, examined in this regard.

There has been a general expectancy that adolescence is a special transitional period, and surely it is in terms of its contents of working toward a career identification, marriage, and independence. From the structural process view, however, it should not necessarily involve any fundamentally different taxonomy of processes nor require any basically different forms of description. A nonstructural view of adolescence is exemplified by Offer's (1969) work. He looked for traditional adolescent anger and rebellion, and when he found that it was not usual, he was inclined to conclude that the classical or Eriksonian description of adolescence was wrong rather than imprecisely drawn—the position taken here.

A further supposition underlies the role of ego processing during transitions: If the person must defend, not merely against sporadic and passing intrasubjective—

intersubjective imbalances, but against the opportunities presented by the transitional period itself, he may not negotiate the transition. Erikson's formulation of premature closure is an example of one such closed system. Such phenomena probably account in part for various horizontal structural decalages observed by the Piagetians and increasingly being suggested as occurring in moral development as well (see Chapter 7 in this volume, Haan, 1975, Rest, 1975). A continued defense vis à vis continued diachronic stress should retard redefinition and therefore development. From clinical experience we know, however, that an overlay of social learning can be achieved while structural retardation is subtle (see Kubie's, 1958, construction of the person who is a public success but a private failure).

With these preliminary statements aside, we can turn to two studies concerned with the childhood and adolescent states of adults whose ego processes were assessed in terms of coping and defensiveness. These subjects, studied by Haan (1974a) and Weinstock (1967a), are members of two different longitudinal samples at Berkeley's Institute of Human Development. The Haan work concerned 97 Oakland Growth Study members who were studied intensively during adolescence and again when they were 37 years of age. At adulthood the subjects, with sexes separated, were divided into "ego groups" of predominantly (1) coping, (2) defensive, and (3) high ego (strongly coping and defending), and (4) low ego (neither saliently coping nor defending). The ego assessments were based on extensive life assessment interviews, which took, on the average, approximately 12 hours. These four groups were compared by one-way analyses of variances on a number of adolescent measures, but primarily on Q sorted measures of their personalities during junior and senior high school.

The general expectancies concerning the processing of diachronic stress developed above were generally supported for both men and women, but more strongly for women: (1) the eventually coping adults seemed to have taken the adolescent experience as an opportunity to change, so that the cognitive aspects of their personality became more salient in the hierarchy of their Q sorted descriptions and (2) they appeared to have experienced a degree of conflict and disequilibrium. The defenders and low ego groups (the latter group characteristically used blanket denial and repressive processes) had done the least changing, generally and cognitively, between adolescence and adulthood, while the high ego group seemed to have increased their self-control and social control rather than to have taken the opportunity to reorganize themselves. Data from interviews with the mothers when the subjects were 16 years old served to confirm the findings based on observations of the adolescents themselves. Interactions with the mothers appeared disequilibrated for the coping groups, bland and unperturbed for the defenders and the low ego group, and socially conventional for the high ego group.

The Weinstock study also concerned the relationship of adult ego functioning to the early family environments of a different longitudinal sample, 39 males of the Guidance Study. The first set of 62 family ratings was made when the subjects were between 21 and 36 months and the second set of 42 ratings when they were between 11 and 13 years of age. A welter of correlations between these early family ratings and the coping and defensive processes at age 30 are reported, but when only those ego processes that had 10% or more significant associations are considered, several patterns emerge that are relevant to the present discussion.

First, more of the adults' defensive than coping processes are related to family environment at both time periods, suggesting that coping tends to be self-constructed (or affected by family styles at different age periods than the ones studied). The three coping functions that did have a substantial number of correlates—tolerance of ambiguity, ego regression, and suppression—are related to the family environment only during the subjects' adolescence. In contrast, six of the defensive processes were significantly related to 10% or more of the family variables. Regression and doubt had a substantial number of relationships with both the early and later family variables, denial with the earlier period only, and isolation with the later period.

Turning now to consider the relevance of Weinstock's investigation to diachronic stress, we can note the first general implication: Adult defensiveness apparently has a lengthy history within the family of origin while coping appears to be self-constructed and relates to the nature of the family only during the subjects' adolescence. This observation is consistent with the supposition that coping is synchronically and diachronically normative, while defensiveness is situationally tied. Moreover, the content of the findings indicate that a family stressed in some degree at the subject's adolescence was the prior condition of adult tolerance of ambiguity and ego regression. The differences between the family correlates for these coping processes and for defensive regression and doubt are important. The defenses' correlates indicated: (1) The early as well as the later family environment was stressed and (2) the mothers had personally negative characteristics (unstable, poor relationship with child, etc.) which were heavily implicated at both time periods. In contrast, the correlates of coping indicated that during the offspring's adolescence the parents themselves disagreed over the child, his discipline, and the family's religion. Weinstock suggested that the child's level of development at the time of family conflict may importantly determine whether he is able to cope or defend and whether or not he adopts either of these strategies as a durable part of his ego repertoire. Presumably the younger child has less ego capability of achieving an intrasubjective—intersubjective balance than the older one and is, therefore, more vulnerable to family conflict. We cannot know with certainty from these analyses, whether or not the adolescent disequilibrium of these eventually coping males was the occasion for the parental disagreement but it seems likely.

Adult denial has substantial correlations with various aspects of the early family environment that describe a particularly bland, even-tempered, self-satisfied type of parent. This parental pattern is consistent with our understandings of denial although it is less undifferentiated. We could suppose, as Weinstock did, that the subjects modeled their parents' denial and accepted the parents' statements at face value.

To complete the account of Weinstock's findings we should add that coping suppression was related to the fathers' granting of freedom and the mothers' protectiveness, demonstrativeness, stability, and sentimentality during the subjects' adolescence. Isolation related only to the family variables at adolescence, and the contents of these items suggested that the fathers were controlling, restrictive, and cold, while the mothers were demonstrative but in open conflict with their boys.

A third study (Haan, Stroud, & Holstein, 1973; Holstein, Stroud, & Haan, 1974) has focused on period-, if not stage-transitional young people who were mostly in their early twenties. They were a dramatically deviant sample—the hippies from San Francisco's Haight–Ashbury district who were interviewed during 1968–69, the time of the "flower children." Many of these young people were de facto runaways from their kin, and many sought to establish new and better "families" in the ideological and drug-taking communes that were being formed. In other words, they were not willing or ready to commit themselves, either critically or accept-ingly, to the world as it is—a definition of social transition. There was ample evidence that many of these hippies were psychologically transitional as well. By their responses to the Loevinger *et al.* (1970) Sentence Completion test, 52% of the sample of 58 were identified as being transitional between conformity and con-scientiousness, and by their reasoning in Kohlberg's moral dilemmas, 50% were relativistic, stage-transitional in the moral structures they used. Other data collected were assessments of ego processes secured from psychiatric interviews. A compari-son of the forms of ego functioning preferred by the morally transitional and nontransitional subjects, all of whom were emotionally transitional by Loevinger's calibration, produced a divergent array of ego strategies: The structurally transi-tional subjects were saliently doubting, intellectualizing, but coping in ego regres-sion, while the nontransitional were more tolerant of ambiguity, were repressive, and received high ratings for their use of reaction formations. The contrasting ego patterns suggest that the transitional subjects were involved in a quest for personal-social meanings while the nontransitional seemed in pursuit of a dogma.

Taken altogether, several aspects of diachronic stress are elaborated by these three studies, which suggest (1) coping at adulthood had a prodrome of adolescent conflict (obviously within some limited range); (2) family conflict at adolescence is particularly related to the development of intraceptive coping (ego regression and tolerance of ambiguity) at adulthood; (3) transition in moral structures during the preadult period is accomplished by ego processes that permit diachronic stress to be experienced and resolved for that period rather than being simply negated.

That development best occurs in open rather than in closed or partially closed systems is an old and familiar idea, although it has more often than not been sentimentalized in the manner of the Rousseauist dictum that the child should be allowed to come into his own like a blossoming flower. But in actuality all open systems are exposed, in the language of general systems theory, to "noise," which can be stressful, and whether coherence is eventually achieved is never certain. The view of development as accumulation necessarily views noise and diachronic stress as unwelcomed interference since clarity and consistency should be maintained to optimize the child's progress.

Kuypers (1974) studied the early adult antecedents of ego processing in 95 elderly people of approximately 70 years of age. Relevant to the present context was his finding that even though the men's earlier and later SES status had a sizable number of significant relations with their coping and fragmenting processes, it was independent of their defensiveness. Instead, their defenses were solely related to various early adult personality attributes. The SES status and attainments of this generation of males were undoubtedly important factors in their being able to view their life with equanimity, live in economic security in their later years, and thus to cope, but, as Kuypers comments, their defensiveness had apparently become habituated by age 30 and continued on to age 70. Kuypers did not specify the kinds of early adult personality attributes involved. The women's pattern is less articulated and comparison with the men is confounded by the fact that a small group of intellective variables were additionally included in the women's analyses. However coping and disorganization are again frequently related to SES status along with the intellective variables. However the character of these women's marriages at early adulthood distinguished a sizeable number of relationships with defensive ego functioning at old age. Thus we can apparently conclude that for the generation of women represented in this sample, marriage was a common source of stress or benefit.

A related finding was reported by Haan (1964a) for the Oakland Growth Study sample of 97 but for a different segment of the life span—from early adolescence to approximately age 37. Men who had been downwardly socially mobile—presumably both an effect and cause of stress—were significantly more regressive, denying, and isolating, and less suppressive, tolerant of ambiguity, empathic, and substituting at age 37, compared to the immobile and upwardly mobile. No defensive pattern was associated with the women's mobility (in almost all cases based on their husband's status). However their downward pattern was negatively associated with the three cognitive coping functions as well as with sublimation and ego regression. Their defensiveness was independent of their social mobility. Various detailed analyses showed that IQ in itself had little relationship to men's mobility but was important for the women's. Neither vocational attainment nor the making of a successful marriage identify (as far as we know) structural stage transitions and achievements, but they do constitute, nevertheless, social tasks of moment in this society. The above results serve to suggest that ego processes bear reasonable relations to them.

A STUDY OF THE ASSOCIATIONS BETWEEN EARLIER ILLNESSES AND HOSPITALIZATIONS AND ADULT EGO FUNCTIONING

A distinction needs to be made between diachronic stress and the long-term effects of early traumatizations. Chapter 8, The Development of Ego Processes, described a study concerned with the associations between changes in family composition and adult ego functioning. This work followed the general line of reasoning represented by the Holmes and Rahe (1967) contention that changes, in themselves, are stressful because they call for readjustment. The results of that

EMPIRICAL STUDIES   **189**

study did not suggest that the outcomes of change are necessarily deleterious even though the experience of change may well be stressful at the time. In fact, earlier changes in the family membership were generally related to later coping intraceptivity, a finding that suggests the necessity of reorganization may have an enriching and a deepening affect on people.

We now turn to a similar problem: the associations between the OGS subjects' ego processing at ages 37 and 47 with the numbers of illnesses and hospitalizations they experienced from birth to their mid-thirties. Again the life change research instigated by Holmes and Rahe's work, as well as common sense, has supposed that the psychological outcomes of physical difficulties are universally "bad." When we regard the person, however, as drawing and constructing complex coping bargains with life, it would seem likely that he will not let himself handle a physical debilitation negatively and in fear for long and will instead make something sensible out of what has happened to him.

The data for these analyses were taken from the medical history forms the subjects completed for the examining physician when they came to the hospital for a medical and physiological workup that necessitated that they stay overnight. The counts for illnesses were based on the number of times they checked a list of 47 items that included symptoms, like abdominal pain and shortness of breath, and diseases, like chicken pox and polio. The numbers of hospitalizations were also counted from the same form and did not include childbirths or abortions unless they were complicated by Caesarian sections, septicemia, and so on. The counts were mutually exclusive, for example, if a subject checked appendicitis, this was not counted as an illness if he had also indicated that he had had an appendectomy. Counts were also made for chronic illnesses, that is, ones extending for more than 2 years and often still present at the time of this follow-up. Subjects with the data needed for these analyses were 28 females and 38 males for the 37-year follow-up, and 36 females and 41 males for the 47-year follow-up. Thus in both instances, the assessments of the ego processes postdate the medical information.

These health data are based, clearly, on the subjects' reports, and as was noted earlier in this chapter, reporting about one's health status immediately brings ego processing itself into play. The context of these reports is, as always, important. These people were not knowingly sick at that time. In part, these longitudinally studied subjects were making their by now traditional, altruistic contribution to science. A more personal advantage for them was the letter and medical reports that the university would send to their private physicians. Thus there was no immediate reason for them to underreport or overreport. In other words, they had no obvious need to solicit the physician's sympathy. However the medical forms listed a number of complaints that physically self-concerned and hypochondrical people might check. Clearly there are others who will decide they do not have a complaint even though a physician might think otherwise. Nevertheless, as medical reports go, these are probably as accurate as any made retrospectively.

To discern the patterns of ego processes associated with these health indices, multiple regression models were constructed with SES being forced into the equations on the first step to control, subsequently for this factor. The ego processes were only permitted to enter the model if their individual F ratios $\geqslant 3.00$. No model or individual process will be discussed that failed to achieve at least the .05 level of probability. Note that the question being asked in all instances is what pattern of ego processes at ages 37 and 47 are associated with illnesses and hospitalizations at earlier dates. In other words, do these experiences leave their mark in preferred patterns of ego processes?

Table XII shows the results of regressing the ego processes for the two different time periods on the total number of hospitalizations, illnesses, and the index of chronic illnesses. For the sake of our comprehending the main trends of these findings, the table does not include all the details of the models. SES is not listed even though it entered each equation first if it did not, in itself, contribute a significant variance. The total variance each model accounts for is given below the model, and indication is made as to how much variance each component contributed, its significance level, and whether it is positive or negative.

From the array of results shown in Table XII we can discern several trends. Women's physical difficulties seem not to necessitate the development of strong or clear patterns of ego processing. Women who have been frequently ill tend to rationalize at age 47, perhaps habitually to justify their incapacities to others. Chronic illness is strongly related to their tendencies to regress at age 47. Men's health difficulties are more closely related to their ego processing, a finding which suggests that illness is of greater social-psychological concern for males. Their hospitalizations are associated with high displacing, little doubt, and little self-justification. In other words, they externalize the blame for their hospital experiences. Illnesses, however, led at age 37 to greater doubtfulness, inability to concentrate, but still, and unlike the women, to nonregressive behavior. At age 47, we first find the relationship between lower SES and physical difficulties in men, which also occurs in both analyses of their chronic illnesses. Beyond the significant contribution from SES, illnesses are also associated with coping suppression at age 47. As public health statistics repetitively show, lower-status men, more than women, have been exposed to physical hazards in their occupations. Moreover, this generation of men has also borne the brunt of economic insecurity since they were solely responsible for supporting their families.

Turning now to the index of chronic illness, we find that mixed patterns of coping and defense are recruited for the males at both time periods. We can assume that a chronic condition is one that a person must especially come to terms with. At age 37 the chronically ill are empathic, express their feelings by *both* coping sublimation and defensive displacing; they are poor at concentration and do not resort to regressiveness. Thus the previously noted sex difference occurs again: Women who have been chronically ill are regressive, while chronically ill men are definitely not and instead angrily externalize their difficulties. The coping pattern of empathy and sublimation suggests that these men have come to some kind of terms with their difficulties; however these coping processes, taken with displacement, indicate that they are unusually emotionally labile. By age 47 they appear to

Table XII
Adult Ego Processes Associated with Physical Illnesses and Hospitalization from Birth to Age 35

	Total hospitalizations	Total illness	Chronic illnesses
		Females	
Age 37	Model ns	Model ns	Model ns
Age 47	Model ns	15% rationalization +[c]	28% regression +[a]
		15%[c]	28%[a]
		Males	
Age 37	Model ns	17% concentration −[a]	16% SES −[a]
		8% regression −[b]	25% empathy +[b]
		16% doubt +[a]	9% concentration −[a]
		52%[a]	12% regression −[a]
			7% displacement +[b]
			4% sublimation +[b]
			72%[a]
Age 47	11% doubt −[c]	8% SES −[b]	17% SES −[a]
	11% displacement +[c]	18% suppression +[b]	16% repression −[b]
	14% rationalization −[b]	26%[a]	8% isolation +[b]
	43%[a]		6% tolerance ambiguity +[c]
			47%[a]

NOTE: Percentages indicate amounts of variance accounted for by the component or the model.
[a] $p \leq .001$.
[b] $p \leq .01$.
[c] $p \leq .05$.

have become more equitable and cognitively defensive: they are more isolating, tolerant of ambiguity, and less repressive.

These analyses of illnesses, taken with those of family change reported in Chapter 8, give us two clear understandings that contradict the main thrust of psychological stress research: (1) these people who were exposed to these real-life stresses of illness and changes in the family living group were not conspicious for their denial or avoidance, in fact such strategies would seem to have been patently unworkable for them; (2) they used mixed patterns of coping and defense and appeared most vulnerable in their attempts to regulate their affect; at the same time they were manifestly coping, intraceptively.

These results indicating that mixed coping and defensiveness typifies those who have been stressed by life events are particularly interesting in view of Hosack's (1968) findings with this ego model. In one of the few longitudinal studies of the stress process, Hosack studied two groups of matched mothers (nine each) who were primiparas. Half had borne malformed infants. Hosack interviewed the mothers three times: a few days after birth in the hospital, 48–72 hours after they went home, and 6 weeks later. The entire sample was highly consistent in their defensive behavior during the two early periods, but their kinds and levels of coping (a description of the experimentation necessarily involved in dealing with a new and a first baby, malformed or not) were highly variable. However, at the later period most mothers of normal infants had polarized into either a predominantly coping or defensive pattern, but the mothers who of abnormal infants had not, by 6 weeks, yet settled into a clear pattern of coping or defense. We can presume that their difficulties would be more acute and that they would need more time.

CHRONIC PSYCHOLOGICAL STRESS

Various references were made throughout this chapter to chronic psychological stress, as opposed to acute stress, and a word needs to be said about it before ending this chapter. Both conditions can be studied within a synchronic or dia-chronic situations. Presumably people are chronically stressed for the following kinds of reasons. The social conditions they experience are relentlessly and irresolvably aversive, so they have a persisting imbalance in matching who they think they are, or should be, with what others or their institutions tell them about themselves. Clearly the well-documented effects of noxious social conditions such as poverty and racial and sexual discrimination represent the kinds of social context that encourage chronic personal stress. Rising hypertension among blacks and women as they gain the confidence to think and act in ways that contradict their social definition is a case in point; but socially promoted chronic stress is not limited to the effects of an unfavorable demographic status. More characteristic of women's situations is the persistent failure of their social environments to confirm their own view of their capabilities.

However, some people prolong their own stress by defending themselves against the implications of their own experience and thereby accumulate a backlog of unresolved problems and vulnerabilities. Thus a new event of even mild stress only further burdens them and makes it necessary for them to re-compartmentalize to continue to protect their intrasubjective valuation. Low self-esteem is often not precisely enough defined: Rather than being the simplistic and direct valuation that the self is worthless, it is probably the social valuation that one assumes is made of one's self. In fact, it seems that everyone must feel that he is worthwhile, and seeming low self-esteem must instead represent a complicated concatenation of defenses that are intended, covertly, to accuse, manipulate, or communicate need to other people. In other words, low esteem is a moral accusation of others. Witness also the theories of depression which suggest that it can be basically explained as anger toward others that is too dangerous to express so that it must be turned on the self.

Prolonged stress makes for the necessity of prolonged defensiveness; it leaves the person ever-vulnerable to the reappearance of threat: it tends, moreover, to be generalized to other like, or not even very similar, situations. Thus chronic stress leaves no time for assimilation and thus for recovery. Even if a person knows, or should know, that the stress situation is in abeyance or no longer exists, he may continue to perseverate. Unrelenting stress, whether it is overtly or covertly experienced, presumably lays the basis for physiological wear and tear, which in its turn contributes yet another situational reason for psychological stress.

Conclusion

This lengthy and multifaceted chapter has barely scratched the surface of stress research; however there was no intention of reviewing and integrating the mass of empirical findings emanating from a variety of fields. Instead the purpose was to outline a point of view about the person's processing of stress and his own distress which, it was hoped, would suggest ways that investigations might be designed and results interpreted. This point of view was basically no different from the one presented in other chapters, but was instead specifically focused here on the problems of stress research.

The core arguments were (1) the person constructs the meanings of his stress; (2) the stress stimuli can be objectively identified on the basis of the investigators' accumulated knowledge or common sense, but still the subject will add something more and make what he will out of the stimuli; (3) imperviousness to stress may be operationalized on the basis of physiological indices and appear "successful," but the ultimate criteria of success must be based on social-psychological grounds; (4) stress does not always have deleterious effects on people; in fact, they may cope and find they have developed or already have capabilities that they did not know they possessed; (5) the variety of research problems concerned with stress means that a psychology of stress is best formed from "primitive" variables that are general in nature, for instance, the ego processes; (6) no clear lines can be drawn among a person's reactions to problems of everyday life, acute synchronic stress, and expectable diachronic stress, since the person is a unity; (7) the formulation here would lead first, in practical public policy, to the reduction of noxious social conditions like poverty and discrimination. Beyond this correction, the results suggest that people's dealings with stress are facilitated, not merely by accommodatory, instrumental attacks but also by periods of reassimilation. The intraceptive processes appear to be of equal or greater importance than the cognitive processes in resolving stressful situations. Thus the question of the temporal reaction and developmental handling of stress is of the essence.

10. The Family, Ego Processes, and Child Rearing

From the process view, the family is an organic center of active interchange among members. Certain characteristics typify families: (*1*) they are corporate bodies, having a structure and a "life" of their own; (*2*) members' ego processes are integral to families' functioning as a whole, in that different individual members, including children, perform various processual tasks that are needed by families to insure their viability, operational efficiency, and continuity (one person is the cool head and another the jester, etc.); (*3*) family groups, and parents particularly, choose and are charged by society with the task of "rearing" the younger members; thus families are task-oriented groups. (*4*) consequently, family groups must change and redefine their ways of operating as the offspring grow and develop.

All of these general characteristics assign basic structure and general function to families but they suggest, in turn, a set of important differential properties that are supported (or not, as the case might be) by members' ego processes: (*1*) If members are accurate with each other (exchanges are preponderantly coping), families should be able to pursue their existences with greater viability, efficiency, and continuity; (*2*) if families cope with younger members' changes, they should be able to facilitate offspring's development and perpetuate group existence as emotional entities, although in this society not necessarily as geolocal collectivities; (*3*) if families facilitate rather than contravene in the younger members' growth, the offspring's developmental course may appear more erratic, but they should eventually be more individuated and coping.

The intent of this chapter is to use the model of ego processes to elaborate and differentiate the ramifications of these characteristics, focusing particularly on the family's child-rearing functions. Consequently, the prevailing themes of child-rearing research are briefly considered first, and then contrasted with a set of reformulations that flow from the process model. Subsequently two formulations—

Swanson's work with ego processes in families and the family interaction research primarily done with clinical concerns in mind—are reviewed and evaluated again within the frame of the present model. Finally the results from empirical analyses of family ego processing, primarily conducted by myself, will be described.

Past Formulations of the Meanings of Families to Children

THE MAIN FORMULATION OF PAST CHILD-REARING RESEARCH

Most child-rearing studies of the past decade were guided by the underlying assumption that parents (usually only mothers) are the efficient cause of the child's behavior and outcomes. Earlier work was based on an even stronger model of linear causality, since point-to-point correspondence between parental behavior and resulting child outcome was expected, for example, severe toilet training at the hands of the parents would produce an anal-retentive adult (see Swanson, 1961, for a detailed criticism of this line of reasoning). Most present investigation attempts to identify more generalized behaviors of parents that *cause* their offspring's immediate responses and guarantee their future character. From this behavioristic perspective, the main dimensions of parental impact have been repetitively identified as various forms of power or love withdrawal, expressed as rewards or punishments that initiate and perpetuate children's behavior. Recent work seems to be moving toward further subdividing or repartitioning parental power and love withdrawal. The family's main meaning to the child's development from this point of view then, is its tutorial, shaping function.

In a review of parent–child research, Becker (1964) suggests that the frequently chosen parental dimensions of love–hostility and control–autonomy could be further subdivided. He proposes a two-fold partitioning of control–autonomy into (1) restrictiveness versus permissiveness and (2) anxious-emotional involvement versus calm detachment. Still he notes, "It is painfully apparent that social scientists who have set for themselves the task of unraveling the consequences of child rearing practices are faced with a problem of infinite complexities [p. 201]." However, Becker goes on to emphasize the advantages of pursuing even more complex patterns of variables, but he notes that the "optimal" levels of parental love and control (e.g., how much control is "good") need to be investigated.

In a recent review Hoffman (1970) states his belief that experimental study might better clarify the causal direction of transmission within families, a view also held by Bell (1968). Parenthetically, we can question whether laboratory study can represent parent–child interactions in their subtle complexities, since O'Rourke (1963) found that families' behaviors markedly shifted between home and laboratory. However, Hoffman's concern about the causal directionality in families does move a bit closer to the present process conceptualization of the child-within-the-family (i.e., the child affects the parents, and vice versa, and the group affects each member). Only a few more steps would be needed to take us to a consideration of the family's reverberatory implications for each member's constructed meanings. In reviewing research relevant to the family's involvement in the child's moral development, Hoffman adds the parent's use of induction to the common, arousing–reinforcing techniques of power assertion and love withdrawal. Induction is identified as the parent's use of explanations or reasons "for requiring the child to change his behavior." Even though induction suggests a class of parental behaviors that could be reactive and counterreactive to the child's own constructions, it is basically another version of control, since Hoffman focuses on the child being "required to change his behavior" to accord with the parents' line of reasoning.

Another recent examination of child rearing is offered by Aronfreed (1968). He, too, considers love and control, but prefers to subsume each under his own constructs of induction and sensitization. He substitutes induction for love and sensitization for control, arguing that his variables refer more directly to the outcomes within the child which result from the parental impacts of love and control. Like other investigators, Aronfreed is also concerned with the question of optimal levels (a question I argue is unanswerable because optimality does not depend on amounts but on the constructed meaning of situations) and the balance between love and punishment. From his point of view, love (induction) is a necessary condition of the child's socialization because it provides the basis for the parents' manipulation of the child's affective responses to provide the necessary motivation for their offspring's internalization. Sensitization (control) is required in itself, so the child can come to anticipate the consequences of his own transgressions.

This brief summary serves to highlight the several issues confronting child-rearing research:

1. What are the relevant dimensions that describe how parents riase their children? If parental love and power or their close relatives are the critical variables, then a question must be raised, as both Becker and Aronfreed have, about their optimal levels. Notice that this is the same question that was raised about competence in Chapter 3 and about measurement of states and traits in Chapter 6. This is not a fortuitous coincidence since this kind of difficulty is endemic to basically deterministic formulations that disregard the processing of immediate circumstances and depend on varying amounts of motivation for the activation of the organism. Moreover for these variables to operate usefully within these kinds of formulations, we must suppose that sizable numbers of parents love and/or control their children too much or too little. No stretch of the imagination is required to see that there can be too little or too much control. With regard to love, what does it mean to love someone too much? If "loving" foolishly is meant, is this really love? I will argue later that the question of love and control is a pseudo-issue—most parents love their children and they could hardly bear living with them if they did not exert a modicum of control (except in the most pathological instances). The

real question is how parents process and formulate their roles with their children— how they express their inevitable lovingness and their inevitable need to stop their children from inevitable indiscretions and violations of others.

2. Is the model of parent causality correct? Do not children affect parents too? Moreover if children ultimately make their own constructions, do they assimilate exactly what the parents had in mind, or something of their own making? If parents reinforce the child by with their own personal dictums, does this mean that children are or will become exact reproductions of their parents?

DEVELOPMENT OF EGO FUNCTIONS IN FAMILIES

In the important early work *Inner conflict and defense,* Miller and Swanson (1960) described their intensive, psychoanalytically influenced investigation of ego functioning with three different samples of males, two composed of adolescents and one of young adults. Two assumptions about the importance of the family guided the substudy of child rearing: (*1*) behavior is learned early in life; (*2*) the family is the main vehicle of socialization. Both of these were considered within the context of social class, which was regarded as an index of general family values and orientations. Thus, a father who solves his own work or career problems conceptually was expected to regulate his son's behavior in the same manner. Considerable evidence was adduced to support social class differences in sons of entrepreneurial families, and, to a lesser extent, in bureaucratic families. The middle class entrepreneurial boys were subjected to the most intense parental pressures and in turn, Miller and Swanson reasoned, had learned defenses which reverse, diminish, or turn aggression against the self. The three *means* of transmitting values and defenses from parent to child were designated as (*1*) identification, (*2*) the parental behaviors of expecting obedience and giving rewards, and (*3*) the early socialization experiences of weaning and toilet training.

From the present point of view, the major conceptual contribution of *Inner conflict and defense* stemmed from its view of the child within the family as a problem solver in his own behalf, albeit exclusively defensive in his means. The study, affected by the thinking of its time, varies from the present effort in several ways: (*1*) the research design made provision only for defensive behavior; as I have commented earlier, "both before and after stimulation, which was intended to arouse increased need and ensuing conflict, a number of their subjects failed to show initial and/or subsequent defensive behavior. Since Miller and Swanson had no conceptual provision for handling nondefensive behavior, they found it necessary to eliminate these subjects from their analysis; this may have excluded from consideration an important segment of the range of normal human behavior [Haan, 1963, p. 2] ;" (*2*) even though the child was seen as defensive and needing to solve his inner and outer conflicts, the parent's impact upon the child, as it was conceived in the design and choice of major variables, could only be viewed as mechanical, linear, and invariably effective; (*3*) the child's own developmental status was not a critical consideration; seventh to ninth graders were studied and pooled, as were 16- to 24-year-olds.

In short order Swanson (1961) became dissatisfied with some of the formulations used in *Inner conflict and defense* and argued that defenses could not be viewed as directly caused, but should rather be seen as aspects of people's social roles that emerge from the interplay of environment and organism. He noted that he and Miller had slipped easily into the tacit assumption that children, confronted by certain minimal but sufficient conditions, necessarily produced specific defenses. Clearly Miller and Swanson had operated from the supposition that family transmission is unidirectional and effectively causal.

Swanson felt that a better approach would seek social conditions that replicate each defense, or, consistent with the design of *Inner conflict and defense,* the defenses that replicate the social conditions of the child. Consequent to this line of reasoning, he also suggested that the parent's socialization of the child moves through stages. As the child's developmental tasks are set out, they are diversely and defensively solved by lower class children in terms of the first family of defenses, essentially those concerned with the avoidance of punishment, or by middle class children in the terms of the second family of defenses, essentially those concerned with reward. He also makes the important and conceptually different suggestion that children's roles may sometimes be compensatory for parents' deficiencies. In this case, children could be seen as working to preserve the solidarity of the family, in the same way that members of small groups do, as a growing body of research in the early 1960s had begun to suggest. However, Swanson's sole concern at the time, with the child's defenses limited the number of accommodatory processes that could be recorded and thus he did not explicate his proposal that children might act compensatorily and in ways other than synonymous with their parents' manifest intentions. However, this behavioristic paradigms of the child's avoidance—avoidance and approach—avoidance conflicts with the parent reinstated the parents' effective causality and portrayed the child as propelled by deficiency and tension-reducing motives in an uneasy and uncertain relationship with his parents.

In subsequent years Swanson has gone on to revise and to elaborate various aspects of his later position in a series of presentations concerned with collective action, group goals, specialization of roles, and decision making. I will turn now to his most recent, but not yet published, programmatic statement (Swanson, 1968), which is directly concerned with reciprocal interactions in collectivities and families.

Swanson now develops a detailed account of ego or self processes as social and moral roles. He observes, "The main innovation in my own work is to view each process of coping or defense as consisting in the establishment, or the exercise of a social *right* or in the acceptance, or the fulfillment, of a social *duty* [1968, p. 1, emphasis added]." Thus Swanson's view of society is that of a normative moral order wherein people's interactions are critically defined by their specific need to sustain their interdependencies. He declares that social influences and social power—both still popular preoccupations of parent–child research, as we saw above—are not germane to his case since both result in people being obliged. Swanson has clearly moved away from a behavioristic model of parent–child relations to a multidirectional organic model. Interdependency, as the special and the most critical description of family interaction, results in mutual obligations and expectancies on both logical and moral grounds. In this context ego processes become necessary, as he says, so that family members can relate to each other's minds in order to discern their own and others' obligations for the family's self-management as an interdependent social system.

Choice of ego operation is also considered from his new position. It follows "that a particular defense or coping process should be differentially fostered in individuals according to the degree to which each process is normatively required of those individuals by social relations. . . . To explain individual differences . . . one should look to social conditions that (a) give exceptional importance to that process and that (b) make it a right or a duty [1968, p. 12]."

Swanson is not as concerned as the present formulation is in drawing sharp distinctions between the three modal aspects of ego processing—coping, defense, or fragmentation. Defenses are thought to follow man's need to protect "his coherence as an actor and his abilities to act [1968, p. 3]." Coherence is probably conceptually very near to the maintenance of self-integration, characterized in Chapter 4 as an important element of the ego model. However, Swanson underscores the necessity of restrictions on the self to achieve self-coherency within social orders that invariably work to morally obligate members. He points out that some misuse (or potential misuse, or even the appearance of misuse) of rights and duties in interdependencies is inevitable so that a person must constantly reestablish and reassert the authenticity of his commitments to others as they must to him. Thus he says, "Something of guilt or shame or self-admonition is therefore as inherent in social relations as are coping and defense [1968, p. 18]." The coping processes themselves are viewed as actions that make it possible for individuals to exploit, to understand, to master, to reshape, and to gain sustenance from their environment, both inner and outer.

FAMILY INTERACTION RESEARCH

We turn now to the contributions that the recent, burgeoning research in family interaction may make to understanding ego functioning in families. Two lines of earlier work—small-group research in academic sociology (for example, Bales, 1950) and research on communications within families of schizophrenics (for example, Jackson, 1960)—converged in the early 1960s. Bales' coding system provided a model for data reduction. Strodtbeck's (1951) earlier invention of the revealed differences technique, wherein individual family members first privately commit themselves to a position and then discuss their differences as a family group, became the prototypic design. Since then, hundreds of families have been observed as they dealt with a variety of problems, for example, differences in attitudes and beliefs among themselves, joint cognitive tasks, role playing, and the simulated planning of a family recreation.

Strodtbeck (1954) reported that unlike small groups, families do not have the same regularities in the distribution of support, nor do high-participating members necessarily dominate the decision making. Bodin (1969) compared real families with matched artificial families that contained the same distributions of age and sex, finding higher all-member and parental agreement and more efficient decision making in real families, but greater maternal compromise in synthetic families. This research has made it quite clear that the special characteristics of the family's primary relationships cannot be simulated so that real families must be studied. O'Rourke (1963) introduced yet another caution when he found that the quantity and quality of various family behaviors changed from home to laboratory. In laboratory settings the positive emotional response of the fathers and children decreased and the mothers' increased, while the group as a whole increased instrumental and negative social-emotional reactions.

Riskin and Faunce (1972) concluded, in an extensive and highly critical review, that literally hundreds of family interaction studies had been done between 1960 and 1970, but that not much had been found in the way of substantiated or replicated findings. In fact, even the lack of clarity and accuracy in the communication within families containing a schizophrenic member, which had once seemed verified, now seems to be in question after recent findings by Reiss (1970, 1971) which contradict, for example, those of Singer and Wynne (1965a,b, 1966a,b). Reiss reports such families are exquisitely tuned into each other, while Singer and Wynne find the communication muddled and convoluted.

Most family research has not considered the status of individual family members; in fact, Riskin and Faunce report that Jay Haley's position is that the "individual" is now obsolete. Very little work has concerned the likely great variety of "normal" families; instead they have been used in undifferentiated contrast to families that contain an offspring who has been diagnosed as having a character disorder or as being schizophrenic. Families classified according to the clinical status of one of its children are frequently studied as a triad of mother, father, and the disturbed child, without other siblings. Apparently no studies have considered children within a developmental framework; Hill and Hansen (1960) proposed a developmental progression for families, but it is more actuarial than conceptual in designating the stages as marriage, childbirth, and the like. The several studies reviewed below represent that small portion of family interaction research that has focused upon formalistic ego processes.

A particularly well designed study of social influence and coping patterns within families of disturbed adolescents was reported by Goldstein, Judd, Rodnick, Alkire, and Gould (1968). Families of adolescents applying to a psychiatric clinic were grouped by judges according to the descriptions of the offspring's presenting complaints. The groups so classified were identified as (*1*) aggressive, antisocial, (*2*) active family conflict, (*3*) passive, negative, and (*4*) withdrawn, socially isolated. In separate interviews each family member was asked to describe specific family conflicts in regard to achievement, sociability, and dating and then to role play his own part in the problem so that the interviewer could elicit "cue statements" that were idiosyncratic for the particular family. Members were also asked to predict each others' responses. Eventually the families were brought together to react to each other's cue statements and predictions. All statements, predictions as well as responses, were coded for each member according to three categories: private dependent power, information-giving, and information-seeking. Results indicated that more power statements were used by the parents of adolescents with extra-familial conflicts. However the adolescents of the active family conflict group were the only teenagers who used more power statements, while their parents did not respond in kind but instead asked significantly more questions. The aggressive, antisocial adolescents and their parents were the most accurate in predicting each other's responses, while the withdrawn, isolated children and their parents were the least accurate. As the authors note, the most interesting finding is that the major group differences in parental behavior were not reciprocated by like group differences among their adolescent offspring.

Reiss has described a series of laboratory, observational studies wherein 16 families with normal or hospitalized offspring diagnosed as schizophrenics or as having character disorders performed a series of elaborate perceptual and cognitive tasks. A factor analysis (Reiss, 1970) reduced the family unit scores to four orthogonal factors. Only the first two—within family responsiveness and environmental responsiveness—distinguished the various kinds of families. Families with normal offspring were significantly higher in family responsiveness than those whose offspring had character disorders and higher in environmental responsiveness than those with schizophrenic offspring.

Reiss (1971) goes on in a subsequent paper to elaborate his growing theory of the family's shared, consensual experiences, contending that there are three main dimensions: problem-solving effectiveness, coordinations, and penchant for closure. His previous investigatory work did not consider these dimensions. He has come to think, however, that the conceptualization of cognitive ego control will be useful in his future work. Reiss's work is noteworthy for its methodological sophistication, but he has not yet demonstrated or suggested the means whereby the family translocates its functioning to the individual child or vice versa.

A very different approach with some conceptual similarities to the present position is that represented by the work of Singer and Wynne, primarily with young adult schizophrenics (see Singer & Wynne, 1965a,b, 1966a,b, for the most relevant reports). The family is viewed in formal, stylistic terms as engaged in transactions, and the individual member's responses to the Rorschach and TAT are assumed to represent a sample of family transactions. Singer and Wynne take the same position as the present investigator in asserting that the contents of transactions are ever-changing, while the formal, stylistic features of processes are more enduring. They note that schizophrenia in itself is "a stylistic disorder of *how* experience and behavior are organized [1966a, p. 1]."

The Singer–Wynne studies are highly successful in producing results with their methodology. Using only the Rorschach records of families, the researchers have been able to predict the global diagnoses of hospitalized young adults (schizophrenic, borderline, or nonschizophrenic), the form of their thinking (amorphous, mixed, fragmented, and constricted), and the severity of their disorganizations. Moreover, groups of offspring were successfully matched with their own parents using only test protocols. Parents who were not themselves psychiatrically disturbed, but who had offspring of various diagnoses, were distinguished from each other on the basis of the parental protocols. Recognizing that all of these results rest upon very expert and sensitive scoring of the projective tasks protocols, the authors developed Rorschach and TAT scoring manuals (Singer & Wynne, 1966b). Cross-cultural studies of families to further evaluate their assertion of formalistic generality are reported to be underway.

The substance of Singer and Wynne's reported findings, beyond these predictive tours de force, are not yet of great consequence. They have generally been concerned with four features of family transaction: styles of communicating and relating, affective disorders, feelings of meaninglessness, and the family's organization in response to threat, involving such maneuvers as pseudomutuality and pseudohostility.

A number of general or inferential remarks made by Singer and Wynne on the basis of their accrued experience are relevant to the present effort. They note that no offspring was schizophrenic unless both parents took aggravating roles in the family and that their predictions were not possible unless both parents were considered. Inferences from sibling data made their predictions more precise, but never drastically revised them. Stylistic, formal differences rather than similarities between parents and children were the rule of their predictions. They note, for instance, that an intrusive parent most often has a withdrawing child, an observation that seems to have a degree of social logic to it.

At this point, research in family interaction is a promise more than a fulfillment. Riskin and Faunce (1972) note that these endeavors are seriously handicapped by a lack of intermediate concepts, necessary for specifying the implications of family interactions and the import of individual members' contributions to children's development. At present the clinical studies of family interaction make richer contributions, but their empirical yield is low; nevertheless their mode of study is based on assumptions that individual members' reactions are in part complementary and reciprocal to the whole family and represent the individual's and the group's solutions to their mutual problems of living.

GENERAL IMPLICATIONS OF PAST WORK FOR EGO PROCESSING IN FAMILIES

Clearly much of the literature reviewed has little relationship to the present conceptualization; however Swanson's recent formulation is very much to the point of the present discourse, and subsequent discussion will continue to consider and draw on his interesting ideas. From this short review we can draw various implications and cautions for studying ego processing in families:

1. To understand families and their implications for children, all members will have to be included in research designs, and families as interacting units (or "interdependent units" which is Swanson's (1968) more heuristic term) will have to be studied. When investigators have included fathers, their results were considerably elaborated and strengthened. Moreover, family interaction in itself can be seen as complementary and reciprocal to the individual's input and to the various dyadic transactions; consequently families or parent–child relations are not likely to be fully understood without knowledge of the group interactions. There has been clear agreement outside of psychology for sometime now that a family is more than and different from the summed composite of the individual members' inputs.

2. The logic of most past family research has been guided by the assumption that linear, unidirectional influence from parent to child is the effective cause of the child's behavior—a supposition that must be more tenable with the translocation of content than with the child's construction of preferred processes and organizations. There is not only increasing recognition that the child affects the parents and that each permuted pair within the family produces effects, but that the linear, investigative model of independent parent and dependent child may not be viable or even correct. A distinction between the baby's real and actual power within the family was made by Erikson (1959). In reality the baby is weak, but in actuality his presence importantly determines the life style of the family. As Spiegel and Bell (1959) note, "This point of view [the family as a subsystem] alters the concept of causality. . . . Putting variables within a total context shifts the question from what in the family causes pathology in the individual, to what processes occurring between the individual and the family are associated with the behaviors which are 'called' pathology? [p. 123]" Riskin and Faunce (1972, p. 388) comment that "although the classical, experimental method may be relevant to the linear causality model, it may not be applicable to the family-as-a-system (mosaic or circular model)."

3. Moreover, a number of the studies reviewed give clear evidence that the action of the child is not necessarily modeled after his parent or even after what the parent intended to bring about in an effective way. Most of this evidence is from troubled (that is, obstreperous) children, since no thoroughgoing attempt has yet been made to record reverberations of reciprocal, complementary, or identical processes in families of the nonpsychiatrically involved. Nor have the researchers in family interaction considered very thoroughly the individual status of family members, separately or prior to observing their interaction. Most clinical studies are preoccupied with the milieus that make children sick rather than with the present question—how do children develop within families?

4. From these various points of view the characterization of families according to processes and structures is likely to produce greater and more general under-

standing than will the further examination of contents such as love and control. Processes are likely the more general and enduring, albeit less obvious, aspects of family transmission. The alternative of continuing to further divide and subdivide the contents of love and control, necessarily attended by attempts to specify how much love or control is "enough," seems not to have been productive, nor does it appear to represent families themselves and the everyday complexities of their reciprocal and complementary implications for children.

We turn now to a full account of family interaction from the process view in order to highlight its implications for child rearing.

Family Interaction from the Ego Process View

If a central theme of family life is the members' intent to sustain and enhance the group and its interdependency, the observations of choice for parent–child study are the ego processes of the members, taken individually and in concert, as they go about fulfilling this group intent. This line of reasoning is related to Swanson's (1961) recommendation, discussed earlier, that the social conditions (including family conditions) that parallel the defenses of individuals should be sought; thus, in his view, social conditions provide the ground for the ego processes. The present perspective is also related in a different way to Witkin's (1969) expectancy that the personally undifferentiated mother will prevent her child from differentiating himself and separating from the family by reason of her own undifferentiation. The present formulation involves both more and less than either of these two views. There is a stronger expectancy that the constructions of individual members must eventuate in complementary, rather than identical, ego processes within family groups (possibly due to the stronger conceptualization of processing taken here). At the same time, the force of social conditions is somewhat diminished by the importance attached to members' developmental states and constructions. Individual members are viewed as obdurately utilizing various ego processes to conserve self-integration even if they must defend or fragment. In this light, extensive parent–child similarity, that is, modeling, unless constitutionally based, may be regarded as an anxious, defensive maneuver taken by the child, and evidence of the price that he feels he must pay to conserve not only his social relations, as Swanson (1961, p. 5) has observed, but also his sense of self-integration.

BASIC DEFINITIONS OF THE FAMILY AS AN ORGANIC UNIT

The following several sections describe a number of postulates, briefly mentioned above, about family functioning that are consistent with the ego process view.

The Family as a Corporate Body

It is assumed that the family is more than the sum of its parts, that it is a corporate body in itself, and that each family is distinctive in its formal and informal regulations and means of operation and governance.

The Family's Integral Operations

Many of the ego patterns favored by individual members perform various functions the family needs to maintain its existence and viability; thus the child's operations come to be congruent, supportive, complementary, or reciprocal to the whole.

Accuracy in Family Interchange

The nature of social interaction comes to involve expectancies and exerts requirements among participants that statements, reports, and comments be made with accuracy; this was noted in previous chapters as the hallmark of coping. In this sense, accuracy is a kind of social integrity. Piaget has more particularly noted that logic itself (as one kind of accurate statement) represents a moral, "categorical" imperative, since it is "indispensable for intellectual interaction and cooperation [1950, p. 156]." Swanson emphasizes that social interaction cannot be sustained without the ego process of objectivity since "people require [of] one another that they actually be what they publicly allowed themselves to seem [1968, p. 9]," another kind of social accuracy.

Accuracy in family communications is obviously important in sustaining the family as a viable, operative unit, since it is the basis for intelligible interactions, but an equally important reason for accuracy is its support for the children's own slowly developing capabilities of achieving integrity in social, logical interchanges. This definition of mutual social accuracy and logic is likely the cognitive basis for the Eriksonian stage of trust, which remains, as he says, a problem throughout life. Accuracy in family members' processes of interchange would be represented not only in their cognitive, coping operations of *objectivity, logical analysis, intellectuality,* and *concentration,* but also by their *tolerance* and recognition of a degree of *ambiguity* in some interchanges, their *empathic* formulation of each other's feelings, and by the social regulation of their own feelings. As Piaget notes, the child first actively attempts to avoid contradicting himself when he is in the presence of others and is just beginning to grasp operational concepts. Undoubtedly his parents and sibs are among the first to feel they can intrude and demand veracity from him. The development of concrete operations frees the child from his own egocentric, intuitive point of view, but he is not able to take a fully hypothetical, reciprocal stance until he is an adolescent, when he may be able to say, "how would I feel if he were to dissemble to me as I contemplate dissembling to him?"

In this light the parents' own accuracy—given the importance of family interchanges and the family's need to maintain a modicum of accuracy for operational viability—should be a necessary, but still not sufficient condition for the child's own development of a respect for accuracy. Up to this point we have broadly discussed how the child's own development is supported by coping functions. However the young child's own inadequate means of ascertaining veracity and achieving accuracy suggest that he is additionally burdened in his developmental attempts if he does not experience a modicum of accuracy in his interchanges with his family. Both parents or all members may not need to be accurate since the child can come to construct contrasts. In clinical practice, children of psychotic parents who have become quite objective about their parents' misconstructions are sometimes seen. Given the frequency of psychologists' recommendations to parents that they should be consistent, I want to underscore the fact that accuracy is not the same as consistency and that the accuracy of the reasons that parents give for being inconsistent or consistent, innovative or noninnovative, is the issue here.

The Self-Perpetuation of the Family

It is argued that families want to perpetuate themselves as units beyond considerations of habit, material and economic security, and affection (see Haan, 1971). The fundamental, integrative ties are thought to relate to the history of individual members' self-constructions. Following George Herbert Mead's distinctions, the self develops in transaction with others—the "I" retains the individual initiative while the "me" assimilates the attitudes of others toward the self. These "others" are importantly the family, as the most closely interacting, continuous, but variegated age group in which the child has membership. If family ties are involved in the development of the individual members' commutative selves, and therefore their self-consistency, it follows, then, that the family has additional reasons for wanting to perpetuate itself. The unit's existence serves not only to conserve self-consistency, but also to corroborate and validate changes in the self. If I have changed for the better (or the worse) who would be better able or more willing to verify it? Clearly the form and value of the members' contribution to the family's perpetuation will vary with the age of the member, but even adult offspring seem to want to perpetuate the idea of their childhood family, even if they do not care to be in its physical locale. In this light, the death of the family contains a self-nullification, an inconsistency of the self, for each of its members. Families appear willing to go to great lengths to sustain themselves as groups even if they must redefine their structures, attenuate their interdependence, or exact undue payment from some or all members.

The Family's Developmental Redefinitions

The family with developing children takes a course punctuated by the necessity of periodically redefining its organization and processes as the children move from one structural stage to another. If the family is unable to redefine itself, the child's development may be impeded or become covert, or, in the case of older children, the family may cease to exist as a corporate body if the late adolescent finds the family's definition of him unbearable and too costly. Runaways are a case in point (see Haan, 1971, for an interpretation of the hippie phenomena in this light). Typically the child's actual development outstrips the family's definition of him as an individual and a participant in its organization. One frequent period of lag in the family's redefinition of itself is during the child's adolescence, a period when children change in ways that clearly entail fundamental parallel changes in the family's organization.

As an example, moral interdependency within families especially require group redefinition in concert with the child's developmental changes. As I have analyzed elsewhere:

When children are very young, the moral exchange of the young with their parents and their society is markedly unequal. In fact, it is essentially unilateral, since adults have moral concerns and commitments to their children that cannot be reciprocated fully or in kind. This imbalance is not only a matter of disproportionate adult moral capability or of adults' greater power and material resources, but is also a commonsense acceptance of the underdeveloped state of children's morality. Whatever the case, children have moral claims as members of both the family and society, and these rights are universally recognized and honored—children are to be cared for. A society that morally neglects its children, whether physically or emotionally, could survive neither long nor well in either a sociocultural sense or in an emotional sense. . . . As children grow to late adolescence, however, expectations about reciprocal moral obligations within the family and with the young are transformed. At this point, the youth's moral capability, in terms of differentiation, integration, and comprehensiveness, equals or exceeds that of his parents, even though his actions may not always be commensurate. . . . His personal power has become sufficient to the logical expectancies of his society, his family, and himself that he will assume moral responsibility for his own actions. This expectation is objectively and rationally based on the level of his development for his particular society—it is thus a normative expectancy. . . . Youth's development, socially, morally, objectively, and logically, obligates him to assume moral responsibility reciprocal to his parents' for him. But equally entailed is the repeal of his parents' unilateral or disproportionate moral concern for him. Typically, however, these requirements for new forms of interaction result in disequilibrium. . . .

In order that the family experience the disequilibrium of reorganization, its ego reactions must permit the comprehension and evaluation of the changed state of the adolescent. In other words, the juncture requires that the family cope in a fairly complex way; it must take in the information of the child's change, evaluate it, and act upon it, to the end that its self-regulating structures are redefined and re-stabilized if moral inequality within the unit is to be revoked and reciprocity established in its stead. The redefinition of the family has advantages for all its members and would, therefore, seemingly be easily accomplished. Undoubtedly it is, in the social milieu of some societies, but this empirical fact does not obviate the logical necessity of structural reorganization or of some kinds of perturbation.

The advantages for the parents lie in their right, now with logical, moral, and social justification and support, to expect and to receive moral consideration from their offspring equal to what they give (when parents are old, societies expect the obverse moral inequality to occur—the young should care for the old). The gains for the young lie in the potentialities for their continued social and moral development.

Since the late adolescent does not move smoothly and instantaneously to principled reciprocity and to the taking of moral responsibility for himself, he presents inconsistent and contradictory cues to his family, which has its own reasons to be perturbed.

Because the young person no longer regards his parents' moral guidance as infallible as a result of their occupation of roles prescribed by convention, and because he knows, formally and hypothetically, in what ways their authority is insufficient and not always rational, the adolescent challenges parental authority, a criticism made possible by his being able to utilize the formal operation of reciprocity. Disproportionate moral concern without sufficient objective grounds is unduly obligating. . . . The parents will need to perpetuate their disproportionately greater moral consideration to ensure their own sense of virtue, since non-reciprocated moral consideration of another is a validation of one's own altruism, whether or not objective grounds exist. Being deprived of their authority, their possibilities for benevolence, and their security in believing in their own virtue, parents are also disequilibrated. Both the young adult and the family view the juncture as an uneasy new era. For the young adult, it is the separateness of self-responsibility, since he can no longer, on logical grounds, pass his responsibility over to the authorities; for the parents, it is the time for redefining the foundations of their virtues and giving up one of its bases by requiring full reciprocity from their offspring as moral equals. . . .

But if the family unit is to promote its own and its member's development beyond this critical period and sustain itself as a unit, it must succeed in transforming its moral relations in these ways—equalizing moral exchange, respecting differences, and accepting separateness. The task is disequilibrating. Some families cannot change because their ego functioning precludes or negates new information, and their moral decisions perpetuate concrete, personalized, or legalized forms of exchange that are intolerant of differences and separateness to the degree that relationships must be dissolved. In these families the young adult, if he remains within the unit, is basically "a chip off the old block," and he forgoes his potentialities for further development. Other families crumble as units—fragment in terms of ego functioning. If the requirements of belonging become unbearable to the late adolescent, he may resign from the unit emotionally, if not physically, and more or less permanently [Haan, 1971, pp. 265-270].

The child's moral development provides a particularly clear instance of the logical necessity of the family's redefining itself in concert with the child's structural developments. However moral change is only one kind of change that the child makes. The family's ability to change its organization and modes of operation along with the child's cognitive and social developments would appear to support the child's development of coping processes, very simply because his family's flexibility does not further complicate his already complex efforts to reorganize himself.

Homogeneity versus Heterogeneity of Processes within Families

Clearly the parents are important sources for instigating the child's learning a great deal of content, that is, information about the world, so that much of his knowledge comes to duplicate that of his parents. However, the child does not necessarily duplicate his parents' operations and structural organization (Haan *et al.,* 1976), and he does not often duplicate their hierarchy of preferred ego operations (see Haan, 1974c). An empirical examination of family ego patterns in these regards is described below. Furthermore, the findings of small-group research suggest that a family group might not be operable if all members favored the same processes. Various studies described earlier in this chapter (e.g., Goldstein *et al.*, 1968; Singer & Wynne, 1965a,b, 1966a,b) suggested that there is sytematic variation in favored processes among the various members of family groups.

Normatively then, a workable family group needs to have a modicum of process heterogeneity at its disposal. At the same time, excessive differences among members' processes, such as a highly logical father, an excessively denying mother, and a projective, displacing teenager, might make it difficult for the family to operate as a unit. In these kinds of families all or most members likely go their own way as a kind of group solution. However, the more frequent nonnormative circumstance—since people are not likely to marry each other and set up families if their ego processes do not mesh reasonably well—is the group's requirement of homogeneity, a standardization of functioning needed by families whose operations cannot withstand too great a diversity. This group intent leads to pressure that the child should imitate his parents, which was discussed earlier in Chapter 4 in regard to the genesis of preferred ego functions. Following the earlier lines of reasoning, extended and durable imitation of parents or authority figures reflects an anxious hyperadaptivity on the child's part, since he overaccommodates to achieve a kind of equilibrium. At the same time, the child's imitative constructions support and promote family homogeneity. Heterogeneity of favored coping operations more likely occurs in families that are better able to tolerate the ambiguity of diversity.

The Parents' Intentions to Enhance Their Offspring's
Development

The vitality and importance of love exchanges in family operation is known and understood by everybody, but so far it has eluded empirical analysis except in its most pallid or calculated forms—either as warmth or its withdrawal, as a means of achieving the child's conformity to parental goals. Of all forms of family interdependency, love, as it is variously formulated, probably explains the most about the parents' actions but not the children's. Swanson (1965) has made a careful, general analysis of the routinization of love in primary relations, and the following analysis of love relations within families owes much to his prior work. The following points seem to be specific to family life: (*1*) Love is the most particularistic, elaborated, and differentiated of all social skills, but the exchange of love within families is permitted and limited by the developed level of children's cognitive-social skills and is disproportionate from the parents to the baby, to the child, and even to the adolescent; (*2*) in love relations the participants make diffused, future-oriented commitments to enhance each other's development and integration in whatever ways are possible and reasonable. Most parents implicitly make such future-oriented commitments when they decide to conceive and bear a child; obviously the baby is not part of the original agreement and does not reciprocate in kind. Even later, the young's commitments to the parents are usually less than the parents'. They cannot and do not often reciprocate in kind, in intensity, or in extensity and only return love in more simplistic forms. Moreover, they are not frequently nor knowledgeably oriented to enhancing, lovingly, their parents' future status. Children's full reciprocation is transferred eventually to the next succeeding generation, their own children. As Rawls (1971) has observed, there is historic injustice between generations.

The parents' love commitment to the child cannot, however, be blind or foolish (or, as Swanson generally observes, love cannot be a matter of being in love with love), since this would obviate realistically aiding the child in his development and assisting him in the resolution of his inevitable difficulties and problems. The parents' task is more complicated since their future-oriented and mature commitment to "bringing up" the child requires that they differentiate and examine their various nourishments.

In light of these considerations and the present focus upon processes, a crucial sector of parent–child relationships lies in the compatibility between the child's structural and ego development and the adults' formulations of how they can best translate their love of the child into enhancing and aiding his future. In extreme cases, parents may not formulate their relationship and responsibility to the child's future at all (he is regarded as a peer), or they may not regard the child as a separate, sentient being, but instead may view him as a possession.

A usual question, asked by clinicians and researchers alike, is whether or not the parents love their child; this seems to me to be a pseudoissue wrought by a behavioristic, unilateral view of family effects. Given the investment that most parents have in their children, it seems self-evident that most parents do love their offspring, but in their own way. Thus the critical questions are how parents formulate their loving, future-oriented commitments and responsibilities with respect to the child's progress, and whether these formulations facilitate, complicate, or deter the child's development. Some parents may make their own disproportionate power and wisdom the point of their loving intentions and thereby come to think they should curb childish impulses to insure the child's future progress. Other parents may not be as concerned with their power and thus think that their responsibility is to facilitate the child's development within his own terms and curb him only when his actions impinge on their moral rights; consequently they view family life as a series of negotiations and mutual accommodations. Some parents may not sufficiently engage themselves in the parental role either to contravene or facilitate the child's development, although most do, given the investments that follow on first bearing and then bringing up a child. In these particular families children, being left to their own devices, must inevitably evoke their own self-gratifications and protective systems against the hazards of their own inexperience. Anna Freud's and Dorothy Burlingham's (1944) preschoolers who had all but raised themselves in concentration camps, had developed their own social system which broke down, however, under tender, loving adult care. In this light, parental intents, which are formulated as responsible contraventions, are expected to promote the child's defensiveness, since the child will need to retrench to protect his own constructions and own integrity. The parental intents to facilitate and catalyze are expected to promote the offspring's coping.

The hallmark of contravention is the parents' organized formulation of their intent to instill competency and social appropriateness within their child, or, in other words, to shape him for his future. The atmosphere may be warm or cool; the general feeling tone, outside of extreme, disruptive circumstances, is probably not critical, although warm atmospheres have been much applauded. In this sense the classical concepts of both power assertion and intentional love withdrawal are the same. In the minds of the parents both are forms of responsible bartering to help their unworldly child gain control and become achieving. Their goals flow from their love and their formulations that their reinforcements are not only crucial and definitive, but also a responsibility that they necessarily bear, given their superior knowledge and the child's uncertain future in a shaky world. Their job is to instill adequacy. Thus the family structure does not reflect the eventual expectancy of reciprocity, but is defined and determined by the parents' strong view that their responsibilities are permanent, logically based, and socially prescribed.

The child, in turn, will probably have to accommodate disproportionately to his assimilation, and in this event he will have to evoke defensive strategies to maintain a workable equilibrium. He comes to know the benefits of social compliance and could very well be a high achiever, given a school environment of like certainty and clarity, and more than likely, he will defensively model his parents.

The crux of parental facilitation is the mutual interchange between parent and child. The parent defines the relationship as a process of mutual accommodation that is disproportionately from him during the child's earlier years, but moves toward actual reciprocity by the end of the child's adolescence. These parents express pleasure or displeasure to the child as inevitable and required feedback, but not usually with the expectancy that the child will definitively and accurately accommodate. Exceptional circumstances occur when the child violates another, including the parent himself, and here the intent of the parents' intervention is partly to protect the child from the unassimilable brunt of his own further indiscretion, but it is also an attempt to restore moral balance between himself and the child and within the family. Facilitative parents expect the child to make his own assimilation and consequent formulation and to invent his own accommodation (without formulating matters in exactly these terms). In other words, they expect that the child will have independent understandings of the world.

This sort of interchange means, of course, that the parents must take chances with the child and tolerate the uncertainty of his present and future directions. The negotiative quality of this parent–child interchange creates periods of family disharmony as the child experiences disequilibrium and as the family accommodates and reorganizes itself within the terms of the child's changes. In turn, the child will develop less consistently as he moves through periods of disequilibrium; consequently his developmental experience will appear more disjunctive. During some transitional periods he may seem less socially appropriate, but he should generally appear to be more spontaneous and more objective in evaluating his parents. Overall he should move toward coping and often be more coping, but the nature of his reorganizations may evoke defensiveness.

Altogether the contrast described above between parental contravention and facilitation represents two conceptually different theories of human development, based on contrasting ontological beliefs, held by people and parents. Thus two different organizations of family life that should have consequences for the child's preferred modes of ego processing are suggested. These organizations, originally designed by the parents and later elaborated by the children, do not lay the basis for clearly coping or defensive actions in transitional adolescents. Instead, the children who are members of facilitative organizations should become more accurate as adults in their dealings with themselves and with others—the hallmark of coping. At adolescence they may appear more perturbed because of their difficulties in negotiating changes on their own. Children who are members of family organizations defined by parents' contravention have less complex experiences since they only need to accomodate to their families' theories of the good. When adolescents are able to do this comfortably and thoroughly, they may well cope, particularly in the outer-directed cognitive sectors and they may be helped to transform their affective reactions to more civil forms, by such means as substitutions and reaction formations.

Prescribed Roles, Role Specialization and Differentiation

Human interchanges, as clinicians and those sociologists persuaded to role theory have known for some time, imply reciprocal definition, that is, people's expectancies of each other work to define selves. The victim finds his victimizer and the ghetto child fulfills his teacher's expectancies by his own academic incompetence. As was noted above, when adults commit themselves to parenthood they come to entertain future-oriented intentions for their children. Understandably, their own past history of successful and unsuccessful self-constructions leads them to some mythological, future-oriented expectancies for their children ("He'll become a mechanic like his father," or "He's going to have the same temper that I do"). The questions for the child's development are (1) the degree to which parents are able to differentiate their own expectancies from the reality of the child; and (2) their capability of reorgnizing their perceptions in the face of the child's own efforts to make something of himself, out of what they have been making out of him. The outcome of this interplay for the child would seem to be affected by two factors, both having to do with the coping or defensive capabilities of the participants: the vigor or torpor of the child's own efforts at unique self-definition and the parents' propensities to cope or defend in response to information contrary to their myths, that is, their degree of objectivity, logical analysis, and tolerance in regard to the ambiguity of the child's future. For the parent it is, in sum, his resistance to the compulsion of historical repetition in intimate interpersonal relations.

Still the requirements of group life, as investigations of small groups have made clear (Parsons & Bales, 1955), call for some degree of role specialization and differentiation that are less liable to gross, affective-laden distortions. The same phenomena can be seen in families as well, and most easily in large families where various children acquire roles—"This one is our mechanic . . . our intellectual . . . our cook." Relevant to the child's development are his possibilities of assuming serious roles of specialization different from being a child and a Jones, along with his family's flexibility in redefining him in concert with his interests in adopting new and different roles to match his evolving developmental capabilities. Thus the family's organization of its various ego potentialities, to the extent that it is an open, responsive system, presents various opportunities for the child to exercise his differing, evolving ego operations. An example is the family's openness to being informed by the classificatory manias (e.g., stamp collecting) of the concrete operational child, as he exercises his newly acquired skills, or to being informed by the social criticism and protest of the late adolescent whose formal operational capacity leads him to envision utopias. In families that are closed systems, children's roles would likely be characterized by fixedness and also by socially prescribed, rather than personally chosen definitions.

CHILD REARING FROM THE PROCESS FORMULATION

When the ego actions of people with respect to others and themselves are taken as the prime observations, the usual picture of the child developing within the family is radically revised. The parents are no longer seen as exerting definite, causal impact upon the child, and room is made for the child's own evolving constructions to have force without these being sentimentally bestowed upon him because he "should" be treated as an individual in a democratic or humanistic society. The force of the child's own constructions are recognized and hypothesized to affect the whole as the whole affects him, whether he normatively progresses in a coping mode, whether he must developmentally evade or retrench by various defensive strategies, or even if he must retreat to fragmentary reactions to spite his parents' intentions.

The foregoing explication has been based on a view of the family as an organic, intimate, human group having some of the characteristics of other small groups but with other attributes singularly and significantly defined by the family's task of child rearing. This view of the family is not new, as was indicated by the earlier discussions of family interaction research and of Swanson's proposal (1968) that ego processes are the means whereby members of groups relate to each other's minds. However, the added treatment here of viewing the child as developing within the family brought additional considerations. Ego processes are the means whereby the family and its individual members work, usually unbeknownst to themselves: (1) to organize their interchanges and their specializations to insure a modicum of accuracy and at the same time to make allowances for the child's earlier inaccuracies; (2) to perpetuate the family and its unity; (3) to redefine its moral, social, and cognitive organizations vis-à-vis the child's developmental changes; (4) to regulate the range of heterogeneity it permits among its members and from its developing, experimenting children; (5) to carry out its intents, of whatever kind, to prepare the child for his future; and (6) to assign and reassign family roles in concert with the child's evolution.

Empirical Findings

Although the present formulation of the family along with its implications for children was not made of whole cloth, its main thrust is different from most past conceptualizations. As a consequence, empirical support from past study is lacking. To examine these ideas further we now turn to findings from a number of analyses of one particular sample and we will, from time to time, consider other work as well.

Since this study will be discussed in depth, it will be economical to describe its methodology first. A prior investigation with the same sample reports even greater detail (Haan, 1974c). Triads composed of mother, father, teenage daughter or son—109 triads in all—who were members of the Institute of Human Development's longitudinal samples, the Oakland Growth Study, and the Berkeley Guidance Study, were seen several years ago as part of a routine follow-up. One parent in each triad was a long-term member of the Institute's longitudinal studies. The offspring were between the ages of 14 and 19, and 31 of the families were represented by both a daughter and a son. Since the sex of the child in each triad would clearly affect the results, 71 families of girls and 69 of boys were constituted for this investigation.

Each family member had been separately interviewed for approximately 1½ to 4 hours about such critical personal-social matters as self, family interaction, occupational involvements, interests, health, and so on. Clinically trained psychologists and a few psychiatric social workers did the interviewing or made second ratings of the 30 ego processes shown in Table II, Chapter 4, after reading the transcripts of each member's interview. (Fragmentation ratings are not included in the analyses to be reported since their distributions in this "normal" sample were decidedly skewed.) At least two evaluations were made of each case, and none was done with the raters having knowledge about other family members, except for what the interviewee himself said. The sets of ratings achieved reasonable reliability (see Haan, 1974c), and the various ratings for each subject were composited to make a single score for the 20 defense and coping functions. Various other data collected by questionnaires, will be considered at later points. These families are generally middle class and somewhat above the average in intelligence and, likely, in emotional stability.

RELATIONSHIPS OF THE ADOLESCENTS' EGO
PROCESSES TO THEIR PARENTS'

To examine the various patterns of association between the adolescents' and the parents' ego processes, stepwise multiple regression models of the parents' ego processes to predict the offspring's processes were constructed separately for the girls' and the boys' triads. In each model, 1 of the 20 ego processes for the adolescents was the dependent variable (analyses were terminated at the point that the next parental process to be added would have had a level of $>.05$; thus each component had a probability level of $\leqslant.05$). The overall number of significant models was large: At the $\leqslant.001$ level, 65% of the girls' and 70% of the boys' models were significant; at the $\leqslant.01$ level, 20% and 15%; at the $\leqslant.05$ level, 15% and 5%. Two of the boys' ego functions—displacement and repression—were not significant. Both of these functions are defensive means of regulating feelings, this suggests that the boys' solutions in this particular regard are independent of their families' modus operandi. The overall strong result, which relates independently assessed ego processes of parents to their adolescent children, is unusual in child-rearing studies and gives some credence to suppositions developed in earlier discussion: Ego processes are apparently a lingua franca of family interchange and may be a useful way of describing the intragroup processes of other intimate groups.

Earlier study (Haan, 1974c) of ego factor scores, based on these same data, had shown that a number of intrafamily ego associations were influenced by SES levels. However at this more specific level of concern with individual processes, the families' SES level made significant contributions to the adolescents' ego functions in only 2 of the 40 models, and both were positive; the girls' intellectuality and reaction formation increase with SES levels. Thus we may assume that SES is a generalized influence which relates to ego functions when these are also represented as general scores. This is not to say that direct associations between ego scores and SES cannot be found (for instance, see Weinstock, 1967b or Miller & Swanson, 1960); however, in these analyses of intrafamily ego patterns, SES was not an important factor in describing the relationship of the parent ego processes to their offspring's.

The individual parental ego processes that made a significant contribution to these multiple regression equations are too numerous for us to consider. (Full details for each model are to be found in Appendix C.) For the explication within this section, each of the parents' ego processes was simply identified as either coping or defense. Consequently the trends depicted for the parents' contributions are more generalized than they actually were. The total amounts of variance explained by each model and the net amounts of positive and negative variances that the parents' coping and defensive processes contributed to each of the adolescents' ego processes are shown in Figures 10 and 11. In analyzing these results, we will not consider the details of predicting single functions, but instead will attend to their broader implications for family ego interregulation.

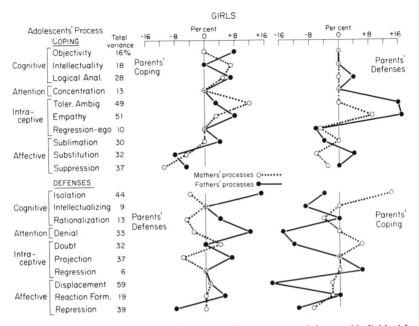

Figure 10. Net variances contributed by parents' processes to adolescents' individual functions.

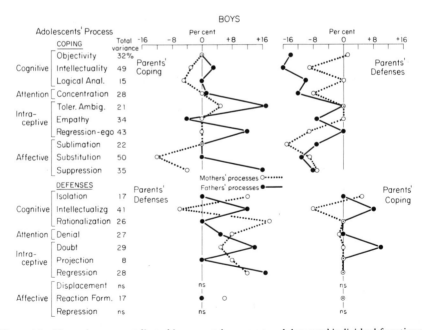

Figure 11. Net variances contributed by parents' process to adolescents' individual functions.

Examining the patterns of total variances explained by the girls' and boys' models, we can see that there is little similarity between the sexes in the functions that are strongly or weakly associated with their parents'. In fact, when each sex's variances for each process were rank ordered and then the boys' and girls' ranks correlated with each other the resulting rho is a $-.45$. Evidently, the implications of parents' processing is very different for each of the sexes, at least for this sample and age group. The two boys' models that have the highest variances are substitution (50%) and intellectuality (49%), findings which suggest that parents' functioning is importantly involved in the boys' achievement and degree of socialization. Girls' displacement (59%) (which was actually insignificant for the boys) empathy (51%), and tolerance of ambiguity (49%) are most strongly associated with the parents' processes. Apparently, then, girls' defensive acting out and coping intraceptiveness are closely associated with their parents' ego processing.

As we turn to the graphic portion of Figures 10 and 11, we need to keep in mind: (1) that the main thrust of the parents' functioning is shown as a net sum which indicates whether the parents' contributions were preponderantly coping or defensive; (2) that the graph should be read across rows to comprehend the overall patterns of mothers' and fathers' coping and defensiveness that are associated with each of the adolescents' functions. In subsequent discussion, the arbitrary convention will be followed of mentioning only those adolescent functions that recruited $\geqslant 10\%$ variance from their parents' processes.

Boys

We will consider the parental patterns associated with the boys' coping processes. Fathers' coping clearly makes strong positive contributions and their defensiveness strong negative contributions to the boys' coping capabilities. In fact, this pattern is the most salient support for the general supposition held by most investigators of child rearing that good begets good. Fathers' coping especially facilitates their sons' intraceptiveness and ability to suppress affective reactions when situationally necessary, while fathers' defensiveness deters the boys' cognitive coping, concentration, and substitution, a pattern probably related to the boys' level of achievement. Mothers' coping has only a weak effect on the boys' coping, and in several specific instances maternal coping actually has an obverse effect on the sons' coping. This is especially marked with the boys' substitution, which suggests that a coping mother does not exert great effort to secure her son's socialization. However, maternal defensiveness tends to prevent the boys' coping, particularly their tendency to sublimate. Thus we can say that coping fathers encourage their sons' coping intraceptiveness and suppressiveness, while fathers' lack of defensiveness encourages the boys' smooth cognitive operation and socialization. Coping mothers have only mild direct effects on their sons' coping and one clear obverse effect, but their lack of defensiveness supports their boys' coping.

Considering the sons' defensive processes, we find that both the mothers' and fathers' defensiveness have important, positive, direct effects. The boys' isolation and rationalization (both cognitive defenses) and regressiveness are encouraged by maternal defensiveness, while their intellectualization, doubt, and regressiveness are encouraged by the fathers' defensiveness. Neither of the parents' coping processes plays an important role in detering the boys' defensiveness. In fact the fathers' coping has an obverse effect, actually encouraging the boy's doubt and intellectualization. Consequently we can say that both paternal and maternal defensiveness draw complementary defensiveness from their sons, a trend that is not importantly deterred by the parents' coping; the boys' cognitive processes are again the most affected; finally the defensiveness of both parents especially contributes to the boys' regressiveness, that is, their tendency to give up when they are faced with problems.

Girls

The immediate, overall impression from the girls' portion of the graph is that their trends are neither as clear nor as salient as the boys', despite the fact that more of their models were significant and the total amount of variance contributed by all the girls' models was actually greater (623% for boys as compared to 652% for girls). At least one important reason for the pallid parent–daughter relations depicted in the graph is that positive and negative variances often canceled each other out when the net amounts were calculated. In other words, even though the girls' processes are more enmeshed with their parents' than are the boys', the parental patterns associated with the girls' processes are more complex and involve more instances of obverse effects, for example, parents' coping being positively associated with the adolescents' defensiveness, or vice versa, or the relationships between coping or defensive functions being negative. (There are 35 such obverse relations for the girls compared to 24 for the boys when a count is made of such instances in all the models.) Obverse relationships occur primarily for the girls' affective regulations and, secondly, for their cognitive processes but occur only for the boys' cognitive processes. Thus we can suggest that the parents' processes have more direct and straightforward implications for their sons than they do for their daughters.

Turning now to the girls' graphs, we can see that the main implication of parents' coping is that their daughters also cope; however obverse maternal and paternal relations occur with the parents' coping diminishing the girls' regulation of feelings in the coping mode (substitution and suppression). Presumably coping parents (as was also the case with mothers and sons) make extra allowances for their daughters' expression of feelings. Moreover, the daughters' coping intraceptiveness—their tolerance of ambiguity and empathy—is strongly and obversely encouraged by their parents', particularly their fathers', defensiveness. Turning to the girls' defensiveness, we find that they generally follow their fathers' suit in defensiveness, most particularly in denying and isolating, but their mothers' defensiveness does not markedly contribute to their own. However, the fathers' coping processes forestall the daughters' defensiveness, most markedly their denial, doubt, displacement, and repressiveness. The most notable effects of mothers' coping on girls defensiveness are obverse: daughters' isolation and, to a lesser extent, their doubt actually being encouraged by maternal coping.

Summary

From this complex set of findings we can make several broad observations:

1. In general, coping parents directly imply coping offspring and defensive parents imply defensive offspring, more strikingly for the boys than for the girls. This direct relationship is an expected one: It follows from the general assumption that when accuracy typifies family interchanges a fertile milieu is provided for the development of accuracy (as well as the reverse for inaccuracy). On its surface the finding is consistent with the theoretical formulation that offspring model their parents. However, this supposition requires, more precisely, that children should prefer and use the *same* process as their parents, and the presentation so far does not address that question.

2. Deterrence effects were found: Boys' coping is prevented by the parents' defensiveness, but the same is not true for the girls. Instead, the mirror image was observed: Daughters' defensiveness is prevented by parents' coping. In other words, the parent–son relationships appear to prevent accuracy in family ego interchanges while the parent–daughter relationships prevent negation. Presumably parents can prevent boys from becoming effective beings if they are markedly defensive. But in a more limited sense, they prevent daughters from becoming ineffective if they are coping—the first is rather like a commission while the second is like an omission. These findings are consistent with the supposition that boys have clear social roles of coping within the family set before them, while the girls are only prevented from becoming defensive by their parents' tendency toward accuracy in family inter-changes. These two contrasting patterns are consistent with the supposition that adolescent boys' relationships with their parents are direct and straightforward, while girls' are more indirect and circuitous, an observation that coincides with Swanson's (1968) suggestion that social conditions should be sought that replicate the ego processes. These girls themselves, their parents, and society are probably not clear about the ways that girls can and should cope, while most everybody has been clear about desired roles for boys.

3. Obverse effects, more numerous for girls, were also found: Most saliently, boys' substitution being obviated by their mothers' coping, boys' doubt by their fathers' coping, girls' suppression and isolation by their mothers' coping, and girls' tolerance of ambiguity and empathy by their fathers' defensiveness. Obverse effects are particularly interesting since they run against the grain of modeling theory, and they may be interpreted here in terms of the integral implications of processing within the family. It seems plausible that coping fathers and coping mothers probably do not compel their adolescent offspring to act in specified ways, but this leaves some uncertainty which probably produces doubt in

the sons in the case of coping fathers or less than effective socialization and restraint of feelings in the girls in the case of coping mothers. The obverse relationship, involving the daughters' isolation, takes a longer clinical reach to arrive at an interpretation. Isolation is a defensive means of not "getting it together," and a particularly strong contribution was made to the girls' isolation by the mothers' own socialization (substitution—14% of the positive variance and doubt, 4% of the negative variance), which suggests these mothers may have presented a problem— perhaps a competitive one—for their daughters by reason of their own smooth socialization and certainty. The obverse relation between the girls' tolerance of ambiguity and empathy and their fathers' defensiveness is probably due to a particular kind of paternal defensiveness. In both instances, the fathers' intellectualizing makes substantial contributions (20% and 18%, respectively) and their repressiveness, contributions of smaller magnitude (3% and 6%). This defensive pattern seems to suggest a degree of paternal passiveness and probably unhappiness that may transfer the initiative for contact and warmth in the father—daughter dyad to the daughters themselves.

4. Of the various sectors of ego processing, the boys' cognitive functions and girls' affective regulations were most reactive to their parents' functioning, suggesting that these two sectors are pivotal concerns for boys and girls personally and for their families as a whole.

5. Some processes appear to be relatively independent of family ego interchange, in other words, self-actional for these adolescents. For boys these processes are defensive affective regulations and for girls, their regressiveness and a mixture of cognitive functions, both coping and defensive (objectivity, intellectuality, intellectualizing, rationalization).

6. Finally, we can note that the inclusion of the fathers in these analyses has been worthwhile; their ego processing has clearly been as important, and in some instances more important, than the mothers' for analyzing the various patterns of family ego interchange.

Thus, we have found direct, deterrent, and obverse implications of parents' ego processing for their adolescent offspring's functioning that suggest altogether a complicated fabric of family ego interchange.

THE FAMILY AS A GROUP

Support for the multidirectional character of the family as a group—as opposed to the view that parents exert causal, unilateral effects—would be findings that a parent—child dyad predicts the other parent as handily as the parents' dyad predicts the child. Although this statement seems self-evident, its implications need more examination particularly in terms of the chronological age of these adolescents. Equal levels of association might occur when children are older and the history of the family involved unilateral effects from parent to child. If mother and father had both exerted like, unidirectional, and additive effects on the child, one could suppose that by near-adulthood either dyad that includes the child might predict one of the parents as effectively as the two parents predict the child. In other words, all members would have come to be as alike as peas in a pod. However, results reported so far already suggest that children do not always do as their parents do. Although we will not be extensively concerned with predicting the parents' functions, they are as handily predicted by the child plus another parent as the child was by two parents (e.g., 75% and 60% of the models predicting the girls' mothers and fathers were significant as the ≤.001 level and 45% and 90% for the boys' parents, compared to 70% predicting the girls and 65% for the boys, a result already reported). In this section we will show that direct, obverse, and deterrent relations, which we have already seen exist between the parent and child, also occur within all dyads, including the parents'. Consequently, the implications of each member's ego processes for all others' are diverse.

Since diversity in family ego processing exists in these samples, we need to inquire about their systematic patterns. If the mother, having preferences for processes *abc*, combines with the father, who prefers processes *def,* will the child use *abc, def,* some combination thereof, or will he construct his own preferred pattern of processes, *ghi*? Here, we suppose that the ego means of resolution used by any two members of these triads constitute an ecology of problem solving paradigms for the third member, so that what the others do is not irrelevant to the third.

John Spiegel's (1972) distinctions among self-actional, interactional, and trans-actional qualities of family exchanges are useful here. If the family's ego patterns do not affect the ego functions of a single member (and the ego scores are reasonably reliable and valid) one could assume that the third member's functions are obdurately his own, in other words, he is self-actional.

If the family's ego patterns directly affect the ego scores of a single member (especially if he is a child) and he reacts in kind, or with some other function, one could assume that the exchange is interactional, that is, an action—reaction para-digm. Much child-rearing research not only assumes the universality and verity of this action—reaction pattern, but also assumes that the parents' actions exert direct effects upon the child and that his reaction is in kind—thus, like begets like. This assumption is accompanied by another—the child contributes little of importance to the parent—child exchange, if in fact he is not entirely a tabula rasa on which his parents write large. Within this condition, the third member's (here the child's) preferred ego functions should come to be identical to those of the other two.

If two family members' ego functions imply (not directly cause) the use of other ego functions by the third member, the exchange may be near to Spiegel's definition of transactional. We say "near" because transactions necessarily involve the construction of reactions that did not exist before in the same precise form. The child must make a redetermination or a reorganization; he *transcends* that which has gone before. Clearly longitudinal study of triads would be necessary to ascertain whether children's adoption of ego patterns not preferred and infrequently used by their parents has this constructivist, emergent quality. Although the design and data of the present study do not permit these phenomena to be tightly analyzed, the results will suggest that it's a good bet that family transactions have occurred and that children have constructed their own actions when their ego functions are strongly associated with, but still not identical to, their parents'. These possibilities are suggested by classifications of obverse and deterrent ego interchanges within family groups.

To examine the suppositions about the integral operations of the family, a count was made within each of three dyads (father–mother, father–child, and mother–child) of the most salient pairings of ego scores. Positive relationships were counted when both members of a dyad had scores that were >60 or <40, and negative relationships were counted when one member's score was >60 and the other's <40. (The ego ratings for the two judges had been composited and then standardized to a mean of 50 and a standard deviation of 10 within each sex and age group.) All such patterns of salient relationship within the entire matrix of family ego scores were counted and classified according to three main patterns: (1) identical—the *same* process for two members, for example, mother's objectivity with father's objectivity; (2) complementary—two *different* coping or two defense functions, for example, mother's objectivity with father's intellectuality; (3) reciprocal—a coping and a defensive process, for example, mother's objectivity and father's isolation. When the positive or negative signs of these relationships are taken into account, they take on the additional meaning of being direct, obverse, or deterrent relations within dyads, patterns of interchange that we already considered in the previous section. This simple method was used after an extensive search of statistical models failed to reveal any more summarizing and continuous score statistics that would permit nonpresumptive comparisons between the three different dyads to be made.

Two main ways of analyzing these counts of salient pairings will be reported: (1) their absolute incidence, in terms of how frequent any one pattern could possibly be, given the ego model of 20 processes and samples of 69 for the boys' families and 71 for the girls'; (2) the relative proportions of the different patterns of pairings within the family ego interchange when the common denominator is the total actual number of salient pairings found. We will consider the analysis of the absolute frequencies first; the results are presented in Table XIII.

Clearly none of these frequencies is great, given all possibilities, but the total array serves to illustrate that members of these families do not duplicate each other's processes more often than they complement or reciprocate with some other process. Moreover, the dyads which include the child do not have a greater incidence of identity than is found for the parents' dyads. However, when all three dyads are taken together to achieve a representation of the family, some kinds of associations are more frequent. The boys' and girls' triads showed only slight differences and were combined for economy's sake, and then their frequencies were ordered. Table XIV shows three systematic trends: (1) Members' defenses generally have stronger direct implications for the family than do members' coping processes. A certain logic underlies this observation: People's inaccuracies within social inter-

Table XIII
Absolute Frequency of Salient Dyadic Patterns in Families

Family Dyads	Identical patterns				Complementary patterns				Reciprocal patterns			
	Positive[a]		Negative[b]		Positive[a]		Negative[b]		Positive[a]		Negative[b]	
	Boys'	Girls'	Boys'	Girls'	Boys'	Girls'	Boys'	Girls'	Boys'	Girls'	Boys'	Girls'
	(Coping—same process)				(Coping with coping)				(Coping with defense)			
Father–mother	5%	5%	4%	4%	5%	5%	4%	4%	5%	4%	5%	6%
Father–child	8	6	2	3	6	6	3	4	5	5	6	6
Mother–child	5	7	4	3	5	6	4	4	4	4	7	6
Total	18	18	10	11	16	16	11	11	14	14	19	17
	(Defense—same process)				Defense with defense							
Father–mother	7	7	6	4	5	6	4	5				
Father–child	7	9	4	4	6	8	3	4				
Mother–child	9	7	6	4	5	6	4	5				
Total	23	24	16	11	16	21	11	13				

NOTE: The indices represent the percentage of dyadic ego patterns found out of the total possible within each classification, for example, reciprocity—10 of mothers' coping × 10 fathers' defense (and vice versa) = 200 × 69 boys' families = 13,800 possibilities; or coping identity—10 of the mothers' matched the same 10 of the fathers' × 69 families = 690 possibilities.

[a]Positive relations: both members score > 60 or < 40.
[b]Negative relations: one member's score > 60 and the other < 40.

223

Table XIV

Rank Order of Various Patterns of Family Ego Interchange by Their Absolute Frequencies (Summed for Boys' and Girls' Triads)

Direction of relationship	Pattern	Sums[a]	Nature of relationship
+	Defensive identity	47	Direct
+	Defensive complementarity	37	Direct
+	Coping identity	36	Direct
−	Coping–defense reciprocity	36	Deterrent
+	Coping complementarity	32	Direct
+	Coping–defense reciprocality	29	Obverse
−	Defense identity	27	Obverse
−	Defense complementarity	24	Obverse
−	Coping complementarity	22	Obverse
−	Coping identity	21	Obverse

[a]Boys' and girls' frequencies together.

changes has the effect of forcing others to act. Meanings must be clarified and social understandings and the moral balance restored; moreover distortion from one member tends to anger and confuse the other, which facilitates his countering distortion (He who lives by the sword will die by the sword?). However, coping by one member makes it more possible for another to choose his own response; (2) the absolute incidence of obverse relationships are not great compared to what they possibly could be, but nevertheless they occur, and in several forms, as can be seen in Table XIII: (3) various direct and deterrent associations occur with moderate frequency in coping interchanges: directly identifying with other members' coping, coping when others are not defensive, or coping in complement to another member's coping.

This analysis is limited in two ways. It assumes that all possible combinations of the 20 processes are equally probable and that all pairs of processes can be expected to have the salient patterns indicated by the standard scores of ≥ 60 or ≤ 40. Therefore, we move on to a description of the relative proportions of the various patterns within the actual family ego interchange. Since there were only slight differences between the boys' and girls' triads they have been merged, and the resulting proportions are shown in Table XV. Two observations can be made: (1) There is no real difference between the three dyads in the size or the patterns of their relationships, and (2) again members' defensive processes are more frequently drawn into association than are their coping processes. Figure 12 shows the overall actual proportions for the various patterns when their signs are taken into account. Clearly, obverse relationships describe more of the family interchange than the absolute frequencies suggested. They account for 43% of the familie's ego interchanges, while deterrent and direct relations are almost tied at 28% and 29%.

In this section, a number of varied and somewhat abstract results have been brought to bear on the question of the family's integral operations. To define and describe these families' interchanges in terms of content would require knowing the

Table XV
Relative Proportions of Salient Dyadic Patterns within Families' Ego Interchanges (Boys' and Girls' Triads Summed and Averaged)

Sign of relation	Mother–father		Mother–child		Father–child	
	Coping	Defense	Coping	Defense	Coping	Defense
	Identity: Within same process					
Positive[a]	1%	2%	1%	2%	1%	2%
Negative[b]	1	1	1	1	1	1
	Complementary: Between two coping or two defensive processes					
Positive[a]	11	13	11	15	12	16
Negative[b]	9	12	8	10	7	10
Totals	22	28	21	28	21	29
	Reciprocal: Between a coping and a defensive process					
	C/D	D/C	C/D	D/C	C/D	D/C
Positive[b]	11	11	11	11	10	12
Negative[c]	13	13	15	15	16	13

[a]Direct relationships.
[b]Obverse relationships.
[c]Deterrent relationships.

Figure 12. Dyadic ego patterns in both samples: proportions of direct, obverse, and deterrent associations.

circumstances and conditions of the specific problems that they face and resolve. Thus later sections are concerned with one family problem we can assume is common to these triads—dealing with the younger members' adolescence and all that this entails for the family group as a whole. We have seen in this section, which has included all members of the triads, that various members' functions do not often imply that other members will use the same function, that is, directly model the member, even if she or he is in the power position of being the mother or father. Deterrent and obverse implications also exist. Finally there is a suggestion in both the major analyses that members' defensiveness forces other members to react in kind, while one member's coping tends not to foreclose on others' options.

PARENTS' INTENTIONS OF DIRECTING OR FACILITATING ADOLESCENTS' DEVELOPMENT

Two kinds of parental intentions, representing different formulations of their responsibilities for child rearing, were described earlier in this chapter and were called contravention and facilitation. In the former instance, parents intend to influence their children in all important ways, but this does not necessarily mean that they are authoritarian or nonhumanitarian, for they may well accomplish their ends by skillfully manipulating rewards and punishment and by offering their children "a vote." Contravention is based on parents' implicit theory of human development. They believe that people are importantly and definitively shaped by the external influences brought to bear on them. As parents, they think they should—in fact, are obliged to—have the most important impact on their children. The second formulation, that of facilitation, is based on parents' suppositions that children and people develop by constructing their own meanings and solutions, but that progress does not occur without input from others. The facilitative parent defines development as the evolution and construction of selfhood.

Thus, the two positions logically lead to the parents' having different anticipations about their roles in building their children's future. Consistent with their views, the facilitative parents feel they must take chances on the child's future, while contravening parents feel they are obliged to insure their child's future by determining his character. In an approximate way the two positions represent a Freudian and a Piagetian formulation of how parents and adults help children grow, most successfully and efficiently, from infancy to adulthood. Parental contravention should relate to the offspring's eventual development of "good" character, that is, one that is well buttressed with effective defenses, while parental facilitation should relate to the eventual development of coping capability. Here we are concerned with transitional adolescents, and we need to remind ourselves that facilitative family situations necessarily result in young members taking a more erratic and self-directed course.

To examine these matters, three scales were generated which represent all family members' views; 16 questionnaire items concerned with various members' views of parental, adult, and peer influences on the adolescents, along with a number of parental values that represent the adolescents' effective socialization—neatness, good manners, and obedience—or their construction of selfhood—curiosity, independence—were submitted to factor analysis and orthogonal, varimax rotation. The three resulting factors accounted for 44%, 29%, and 31% of the variance. The first factor, called *contravention/parents,* represents the parents' views that contravention is not only important but also effective with their children. The second factor, called *contravention/child,* primarily represents the adolescent's perspective that both parents are contravening and not facilitative, along with several other items that reflect the father's view that contravention is the method of choice. The third factor, called *parental facilitation,* represents the adolescent's view that the father is facilitative, as well as the mother's indication that she values facilitation over contravention. These three factor scores became the dependent variables on which the families' SES levels and the adolescents' ego processes were regressed. The number of families having these parental intention scores and all succeeding ones representing parental actions was less than before—47 girls' and 42 boys' triads. The results for these analyses are shown in Table XVI.

Contravention/parents is significantly and positively related to defensive regression in the girls but to coping intellectuality in the boys, qualified for the boys by a substantial negative association with tolerance of ambiguity. Thus parental attempts to determine the adolescents' course has differential meanings for the two sexes: A readiness in girls to retreat to irresponsible, non—age appropriate strategies in dealing with problems, and a heightened but likely rigid intellectuality in boys. Evidently contravening parents are somewhat more "successful" with boys than with girls. *Contravention/child* is associated with the girls' lack of intellectuality and their inability to restrain their affective expression in a coping way (suppression). For the boys, *contravention/child* is negatively associated with both their defensive and coping regression and the families' SES levels, but is positively associated with their doubt, intellectualizing, and suppression. Again contravention seems most deleterious for the girls, but the boys' status, as it is described by this pattern of results, again seems brittle and uncertain. Finally we see that *parental facilitation* is strongly and positively associated with girls' task orientation, but is evidently not important for the boys' use of various ego processes.

Taken altogether, these results for boys generally, but not strongly, support the expectancy that contravention should build character. However, contravention by parents appears to present problems for the girls, who were probably more adult-determined—or oversocialized—when they entered adolescence than were the boys, and so additional pressure may have complicated their development.

FAMILIES' RECOGNITION OF ADOLESCENTS' DISEQUILIBRIUM

The family's reactions to its young members' developmental movement are integral to formulating the role of processes, since families must reorganize themselves when any one of their members make fundamental changes in themselves. To

Table XVI
Adolescents' Ego Processes Related to Parental Intentions

| Girls | | | | | Adolescent process | Boys | | | |
Adolescent process	β	F Ratio	%	r		β	F Ratio	%	r
					Contravention/parents				
Regression	.32	4.91[c]	10	.32	Intellectuality	.45	9.42[b]	14	.38
Model		4.91[c]	10	.32	Tolerance of ambiguity	-.31	4.33[c]	9	-.19
					Model		5.60[b]	23	.48
					Contravention/child				
Intellectuality	-.33	6.18[a]	15	-.39	Regression-ego	-.44	9.71[b]	9	-.30
Suppression	-.32	5.87[a]	10	-.38	Regression	-.43	6.49[b]	7	-.30
Model		7.22[b]	25	.50	SES	-.43	8.45[b]	7	-.16
					Doubt	.38	5.69[b]	8	.05
					Intellectualizing	.35	5.85[b]	8	.12
					Suppression	.29	3.29[c]	5	.20
					Model		4.55[b]	45	.68
					Parental facilitation				
Model		7.22[b]	25	.50	(not significant)				
Concentration	.37	6.84[b]	13	.37					
Model		6.84[b]	13	.37					

[a] p
[a] p ≤ .001.
[b] p ≤ .01.
[c] p ≤ .05.

illustrate, a recent study (Haan, 1974d) found that well-functioning elderly people are considerably more intraceptive and interpersonally engaged but, not surprisingly, less cognitively invested and ambitious than younger people. These changes would necessitate changes in other family members as well. Berman (1973) has made a very interesting and detailed clinical study of a family over a year's time as it prepared itself for the father's open-heart surgery. He found distinct patterns of reorganization. Changes in adolescents probably demand special validation from their families, since the achievement of adulthood involves a primary and ritualized recognition of the young as social equals. In writing of his own youth, George Bernard Shaw made the point: "All men are in a false position in society, until they have realized on their possibilities and imposed them on their neighbors [1952, p. 103]." Establishing one's self as a social equal entails being a moral equal, and neither step is easily taken by the adolescent. Moreover long-established groups, like families, are often lethargic about reorganizing their structures and processes of operation, and some families experience the adolescents' pressure toward self-redefinition as a threat to their integrity. Changes in the young foreshadow important shifts in parental roles as well. Hypotheses elaborated earlier suggested that the family's ability to recognize and accommodate to its members' changes should facilitate the adolescent's coping, since this type of familial context would support his open-ended problem solving. The family's reluctance to change may make it necessary for the adolescent to engage in a series of complicated defensive maneuvers, not merely in reaction to his parents, but also in response to his own sense of uncerainty about the legitimacy of his self-redefinition. Recognition of families' "stickiness" in these regards is the basis of some psychotherapists' contention that the young individual cannot change without his family's changing.

To test these hypotheses, three scales of the families' reactions to adolescent changes were developed. The original items, 29 in all, were mostly from questionnaires that all family members had completed. Their contents represented various members' views of the adolescents' concern with their own position in regard to questions of right and wrong, the parents' reactions to these adolescent concerns, and all members' admission or denial that family disagreements did occur. The adolescents' vigor in defining their own moral positions was assumed to be one important indicator of their own attempts at self-redefinition, while their families' reactions were expected to represent the context of their efforts. The items were submitted to factor analysis with varimax rotation; three factors of approximately equal power emerged that accounted respectively for 32%, 33%, 35% of the total variance.

The first, called *disequilibrium/mother,* is defined by items that indicate both the mother's and adolescent's views that the offspring is actively addressing issues of right and wrong, that the mother encourages this process and that there are disagreements within the family. This factor represents, then, an open admission and an active, mutual negotiation of adolescents' disequilibriums.

The second factor variable, called *disequilibrium/father,* is defined by items that indicate the father takes somewhat the same role as was described for the mother in the first factor: The father reports that the adolescent is actively addressing moral issues and that there are family disagreements, but a few other items indicate that the mother denies that such is the case and she instead describes a harmonious family context.

The third factor, called *usual adolescent problems,* includes items that reflect parents' feelings that adolescents are unpredictable. Both mothers' and fathers' items are included, and the fathers, taking the traditional paternal role, report that they take definite measures to prevent their adolescents from wrongdoing.

These three scores became the dependent variables on which the adolescents' ego functions and the families SES scores were regressed. All these analyses were significant for the girls while only *usual adolescent problems* was for the boys.

Turning now to the separate models, shown in Table XVII, we can first see that the adolescent's defenses are independent of these measures of disequilibrium. Only coping functions are recruited, and they do not always make a positive contribution. The girl's ego regression and objectivity appear to be encouraged, but their concentration and affective regulation via substitution are discouraged by the maternal context of *disequilibrium/mother.* The pattern associated with *disequilibrium/father,* although similar to the mothers', has important differences: Again ego regression, but not empathy, is positively encouraged, while suppression of affect is discouraged by the paternal context of disagreement. The differences between the two patterns seem to suggest that the girls' disagreements with their mothers imply more detachment and less social compliance for daughters, while their disagreements with their fathers imply more interpersonal sensitivity and expression of feeling.

The variable *usual adolescent problems* is associated with ego regression and objectivity for girls, again suggesting that the daughters' detachment and working through the past in terms of the present occur within a context of family problems. The boys' intellectuality and tolerance of ambiguity (probably here a tolerance of dissonance) is positively associated with this variable along with a means of problem resolution that represents a here-and-now attitude (low ego regression).

The analyses of the family disequilibrium, taken altogether, lend further support to the suggestion that the girls in this sample are much more actively involved than are the boys in attempting to renegotiate their status within their families. The girls as well as the boys who are in disequilibrium with their families, are not *all* coping; instead, they are coping in some ways but not in others. Moreover these results clarify some of the occasionally anomalous descriptions of the girls' processes that have been made so far. They suggest, first, that the adolescents' questionirg and family disagreements are more differentiating of girls' ego functioning than of the boys'. Second, the content of the results indicates that the *lack* of disagreements does not generally promote either sex's coping, as is generally expected by the design of most research. A particularly interesting result is that the adolescents' ego regression significantly and positively participates in each of the girls' models but makes a negative contribution to the single, significant model for the boys. If any

Table XVII
Adolescents' Ego Processes Related to Family Disequilibrium

Adolescent process		Girls			Adolescent process		Boys		
	β	F Ratio	%	r		β	F Ratio	%	r
					Disequilibrium/mother				
Concentration	-.58	14.57[a]	18	.42			(Not significant)		
Regression-ego	.44	13.38[a]	13	-.30					
Objectivity	.36	5.98[c]	10	.06					
Substitution	-.24	3.77[c]	6	-.36					
Model		9.17[a]	47	.68					
					Disequilibrium/father				
Regression-ego	.52	12.93[a]	11	.33			(Not significant)		
Suppression	-.31	4.70[c]	12	-.30					
Empathy	.29	4.30[c]	7	-.14					
Model		6.17[a]	31	.55					
					Usual adolescent problems				
Objectivity	.26	3.11[c]	10	.32	Regression-ego	-.47	8.80[b]	11	.29
Regression-ego	.25	3.02[c]	6	.32	Intellectuality	.39	6.58[b]	9	-.19
Model		4.17[c]	16	.40	Tolerance of ambiguity	.33	4.82[c]	8	.25
					Model		4.95[b]	29	.54

[a] $p \leqslant .001$.
[b] $p \leqslant .01$.
[c] $p \leqslant .05$.

of the ego functions reflect the developmental process of reworking one's past in terms of one's present, this function should.

FAMILY PRESCRIBED ROLES

The integral quality of family interchange produces some pressure for assigning and limiting the number and character of roles that members may take, as it does in other intimate groups. Although this pressure may serve to unify groups, it is logically countered in families by the consequences of the children's development. Their changes mean they will want to define themselves, and to work toward leave-taking and eventually attenuating their family participation. Families' expectancies that their developing members will set their own roles should encourage adolescents' coping. Families' prescriptiveness with regard to roles was expected to complicate the adolescents' course and confront them with the alternatives of premature emotional withdrawal, actual leave-taking, or restricting their own self-development. Whatever the course, the offspring will need to evoke defenses to protect his integrity, but in each case the pattern of defenses would be different.

Again three scales were generated from an initial group of 12 questionnaire items by means of factor analysis; the resulting factors accounted for approximately equal amounts of variance: 31%, 36%, and 33%. The first factor, called *prescriptiveness/child,* is composed entirely of items that represent the adolescents' contention that their parents expect conformity to parental values as well as to their ideas of worldly success, and, negatively, that their parents are interested in their offspring's developing toward individually chosen goals. The second factor, called *child adherence/parents* is composed of items that indicate both parents' suppositions that the adolescent adheres to parental values in regard to a variety of moral, social, interpersonal, and political issues. The third factor, called *child adherence/child* represents the adolescent's views on these same issues and his indication that he does adhere to his parents' values. The results of these analyses are shown in Table XVIII.

Girls who report that their parents are prescriptive in regard to family roles are particularly task oriented; the same result occurs if the parents themselves report that their daughters adhere to family standards, but here the girls' concentration is accompanied and qualified by regressiveness, suggesting that the pattern represents social compliance rather than self-directed accomplishment. Neither of the first two analyses of *prescriptiveness/child* or *child adherence/parents* is significant for the boys. The adolescents' view of their own adherence to parental standards is significant for both sexes, being negatively related to the girls' suppression, but strongly and positively related to the boys' suppression and their lack of intellectuality. As has occurred before, the impact of the parents' more deliberate child-rearing actions has diverse, even opposite effects for the two sexes. In these analyses of role prescriptions and standards, it appears that the adolescents' task orientation and impulse control are most affected, the girls in a general negative way. In

Table XVIII
Adolescents' Ego Processes Related to Parents' Role Prescriptions

Adolescent process	Girls				Adolescent process	Boys			
	β	F Ratio	%	r		β	F Ratio	%	r
					Prescriptiveness/child				
Concentration	.29	4.37[c]	9	.30			(Not significant)		
Model		4.37[c]	9	.30					
					Child adherence/parents				
Concentration	.43	8.06[b]	9	.30			(Not significant)		
Regression	.32	4.30[c]	8	.13					
Model		4.50[b]	17	.42					
					Child adherence/child				
Suppression	.29	−4.18[c]	9	.29	Suppression	63	18.02[a]	22	−.47
Model	.29	4.18[c]	9	.29	Intellectuality	−37	6.06[c]	11	.09
					Model		9.22[a]	33	.37

[a] $p \leq .001$.
[b] $p \leq .01$.
[c] $p \leq .05$.

233

contrast, the boys, although highly restrained emotionally, are not particularly intellectual.

DIVERSITY OF PREFERRED EGO PROCESSES WITHIN FAMILIES

Families' degrees of tolerance toward their members' use of diverse and different ego processes was earlier described as an intrinsic aspect of family life. For instance, we wonder sometimes whether a family can continue to relate to a member who has become different in some way—because he has been away and changed, or is unexpectedly seized by an odd and new passion that is outside his family's ken. Some families work energetically to preserve homogeneity, that is, they insist upon standardizing their members' ways of operating so that their differences will not threaten the fabric of family solidarity. Others tolerate diversity without seeming to fear disintegration. Logically, there has to be a limit to the diversity that a group can permit and still maintain unity since groups are not groups unless they share a modicum of commonality. However, this study is of intact family units. Still, diversity is probably a strain even in these families. Chilman (1968) notes that unhappiness is reported to be the greatest for women during the ages of 40 to 50 and for men between 50 and 60. Whatever are the problems that adults personally experience at these ages, it is usually the time of their offspring's late adolescence— a time when the younger members strain family solidarity by engaging in new, experimental forms of problem solving, and in fact, force reorganization of the family's modes of operation by leaving home. From a different theoretical perspective, Neugarten (1968) and others have called this phenomenon the period of the "empty nest."

In general, family members' coping should be encouraged when diversity is permitted, while defensiveness—a retrenchment to serve individual integrity—should occur when diversity is discouraged. However the transitional, and therefore defensive-prone, state of these adolescents makes a strict test of this supposition impossible, at least in regard to them.

Nevertheless, to explore this conceptualization, scores were generated for each family group's coping and defensive homogeneity—heterogeneity. Squared deviation scores were calculated for the ranges of each of the ego functions within families (including all available offspring); these were divided by the number of members to adjust for family size, and then summed for the coping and defensive modes. To identify the family patterns associated with diversity, the ego functions of *all* members were regressed on each of the homogeneity scores. As can be seen in Table XIX, all models were significant at the .001 level. Thus heterogeneity does have systematic relationships with various patterns of family ego functions, but the question remains as to what kind.

In the girls' families, homogeneity in coping is primarily related to the mothers' task orientation (concentration), their projectivity, intolerance of ambiguity, and

Table XIX
Relationship of Members' Ego Processes to the Coping and Defensive Homogeneity of the Family

β	Fathers' processes	β	Mothers' processes	β	Adolescents' processes
			Coping homogeneity: Girls' families		
		.63	Concentration	−.41	Projection
(Not significant)		.49	Projection	−.21	Tolerance of ambiguity
		−.35	Suppression		
		−.30	Tolerance of ambiguity		

Model R = .68; F = 7.91[a]; total variance = 46%

β	Fathers' processes	β	Mothers' processes	β	Adolescents' processes
			Coping homogeneity: Boys' families		
		−.43	Empathy	−.27	Doubt
				.21	Projection

Model R = .52; F ratio = 7.88[a]; total variance = 27%

β	Fathers' processes	β	Mothers' processes	β	Adolescents' processes
			Defensive homogeneity: Girls' families		
−.31	Reaction formation	.48	Denial	−.42	Objectivity
−.31	Denial	.29	Concentration	.31	Tolerance of ambiguity
−28	Intellectuality	.24	Logical analysis		
.26	Repression				
.23	Sublimation				

Model R = .52; F 6.56[a]; total variance = 27%

β	Fathers' processes	β	Mothers' processes	β	Adolescents' processes
			Defensive homogeneity: Boys' families		
.41	Doubt			−.40	Reaction formation
.36	Repression			−.21	Doubt
−.35	Reaction formation			−.24	Rationalization
				.20	Tolerance of ambiguity

Model R = .73; F = 9.53[a]; total variance = 53%

[a] $p \leqslant .001$.
[b] $p \leqslant .01$.
[c] $p \leqslant .05$.

inability to suppress their feelings; the fathers' processes are not involved. Like their mothers, the daughters are intolerant of ambiguity, but they are not projective. In the boys' families, coping homogeneity again does not involve the fathers' processes, but it is associated with the mothers' lack of empathy. The sons are projective, but not doubting. These characterizations of family homogeneity accord with our expectancies since the mothers' defensiveness and lack of coping intraceptiveness are associated with family standardization in both samples; however the picture of the adolescents' themselves is one of mixed coping and defense. Fathers' processes are independent of the familys' coping diversity in both samples.

The fathers' processes are saliently involved, however, in predicting defensive homogeneity in both sets of families; moreover, two replications of fathers' processes occur between the triads: Fathers' repressiveness is positively associated and their reaction formations negatively associated with the family's defensive homogeneity. Further, in the girls' families defensive homogeneity is positively associated with the fathers' sublimation but is negatively associated with their denial and intellectuality. In the boys' families, fathers' doubt also encourages homogeneity. The girls' mothers again contribute to homogeneity if they are task oriented, but this time only if they are also denying, though still logical. The girls lack of objectivity but tolerance of ambiguity contributes to family's defensive homogeneity. The boys are negatively described. Like their fathers, they do not evoke reaction formations, nor are they doubting nor rationalizing. Like the girls, the boys are tolerant of ambiguity within the family context of homogeneity.

The description of the parents' ego processes seems to be consistent with their not tolerating diversity. The curious matter is that adolescents of both sexes are tolerant of ambiguity within the family context of defensive homogeneity—it may be that this is the only way they can survive at this stage in their development within these families that evidently require standardization.

SELF-PERPETUATION OF THE FAMILY

No empirical support can be offered in regard to these families' interest in perpetuating themselves, since they are still together geographically, and from all appearances psychologically as well. A follow-up at a later date should permit some of the following assumptions and questions to be examined: 10 years from the last observations, most of these families should still exist as emotional but not geolocal units. The questions relevant to the present view of adolescents and their families will be, At what costs and benefits? With what psychological and social arrangements? Beyond affection and material security, there should be psychological benefits since the family is regarded as serving not only to conserve the continuities of historic self-definitions, but also to corroborate and validate the fact that changes in self-definition have actually occurred. On the other hand, expenses are also assumed since the interdependencies of families require some degree of giving-in, giving-up, and re-negotiation to reconcile the individual enterprises of all members.

Presumably one of two conditions should obtain with the families of great homogeneity, who prescribed roles, who were unable or unwilling to negotiate their adolescents' disequilibriums, and whose parental members thought they should contravene in the younger members' development. At a later date these families should be either: (1) organized much as before and likely still in propinquity; however there should be evidence that some toll was taken on the younger members' development, or (2) the pressure of the younger members' bid for selfhood will have resulted in the disintegration of the family with different expense to the younger members' development. In the first instance, the expense should be the constriction of the young person's selfhood and means of ego operation, and in the second a diminished intraceptiveness and a defective regulation of emotions and impulses. Presumably one general condition should obtain in the families of ego heterogeneity who negotiated the adolescents' disequilibriums, who did not prescribe roles, and whose parent members intended to facilitate their younger members' development. The general condition of family intactness through reform of its means of operation may or may not involve geolocality, depending on various members' environmental opportunities, but the younger members should be characterized by a repertoire of coping functions and therefore a clearer sense of self.

Since we cannot know the fate of these particular families at this time, we will turn to a synthesis of findings from a number of studies (see Haan, 1971) made several years ago. The occasion was an attempt to define what is meant by "the generation gap," and the young people of interest were college students who were not activists, student activists, and "hippies" or "underground" people. A particularly intriguing observation within the present context was the fact that the hippies, who had less contact and interaction with their parents in any of the other groups, typically wanted to form an ideal family of nonconsanguinous people.

General findings from a number of studies (Braungart, 1969; Flacks, 1967; Haan et al., 1968, 1973; Holstein et al., 1974; Watts & Whittaker, 1968) showed that the students, particularly those who were morally conventional, had the most frequent contact with their parents, the activists next, and the hippies the least. Germane to the present formulation are these young people's views of their parents' child rearing styles. The hippies described their parents as muting family aggression and as being overinvolved with their parenting roles—intrusive, warm, overprotective, worried about their offspring's future and possible failure. These family-alienated youth appeared to have experienced parental contraventions delivered with loving, permeating care. The students, who were still family-tied, seemed to feel that they had experienced parental styles that represented a more direct version of parental contravention. They described their parents as operating according to clearly defined rules and schedules of contingent privileges and punishments based on the assumption, which was correct from the students' point of view, that the family was value-congruent. Finally the activists (these were the activists of the early 1960s, more of whom had been identified as morally principled) seemed to have experienced a variety of parental facilitation. They described their parents as being very clear about their offspring's responsibility over their own fate: Thus the parents were characterized as having encouraged independence, curiosity, and reasoning in their offspring, but that they were comparatively less warm.

Clearly the ex post facto interpretation of these findings cannot be a convincing support for the varying natures of family self-perpetuation in relationship to earlier familial context as the results of longitudinal study would be. There is one study of young people's leave-taking that has relevance to the present formulation (Silber, Coelho, Murphey, Hamburg, Pearlin, & Rosenberg, 1961). Highly competent, college-bound adolescents were selected while they were still high school seniors; their methods of coping with problems of college selection and eventually with their adjustment away from home were intensively investigated. Of particular interest here were the investigators' observations that the adolescents were objective about their parents' values—concerned but not necessarily complying. Parents unequivocally expressed their preferences of colleges, and if the offspring took a contrary position, the parents accepted it, even though they were sometimes frankly disappointed, but not, it is reported, in a way that was disrespectful of the adolescents. One mother is quoted, "She is very independent. I tried to steer her in the right direction, but she has her own ideas [p. 523]." It would appear that open negotiation but eventual adolescent determination occurred within the families of these especially competent younger people.

We have been concerned with the nature of adolescent leave-taking and have assumed that it makes for strains. The family status quo not only represents the continuities of social conditions for all members, but it is also integral to all members' self-constructions. That the young adult's leave-taking is a time of disruption seems to square with common experience. Consequently, another way to evaluate the meaning of the family tie is to consider family cohesion in disastrous situations when it might have been better for members to separate. Several examples come to mind. The first is Bettelheim's (1964) graceless criticism of the Jews who went to their death—he uses the Anne Frank family as an example— because they maintained their family groupings rather than separating. The other two are empirical studies of natural, not man-made, disasters. Drabek's (1969) study of families threatened by a flood in Denver, Colorado, and Moore's (1963) study of families forewarned of a hurricane. Both investigators reported that their subject families remained together, sometimes at cost.

Conclusion

This lengthy and complex series of analyses has produced a plethora of specific results that will not be reiterated here. Instead, I want to focus on their main implications for describing individuals in families, families as groups, and perhaps groups in general:

1. Processes have proven to be a productive means of characterizing (a) the intrafamilial activity of the groups as a whole—describing a kind of ecology—and (b) the developmental efforts of the child as he moves through adolescence toward his own preferred methods of problem solving.

2. Presumably the formulation of process is as good a candidate for describing the family's transmission of sophistication to the young as other variables that have been used to represent the child's learning. However there was little indication that he learns (or here that he comes to prefer) the same means as his parents. Instead it seems likely that he constructs his own preferred processes in transaction with his family. Evidences of identity, complementarity, and reciprocality within and between the coping and defensive modes were found, and their positive or negative

forms indicated that processes within dyads have direct, deterrent, or obverse effects. Defensiveness in one member evidently compels defensiveness in another to a greater extent than does a member's coping. It was argued that defensiveness in one dyadic partner narrows the other's options since he must work then to correct the balance within a context of mild social disruption. Moreover one person's defensiveness can come to be a kind of life solution for another or for the family or the group.

3. The character of the parent–child patterns showed that boys have more expected, straightforward relations with their parents than do girls. Various aphoristic statements fit the parent–son relationships: Coping begets coping, defensiveness begets defensiveness, defensiveness deters coping. However, the clearest findings for the girls suggest that coping only deters defensiveness, an observation that suggests nothing about how family transmission might positively affect girls. As a matter of fact, obverse relations were more frequent for girls. However, the analyses of family actions were frequently significant for girls and most predictive of their coping. Boys are evidently more reactive to who their parents are, while girls are evidently more responsive to what their parents do. I expect this pattern obtains because parents want to "do" more to their girls than to their boys. Congruent with these observations are the contrasting patterns of (a) persistent associations between the girls' affective regulations and their parents' processes, and (b) persistent associations between the boys' cognitive processes and their parents' processes. The pivotal problem of family exchange for girls appears, then, to be their emotional regulation, but for boys it is the effectiveness of their thinking.

4. That parents' intentions, the families' reaction to the adolescents' disequilibrium, their requirements as to role assumption, and the families' diversity should predict coping was more strongly supported for the girls than for the boys. When the boys' results were significant, they tended to suggest that the families' requirements, rather than their openness, built "good character" at the expense of individual liberation. Perhaps the most useful aspect of the processes, as the primitive elements of these analyses, was their arrangement as a "complete" map with various topographical features that made it possible to ask questions concerning the comparative patterns of coping and defending within the different ego sectors as these converged or diverged between and within generations. If the foci had been the contents of personalities, the generational differences in life time within the families would have made it difficult to address these questions clearly. The process view has the advantage, compared to formulations of states or traits, that children (and people of different cultures) can be seen to use the same processes which differ for the various age groups only in their complexity and integration, even when the young clearly are not as competent in kind as adults (or people of other cultures).

The variables used in these analyses—that is, family homogeneity, disequilibrium, parental intentions, role prescriptions, family self-perpetuation—are processes too, group processes that are specific to the ongoing functioning of families that have the unique task of rearing adolescents. Thus the analyses related intraindividual processes to social processes shared by members of family groups. The latter were defined not only by the personal commitments parents themselves make but also by the accomplishments that children and society expect from families. When children's development is seen within this context, the family's processes are integral to the younger members' growth. In the light of the present results, families seem irreplaceable unless the child can develop within some other similarly structured, intimate primary group. How else might a young person experience a context of particularized requiring and loving that provides the feedback and a sounding board for his trial runs at being a moral and social equal? Less-personalized collectivities surely do not have the investments in their own perpetuation, their own self-definitions, and in the young member to go to the trouble of providing these kinds of feedback. Foster care families are an example of family groups that readily and frequently dissolve and re-form with new memberships. Their inadequacies as vehicles for child rearing are well known, but these are usually regarded as being due to deficiencies in loving or inappropriate child-rearing techniques.

Just as the taxonomy of the ego processes is offered by the ego model, a taxonomy of group processes, specific to families containing adolescents, was offered here along with a description of the interregulation of the two sectors as representing the interchange between intraindividual and social context. Just as the definition of ego as a state was rejected earlier, a definition of family status in terms of the quantities of love and power exerted by the parents was rejected here. The family processes were meant to reflect what families do, and the intraindividual processes became descriptions of what individual members do within the social context. Clearly the more formal aspects of the family's organization and decision making, which were not included in these analyses, are also important to consider. Swanson (1968) is concerned with such formulations of formal structures and has so far made one report (Swanson, 1974) which presented consistent associations between forms of family decision making and adolescents' cognitive structural developments.

The well-functioning family group was defined in terms of the family's basic notions of child-rearing tasks and by the criterion of generally coping parents' producing generally coping offspring. (This definition, which featured the family's openness to the adolescent's changes, seems to be very near to Argyris' [1975] recent description of his Model Two organizations.) However, there was no expectancy, given the adolescent's cognitive structural changes and the family's complementary needs of social structural change, that offspring between the ages of 14 to 18 years belonging to coping families would themselves be consistently coping. Malfunctioning families were defined in the analyses as (1) those that exact irrecoverable costs from their members or (2) those that fail to perpetuate themselves as emotional groups beyond the time when the younger members have free choice about whether or not they will continue their participation in some meaningful form. Moreover, well-functioning and malfunctioning people cannot be defined, simply and naively, by the criterion of their family's coping, since we know from common experience that some people "rise out of ashes" and cope despite their "bad" backgrounds; moreover, the results themselves suggest that more than infrequently, coping parents do not always have coping children, at least during the age range we have considered. The ego model led to a hunt for the elements—the primary variables—of family life that would be conceptually consistent with the view of individual adolescent members as perpetually and mutually negotiating their roles, obligations, and responsibilities and reaffirming their love commitments to one another.

Within this view, too, various reverberatory patterns of ego interchanges could be found since the search was not constrained by the more simple and usual supposition that like begets like. Identity between parents' and adolescents' ego processes does occur; in fact, it is a frequent occurrence, given its absolutely lesser number of possibilities compared to the absolutely larger numbers of complementary and reciprocal patterns. However it was rare when the base denominator was the actual number of family associations. Moreover, identity between family members was most often found to be a measure of quiet desperation—an identification of mutual defensiveness. In fact, defensiveness was generally more implicated in family interchanges, an observation that implies that coping is more self-actional. The evidence for complementary and reciprocal interchanges—direct, obverse, and deterrent—was considerable and appears to support and further define the contention that families are interdependent collectivities with patterns that are integral to the whole. Finally, there is no reason to suppose that the ego interchange from parent to child is any more determinative than that between husband and wife.

11. Implications, Limitations, and Perspectives

Suggestions for Evaluating This Work

Now that this endeavor is nearing its conclusion, I can (assuming I have communicated with readers) state more freely and sweepingly, what I think I have done and suggest strategies readers might use in evaluating this work.

1. I intended to draw an integral formulation that revamped and reorganized cognitive and psychoanalytic theories around the central idea that personality can only be from the standpoint of the empirical sciences, about processes and their organizational activities. I argued that from the standpoint of biography, psychotherapy, one's own intimates or spiritual systems, personality is always much more. However these approaches are concerned with a different kind of reality and phenomenology—that of individual people—which is too particularized ever to be the business of science. I argue that we would be better off shedding our secret supposition, left over from the age of heroic materialism, that social science will eventually predict all important choices and actions of all individual people in any particular context. However this is not to say that when biographers, psychotherapists, relatives, or religionists seek to understand individual people that scientific generalities, abstractions, and hypotheses are not helpful or that their use does not serve to correct suppositions we privately cherish or we grew up with. The process formulation approximates the level of generality required for laws of personality, but it is contentless, while one hallmark of an individual life is its distinctive content.

2. The secondary intent of this work was to illustrate and test the implications of the first premise that personality is process. Considered were how this idea affects the endemic problem of value choice in theory and research, how it affects

the methods, designs, and interpretation of research findings, and finally what its application produces in the way of substantive, empirically based understandings in several fields of research. Two of the empirical chapters were required by the pivotal claims: (a) that ego processes and structures constitute the integral intrapersonal and extrapersonal means of interregulation and (b) that processes undergo development as a concomitant of structural evolution. However, the stress and family chapters, although obvious areas for the application of the process model, were not necessarily demanded by the structure of the theory and, therefore, were chosed with less constraint. Both stress and family research are areas that especially stand to benefit from an elaborated process formulation, and, I hasten to add, this possibility has certainly not escaped the attention of the experts already actively engaged in investigating each field. However, extant notions of process and their application, as was brought out in the literature reviews accompanying each of these chapters, have been piecemeal, adevelopmental in approach, and unclear about the difference between self-accuracy and self-deception. Thus, the particular contribution of this work may be its fuller, systematic exploitation of possibilities inherent in the process view. I do not want to give the impression, however, that the topics actually chosen were exhaustively examined, within themselves, and I will suggest further lines of study later in this chapter.

Other or additional chapter headings could have been chosen instead, for instance, ego processing in social groups, in psychotherapy, in psychosis, in psychosomatic disorders, in creative productions, in different cultures, in language development, in handicapped people, in altered states of consciousness, and so on.

Readers will now have to evaluate the process model on the basis of its performance in two main ways: (1) in the conceptual sense of how well it handles the nondisposable question of values, inherently involved in constructing a model of the well-functioning system and how sensibly it structures the nature of investigation as a social enterprise in itself; (2) in the empirical sense of how thoroughly and logically it identifies and ramifies the relationships between processes and structures, the nature of development itself, the main questions of stress research, and the structures of the family group and of the individual persons within the family.

Implications

I want to emphasize one last time that I do not think the particular model of ego processes I describe here is the best one or even necessarily complete in itself. The more important and durable idea is that personality is processes. Having presented the case as fully as I now can, I want to point to the general implications of this formulation of personality now that it has been seen in action:

1. The distinction between coping and defense seems vital and indispensible because (a) it points to a solution for the value choices of social scientists that

seems palatable enough that serious persons dedicated to the scientific ethic would want to choose it, or at least would not want to refute it. In fact, accuracy (I mean here the broader, completely social version of accuracy, namely, integrity) is the hallmark of both coping and the scientific ethic itself. Coping merely extends accuracy so that it becomes integrity, the proposed hallmark of the well-functioning person. We understand how to assess intersubjective accuracy—we base it on consensual validation—but we are less certain about how to observe the accuracy of people's self-assessments—their intrasubjectivity, or in George Herbert Mead's terms, their "me." But if we can come to identify and understand a broader array of structures, we will know how to assess them and will be well on our way to knowing more about intrasubjectivity. If we are willing to entertain the possibility that there may be social and moral and possibly affective-cognitive schemata as well as cognitive, we have to agree that the search for intrapersonal, organized systems of knowing and meaning is still in its infancy; (b) the nonbipolarity of coping and defense permitted people in action to be represented as neither all coping nor all defensive, but as functional mixtures of both. We found in the chapter about families that the standard equations of family research that good begets good and bad begets bad were considerably more complicated; we found in the chapter about interregulation of structures and processes that measures of achievement, like moral and cognitive stages and IQ, were supported not solely by coping, but also by certain defenses (once generally advantaging social conditions were removed).

Although future process models may look different, it seems to me the distinction between self-accuracy and self-deception will endure. It was the exploitation of this distinction and the elaboration of its various implications as two parallel but mutually influencing trends that permitted the integration of the Piagetian and Freudian theories proposed here. Our conscious disregard of the social difference between self-accuracy and self-deception is probably motivated by our wish to emulate those scientists whose subject matter permits them to observe, impartially, physical matter or infrabeings. From my point of view, the failure to recognize this distinction is the key log in the jam. We cannot treat all actions of man, as if they were the same utility to him and to his intimates.

2. The particular integration of Freudian and Piagetian theories described was based (a) on a refurbished psychoanalytic theory that was no longer beholden to the instincts and was therefore freed to regard defenses as constructivist, self-regulative, and even "creative" efforts, and (b) on a Piagetian theory that was extended to become more a psychology of ecosystems and less one of entities. Thus integration was obtained by realigning old ideas so that they were in accord with new perspectives of processes and structures. The result is a personal-social psychology of meaning systems that is unabashedly constructivist and admitted to be so from both the investigator's and the subject's points of view. I think this proposal may be a small indication that a zeitgeist is emerging that we do not yet entirely appreciate, but which will eventually result in sharp contrasts between the enterprises of physical and social scientists. However, to paraphrase and bend Quine (1969) a bit, we are still attempting to reconcile our past positivist view of man

with the constructivist one we are coming to see, by cunningly readjusting our translations so as to compensate for the ontological switches we have already partly made. But as a consequence of our state of flux and indecision, the language we use to describe people is now an undigested mix of positivism and constructivism.

Academicians and clinicians are far apart, but the time may soon come when the accrued common knowledge of clinical practice can be re-sifted by clinical and academic theorists alike to discard the nonsense and salvage the sense for the enrichment of personological theory. In this realm, the psychoanalytic theories of therapeutic techniques are without peer.

3. By all common sense definitions, personality refers to the central, ineffable essence of the person; thus, whether admitted or not, most personality theorists operate on the strong premise that people are unified wholes. However, some like Mischel (1968) would probably want to wait to construct the person's unity until the nature of all his situationally specific parts are established; but Mischel surely cannot mean there is no unity. Such a contention would violate the meaning of the English word, "personality," and would fly in the face of substantial evidence that people are traumatized when they are forced to be someone other than themselves or when they discover that they have made choices not recognizable as their own (e.g., battle neuroses or Milgram's subjects). Reasearchers in some fields can afford to ignore, control, or minimize the comprehensively organized aspects of the person. However, the personologist's raison d'être is the study of the person.

The ego conceptualization represents the person, at the outset, as a whole or a being trying to be a whole; processes are the primitive elements of the system and they are the handmaidens of the person's unified intent to maintain his sense of his sensibility. However, the formulation of processes would be vacuous, a spectacle of perpetual motion, without the additional stimulations that ego processes coordinate not only the various structures' functions but also the person's intents to sustain a dynamic intersubjective—intrasubjective balance. However, the structualists' psychology of the person, as the general system theorists would probably agree (for instance Wilden, 1974 and implied by Maruyama, 1968), is more a psychology of entities than of unities. This outcome is inevitable, I think, when the intersubjective—intrasubjective balance is not fully exploited for its implications, particularly its social implications. Cognitive theory can never be more than a psychology of entities unless it regards people as ecosystems—dynamic unities operating and surviving within ecologies that are noisy and in flux. From the standpoint of the personologists, people's adaptive capabilities are not directed solely to the environment, but are also determined by the necessities of adapting the self to the self, the I to the me and the me to the I, to use George Herbert Mead's terminology again.

Personology's excessive preoccupation during this century with instrumental kinds of processing, which has historically paralleled society's heroic materialism, is reduced in this proposal by the acceptance and reification of "noise." However, this exposition has done all too little with that idea. From the intrapsychic standpoint all the intraceptive and affective regulatory functions, which are not immediately concerned with instrumental processing, permit the "creative chaos" that is the precursor of new, emergent solutions and self-organizations as well as of the self-disorganization and dedifferentiations that may result in plain chaos and nothingness if the person should give up his interest in unity or his environment gives him no other choice. In this sense, all change, developments, and emergences involve risk taking, so much so that some people will defend themselves against these possibilities and confine their processing only to instrumental forms directed toward the logical solution of external problems.

4. A personology that arises from, and therefore requires, a developmental account was described here. The formulation of structures was necessary to that developmental description to provide a central, durable core of knowingness which requires processes for expression. But a critical difference between structures and their functions, on the one hand, and the ego processes on the other, was implied. Psychological structures do not arise until there is development, while some form of ego processing is synonymous with life from its beginning to its end. However, it was repeatedly pointed out that even though we know a fair amount about the cognitive structures, we know only a little about moral structures and next to nothing about social structures. Moreover we have not yet decided whether something like affective-cognitive structures exist, although pure affective schemata probably do not. The term "affective schema" is internally contradictory because we cannot schematize affect without the aid of cognition.

Although structures can arise only following commerce with the environment, two different foci were taken in regard to the relationships between processes and structures—from the standpoint of intrapsychic regulation, described in Chapter 7 and from the standpoint of extraintrapsychic regulation in Chapter 10, where the family as a human group was the concern. Since both of these areas require structural descriptions—disproportionately cognitive for the intrapsychic and disproportionately social for the extrapsychic realms—both require developmental accounts that go hand-in-hand with the development of processes. Ultimately too, an assumption was made, which is shared by most child psychologists, that one is not likely to understand a psychological phenomenon unless one understands how it came into being.

5. If the recommendations made in this work were taken seriously, personologists would be sobered, and their ambitions would be reduced for several reasons. First, it was argued that subjects always construct their own versions of everything that happens to them, whether it be experiencing the procedures of somebody else's data collection or the intents of loving, caring psychotherapists. Ever more complex forms of blinding the subject only whet his need to construct ever more complicated hypotheses about what is happening to him. Thus it was argued that experimentation that employs deception ends up studying defensive behavior that may not—in fact, it is likely that it does not—represent what the subject is usually like, but still this defensive behavior is his behavior so it may represent how he acts when he is stressed, mildly or severely, depending on the circumstances. The subject is cooperative only because he has decided to cooperate (as did Alker's, 1971,

"paranoid" subjects when the testing situation was less certain) and the investigator will still not know whether the subject is being his usual self or being cooperative. As a consequence of these considerations it was argued that the personologist's craft is always approximate and that his results are beholden to his subjects' decisions.

Second, an attempt was also made to temper our ambitions by arguing that we need to seek very general laws based on abstract variables and to release ourselves from the grip of the materialist notion that there will eventually be a science of personology with the predictive power to foretell the particular choices of particular individuals in particular situations. Even when we achieve a "correct" statement of the laws of personology, they will not explain; they would describe people in probabilistic terms.

Limitations and Perspectives

Of course it is difficult, if not actually impossible, for me to see what general or fundamental conceptual limitations exist in this proposal, since I put it together in the best way that I now know. I have every expectancy that colleagues of different ontological persuasions will disagree with this formulation. However with careful clarification of terms, these kinds of disputes readily resolve themselves into agreements to disagree, because they are based, ultimately, on unmalleable, oppository beliefs about the basic nature of man. However there are facets of this formulation that have empirical support. Furthermore, some segments of the underlying conceptualization of the empowering structures themselves (e.g., social structures) have not yet been developed by me or anybody else. Of course, there is also the need for other investigators to test the most certain and therefore potentially worthwhile findings. I want now to concentrate on the question of what additional empirical evidence is needed to test, so as to support or to refute, the model as it now stands.

1. The developmental relationships of the ego processes to structures are neither well nor sufficiently documented in this work. I am including here not only cognitive structures but also the moral, social, and affective-cognitive. To address the ego processes' interegulation of cognitive and affective-cognitive schemata, data are needed, preferably longitudinal data (although cross-age data would help) that track structural developments in concert with the appearance, use, and enhancement of the various ego processes. We already know fairly well how to undertake this kind of research. To address the concern of the more extrapsychic developments of moral and social structures, conceptualizations are first needed that identify those social structures that develop and become resident in the person and serve to organize and direct his understandings of his embedment and commerce with others. Swanson (1974) has reported and is still at work investigating the structures of decision making in families as they become manifest in offspring's

cognitive development and ego processing; but we have little more to guide our formulations about the unions between social structures' and the processes' development.

Another logical step would be to study families that contain children who are younger in age than those adolescents whose families were the target in the study described in Chapter 10. Presumably, if the basic formulation is correct, such analyses would indicate that family groups with younger children are engaged in different social structural tasks and that the intrafamilial ego patterns and the individual members' ego processing are also different since the children's structural development would be at different stages. Another obvious move is to follow the families described in Chapter 10 or other like families through the period of the offspring's leave-taking, since this disjuncture in the groups' functioning should also result in different and predictable shifts within the family's social structures, the members' understanding of social structures, and the members' ego processing.

2. The intraceptive and affective regulatory aspects of the ego processing need a great deal more direct and focused attention than was given here. This kind of information is critical to the further development of the formulation since the intraceptive and affective regulations represent noninstrumental strategies of ego processing that we now call, in our ignorance, "noise." (In other words, what we cannot fit into our present logical, instrumentally based understandings we call "noise" because we cannot rationalize it.) I am inclined to think that understanding noise may be as important to the future development of personology as is further understanding of peoples' direct instrumental attacks on the problems of living. Intraceptive and affective regulations were only considered in passing as they happened to appear as results in various analyses that were reported.

3. I think we can assume that the recommendations for adopting the value aspect of coping will not be accepted, forthwith, by many of our fellow social scientists. Consequently, even though I find comfort in the notion, there is clear need for considerably more empirical work that directly examines the ramifications of sorting people by the criteria of coping as compared to other sets of valued criteria. One such study (Haan, 1974a) was reported in Chapter 7. One of the difficulties with carrying out this proposal is that even though all systems of personology now contain value, few values are objectified so that their ramifications can be clearly tested. (How do you operationalize self-actualization? Which competence should one choose? What is mental health?) A selection of one system of value over another probably can be based, at least partially, on pragmatic grounds, since an empirical test is one way to clarify the implications of one point of view compared to another. In fact, my argument that social science should choose its model of the well-functioning personological system according to the criterion of coping accuracy or integrity is pragmatically based, that is, it should work because scientists are likely to agree to it. However there will always be in some people's minds additional grounds that are crucial and political: What values do you, I, or we *wish* to impart by implication to all man in our research designs?

4. More research is also needed about the ego processing of people as subjects beyond what Alker (1971) and Folkins (1970) have already done with some aspects of this model. The argument that subjects will make what they need to make out of situations of data collection can be empirically examined.

5. A number of other headings for chapters were suggested above. If this model was general worth and validity, its capability for describing the person in all areas of research, and especially in those areas where a formulation of personality is directly needed, must be demonstrated.

At this point, I will rest my case, along with the qualifications, assertions, self-criticisms, and suggestions for further study, and turn the reader over to Richard Morrissey, who evaluates all previously published research concerning this model. Paul Joffe and Murray Naditch follow in the next chapter by describing their recent work in improving ego scales to measure coping and defensive processes.

12. The Haan Model of Ego Functioning:
An Assessment of Empirical Research
Richard F. Morrissey

Introduction

Since its introduction into the psychological literature in 1963 (Haan, 1963; Kroeber, 1963), the Haan model of ego functioning has received some attention as a potentially valuable scheme for specifying optimal and nonoptimal modes of psychological functioning. The model's distinction between 10 coping and 10 defensive processes and its subsequent extension to include a dimension of ego fragmentation (Haan, 1969) show promise as a useful taxonomy by which the relative strengths and weaknesses of ego transactions can be abstracted, ordered, and assessed. Despite the model's provocative theoretical stance, however, the true test of any conceptual innovation lies in its potential utility in guiding empirical research. The purpose of this chapter is to provide some basis for assessing the model's adequacy along these lines by systematically reviewing all the available literature which has used the model, in whole or in part, in research studies. My intent is to be inclusive and exhaustive regarding the selection of studies bearing on the Haan model, and I have attempted, wherever possible, to include dissertations, working manuscripts, and papers presented at professional meetings, as well as reports appearing in the research literature.

The review includes 30 studies, distributed fairly evenly over the 13-year period since the model's introduction. A useful breakdown for discussing the studies seemed to revolve around the procedure used in determining scores for the ego process variables. Two methods have been used, one employing judges' ratings based on interview data, the other involving the use of empirically derived scales from the item pools of the Minnesota Multiphasic Personality Inventory (MMPI) and the California Psychological Inventory (CPI) (Haan, 1965). Since these measures were not cross-validated, the observed relationships between the scales and other measures of interest should be accepted with caution until a firmer case is established for their construct validity. The rationale for the present review, then, breaks down into two parts: (1) gauging the extent to which studies employing the ego ratings have successfully established the ego model as a useful framework in the analysis of specific substantive areas, and (2) assessing the construct validity of the psychometric measures derived from standard personality inventories.[1] Following the discussion of specific studies, an attempt will be made to assess the implications of these findings from both theoretical and methodological perspectives, as well as to suggest possible areas for future research.

Studies Employing Ego Ratings

There are 14 studies using judges' ratings that have attempted to assess the implications of Haan's ego model for such diverse areas as projective and psychometric test taking (Haan, 1964b, 1965; Kroeber, 1963), intellectual functioning (Haan, 1963), social functioning (Haan, 1964a), moral and ego development (Haan et al., 1973), stress (Folkins, 1970; Hunter & Goodstein, 1967; Margolis, 1970), locus of control (Kuypers, 1972), and early antecedents of later ego functioning (Haan, 1974a; Kuypers, 1974; Weinstock, 1967a,b).

The introduction of the model into the literature (Kroeber, 1963) included the results of a pilot study performed on a sample of 39 males and 33 females selected from Berkeley's Oakland Growth Study (OGS). Ego ratings were based on a series of intensive interviews with these subjects at age 38–40 (average interview length: 12 hours) and were made by two independent raters, the interviewer and a second staff member who assigned ratings on the basis of interview transcripts. Reliability ratings were calculated by means of a χ^2 analysis on each ego variable. Although significance tests revealed that interrater reliability was acceptable, the use of the χ^2 statistic in preference to the more conventional correlation coefficient makes the results difficult to compare with reliability assessments in later studies. There are some indications that men are rated more consistently than women, since probability levels for the χ^2 for men were never greater than .005, while for women the probability level for some variables was .06. Although the disparity may seem minor, it is worth noting since it appears in later studies as well.

[1] The present discussion focusing on the psychometric scales may have a somewhat untimely flavor in view of the construction of new measures reported by Naditch and Joffe in this volume. Nevertheless, to omit these studies from consideration would involve a gross injustice to the purpose at hand, namely, an evaluation of all the available empirical evidence bearing on the model.

The criterion against which the ego ratings were assessed were Rorschach protocols, rated independently by three clinical judges. Reliability ratings here were poor, with almost 30% of all scores unreliable. In addition to the standard Rorschach categories, special ratings of the test taking situation itself such as "affective enjoyment of the test," were scored. Of the 42 expected relationships between the coping and defense processes and the Rorschach scores, 4 were not possible to test because of the poor quality of the Rorschach results.[2] Of the remaining 38 hypotheses, 21 were confirmed as statistically significant (55%), with 33 in the predicted direction (87%).[3] Although Kroeber did not analyze the results separately for the coping functions, I have done so, since the coping dimension is the unique contribution of the model. Results closely parallel those presented above, with 8 of the 15 coping hypotheses confirmed (53%) and 12 in the predicted direction (80%). Especially suggestive are the results confirming relationships between (1) ego regression and the number of original responses, (2) intellectuality and cognitive enjoyment of the Rorschach, and, for the defense functions, (3) between reaction time and projection, doubt, and repression. Despite some problems with the reliability of the criterion, results are generally supportive of the model's usefulness in calling attention to the role of ego functioning in facilitating and moderating the relationship between cognitive structures and their behavioral expression in a test taking situation. One drawback of the Kroeber study is its failure to analyze the data separately for males and females, thus masking possible interaction effects between ego functioning and sex.

A more extensive look at the model's potentials in relationship to intellectual functioning was undertaken by Haan (1963). This study drew on the same subject pool and ratings. Interrater reliability coefficients are reported by Haan that show wide variability—they range from −.11 (tolerance of ambiguity: women) to .83 (logical analysis: men; intellectuality: women), with four variables unreliable (male reaction formation and female isolation, tolerance of ambiguity, and substitution). My own calculations for the coping variables reveal average reliabilities of .69 and .43 for men and women, respectively. For the defensive functions, results are similar, with a male mean of .62 and a female mean of .52.[4] If we adopt a criterion of roughly .70 for acceptable reliability, it is evident that interjudge agreement of identifying the coping and defensive functions is generally only moderate for males and poor for females. The latter point is underscored by the following: Only one defense and one coping function for women achieved a reliability of over .70, and

---

[2] It should be noted that Kroeber lists only 40 hypotheses and reports that no test was performed on 4 of these. At no point does he give any indication what the remaining two hypotheses were.

[3] My figures differ from Kroeber's in that he claims 24 significant relationships. I have excluded 2 significant findings which ran counter to the predicted direction, and after a fruitless search have yet to locate the remaining case from his tabular data.

[4] These means are smaller than those reported in later papers by Haan (1964a, 1964b, 1965) which used the same data, since she excluded the unreliable variables before averaging.

in only 2 out of 22 cases was a female reliability rating higher than a male rating for particular ego processes.

The poor overall interrater reliability may be due to inadequate specification of constructs, to the difficulty in assessing some processes from interview data, or perhaps to the different raw materials from which ratings were made. The interviewer, in addition to the content of the subject's discussion, has as its disposal a wealth of nonverbal cues, including hesitations in speech patterns, tone of voice, facial expressions, and body movements. The judge rating transcripted material, on the other hand, must form his judgment solely on the basis of the content of the interview. The end result of this difference in raw materials may be a fair amount of "slippage" between the two sets of ratings. Seen in this context, the sex differences observed may be a function of women's more extensive use of such nonverbal communications during the interview, or the increased importance attached to these behaviors by the interviewer. It would be instructive to estimate the difference in reliabilities when the sex of the rater is varied. Perhaps female raters would more consistently agree on the ego functioning of another female.

Following the ratings procedure, Haan performed a factor analysis of the 20 ego functions separately by sex; this yielded five factors for each sex, four of which were parallel. Although the validity of a factor analysis of 20 variables carried out on samples of under 50 is open to question on statistical grounds, the four parallel factors correspond to clearly identifiable dimensions, with two of the factors related to coping (controlled and expressive coping) and two to defense (structured and primitive defense). (Note, however, the factor analytic study done by Joffe and Naditch, reported in Chapter 13, replicates this analysis with a larger sample.) For both sexes, controlled coping included high loadings for concentration, logical analysis, objectivity, substitution, and sublimation, while expressive coping was characterized by tolerance of ambiguity, empathy, and regression in the service of the ego. Displacement, rationalization, projection, isolation, and reaction formation yielded high loadings on the structured defense factor, while primitive defense was characterized by positive loadings for repression and denial, and a negative loading for logical analysis.

In comparing the means of all the coping and defense variables, some sex differences were noted. Males were significantly rated higher on the coping functions of objectivity, intellectuality, logical analysis, concentration, and total coping, and on one defense, intellectualizing. Although these findings might be predicted, given traditional sex role expectations regarding male preferences for cognitive activity, the failure of other, more expressive, coping variables to differentiate along sex lines is notable. Although female means were higher on empathy, sensitivity, and expressive coping, the differences did not reach statistical significance.

In addition to establishing the groundwork for the analysis of the ego functions themselves, Haan's study (1963) attempted to demonstrate their relevance in moderating intellectual functioning. As predicted, coping functions (particularly the cognitive processes) tended to correlate positively with the Stanford–Binet IQ ratings taken over 20 years earlier, with the trend more marked for males. Defenses, on the other hand (with the notable exception of intellectualizing), tended to correlate negatively with IQ. One general problem which mars the latter finding is that, of 20 hypothesized negative correlations, only two (displacement and total defense for males) reached statistical significance.

Using group-administered intelligence tests given in 1933 and again in 1955, Haan then related ego functioning to IQ acceleration and deceleration. The results showed little relationship to total IQ change, with no significant relationships for males and two for females. Among the latter, projection was associated with female acceleration, while empathy was associated with deceleration, suggesting that absorption in the feminine role has detrimental impacts for female intellectual development. A number of significant relationships between ego functioning and the subtests of sentence meaning and arithmetic were also uncovered. Accelerators of both sexes were characterized by objectivity, total coping, and a general reliance on cognitive processes. Defensiveness, on the other hand, showed strong sex differences, with structured defense correlating significantly with female acceleration and defensive impulse regulation with male deceleration. As Haan suggests, to be an intelligent woman in our society may involve a certain degree of defensive functioning. When holding Block's MMPI Ego Control factor constant, the relationships remained significant, with the exception of denial, which proved to be associated with IQ deceleration for both sexes. These findings gain added strength since IQ change was also shown to be unrelated to previous IQ levels.

In summary, the original Haan paper (1963) presents initial reliability and validity data on the coping and defense model, as well as suggesting its relevance in studies of intellectual functioning. Certain themes emerge: moderate to poor interrater reliability, due perhaps to the differences in raw data rates; the importance of considering sex differences in ego functioning and its assessment; the necessity of analyzing correlates of ego functioning separately by sex; and the general relevance of the model in helping to explain accelerations or decelerations in aspects of intellectual functioning. One difficulty in endorsing the study wholeheartedly is the lack of statistically significant results in relating ego processes to total IQ change.

Two other papers by Haan, using the same subject pool and ego ratings, investigated relationships between ego processes and social functioning (1964a) and Rorschach test taking (1964b). The first of these focused specifically on the relations between childhood and adult social status and adult ego functioning, between social mobility and adult ego functioning, As in the previous study, all data were analyzed separately by sex. Results revealed little relationship between childhood socioeconomic status (SES) and ego processes. No significant correlations were found for females, while for males, the cognitive processes of objectivity, intellectuality, intellectualization and logical analysis tended to show positive associations with childhood SES. However, relationships between ego processes and adult SES were marked, with some sex differences. Of 19 tested relationships for males, 13 (68%) were significant, and 18 (95%) in the predicted direction. Four of nine defenses correlated negatively with male SES, with only intellectualizing showing a positive association. Stronger relationships were evident for the coping dimension, as 9 of 10 associations significantly correlated with male adult status. The only exception here was regression in the service of the ego, suggesting that playfulness is not a critical factor in influencing social position in an achievement-oriented society. For females, the pattern is similar, but weaker. Of 17 tested relationships, 8 (47%) were significant, with 15 (88%) in the predicted direction. There is perhaps less reason to expect clear relationships there, since a woman's social status has been traditionally determined primarily by her husband's position. For both sexes, total coping showed strong relationships to adult SES ($r = .61$ for males; $r = .55$ for females). In general, controlled coping, rather than expressive coping, was linked with adult SES, while primitive defense showed a significant negative relationship with social status. One methodological problem which complicates these findings is that the judges who rated the subjects on the ego variables had information concerning their social position. Some spuriousness in the observed relationships cannot be ruled out because of this bias.

Results comparing ego processes to social mobility support the general hypothesis that total coping is related to SES gains. For males, there are indications that upward social mobility is contingent on control of impulses (substitution and suppression) balanced by intraception (empathy and tolerance of ambiguity). For females, such mobility is linked more with affective expression (sublimation and playfulness) balanced by cognitive control (logical analysis, objectivity, and intellectuality). Downward mobility, on the other hand, is associated with male isolation, denial, and regression. When the effects of IQ were controlled, the relationships between the ego variables and adult SES and social mobility were relatively unchanged, although the effect of intelligence on female social mobility was itself moderate.

Data concerning the adolescent personality correlates of adult ego functioning revealed marked sex differences. Of particular interest are the later ego correlates of adolescent autonomy and achievement-orientations. For males, no relationships emerged between autonomy and later adult ego functioning, while achievement was negatively related to adult isolation, denial, and total defense. Adolescent female autonomy and achievement, however, were linked with adult objectivity, intellectuality, logical analysis, sublimation, and total coping. Evidently, for males, being autonomous and achievement-oriented requires and nurtures no particular coping skills, and perhaps only a lack of defensiveness. Females who rate high on these variables, however, seem to possess the cognitive coping capabilities which may aid in their rejection of sex-stereotyped behavior.

In all, the results of this study (Haan, 1964a) offer strong evidence for the utility of the ego model. Social achievement can be partially understood as a result of possessing coping skills which facilitate effective transactions with the environment in seeking valued goals. An important side issue here is the finding that the effect of IQ itself on male social mobility is negligible when the effects of ego functioning are controlled. Since much of social mobility research in the past has considered the potential effects of IQ on social performance, this study raises some question as to whether the more profitable research strategy might be to focus on ego processes, rather than intelligence itself, as predictors of later social success.

Where the mobility study called attention to the importance of controlled coping, Haan's Rorschach study (1964b) places emphasis on the potentials of affective expression. Using a subsample of 46 men and 42 women from the previous sample, Haan related ego functioning to different aspects of the Rorschach test-taking situation. The methodology closely parallels that employed in the Kroeber study (1963), but the data here were analyzed separately by sex. Although specific hypotheses were too numerous to be reported here, it was generally expected that certain coping and defense functions (particularly free expressive coping) would be related to Rorschach scores, patterns, and test-taking attitudes. Although the results of the study are considerably clouded by the use of a liberal criterion for statistical significance ($p < .10$), Haan found support for her contention that test-taking response is related to coping. Logical analysis related to intellectual enjoyment of the Rorschach, while playfulness showed positive associations with affective enjoyment of the test. Although the results reported are of only moderate statistical significance, their practical significance may be considerable. In essence, they argue for an examination of the entire Rorschach test-taking situation itself, rather than particular responses, for providing potentially valuable information regarding ego functioning, particularly coping functioning.

An attempt to assess the model's relationship to standard personality inventories was undertaken by Haan (1965). Using the same subject pool and ratings described earlier, an effort was made to determine if the CPI, as an inventory of nonpathological functioning, would be more efficient at discriminating high and low groups on the coping dimensions than would be the MMPI. Similarly, the MMPI was expected to differentiate more effectively along the defense dimension. Results generally supported this contention, but more so for the coping variables than for the defense.[5] A more extended treatment of the results of this study will be given in a later section of this paper in which the empirical scales are discussed. Of interest here is the finding that neither item pool was particularly successful in assessing a dimension of suspension of ego control, suggesting that use of available inventory items may render the assessment of such a dimension difficult.

Two studies by Weinstock (1967a, b) reported the results of an investigation of the antecedents of defense and coping functioning. Although his sample size is small ($N = 39$) and consists only of males, Weinstock's data, derived from a different longitudinal subject pool, provide some comparison to the previous findings reported by Haan (1964a). Mean interrater reliabilities for Weinstock's ego ratings are generally comparable to, and slightly higher than, Haan's.[6] The latter is perhaps

---

[5] The following ego variables did not differentiate items: sublimation, expressive coping, rationalization, structured defense and total defense.

[6] Mean reliability for male coping was .75 for Weinstock (compared with .69 for Haan), while mean reliability for male defense was .64 for Weinstock (compared with .62 for Haan).

a function of both judges working from the same transcripted material. Reaction formation, which was unreliable in the Haan studies for males, also was unreliable for Weinstock (Haan, $r = .20$; Weinstock, $r = .37$). This consistent finding suggests that this particular ego defense is difficult to identify with reasonable consistency in social transactions.

In the study focusing specifically on familial antecedents of defense and coping (1967a), Weinstock's substantive findings lend some support to theoretical formulations that have stressed the notion that "primitive" defenses such as repression and denial are rooted in early family environment, rather than in adolescence. Other defenses, such as isolation, displacement, and projection were related more closely to family variables in adolescence. Although arguing his results in support of modeling theory, Weinstock also notes that his findings are consistent with a more cognitive formulation which would posit that an individual's level of cognitive functioning at the time of family difficulties is an important element in influencing which ego functions eventually become part of his more enduring personality. A child with an immature ego encountering stress might resort to denial, while one with a more differentiated ego structure would adopt more complex methods of defensive adaptation. Adult coping showed fewer associations with family environment variables. Interestingly, tolerance of ambiguity and regression in the service of the ego showed some relationship to familial antagonisms in adolescence, suggesting that expressive coping follows less from unconflicted development than from the active working through of adolescent conflicts.

Weinstock's next study (1967b), using the same data for ego ratings, sought support for the hypothesis that certain defenses would be associated with childhood social class. Significant relationships were observed for intellectualization and projection, which correlated positively, and denial, which correlated negatively, with childhood SES. Comparing these findings with those reported by Haan (1964a), the association between intellectualization and high childhood SES is replicated, while Haan's results on the other two variables are in the same direction, though not significant. Despite these patterns, perhaps the clearer finding is the *lack* of relationship between the majority of the defensive functions and childhood social position. With some exceptions, it would seem that defensive ego functioning has fairly democratic roots.

In addition to specifying a set of individual difference variables whose correlates may be empirically observed, the Haan model has been used as a scheme for coding responses to experimentally induced stressors. Hunter and Goodstein (1967) administered a difficult symbolic reasoning test to 40 college students classified as either high or low on Barron's Ego Strength (Es) scale. Students were asked to explain their "poor" performance in taped interviews, which were transcribed and rated by three independent judges for denial, rationalization, total defensiveness, and logical analysis. The authors present no reliability data other than the statement that ratings were "adequately reliable." Hypotheses that high-Es subjects would use more logical analysis than low-Es subjects, and that low-Es subjects would be rated as more defensive were confirmed. While an hypothesis that low-Es subjects would use more denial was in the predicted direction, it was not significant. Contrary to hypothesis, low-Es subjects used significantly more rationalization responses than high-Es subjects. Although the study gives general support for the usefulness of the Haan model as a coding scheme for behavior under moderate stress, the lack of scope of the responses studied and the failure to specify the sex of the subjects present problems in assessing its importance.

A similar paradigm was employed by Margolis (Hunter) in her published doctoral dissertation (1970). Using 40 students rated high or low on Es and matched for sex and intelligence, role plays were performed that induced varying levels of stress. The following pairs of ego functions were used to classify verbal responses: rationalization–logical analysis, projection–empathy, doubt–tolerance of ambiguity, denial–concentration, total coping–total defense. Two independent judges rated the taped role play dialogue, with reliability "exceedingly high" for the global ratings but only moderate for the specific mechanisms. Results indicated that high-Es subjects showed significantly more total coping responses than did low-Es subjects, and the manipulation which presented students with a moral dilemma elicited significantly more defensive responses than a condition of no-dilemma. Perhaps more important, a χ^2 analysis found no significant relationship between level of ego strength and any individual ego functions. This is inconsistent with results from the previous study by Hunter and Goodstein (1967), which had noted associations between Es level and the use of logical analysis and rationalization. Margolis concluded that the Haan model "does not carry us very far in our search for new ways to categorize behavior" and that the "specific coping mechanisms cannot be clearly operationalized at this point [Margolis, 1970, p. 427]."

A third study which utilized the model to classify responses to stress was reported by Folkins (1970), who employed all three dimensions of the tripartite model: coping, defense and fragmentation. Using a sample of 90 males, Folkins measured physiological and psychological reactions to the threat of shock, with anticipation time as his primary independent variable. Following the manipulation, subjects were given 10-min interviews, and the transcripts were rated by two independent judges. Although exact reliability data was not reported, Folkins noted that the reliability range was $-.25 < r < .82$, with regression in the service of the ego, sublimation, and suppression as unreliable. The average reliability of the remaining ego functions was .51. Since none of the coping functions above was unreliable in the Haan (1963) or Weinstock (1967a) studies, and since the mean reliability is notably lower than results obtained earlier, we might conclude that the interview period was too brief to allow for the identification of specific ego functions or that material elicited following stress is particularly difficult to identify, especially along an expressive coping dimension.

Following the rating procedure, Folkins performed a cluster analysis to isolate dimensions of ego functioning which could be empirically grouped together. Three general factors could be identified, which paralleled each of the ego dimensions of coping, defense, and fragmentation. Empirically as well as theoretically, "copers," "defenders," and "fragmenters" can be differentiated under stress conditions.[7] It is interesting to note that the factors described earlier by Haan (1963) did not emerge from the data, but this may be due to the inclusion of the fragmenting dimension and the conditions under which responses were obtained.

Folkins' results argue for the utility of the general classification of coping, defense, and fragmenting as potentially distinct responses to stress. Shorter intervals of anticipation time were generally associated with more coping and less fragmentation. For the longer intervals, more ego failure was noted. Efforts to relate individual differences (as cluster scores) to measures of stress actions were suggestive, but generally weak. As predicted, "copers" had the lowest physiological stress reactions, while "fragmenters" recorded the highest. The only significant relationships with the psychological indicators of stress were negative correlations between the defense cluster and three measures of self-reported tension.

The general failure of the clusters used as individual difference variables to relate to stress indicators is perhaps a function of the design itself, which recorded ego functioning only following stress. Perhaps it would have been profitable to add to the design some a priori classification of subjects along ego dimensions. This would enable some analysis of the data in a Person X Situation framework and could address the question of how "controlled copers," for example, react under varying degrees of threat. Stronger associations might then have been observed between ego functioning and stress response. The prestress and poststress assessments might have also yielded information on relative consistency of coping and defensive postures under conditions of no threat and also under conditions of moderate or severe threat.

Two studies which explored the relatively uncharted region of personality functioning in old age were reported by Kuypers (1972, 1974). The first investigated the relationship of the Haan model to the construct of locus of control (Rotter, 1966) using a sample from the OGS. The mean age of the 25 males in the study was 67.7, and the mean age of the 39 females was 68.8. As Kuypers notes, the sample can be characterized as a generally advantaged group with levels of education and income well above national norms. Ratings of coping, defense, and fragmenting were established by two independent raters from interview transcripts, while locus of control was assessed by a short form of the Internal−External (I−E) scale (Rotter, 1966). Reliability ratings for all ego ratings were all over .50, the most consistent set of ratings yet reported. It appears that to facilitate data analysis, Kuypers excluded the middle third of I−E scorers, since he reports comparisons on ego functions between only the lowest third on the I−E measure (*N*

---

[7] The following ego functions secured high loadings on the factors: Factor 1 (coping)−intellectuality, logical analysis, substitution, objectivity, tolerance of ambiguity; Factor 2 (defense)−projection, enologisms, unstable alternation, intellectualization, reaction formation, denial, displacement; Factor 3 (fragmenting)−depersonalization, decompensation, pollyannish responses, regression, delusions, impulse preoccupation, tangentiality, confabulation, immobilization.

= 31, external) and the highest third (N = 33, internal). The results indicate that internals scored higher on all coping functions (6 of 10 comparisons significant), lower on 9 of 10 defense functions (1 of 10 comparisons significant) and lower on all fragmenting functions (3 of 10 comparisons significant).[8] Results are generally supportive of the link between locus of control and coping as related, and perhaps complementary, approaches to the study of effective personality functioning.

The second study (Kuypers, 1974), focusing on the same sample, attempted to examine early adult life antecedents of ego functioning in old age. Using data collected 40 years previously on his elderly subjects, Kuypers examined the potential impacts of five areas of early adult functioning on later ego functioning: health, intellectual functioning, socioeconomic status, personality, and family interaction patterns. Data in these areas were available for 95 elderly persons, 71 women and 24 males. In contrast to the previous study, results were analyzed separately by sex. Of the five areas considered, health status and personality characteristics assessed during early adult years showed poor associations with the coping, defense, and fragmenting functions for both sexes in old age. Intelligence, especially in women, showed high associations with coping capabilities in later years, as did socioeconomic status with both coping and fragmenting for both sexes. Disruptions in marital and family relationships during early years also was associated with later ego disorganization, especially for females. Kuypers notes the possibility that a combination of high socioeconomic status and intelligency may best predict coping functioning in later years, while a combination of low socioeconomic status and family tension may often lay the groundwork for later ego failure. Although this pattern suggests the need for examining interactive effects among the variables considered, Kuypers seems not to have examined these propositions empirically. The study as a whole, however, yields support for the model's viability in specifying modes of optimal and nonoptimal personality functioning which can be identified in older subjects and whose antecedents can be traced to experiences in earlier years. The results also provide some comparability to earlier findings which suggest a relationship between intelligence (Haan, 1963), socioeconomic status (Haan, 1964a), and coping.

The final two studies to be reviewed in this section were published recently by Haan. The first (Haan et al., 1973) investigated relationships between three theoretical schemes which posit ideal modes of psychological functioning: Kohlberg's cognitive theory of moral development, Loevinger's theory of ego development, and Haan's model of coping. Although interesting in its own right, the sample of 58 "hippies" was not representative of San Francisco's Bay Area hippies, and certainly not comparable to other, more conventional populations. Reliability data was excellent, with a mean coefficient of .77 for coping, .71 for defense, and .77 for ego fragmentation. The only rating under .50 was neologisms, perhaps due to the

---

[8] Internals scored significantly higher on objectivity, logical analysis, tolerance of ambiguity, empathy and sublimation; externals were significantly higher on isolation, confabulations, delusions and impulse preoccupation.

raters' disagreement on countercultural argot. Unfortunately, no sex differences were treated because of the small sample size.

Preliminary analysis revealed the only associations between intelligence (WAIS performance) and ego functioning involved the defenses. IQ had significant positive correlations with isolation, intellectualizing, projection, and reaction formation. This is in contrast with previous findings which had reported a positive link between coping and IQ (Haan, 1963) and is perhaps a function of the sample under consideration. As Haan notes, to do well on an IQ test when one is a hippie may necessarily involve a fair amount of defensiveness.

The results comparing ego functioning and moral and ego development are complicated by the use of a significance level of $p < .10$. Generally, the cognitive coping processes, in contrast to those dealing with affective regulation, showed associations with moral development. In contrast, coping showed no clear relationships with Loevinger's ego stages. An opposite pattern was evident for the defensive processes, as no defensive function could be significantly differentiated by moral stages, while intellectualization and projection were significantly differentiated by ego stages. Haan interprets these findings as suggestive that moral development is accompanied by coping (in line with the cognitive character of each) and independent of defense, while ego development as defined by Loevinger is independent of coping and, if anything, characterized by "successful" use of defenses. An interesting interaction effect emerged when individuals at incompatible moral and ego stages were observed to be significantly higher on six fragmenting variables, including total fragmenting.

In short, the results of the "hippie" study are very suggestive in estimating the extent of the relations among the Kohlberg, Loevinger, and Haan models, but because of the nature of the sample under study, the failure to specify sex differences, and the use of a liberal significance criterion, they must be accepted with some caution.

The final study using judges' ratings to be reviewed here was performed by Haan (1974a), using the identical pool of OGS subjects reported in earlier studies (Haan, 1963, 1964a,b, 1965). This study attempted to identify adolescent antecedents of later adult functioning and also compared Q sorts and ego ratings of the subjects as adults. One important aspect of the study is that it is the first to examine the *patternings* of particular coping and defense configurations in an effort to isolate global "types" of ego functioning. Haan examined only the total coping and total defense scores and separated these into four groups: high coping, low defense (coping group); low coping, high defense (defense group); high coping, high defense (high ego group); and low coping, low defense (low ego group).

Marked differences were observed between the groups in antecedent personality variables, which had been rated by judges at the time of the subjects' adolescence. During adolescence, women copers valued independence, saw themselves as causative agents, were poised with peers and were the least respectful to parents. This autonomous stance was corroborated by mothers' statements at the time, and also compares favorably to results reported earlier by Haan (1964a) that female autonomy in adolescence was related to later adult coping. Male copers were characterized as ascetic, haughty, and intellectually arrogant as adolescents, and were described by their mothers as spending too much time on outside activities. These observations afford an interesting parallel to Weinstock's data (1967a), which noted traces of conflict in adolescence in the homes of male copers. The overall portrait of the "coper" which emerges is that he or she values freedom, prefers to initiate action, likes intellectual activity, and can be arrogant around others. The coping stance, moreover, seems to be the result of a period of cognitive restructuring, beginning in a conflicted adolescence, and marked by a successful working through of this disequilibrium. In contrast to approaches to optimal personality functioning which emphasize socialization into social roles and increasingly effective control, coping seems a much more active, ego-involving process, in which the growing person attempts to synthesize an identity amid conflict and to structure his or her own responses to new circumstances.

Equally detailed descriptions of the other groups are beyond the present scope, but a short synopsis is in order. In adolescence, defenders were characterized as anxious and uncertain, and seen by mothers as nonassertive. Those in the high ego group had been relatively conventional, nonquestioning, and liked by their peers; while those in the low ego group were the least cognitively oriented, the most dependent on peer support, and were seen by their mothers as low in energy and creativity. The Q sort and ego process comparisons yielded close agreement on nonoptimal aspects of functioning but tended to diverge in their conceptions of ideal men and women. In all, results were supportive of the model's usefulness in specifying an alternative conceptualization of psychological "health" and provided some evidence for its development.

Studies Using Empirically Derived Scales

Haan's effort (1965) to isolate items distinguishing high and low groups on each coping and defense variable resulted in provisional scales, which were not cross-validated on other populations. The review of studies which follows is therefore an attempt to assess the construct validity of these measures by estimating the extent of their correlations with other scales and by noting the degree of support which has been given hypotheses relying on their measurement potential.

Initial reliability data presented by Haan (1965) indicates adequate internal consistency, as assessed by the Kuder–Richardson formula, with both coping and defense scales having a mean reliability of .70. Validity data, assessed by comparing the ego scales to standard and special scales of the CPI and MMPI, was also favorable. Total coping correlated significantly with all standard CPI scales with the exception of Socialization, Self control, Good Impression, Communality and Femininity. From the descriptions of copers sketched earlier, associations with these measures of more socially conventional attributes would not be predicted. Of the individual coping scales, those concerned with cognitive capacities showed stronger associations with CPI scales than those dealing with intraceptive processes which involve suspension of control. Haan does not present correlations of all the defense scales with the standard clinical scales of the MMPI, but interesting patterns are pointed out for the Denial and Doubt scales. Consistently, the Denial scale is *negatively* associated with psychopathology as judged by the anxiety ($r = -.50$), depression ($r = -.27$), neurotic overcontrol ($r = -.46$), neurotic undercontrol ($r = -.50$), schizophrenia ($r = -.43$) and paranoia ($r = -.51$) subscales. Denial also showed strong positive correlations with the social desirability ($r = .52$) and lie ($r = .44$) scales. It would seem that deniers consistently disavow all signs of malfunctioning and need to present themselves in a conventional, acceptable light to others. The pattern is dramatically reversed for Doubt, which correlates positively with the anxiety ($r = .75$), depression ($r = .57$), neurotic overcontrol ($r = .65$), neurotic undercontrol ($r = .45$), schizophrenia ($r = .55$) and paranoia ($r = .68$) subscales, and negatively with social desirability ($r = -.69$). These findings suggest that doubters are acutely aware of psychological distress and are willing to disclose such signs publicly. Relationships between the projection, repression, and primitive defense measures and the MMPI scales were "not impressive" in magnitude, while the regression scale had predictable positive associations with *Hs*, *Pd* and *Sc*.

Since the construction of the scales, I have located sixteen studies which have reported results of their use, including one doctoral dissertation for which results are available. Without exception, these studies have examined the usefulness of some part of the model, rather than its relevance as a whole. As a result, evidence for construct validity is somewhat piecemeal and does not integrate easily into a clear picture.

The first study using the scales was reported by Alker (1967), who suggested that the theoretical linkage posited between pairs of coping and defensive processes had an empirical base along the dimension of cognitive style. Specifically, Alker hypothesized that the cognitive control aspect of extensive scanning and narrow category width would form the basis for the pairing of the interpersonal sensitivity processes of defensive projection and coping empathy. Using a sample of Berkeley undergraduates, Alker obtained multiple measures of empathy and projection. Empathy was assessed by Haan's scale (1965) and also by a procedure of matching photographs of persons to tapes of their voices. Projection was operationalized in three ways: by a combination of Haan's projection and displacement scales, by a form of Byrne's sensitization scale (Ullman, 1962), and by a photographic rating procedure. No substantial correlations were found between Haan's two scales and the other parallel measures—Alker's final assessments of empathy and projection, which were based solely on the photograph procedures. Although the findings of this study lend support to the hypothesis that a cognitive control dimension of scanning underlies the ego process pair of empathy–projection, this achievement is complicated by the sex differences which emerged and also by Alker's use of a similar perceptual method to assess both the ego processes and cognitive style. The lack of convergent validation between the empathy and projection scales and other measures of these constructs is not supportive of the scales' construct validity, although Alker notes that all ego processes are "multifaceted constructs" only one dimension of which may be tapped by a single measure. In view of the variation in method used, it is not surprising that the ego scales did not correlate with the photographic rating procedure, a method whose validity is itself not well established. More problematic is the failure of the projection scale to correlate significantly with Ullman's measure (1962), which was also empirically derived from the MMPI.

An exploration of the political correlates of projection and empathy was reported in a later paper by Alker (1971), who again used Haan's scales for these constructs as his main personality measures in a Person X Situation experimental design. As hypothesized, the use of projection was associated with extreme leftist, anticolonial attitudes when the responses were elicited in a suspicion-allaying condition. The association remained significant while controlling for the possible effects of empathy, social insight, and other cognitive variables. The results of this study are generally supportive of the projection scale's utility.

Powers and Alker (1968) undertook an investigation of the paired processes of repression–suppression as variables affecting the recognition and reporting of taboo words elicited in an experimental condition encouraging such reports. Subjects were 40 undergraduate females, who, after initially completing the suppression and repression scales were presented with 22 words, 4 of which were taboo. Galvanic skin response (GSR) was monitored as subjects were presented with each word at gradually increasing stages of legibility. The authors hypothesized that suppressors, accurately perceiving that the GSR situation called for the honest reporting of taboo words upon their detection, would require lower identification levels for reporting taboo words than would repressors. This hypothesis was confirmed, although the lack of a control group complicates the findings. If the main purpose was to show that suppressors rather than repressors are particularly sensitive to cues in the experimental situation which affect differential reporting of taboo words, an alternative design might have employed an experimental GSR group, a control non-GSR group, and groups of repressors and suppressors within the context of a factorial design. Allowing for an adequate sample size, this would have permitted the analysis of the main effects of the manipulation, the individual difference variables and their interaction on taboo word reporting. Since no controls were employed and repression scores were subtracted from suppression scores in the actual study, it is difficult to estimate the overall impact of the manipulation and the independence of the repression and suppression effects on the dependent variable. Because of these methodological shortcomings, the findings of this study should be accepted with some caution, though they do provide some data supporting the validity of the repression–suppression distinction and the measures of these constructs.

Alker (1966, 1968) has also reported results of an investigation of item characteristics of the defense and coping item pools. Eliminating items from the item pools which were included in both defense and coping measures, Alker examined the remaining 286 items (129 coping, 157 defense) for social desirability values and controversiality, as indexed by the standard deviation of the social desirability values of each item. With regard to controversiality, a significant association between the controversiality of coping items and their empirically keyed direction was found that was absent in the defense item pool. Specifically, Alker found a greater tendency for highly controversial items to be affirmed and minimally controversial items to be negated in the coping set. In addition, the presence of socially desirable characteristics was inferred by affirmative responses to high-desirability items and negative responses to low-desirability items. A comparison of the frequency of such socially desirable responses in the coping and defense item sets showed significant differences, with a higher proportion of such responses among the coping items. Alker's conclusion, that endorsement of socially desirable items may actually reflect the performance of genuinely valuable social behavior (coping), argues against the elimination of high-desirability items from personality inventories, as well as shedding additional insight on coping characteristics. Although the results of this study have no bearing on the validity of particular defense and coping scales, they provide data suggesting that copers may be broadly differentiated from defenders by their controversial commitments and genuinely valued social behavior.

The most stringent test of the defense scales is reported in a validation study of the Defense Mechanism Inventory (DMI) by Gleser and Ihilevich (1969). The DMI is an instrument devised for measuring responses on five dimensions of defense. Subjects are presented with a series of stories, after which they are asked to indicate which of five structured responses best characterizes a response to the story. The DMI has been cross-validated and subjected to fairly extensive reliability and validity tests (Barclay, Weissman, Ritter & Gordon, 1971; Clum & Clum, 1973; Gleser & Ihilevich, 1969; Gleser & Sucks, 1973). Because of the conceptual similarity to the Haan defense model, it may be of interest to examine the instrument more closely here.

The following descriptions of the five defense classifications of the DMI have been taken from Gleser and Ihilevich (1969, p. 52):

1. *Turning against Object* (TAO). This class of defenses deals with conflict through attacking a real or presumed external frustrating object. Such classical defenses as identification-with-the-aggressor and displacement can be placed in this category.
2. *Projection* (PRO). Included here are defenses which justify the expression of aggression toward an external object through attributing to it, without unequivocal evidence, negative intent or characteristics.
3. *Principalization* (PRN). This class of defense deals with conflict through invoking a general principle that "splits off" affect from content and represses the former. Defenses such as intellectualization, isolation, and rationalization fall into this category.
4. *Turning against Self* (TAS). In this class are those defenses that handle conflict through directing aggressive behavior toward S himself. Masochism and autosadism are examples of defensive solutions in this category.
5. *Reversal* (REV). This class includes defenses that deal with conflict by responding in a positive or neutral fashion to a frustrating object which might be expected to evoke a negative reaction. Defenses such as negation, denial, reaction formation, and repression are subsumed under this category.

From this scheme, some straightforward hypotheses can be formulated regarding the relationship of the DMI categories to Haan's defenses. Isolation, intellectualization, and rationalization should show positive correlations with PRN; denial, reaction formation, repression, and primitive defense should be associated with REV, projection with PRO, and displacement with TAO. Doubt might possibly be linked with TAS. Regression does not seem to fit easily into the DMI's classification scheme. Gleser and Ihilevich report validity data for the DMI which compare their measures against Haan's scales, and the significant associations are reproduced here as Table XX.

The subject population included two samples of psychiatric clinic outpatients. Of the 10 hypotheses suggested above, only 9 were testable because of the lack of a rationalization scale. The data indicate good results for 3 of these (denial, primitive defense, and doubt), fair results for 2 (intellectualizing and projection) and poor results for 4 (isolation, reaction formation, repression, and displacement). Other correlations tend to support relationships between the two models. Denial correlates negatively with TAO and positively with PRN, which is consistent with the lack of aggressiveness presented by the denier, along with his reluctance to admit to experiencing unpleasant affects. The latter point is underscored by the positive relation between primitive defense and PRN. Doubt, on the other hand, reverses the relationships, correlating negatively with REV and PRN, suggesting that the doubter does not neutralize or disavow his conflicts and is painfully aware of his

Table XX
Correlations between Scores in the Defense Scales of the DMI and Those of Haan

	Males		Females	
Scales	Clinic 1	Clinic 2	Clinic 1	Clinic 2
TAO × Displacement	.12	.04	.00	−.05
TAO × Denial	.00	−.40**	−.43*	−.26*
TAO × Repression	−.14	−.33	−.33	−.20
PRO × Projection	.06	−.04	.36	.01
PRN × Intellectualizing	.29	.09	−.21	.19
PRN × Doubt	−.50**	−.17	−.28	−.26*
PRN × Denial	.34	.33**	.26	.48**
PRN × Primitive defense	.22	.33**	.24	.07
TAS × Doubt	.33	.26*	.35	.30*
TAS × Repression	.29	.35**	−.10	−.36**
REV × Doubt	−.01	−.25*	−.08	−.10
REV × Denial	.24	.48**	.50**	.30**
REV × Primitive defense	.23	.37**	.48**	−.08

Source: Data from Gleser and Ihilevich (1969).
NOTE: For males (clinic 1, $N = 23$; clinic 2, $N = 67$); for females (clinic 1, $N = 24$; clinic 2, $N = 93$).
*$p = .05$
**$p = .01$

affective distress. An interesting sex difference appears in the association between repression and TAS, which correlates positively for males and negatively for females in both samples.

The findings comparing the DMI to the Haan scales begin to suggest differences in the scales' worth. Here and in the Haan study (1965), denial and doubt show consistent and predictable relationships to other variables. Projection, primitive defense, and intellectualization receive some, though qualified, support here, and Haan has also noted fair results for repression and regression. The scales for isolation, displacement, and reaction formation, on the other hand, show no clear relationships to other variables.

An investigation of the coping dimension of the model was undertaken by Saffer (1968) in his dissertation research investigating personality characteristics associated with obesity. Administering the CPI to a sample of 30 obese males attending a reducing clinic and 30 male controls matched for age, intelligence, occupation, and education, Saffer predicted that the control group would outscore the obese on seven coping variables: objectivity, intellectuality, regression in the service of the ego, empathy, suppression, controlled coping and total coping. Significant results in the predicted direction were observed for all coping variables considered with the exception of regression in the service of the ego and total coping, which failed to differentiate the groups. The results of the study are interesting in several respects. First, if some selection bias was incurred by choosing obese subjects who had voluntarily enrolled in a treatment program rather than an unselected group of obese individuals, this bias would result in a conservative test of the null hypotheses under consideration. That is, one would expect that self-identification of problems of obesity and subsequent enrollment in an appropriate treatment program presume a fair degree of accuracy, rationality, and purposefulness on the part of the obese subjects included in the study. To obtain significant relationships despite this qualification speaks well for the measures used. Second, the Saffer study suggests the utility of conceptualizing clinically oriented problems from the point of view of a lack of adequate coping resources, rather than simply the presence (or absence) of certain defenses.

The broadest test of the scales for the entire model was undertaken by Thelen and Varble (1970), who attempted to differentiate 65 college students who had sought psychotherapy from 112 no-therapy controls. One problem in this study is that the matching procedure was not rigorously controlled by sex, age, intelligence, or SES. The coping scales used in the study were objectivity, intellectuality, logical analysis, concentration, empathy, regression in the service of the ego and suppression; the defense scales used were intellectualization, doubt, denial, projection, regression, displacement, and repression. It was hypothesized that the controls would score significantly higher on the coping measures and significantly lower on the defenses. Since the data were analyzed separately by sex, 28 hypotheses in all were tested.

Results generally showed support for the measures. For the coping dimension, suppression and concentration significantly differentiated the groups in the predicted direction for both sexes, and objectivity did so for males. Interestingly, logical analysis also yielded significant results for both sexes, but the direction of the relationship reversed, with the therapy group outscoring the controls. Of the scales which did not differentiate the two groups, it is interesting that two, playfulness and empathy, involve suspension of control, suggesting that ego expressiveness may not be relevant for identifying pathology in a culture where control is more characteristic of normative social functioning.

The pattern of results was similar for the defense scales investigated. Displacement and projection significantly differentiated the groups for both sexes in the predicted direction, and doubt did so for males. Denial produced a reversal of the hypothesis for both sexes, with the therapy group scoring less than the controls. In view of the consistent negative correlations between the Denial scale and indices of psychological distress, this result is clearly in line with previous findings and provides more evidence for the scale's validity. Help-seeking behavior is contingent on the acceptance of psychological distress and its public admission, both of which are incompatible with denial. Measures of intellectualization, regression, and repression failed to distinguish the groups for either sex.

Although the Thelen and Varble (1970) and Saffer (1968) studies have some relevance in the investigation of the relationship of ego processes to variables of clinical interest, the most systematic attempt to assess the utility of the Haan model for psychopathological problems has been made by Naditch and his associates in a series of studies focusing on acute adverse reactions to psychoactive drugs, (Naditch, 1974, 1975a,b), drug usage (Naditch, 1975c), drug flashbacks (Naditch & Naditch, 1975), depression (Naditch, Gargan, & Michael, 1975) and problem drinking (Naditch, 1975d).

In an investigation of correlates of drug usage and acute adverse reactions to drugs in a sample of 483 male drug users, Naditch (1974) found that regression was associated with LSD–mescaline usage and strongly related to acute adverse reactions to both marijuana and LSD–mescaline. The relationships observed were attenuated, but remained statistically significant, when the effects of other personality variables were held constant via path analytic techniques. Naditch observed that results supported the hypothesis that regressive individuals may take drugs as a passive attempt to handle personal problems and consequently increase the likelihood of having an adverse reaction to the drug experience. A moderately strong negative correlation between the regression scale and a measure of personal adjustment was also reported in this study, supporting the position that persons utilizing regressive defenses are particularly vulnerable to interpersonal, financial, or sexual stresses. In further analyses of these data (Naditch, 1975a,b), regression continued to show strong, independent associations with adverse reactions to the drug experience when considered in multiple regression equations including motives for use (Naditch, 1975a) and other ego process variables (Naditch, 1975b). In addition to regression, the latter study examined the relationship of denial, repression, projection, intellectualization, regression in the service of the ego, tolerance of ambiguity, and total coping to the development of acute adverse reactions. The only ego variable consistently showing no relation to the dependent variable was projection;

hypothesized associations between each of the other processes and adverse drug reactions were confirmed.

Naditch (1975c) also has presented the results of a discriminant function analysis, using the same data, which attempted to differentiate marijuana users from those users who also employed more potent psychoactive drugs. Results suggest interesting personality differences for these different types of drug users. Regression, regression in the service of the ego, and total coping each emerged as independent discriminating variables for the two groups, suggesting that users of more potent drugs differ from marijuana-only users by greater employment of defensive regression and poorer coping capacity, as well as by more characteristic use of regression in the service of the ego. Naditch suggests that one factor which may predispose some marijuana users to go on to use more potent, illicit drugs, may be a lack of effective coping skills and the use of primitive psychological defenses such as regression.

Naditch and Naditch (1975) investigated the occurrence of flashbacks in a subgroup of 235 LSD users from the sample described above. Results indicated that subjects experiencing flashbacks were more likely to employ repression and regression, were less likely to use intellectualization, had less tolerance of ambiguity and less total coping capacity than those who did not report flashbacks. Interestingly, most of these associations were attenuated to nonsignificant levels when the effects of acute adverse reactions to LSD were taken into account. The authors suggest that the occurrence of flashbacks can be understood not as a direct result of ego functioning, but as an indirect consequence of the tendency of individuals with impaired ego functioning to experience more acute adverse reactions.

Relationships between denial, locus of control, and self-reported depression and anxiety were examined in a study of 547 males in Army basic training conducted by Naditch et al. (1975). Employing the denial scale, Naditch et al. found significant negative correlations between denial and depression, anxiety, and locus of control. The first two associations offer a replication of previous findings concerning denial and psychopathological symptoms, while the relationship between denial and Rotter's (1966) I–E scale suggests that deniers may also disavow any suggestion of manipulation or control from external sources. In view of the high correlations observed between denial and social desirability (Haan, 1965), it is also possible that deniers are acutely sensitive in presenting themselves in a socially acceptable light and are more inclined to endorse internal items because of this characteristic. Since the I–E scale shows a moderate and consistently negative relationship with social desirability across different populations (Rotter, 1966), the association between denial and locus of control may be a function of this third variable.

In a further investigation of these data, Naditch (1975d), examined the relationship between several ego processes and problem drinking behavior. Regression, denial, total coping, repression, and displacement each demonstrated linear relationships with problems in drinking. Four of these (with the exception of denial) remained significant when the effects of the others were controlled by multiple regression analysis. This study also provides some data on the relationship of the ego variables to paper-and-pencil measures of extraversion, aggression, and anti-social behavior. Denial, repression, and total coping correlated significantly and negatively with aggression and antisocial behavior, while regression reversed this direction, perhaps indicating the tendency of regressive individuals to "act out" in impulsive, socially undesirable ways. The ego variables considered showed few clear relationships to extraversion, with the exception of denial, which yielded a moderate positive correlation. A somewhat puzzling aspect of the analysis was the lack of association between displacement and aggression and the negative association between displacement and antisocial behavior. Such results are inconsistent with the notion that individuals utilizing displacement tend to deal with impluses in the socially inappropriate modes which aggression and antisocial behavior suggest.

An attempt to integrate the findings of the Naditch studies from the point of view of scale validities suggests that the regression, denial, and total coping scales provide fairly consistent and predictable associations with different indices of psychopathology. Some support for the defense scales of intellectualization and repression and for the coping scales of regression in the service of the ego and tolerance of ambiguity was also evident. More questionable are the results for the projection and displacement measures, which yielded relatively inconsistent effects for the hypotheses tested.

The final study to be reviewed here used the defense scales in an attempt to assess general MMPI scale consistency over time when used in an ideographic manner. Dahlstrom (1972) reports an attempt to estimate the degree of fluctuation in standard and special MMPI scales (including Haan's) for two individuals at different points in time. The first case involved a young married male student who, when originally tested, showed high levels of primitive defense and intellectualization. When tested $1\frac{1}{2}$ years later in the midst of a marital crisis, some changes were noted; primitive defense, denial, and intellectualization scores dropped, while doubt rose dramatically. When tested after the crisis had been resolved, doubt dropped, primitive defense remained low, and intellectualization returned to its previous level. A second case, that of a female nurse, showed a different pattern. Originally showing high scores on intellectualizing and projection and low scores on primitive defense, the nurse later experienced a psychotic episode, during which she attempted suicide. Tested during this period, scores reflected a drop in intellectualization and projection, with a rise in denial, primitive defense, and displacement. Doubt remained relatively unchanged. These two examples are instructive in that they suggest that the scales may be profitably used to record shifts in defensive patternings as individuals enter and resolve crises. The two cases are illustrative of the marked extent of individual differences in the use of defenses preceding and following stress. The student, originally exhibiting a cognitively "primitive" way of dealing with conflict (with the exception of the classic student defense of intellectualization), drops this mode under stress and becomes intensely self-questioning, which seems to result in an abandonment of his earlier primitive defense patterns. The nurse chooses the opposite strategy, moving from a more differentiated pattern of defense to one characterized by denial and primitive defense. Although Dahlstrom's data are based solely on the MMPI item pool, it would also be instructive to examine shifting patterns of coping on an idiographic level, as they naturally develop through the life cycle, and at specific crisis points.

Dahlstrom also describes administering the MMPI to 16 dental and medical students 2 weeks prior to LSD administration, again at the height of the drug effect, and a final readministration within 3 days following the experience. Under LSD, marked rises were observed on the regression, displacement, and doubt scales. Postdrug administration documented a return to original levels. The results for the regression and doubt measures are particularly instructive in that they signal a diminishing of effective contact with external reality accompanied by an acute awareness of conflicting and disturbing subjective states, both of which are consonant with the drug experience.

In all, the Dahlstrom findings argue for the clinical utility of the defense scales, which may provide a constructive method of capturing idiographic patternings of ego processes over time. The shifts recorded during crisis points and under drug influence also present more evidence for the construct validity of particular defense scales.

Theoretical Implications

The preceding section of this chapter has demonstrated that the Haan model has been found useful by a number of researchers working in a variety of psychological subfields. The questions to be addressed now involve consideration of how this body of empirical findings bears on the theoretical claims of the model. For purposes of the present discussion, four such theoretical issues will be discussed: the existence of coping, the differential correlates of coping and defense, the origins of ego processes, and the normative nature of coping.

THE EXISTENCE OF COPING

There has been some reluctance, especially on the part of psychoanalytically oriented writers, to admit to the existence of coping activity, that is, personality processes which are nondefensive, accurate, and flexible with regard to reality transactions. The resolution of this question relies on obtaining adequate intersubjective agreement that an observed action does indeed conform to the criteria specified by the coping constructs. Issues of the identification of coping processes from ongoing transactions and the reliability of such identifications are paramount.

The studies cited above which utilize the empirically derived scales do not have a direct bearing on this issue since they presuppose the existence of coping by investigating its correlates. With regard to the studies employing ego ratings, evidence is mixed, but generally supportive of the construct. Transcripts of the interviews obtained from the Folkins (1970) experiment, for example, contain statements by subjects who did not distort the reality of the threatening shock stimulus while waiting for its occurrence, but who instead attempted to place the event in perspective by using other information available to them (see Haan, 1969). These subjects recalled their freedom to terminate their role as subjects at any time, reasoned that university ethical procedures would prohibit the use of a heavy shock of long duration, or noted that the experimenter had not arranged for physical examinations and thus decided that the shock would not be great. Others, having considered some of the ramifications of the threat situation, deliberately diverted their attention to other matters. Seen in the context of the ego model, these cognitive strategies give evidence of objectivity, logical analysis, intellectuality, concentration, and suppression in the face of threat.

In a recent study, Viney and Clarke (1974) found the concept of coping useful in explaining the results of an experiment which examined children's responses in an induced "crisis." In the experiment, a series of rewards were abruptly terminated and the responses of the children monitored following reinforcement cessation. The children responded in a variety of ways, from attempts to create new responses to regain the reward, to "giving up," or to "frustration" responses signifying a rigid adherence to behavioral patterns which no longer produced their customary effects. The authors note that Haan's distinction between coping and defense is useful in identifying purposive and reality-oriented behavior, such as the initiation of original responses, as well as those actions which are fixed and maladaptive.

Estimates of the consistency of such identifications are more problematic. With the possible exceptions of the "hippie" study (Haan et al., 1973) and the recent Haan follow-up of OGS subjects (Haan, 1974a), both of which reported good interjudge agreement on the coping processes, and the study of ego functioning in old age (Kuypers, 1972, 1974), which reported no reliability coefficient below .5, empirical research has shown mixed results regarding interrater reliability.

Folkins (1970) found three coping ratings (regression in the service of the ego, sublimation, and suppression) unreliable, though this may have been a function of the conditions under which the ratings were obtained. Hunter and Goodstein (1967) and Margolis (1970) obtained only moderate reliability ratings, with the exception of the global coping rating, on which agreement was excellent. Weinstock (1967a) and Haan (1963) report mean reliabilities of acceptable magnitude for the coping functions, although this is somewhat clouded by the sex differences noted earlier. Despite the fact that reliability coefficients for the coping functions are not overwhelming, it should be noted that in each study investigated, identification of the coping processes fared no worse than specification of the defense functions, whose acceptance by both clinicians and researchers is commonplace. In fact, in three studies for which exact data are available (Haan, 1963; Haan et al., 1973; Weinstock, 1967a), mean reliabilities for the coping processes exceeded the mean ratings for defense.

In summary, the studies reviewed indicate that coping functioning can be identified with moderate consistency by independent judges during interview situations. Given the prodigious problems of personality assessment using any measurement device, the magnitude of the ratings obtained should probably be taken less as indicative of a spurious construct than as signaling the need for conceptual clarification in the coding scheme provided to raters. It is also likely that even if this were to be accomplished, some coping processes (e.g., substitution and sublimation) would be more difficult to identify than others (e.g., logical analysis and concentration), especially using only interview data.

DIFFERING CORRELATES OF COPING AND DEFENSE

The original rationale for the broad division of ego processes into coping and defense presupposed that the employment of more differentiated and purposive modes of personality functioning could be expected to lead to more positive consequences for the person than would defensive modes. Although Haan notes (Chapter 4) that coping never guarantees success or mastery, it does involve the notion of "open system" functioning, which should increase the probability that interchanges with the environment will be productive, life-enhancing experiences. This situation is in contrast with "closed system" defensive modes which, in their negation and distortion of life events, may rob the individual of chances to profit from experience and may render maladaption more likely.

The evidence on this point is not unequivocal, but is clearly suggestive of the utility of distinguishing between the two modes. Coping has generally been found to have positive associations with intellectual functioning and IQ acceleration over time (Haan, 1963), adult SES and social mobility (Haan, 1964a), intellectual and affective enjoyment in a test-taking situation (Haan, 1964b), measures of nonpathological functioning (Haan, 1965), high ego strength (Hunter & Goodstein, 1967), belief in internal control (Kuypers, 1972), and moral development (Haan et al., 1973), while negative associations have been observed with obesity (Saffer, 1968), help-seeking (Thelen & Varble, 1970), acute adverse drug reactions (Naditch, 1975b), and problem drinking (Naditch, 1975d). It would seem that copers can more easily draw on their well-developed intellectual and moral capacities to facilitate effective transactions with their environment in the attainment of valued goals. In the process, it is likely that copers come to feel some confidence in their ability to handle events and become resistant to signs of psychological distress.

Defense, on the other hand, has been shown to be negatively related to IQ and positively associated with male IQ deceleration (Haan, 1963), low adult SES, and downward social mobility (Haan, 1964a), measures of psychopathological functioning (Haan, 1965), low ego strength (Hunter and Goodstein, 1967), belief in external control (Kuypers, 1972), extremist and political attitudes (Alker, 1971), help-seeking (Thelen & Varble, 1970), acute adverse drug reactions (Naditch, 1974, 1975a) and problem drinking (Naditch, 1975d). It is possible that defensive individuals, because of their tendency to bend perceptions to their own needs, fail to take advantage of realistic opportunities for achievement and enjoyment. Fatalistic, rigid expectancies regarding their abilities to influence events may develop and render them more vulnerable to symptoms of psychopathology. There is reason, however, to be cautious regarding such a formulation. In contrast to the evidence presented on coping, some of the studies cited above suggest that the use of defenses need not be self-defeating nor indicative of acute psychological difficulties. Structured defense, for example, was found to be associated with IQ gains for women (Haan, 1963), and with intellectual functioning and ego development in "hippies" (Haan et al., 1973), while specific defensive postures (e.g., intellectualization) have been consistently related to SES (Haan, 1964a; Weinstock, 1967b). In addition, the data provided by Naditch (1975b,d) suggest that the inability to employ defenses such as denial, displacement, and projection can also lead to problems in effective functioning. These findings, combined with the consistent failure of the total defense variable to differentiate items in personality inventories (Haan, 1965; Naditch and Joffe, this volume), suggest that global conceptualizations of defensiveness may be misleading, and that specific defensive postures may be facilitative under certain circumstances for certain groups and individuals.

Such a formulation is not inconsistent with Haan's framework, since a simple good–bad dichotomy is deliberately eschewed by the conceptualization of coping and defense as independent, rather than bipolar, processes. Rather than anticipating consistent positive correlates of coping and consistent negative correlates of defense, one would expect that, on the whole, coping should be associated with more intellectual, moral, and social gains while defense should render these outcomes less likely, but not impossible. The evidence to date supports such a conclusion.

ORIGINS OF EGO PROCESSES

Central to the conceptual formulation of ego functioning developed in this volume is the notion that ego processes are created within the matrix of family interaction patterns during childhood and adolescence and continue to be employed as strategies throughout life. As Haan has noted (Chapter 4), this view implies that ego functions are not states which result from social learning via modeling or reinforcement effects, but relational modes which the person actively constructs in the process of giving organization to his experience, within the constraints imposed by external pressures and internal levels of cognitive and moral attainment.

Although direct evidence on the constructivist-versus-learning argument is extremely difficult to obtain, a number of studies bear on the issue. Perhaps the most important of these is the Haan study (found in Chapter 7) which compares ego processes of family members with one another. Although the specific findings of the study are too complex to be summarized here, it should be noted that Haan found evidence for both identity and complementarity in comparing parents' and adolescents' ego processes. Daughters of affectively controlled and nonempathic parents, for example, seemed to disavow affective regulation and develop empathic modes of relating interpersonally. Boys whose mothers' coping capacities were low showed signs of cognitive coping. On the other hand, there was the suggestion in the data that families in which identity of ego functioning was found were characterized by mutual defensiveness. Whether such styles are the result of direct learning or the result of constructed cognitive retrenchments in the fact of interpersonal difficulties is an intriguing question that cannot be answered with the available data.

Other studies show similar equivocal results. Weinstock (1967a) found that primitive defenses were rooted more in early childhood experience than were structured defenses, which showed stronger associations with family variables in adolescence. Weinstock argues that his results support both social learning theory and also a cognitive-developmental position. Use of defenses such as denial, repression, regression, and doubt by his male subjects seemed to mirror similar behavior on the part of the parents, with the strongest relationships evidenced in early childhood. On the other hand, conflict in the home during adolescence was generally predictive of expressive coping in later years. Weinstock (1967a, p. 74) notes that "the immature ego seems to react to conflict in the early family environment by rigid imitation of the parents' ways of handling conflict, while the more mature ego learns to confront conflict and impulses and to deal with them in an adaptive way."

The relationship of adolescent conflict to later coping is reflected in Haan's longitudinal study of OGS subjects (Haan, 1974a). As adolescents, women copers valued independence, were socially poised, and showed little respect for parental authority. Male copers were described as haughty, intellectually arrogant, and also gave evidence of conflict with parents. It seems plausible to suggest that copers may have used this conflict in a productive way to restructure their experience and actively develop flexible modes of dealing with their environments. However, not enough data concerning the ego processes of the parents of these adolescents is available in the Weinstock (1967a) and Haan (1974a) studies to decide the constructivist-learning issue with any certainty.

COPING AS THE NORMATIVE EGO MODE

Perhaps the most difficult problem which the Haan formulation raises is the ever-thorny value question. There seem to be at least two different ways in which Haan has discussed the normative nature of coping. First, from a metatheoretical perspective, she notes that values are implicit in all personality theorizing and that the concept of coping requires only weak assumptions with which most observers would agree, namely, that flexible, open, responsive transactions with self and environment are preferable to self-deceptive, reality-distortive transactions. Adherence to the coping formulation requires only acceptance that certain processes are more valuable than others and allows for wide differences in the end-goals particular individuals wish to achieve. Second, from an empirical perspective, Haan notes that coping actually is the preferred method which most individuals use in their daily transactions. It is in this context of emphasizing the utilitarian hierarchy of ego functions that she writes (this volume): "Coping is then very simply the *normative* mode. All other matters being equal, the person will cope. . . ." Again, "[The] person will cope if he can, defend if he must, and fragment if he is forced to do so." The former proposition suggests that coping should be adopted by psychologists as a criterion for optimal personality functioning, while the latter implies that most people have, in effect, already done so.

If the first formulation is indeed metatheoretical, empirical evidence supporting its validity can be considered tangential at best, since value questions are nonempirical by definition. Nevertheless, the positive correlates of coping described above are interesting, despite the fact that most of them (e.g., social mobility) reflect end-goals that are especially valued in our culture. Alker's studies (1966, 1968), examining the characteristics of the coping and defense item pools, are also of relevance here. It will be recalled that coping items were found to reflect more genuinely valuable social characteristics than were the defense items. If response to the coping items actually is reflective of real-life behavior that mirrors item content, it is possible that coping could be considered to facilitate valuable social performance. Here, too, results may be limited to our society, but cross-cultural and subcultural applications of the model might yield generally positive associations between coping and the particular valued goals under consideration.

Compared with previous approaches to the study of optimal personality functioning, coping presents a slightly different portrait of the "healthy" person. Haan (1974a) has provided some data indicating that ego ratings and ideal Q sort descriptions of subjects show good convergence regarding nonoptimal personality characterizations but diverge substantially in their characterization of optimal functioning. In short, copers seem less conventional and less conflict-free than Q sort characterizations of the "ideal" personality suggest. Coping, often presaged by conflict and autonomy in adolescence, seems marked by productivity, fluency, introspection, independence in judgment, and controversiality in adulthood.

Haan's second formulation, regarding the actual preferred ego modes of individuals confronting life situations, is eminently researchable, but as yet virtually untested. One finding that has some bearing on the issue is the Folkins study (1970), which examined anticipation time and its effect on stress reactions. His results indicate that for shorter time intervals between threat of shock and termination, coping was more marked, while longer intervals produced more ego failure. This result lends tentative support to the thesis that individuals may initially prefer to utilize coping functions rather than defensive or fragmenting processes in dealing with situations.

Methodological Problems and Research Lacunae

Although the present review has found the empirical results bearing on the Haan model encouraging, a number of methodological problems have also been noted, including the use of nonrepresentative samples (Haan et al., 1973), liberal significance criteria (Haan, 1964b; Haan et al., 1973) and potentially biased rating procedures (Haan, 1964a). An equally serious drawback to the present line of research is that its conclusions are drawn largely from the investigation of a single population, subjects in longitudinal studies at Berkeley. Of the 14 studies utilizing judges' ratings in ego assessment (Haan, 1963, 1963a,g, 1965, 1974a; Kreober, 1963; Kuypers, 1972, 1974; Weinstock, 1967a,b) 10 have employed either subjects, parents of subjects, or offspring of subjects from either the Oakland Growth Study or the Berkeley Guidance Study. Although the breadth and depth of coverage on these subjects has been great (and all too rare in psychology), it is nevertheless important to extend the research findings on this population to other samples, across age, occupational, educational, and regional lines. Similarly, the five research reports relating ego processes to drug-related variables (Naditch, 1974, 1975a,b,c; Naditch & Naditch, 1975) have been generated from one subject pool. Replication and extension of these efforts to other groups is now underway and, if successful, will greatly enhance the suggestive findings reported earlier. Problems of adequate interrater reliability have been discussed in previous sections of this chapter and need not be repeated here except to reemphasize the possibility for conceptual clarification of some aspects of the model.

One interesting test of the conceptual soundness of the entire scheme would be to subject it to a multitrait–multimethod analysis (Campbell & Fiske, 1959). Now that cross-validated empirical measures are available, one could use both judges' ratings and the scales to operationalize the model and determine if the measures show adequate convergent and discriminant validity. It may be that correlations between estimates of the same ego process obtained from different data sources are consistently lower than associations between different ego processes obtained by the same method. A similar methodological analysis between selected ego variables (e.g., logical analysis and intellectuality) and conceptually similar, but more generally accepted variables (e.g., intelligence), might also be useful in determining whether the formulation of ego variables described by Haan actually has any measurable advantages over more traditional personality variables.

It would also be instructive along these lines if investigators would publish intercorrelations among the ego measures. Although factor analyses might have been performed (Haan, 1963; Folkins, 1970), inspection of the interrelationships of ego processes would be helpful in determining how ego functioning relates to other variables of interest. For example, in assessing the implications of the ego model for social mobility or intellectual functioning, how much of the observed relationship between cognitive processes and these variables is actually due to shared variance among the ego process variables themselves? Although the general relationship between the ego functions and the dependent variables is clear, only an analysis which takes into account intercorrelations among the specific ego variables would clarify whether their contributions to the explained variance are unique. Multiple regression analysis would be helpful along these lines, to determine both the independence and relative importance of different ego processes in relation to different dependent variables of interest. Naditch (1974, 1976a,b,c), for example, has used this technique to advantage in his studies of drug usage.

Although the newly derived empirical scales whose construction is reported in this volume by Joffe and Naditch will supplant the previous ego scales (Haan, 1965), some assessment of their worth is central to the purpose of this review. Generally, encouraging support for their validity has been found, although some differences in quality among the individual scales is evident. The defense scales have generally received more attention in research, and consistent results have been observed particularly in connection with the denial scale (Gleser & Ihilevich, 1969; Haan, 1965; Naditch et al., 1975; Thelen & Varble, 1970), the doubt scale (Dahlstrom, 1972; Gleser & Ihilevich, 1969; Haan, 1965; Thelen & Varble, 1970), and the regression scale (Dahlstrom, 1972; Haan, 1965; Naditch, 1974, 1975a,b). The projection measure (Alker, 1971; Gleser & Ihilevich, 1969; Thelen & Varble, 1970) shows promise, but contradictory evidence has been reported (Alker, 1967; Gleser & Ihilevich, 1969; Naditch, 1975b). There is also some positive evidence for the intellectualization, displacement and primitive defense scales (Dahlstrom, 1972; Gleser & Ihilevich, 1969; Naditch & Naditch, 1975; Thelen & Varble, 1970). Although the coping scales have not been adequately tested, preliminary results show that the suppression and objectivity measures have differentiated psychologically atypical groups from normals in two independent samples (Saffer, 1968; Thelen & Varble, 1970), while promising results for the tolerance of ambiguity, regression in the service of the ego and total coping scales have also been noted (Haan, 1965; Naditch, 1975b). More research is needed on the coping dimension, particularly using the scales for the intraceptive processes.

Extended use of the psychometric measures in assessing ego functioning will allow extension of some of the previous work relating ego functioning to intelligence, social functioning, and moral and ego development to larger populations. The systematization which the Haan model brings to the study of ego processes offers promise not only in the substantive areas mentioned above, but also in other areas of long-standing concern in psychological research. Creativity research might benefit from a perspective which allows scope for suspension of control (tolerance of ambiguity, regression in the service of the ego), the disciplined application of cognitive activity (concentration, objectivity) and the resultant creative accomplishment (sublimation, substitution). Inclusion of the defense dimension might also shed some light on the oft-observed connection between creativity and neurosis.

Research in psychotherapy might take the model as a scheme for analyzing movement during the course of therapy, from defensive to coping modes of functioning. In addition, it might also be possible to clarify which therapist and client variables are the most promising in predicting positive therapeutic outcomes, and may even help to specify particular interactive combinations of ego functioning between therapist and client which would facilitate client growth. Would a client who prefers an ego strategy based on logical analysis, for example, respond more positively to a therapist whose strengths lie in the same cognitive direction, or would some aspect of ego complementarity prove more facilitative of the interaction? Although the effects of therapist empathy have received much attention in psychotherapy research, perhaps other processes (e.g., tolerance of ambiguity, objectivity) are equally important, particularly for clients whose own ego functioning meshes well with these characteristics.

The model's usefulness as a scheme for organizing reactions to experimental stressors has already been investigated, but its use in naturalistic studies of stress has yet to be tapped. In view of the recent concern in identifying the "resistance resources" that individuals bring to situations of life change (Antonovsky, 1974), the ego model represents one of the most fruitful methods of specifying individual difference variables that might act as resources under situations of stress. Individuals with high coping capacities, including the ability to view threatening situations objectively, reason about their causes and consequences, and tolerate the ambiguity of shifting life patterns, might be expected to be spared the psychological and physical distress of life change and more easily mobilize their energies to meet such situations in realistic, constructive ways. Regressive individuals, when undergoing similar changes, would probably be likely to experience more distress, give the distress more attention and seek help from health authorities. Deniers, on the other hand, might continue to disavow symptoms of ill health, whether psychological or physical, while experiencing life stress. Clearly, the model yields a number of fertile, testable hypotheses in this area.

This chapter has reviewed the research utility of the Haan model and has found the evidence encouraging and suggestive of further exploration. In contrast to constructs of personal traits, motivations or expectancies, the model calls attention to the general processes individuals use in relating to themselves and to their social environments and so, by definition, has wide applicability. Research on the coping dimension in particular should yield profitable results if Haan is correct in assuming that coping is the norm, rather than the exception, in much of human action. By focusing equally on the rationality, accuracy, and flexibility of individuals' social transactions, as well as on their distortive, defensive aspects, future research may be able to achieve a more balanced assessment in viewing different topics of concern.

13. Paper and Pencil Measures of Coping

and Defense Processes

Paul Joffe and Murray P. Naditch

Most personality scales measure traits, as does the California Personality Inventory (CPI), or symptoms, states, or conformance to diagnostic categories, as does the Minnesota Multiphasic Personality Inventory (MMPI). However, as researchers try to formulate the meaningful interrelationships within various personality systems, they may also want to measure processes. Although processes are probably more directly observed and measures by observational procedures, many research projects are not designed to include such expensive possibilities. Haan (1965) earlier developed a series of preliminary scales for measuring coping and defense, but the present work was undertaken with the thought that these earlier scales could be improved by using greater numbers of subjects and more refined procedures, notably those developed by Darlington and Bishop (1966).

Richard Morrissey reports in his review of research concerning the ego process model (see Chapter 12) that sixteen studies have used the earlier Haan scales and that they have generally yielded consistent findings in a variety of contexts, although some anomalous results have been reported. None of those studies provides a confirmation of the model as a whole; instead, they concern the effectiveness of individual scales. This chapter describes the development of new

The authors would like to thank Richard Darlington for the use of his computer programs as well as his generous comments and suggestions. We also appreciate the helpful comments of Margaret Gargan, Henry Alker. Lewis Goldbert was most generous in permitting us to use the data for the reliability study described in this chapter. Finally, we thank the Institute of Human Development at Berkeley and Norma Haan for the use of these data.

scales using interviewer ratings, CPI and MMPI data, larger samples, and more sophisticated methods. The statistical procedures will include cross-validity coefficients, which measure the scales' ability to predict the criterion in samples other than those on which they were created.

Method

SUBJECTS

Two separate samples were used to create the new version of the scales. Both samples were provided by the Institute of Human Development at Berkeley. The first sample included those members of the longitudinal Oakland Growth Study who had completed the MMPI and who were interviewed when they were approximately 37-years old (Females, $N = 36$; Males, $N = 37$). The second sample was secured at a later follow-up and contained many of these same Oakland Growth subjects, their spouses, as well as two smaller but substantial samples from the Guidance Control Study (total N: Females = 132; Males = 111). All members of the second sample had completed the CPI but not the MMPI. The mean age during the second follow-up was 49 years for the Oakland Growth subjects and 42 for the Guidance-Control subjects. The subjects are almost all white, generally above the national average socioeconomically, and include a range of emotional adequacy from effective, successful individuals to a few who have had one or more experiences as hospitalized psychotics.

INTERVIEWER RATINGS

At both time periods, 20 ratings of ego processes (the 10 coping and 10 defense functions) were made by interviewers, and independent ratings were also made by other clinical psychologists on the basis of typescripts. Interviews concerned the subject's present status, past memory of self, social interactions, and other like matters. The interviews required 12 hours for the first follow-up and between 2 and 4 hours for the second. The details of the interviewing and rating procedures have been previously reported (Haan, 1963, 1974c).

Ratings of these defense and coping processes were generated by adding the interviewer and independent judge's ratings on five-point scales. In addition, results will be reported for two summary measures: (1) summed coping (the summation of the 10 coping processes), and (2) summed defense (the summation of the 10 defense measures). The mean interjudge reliability of the ego processes for the first sample, calculated by a z tranformation was .68 for the men and .55 for women (cf. Haan, 1963, for individual reliabilities).[1] The mean interjudge reliabilities were .70

---

[1] These ratings for females failed to reach acceptable levels (less than .36): isolation, tolerance of ambiguity, and substitution. Reaction formation was unreliable for men.

for male subjects in the second follow-up, .70 for female subjects, .67 for male spouses, .63 for female spouses (cf. Haan, 1974c, for individual reliabilities).

PROCEDURES OF SCALE DEVELOPMENT

Following procedures developed by Darlington and Bishop (1966), the samples were randomly divided into two groups, the first being the test creation sample and the second the cross-validation sample. To increase stability of the measures that were to be generated, more subjects were assigned to the test creation sample than to the cross-validation sample. The MMPI test creation group contained 22 males and 22 females; the cross-validation group contained 15 males and 14 females. The CPI creation group contained 61 men and 82 women, the cross-validation group 50 men and 50 women.

The scale construction procedures were identical for the CPI and MMPI, but will be described only for the MMPI. The first step, taken with the test creation subjects was to correlate 566 item responses with their criterion ego ratings. The second was to generate a preliminary "scale" by successively adding the highest correlated items (most valid items) one at a time in order of descending significance. Thus a 1-item test was constructed from the subjects' score on the single most valid item. Their responses to the second most valid item were added to that to create a 2-item test. This procedure was repeated until there were approximately 60 tests ranging from 1 item to 60 items for each of the ego ratings. The third step involved assigning scores to the subjects in the test validation group ($N = 29$) for each of the 60 individual tests for each rating. Subsequently, the test which resulted in the highest cross-validity, or in other words was best able to predict the actual ego ratings, was selected as the first stage test.

As an example, the first stage test for the defensive function of regression resulted in 21 items. The 1-item test consisted of item 483 (Christ performed miracles such as changing water into wine; scored false). Among the test creation subjects it correlated .50 with the judges' rating of regression and .18 among the test validation subjects. The 2-item test consisted of item 483 and item 55 (I am almost never bothered by pains over my heart or in my chest; scored false). Among the test creation subjects the correlation was .59, the cross-validity .41. Items added after the first 21 failed to improve the test's ability to predict the clinical rating of regression in the cross-validation sample.

The next major procedure was to find those additional items which would add the most variance to the 21-item test's correlation with the clinical rating of regression. This was accomplished by computing partial correlations, among the test creation subjects, between the criterion rating of regression and all 566 items in the pool, controlling for the effects of the first stage test. As before, the most valid items were added one at a time to the 21-item test, creating a 22-item test, a 23-item test, and so on to a 60-item test. Items included in the first stage were removed during the second stage if they developed negative correlations with the clinical rating. The cross-validity of each second stage test was then calculated using the cross-validation group. The second stage test with the highest cross-validity was chosen at the final "preliminary" test. The procedures used for the CPI items were identical.

One interesting characteristic of the items added during the second stage was their markedly reduced face validity. Items were recruited that were seemingly unrelated to the criterion in question or were scored in a direction opposite to what might be expected. The use of partial correlations and the procedure of removing items already included in a test reduced the possibility of overrepresenting or overweighing individual surface components of the criterion.

Most personality test constructors combine males and females during their analyses and later report separate norms. To add stability to the measures, first stage tests were created on a combined sample of men and women. To account for sex differences, which later proved to be substantial, partial correlations were computed for three samples; females and males combined, males only, and females only. Each set of partial correlations was based on the first stage test, created on a combined sample (21 items in the case of regression). Second stage validities were calculated for each group separately. Sex differences were considerable; consequently, only results found when analyzing the sexes separately will be reported.

Following usual test construction procedures, the next major procedure involved recombining the creation and validation samples into one creation sample and repeating the previous procedures. Instead of selecting tests on the basis of cross-validity, tests were selected on the basis of the strength of correlation between the test and clinical rating for all subjects.

There are no established standards for determining the level of acceptability for coefficients of cross-validation. Researchers usually select tests on the basis of their length and their predictive power. A cutoff point of .30 was arbitrarily selected for the MMPI scales and .20 for the CPI because this sample was larger. Although these predictive coefficients appear small, they compare favorably with similar criteria used in other work with scale construction (e.g., Cronbach, 1970; Megargee, 1972).

Combining the subjects into one large creation pool substantially increased the sample size on which the scales were created. This strategy increased the size of the male sample by 82% and the female sample by 61%. Increasing the number of subjects should improve the predictive stability of the scales, although no means of estimating the extent of improvement exists. For this reason, final scales were created on the CPI for all 22 measures regardless of their cross-validity coefficients.

Results

DEVELOPMENT OF MMPI-BASED EGO SCALES

An initial attempt was made to construct the defense scales on the MMPI since Haan (1965) has shown that the item pool of the MMPI was more productive of items that differentiated the defense processes than was the CPI. The CPI had been more productive of items distinguishing the coping processes. However, the necessity of segmenting the samples and the small number of subjects, 37 men and 36 women, who had been interviewed and had completed the MMPI made this work difficult.

Only two defense scales, projection and regression, achieved cross-validities ≥ .30 when MMPI items were the basis of their construction (these results, which range from .36 to .62, appear on the bottom of Table XXI.) Consequently, the remaining defense scales and all of the coping scales were created with CPI items.

DEVELOPMENT OF THE CPI-BASED EGO SCALES

The cross-validities based on the CPI items and the second follow-up subjects were considerably more consistent. The median validity coefficient of acceptable scales was .36 for men and .38 for women. Of the coping scales, 8 out of a possible 11, and 9 of the 11 defense scales yielded acceptable validity coefficients for men (greater than .20). Only 3 coping scales could not be created for women. The coefficients for men ranged from .21 for denial to .57 for intellectuality. The lowest validity coefficient for the female version of the scales was .21, for rational-

Table XXI
Validity Coefficients of the Ego Scales

	Coping				Defense	
	Male	Female			Male	Female
CPI-based scales						
Objectivity	.29	.25	Isolation		.28	.39
Intellectuality	.57	.44	Intellectualization		.37	.38
Logical analysis	.53	.41	Rationalization		−	.21
Concentration	−	−	Denial		.21	.57
Tolerance of ambiguity	.42	.43	Doubt		.36	.44
Empathy	.34	.22	Projection		.42	.24
Regression-ego	.38	.32	Regression		.31	.39
Sublimation	−	.23	Displacement		.29	.49
Substitution	.25	−	Reaction formation		.46	.31
Suppression	−	−	Repression		.34	.38
Total coping	.49	.36	Total defense		−	.35
Controlled coping	.29	.27	Structured defense		−	.47
Expressive coping	.20	.24	Primitive defense		.27	.40
MMPI-based scales						
Concentration	.82	.64	Projection		.36	.49
Suppression	.66	.50	Regression		.62	.46

ization, and the highest was .57, for denial. There were large sex differences in the predictive ability of a number of defense scales, such as denial and displacement.

An attempt was made to create MMPI scales for those coping processes—concentration and suppression—that did not achieve acceptable predictive coefficients with CPI items. Both processes were well discriminated, and their validity coefficients are also presented in Table XXI. To facilitate practical administration of the scales, regression and projection, originally generated on the MMPI, were also created on the CPI. All coping and defense processes with acceptable cross-validities, except for the coping scales of suppression and concentration, can be measured using the CPI.

DEVELOPMENT OF FACTOR SCALES ON THE CPI

A number of test reviewers (Goldberg, 1972; Kelly, 1970; Thorndike, 1970) have objected to the necessity of administering 19 standard CPI scales to achieve a general profile. Various factor analytic studies (Bouchard, 1969; Crites, Bechtoldt, Goodstein & Heilbrun, 1961; Shure & Rogers, 1963; Parloff, Datta, Kleman & Handlon, 1968) have shown that a high degree of redundancy exists among the scales, since four or five stable configurations have consistently been found. Haan has used two summary measures for the ego processes, summed coping and summed defense, but these measures may not reflect the "natural" or underlying configurations of ego functioning. Nevertheless, the decision was made to factor analyze the coping and defense ratings and then extract scales based on the resulting factors, since a smaller set of measures that reduced redundancy would facilitate evaluation. Haan (1963) had previously factor analyzed the ratings for the ego processes and found four factors that had parallel loadings for men and women and a fifth factor that escaped interpretation. She labeled the four factors controlled coping, expressive coping, structured defense, and primitive defense.

The Factor Analysis of the Clinical Ratings

This factor analysis of the ego ratings included all those subjects described in the previous section in addition to 100 subjects who had interview ratings but who had only completed the CPI (total N: females, 188; males, 175). The scales construction was, of course, restricted to those 243 subjects who had both measures.

Separate Pearson product moment correlation matrices were computed for men and women. Four factors with eigenvalues greater than 1.00 were extracted from each group and were submitted to varimax rotation. The factor loadings for men and women appear in Table XXII. The first factor for males was characterized by positive loadings on the coping processes, notably objectivity, intellectuality, and substitution, and negative loadings on displacement, regression, and projection. The

Table XXII
Factor Analysis of Ego Processes

| | Factor Loadings | | | | | | | |
| | Factor 1 | | Factor 2 | | Factor 3 | | Factor 4 | |
	Male	Female	Male	Female	Male	Female	Male	Female
Objectivity	.74	.64	.34	.34	-.15	-.19	-.16	-.31
Isolation	-.02	-.01	-.52	-.38	.58	.66	.19	.20
Intellectuality	.72	.74	.47	.38	.07	.08	-.09	-.19
Intellectualization	.39	.32	.02	-.10	.74	.75	.17	.04
Logical analysis	.70	.74	.44	.38	-.07	-.15	-.23	-.25
Rationalization	-.21	-.23	-.22	-.10	.66	.70	.28	.06
Concentration	.69	.70	.12	-.03	-.06	-.20	-.48	-.09
Denial	-.30	-.36	-.46	-.09	.33	.10	-.18	.70
Tolerance of ambiguity	.38	.54	.65	.27	-.12	.05	.12	-.45
Doubt	-.07	-.36	-.09	.19	.27	.58	.80	-.02
Empathy	.16	.23	.75	.77	-.04	-.13	-.19	-.25
Projection	-.47	-.18	-.15	-.24	.61	.58	-.04	.36
Regression-ego	.17	.33	.79	.65	-.07	-.02	-.05	-.21
Regression	-.51	-.32	.15	.07	.43	.77	.49	.16
Sublimation	.15	.12	.44	.18	-.01	-.30	-.53	-.18
Displacement	-.61	-.15	-.15	-.25	.46	.60	.01	.15
Substitution	.71	.62	.17	.33	.04	-.19	.01	.19
Reaction formation	-.11	.12	-.56	-.10	.47	.30	.11	.73
Suppression	.40	.25	.51	.67	-.26	-.40	-.10	-.05
Repression	-.18	-.34	-.74	-.32	.11	.16	.13	.67

Males, N = 175; females, N = 188. The following labels were offered for the factors: factor 1, controlled coping; factor 2, expressive coping; factor 3, structured defenses, factor 4, primitive defenses.

first factor for females is similar, except for the absence of negative defense loadings. This factor seems to describe a personality that is cognitively capable and well socialized. This factor was labeled controlled coping because of its similarity to a corresponding factor in Haan's (1963) earlier work.

The second factor extracted for males was also marked by positive loadings on coping and negative loadings on defense. In contrast to controlled coping, the highest loadings were regression in service of ego and empathy followed by negative loadings on repression and reaction formation. Although there were a number of loadings in the cognitive sector of the model, they did not dominate the factor as they had with controlled coping. Among the females, only three coping processes, empathy, suppression, and regression in service of ego had loadings greater than .40. This configuration, labeled expressive coping, seems to reflect an emphasis on intrapersonal and interpersonal accuracy as well as a heightened flexibility and creativity.

Factor three for males consisted of loadings on seven defense functions. The highest loading was for intellectualization, followed by rationalization, projection, and isolation. This pattern is replicated for females, which also had substantial loadings on seven defense processes. The ego processes with the highest loadings on the female's factor were regression, intellectualization, and rationalization. The factor, which we labeled structured defense, seems to represent a sophisticated and well-integrated pattern of self-protection. The relative importance of regression in the females' analysis is interesting in contrast with its lesser importance in the males' analysis. Regression may be a more acceptable means of defense for women than for men, given the predominant sex-role stereotype for men.

The last factor extracted for males consisted of positive loadings on the defense processes of doubt and regression, and negative loadings on concentration and sublimation. The last factor for females was characterized by positive loadings on reaction formation, denial, and repression, and a negative loading on tolerance of ambiguity. The last male and female factors shared no major loadings on the same ego processes. Nevertheless, both reflect a thin, disorganized, and poorly integrated defense pattern, in contrast with structured defense. While doubt and regression seem to represent an isolated and primitive defense pattern for men, they are enlisted as major components in the structured defense factor for women. The repression, denial, and reaction formation triad for women is reminiscent of classical hysteria. This factor was labeled primitive defense, following Haan (1963).

The Construction of the CPI Scales Based on the Factor Analysis

The results of the scale construction for the four factors, shown at the bottom of Table XXI, were generally poorer than those constructed on the basis of individual ratings. Although seven out of the eight measures had validity coefficients greater than .20, only two scales, primitive defense and structured defense, both for women, had coefficients greater than .30. These lower coefficients suggest that the effects of the data reduction involved in factor analysis overgeneralizes the ego processes and that important distinctions are preserved by the individual scales.

TEST–RETEST RELIABILITY

A different sample of subjects was used to calculate the reliability of the CPI- and MMPI-based ego scales. These included 95 male and 108 female students enrolled in a general psychology course at the University of Oregon.[2] Two sets of tests were administered to these students separated by a 4-week interval. The results are reported in Table XXIII. The test–retest reliability coefficients for men ranged from .49 for substitution to .83 for controlled coping, with a median of .71. Coefficients for females ranged from .46 for isolation to .81 for repression and intellectualization. The median reliability was .70. Scales with lower cross-validities, such as the CPI versions of suppression, concentration, substitution, sublimation, reaction formation, and rationalization, generally had less than average reliability coefficients.

CORRELATIONS WITH ESTABLISHED SCALES ON THE CPI AND MMPI

A series of correlation matrices were computed between the newly created ego scales and the established scales on the MMPI and CPI. The results provide some consistent validation for the scales. On the CPI, coping tended to be positively related to the standard scales and defense was negatively related (see Table XXIV and XXV). The coping scales were correlated more strongly with (Gough, 1957) Class One Measures (poise, ascendancy, self-assurance, and interpersonal adequacy), Class Three (intellectual efficiency and achievement potential), and Class Four (intellectual and interest modes) than they were with Class Two Measures (re-sponsibility, socialization, maturity, and intrapersonal structuring of values). Moreover, there were several small but significant negative correlations with the Class Two Scales of communality, good impression, self-control and socialization.

Two exceptions to this trend were noticed with regression in service of ego and expressive coping (of which regression in service of ego is a major component). There were strong negative correlations between regression in service of ego and the CPI scales of sense of well-being, socialization, self-control, good impression, communality, and achievement via conformity for both men and women. While the female scale of ego regression correlated positively with a number of Class One measures, particularly social presence and self-acceptance, the same relations either did not occur or were weaker with the males. Both the male and female versions of

[2] The authors wish to thank Lewis Goldberg for his generous help in allowing us to use this data.

Table XXIII
Test–Retest Coefficients

| | Coping | | | Defense | |
	Male	Female		Male	Female
CPI-based scales					
Objectivity	.70	.61	Isolation	.54	.46
Intellectuality	.81	.77	Intellectualization	.78	.81
Logical analysis	.80	.69	Rationalization	.65	.63
Concentration	.56	.58	Denial	.69	.79
Tolerance of ambiguity	.76	.80	Doubt	.78	.80
Empathy	.59	.75	Projection	.73	.61
Regression-ego	.67	.78	Regression	.74	.69
Sublimation	.58	.67	Displacement	.82	.71
Substitution	.49	.52	Reaction formation	.57	.68
Suppression	.64	.55	Repression	.78	.81
Summed coping	.68	.69	Summed defense	.68	.58
Controlled coping	.83	.72	Structured defense	.77	.70
Expressive coping	.73	.71	Primitive defense	.70	.77
MMPI-based scales					
Concentration	.76	.76	Projection	.56	.67
Suppression	.75	.71	Regression	.74	.75

CPI: Males, $N = 95$; Females, $N = 108$.
MMPI: Males, $N = 79$; Females, $N = 108$.

regression in service of ego were strongly related to flexibility. Similar patterns of correlations were found with expressive coping.

Mackinnon (1961b), in a study of architects, found that their creativity ratings correlated with 11 of the CPI scales, mostly in the negative direction. Of the 9 significant correlations found here between the CPI scales of ego regression for males, 8 were also observed in Mackinnon's study, and all were in the same direction. Thus the results of Mackinnon's study seem to offer indirect support for the validity of this scale.

In general the defense scales were negatively correlated with the standard CPI scales among both males and females. This relationship was pronounced with rationalization, doubt, projection, regression, displacement, summed defense, and primitive defense. Intellectualization, theoretically a more sophisticated defense, was an exception, since its pattern of results resembled the coping scales. Among the males, intellectualization was more positively associated with the CPI scales than any other ego process, summed coping included. The CPI scales appear to be measuring the intellectualizer's socially dominant, ongoing, intellectually capable manner.

The male versions of reaction formation and denial produced interesting sets of correlations. Both scales had small positive correlations, with several CPI scales including good impression (intended as an index of social desirability) and com-

Table XXIV
Correlations between Standard CPI Scales and CPI-based Coping Scales

	Objectivity		Intellectuality		Logical analysis		Concentration		Tolerance of ambiguity	
	Male	Female	Male	Female	Male	Female	Male	Female	Male	Female
Dominance	.32[a]	.46[a]	.50[a]	.66[a]	.25[b]	.38[a]	.51[a]	.52[a]		.37[a]
Capacity for status	.51[a]	.50[a]	.69[a]	.66[a]	.46[a]	.41[a]	.32[a]	.43[a]	.39[a]	.49[a]
Sociability	.23[c]	.44[a]	.34[a]	.51[a]		.24[b]	.31[a]	.46[a]	.24[c]	.38[a]
Social presence	.21[c]	.45[a]	.42[a]	.58[a]		.27[b]	.30[a]	.41[a]	.39[a]	.55[a]
Self acceptance	.25[b]	.38[a]	.50[a]	.54[a]	.28[b]	.36[a]	.29[b]	.34[a]	.34[a]	.42[a]
Sense of well being							.57[a]	.35[a]		
Responsibility	.48[a]	.37[a]	.41[a]	.21[c]	.48[a]	.25[b]	.31[a]	.34[a]	.21[c]	.19[c]
Socialization	.24[c]			−.30[a]	.19[c]	−.18[c]	.52[a]		−.23[c]	−.25[b]
Self control				−.18[c]			.24[c]		−.35[a]	−.25[b]
Tolerance	.36[a]	.32[a]	.45[a]	.44[a]	.37[a]	.27[b]	.30[a]	.35[a]	.23[c]	.29[a]
Good impression	.23[c]		.20[c]				.31[a]	.27[b]		
Communality			−.39[a]	−.20[c]	−.25[b]	−.22[b]			−.32[a]	−.21[c]
Achievement conformity	.39[a]	.30[a]	.41[a]	.29[a]	.46[a]	.25[b]	.61[a]	.47[a]	.41[a]	.19[c]
Achievement independence	.45[a]	.41[a]	.54[a]	.45[a]	.56[a]	.37[a]		.34[a]	.36[a]	.35[a]
Intellectual efficiency	.47[a]	.52[a]	.50[a]	.56[a]	.44[a]	.38[a]	.52[a]	.53[a]	.28[b]	.46[a]
Psychological mindedness	.46[a]	.30[a]	.53[a]	.39[a]	.47[a]		.24[c]	.37[a]		.23[b]
Flexibility	.24[c]	.34[a]	.36[a]	.49[a]	.28[b]	.30[a]	−.21[c]		.62[a]	.58[a]
Femininity		−.21[c]		−.24[b]	.19[c]		−.20[c]	−.34[a]		

290

	Empathy		Regression ego		Sublimation		Substitution		Suppression	
	Male	Female	Male	Female	Male	Female	Male	Female	Male	Female
Dominance				$.22^b$	$.24^c$	$.35^a$	$.34^a$	$.40^a$		$.22^b$
Capacity for status		$.18^c$		$.24^b$	$.40^a$	$.39^a$	$.43^a$	$.40^a$	$.26^b$	$.38^a$
Sociability					$.31^a$	$.40^a$	$.30^a$	$.32^a$		$.27^b$
Social presence		$.21^c$	$.25^b$	$.43^a$	$.31^a$	$.42^a$	$.40^a$	$.43^a$		$.36^a$
Self acceptance			$.23^c$	$.35^a$	$.26^b$	$.45^a$	$.33^a$	$.36^a$		$.34^a$
Sense of well being	$-.26^b$	$-.18^c$	$-.45^a$	$-.30^a$	$.49^a$	$.30^a$	$.30^a$	$.40^a$	$.38^a$	$.40^a$
Responsibility					$.30^a$	$.30^a$	$.26^b$	$.27^b$	$.31^a$	$.30^a$
Socialization	$-.23^c$	$-.17^c$	$-.41^a$	$-.38^a$	$.25^b$		$.29^b$		$.36^a$	
Self control	$-.30^a$	$-.23^b$	$-.61^a$	$-.64^a$	$.21^c$				$.34^a$	
Tolerance			$-.56^a$	$-.48^a$	$.36^a$	$.38^a$	$.33^a$	$.39^a$	$.41^a$	$.19^c$
Good impression	$-.25^b$		$-.30^a$	$-.27^b$	$.29^b$				$.19^c$	$.46^a$
Communality			$-.40^a$	$-.22^b$						$.24^b$
Achievement conformity	$-.22^c$	$-.30^a$			$.40^a$	$.25^b$	$.43^a$	$.30^a$	$.39^a$	$.36^a$
Achievement independence					$.19^c$	$.22^b$	$.34^a$	$.30^a$	$.46^a$	$.46^a$
Intellectual efficiency					$.50^a$	$.51^a$	$.39^a$	$.44^a$	$.43^a$	$.45^a$
Psychological mindedness					$.30^a$	$.28^a$	$.24^c$	$.37^a$	$.29^b$	$.28^c$
Flexibility	$.45^a$	$.32^a$	$.58^a$	$.50^a$			$.33^a$	$.34^a$	$.21^c$	$.18^c$
Femininity	$.35^a$	$.31^a$				$-.31^a$		$-.25^b$		$-.19^c$

Significance levels based on a two-tailed test.

$^a \leqslant .001$.
$^b \leqslant .01$.
$^c \leqslant .05$.

Males: $N = 111$; Females: $N = 132$.

Table XXV
Correlations between Standard CPI Scales and CPI-based Defense Scales

	Isolation		Intellectualization		Rationalization		Denial		Doubt	
	Male	Female	Male	Female	Male	Female	Male	Female	Male	Female
Dominance	.25[b]		.71[a]	.65[a]	-.27[b]	-.35[a]		-.19[c]	-.73[a]	-.53[a]
Capacity for status			.71[a]	.59[a]	-.36[a]	-.34[a]			-.55[a]	-.57[a]
Sociability			.54[a]	.46[a]	-.27[b]	-.39[a]	.31[a]		-.63[a]	-.68[a]
Social presence	.23[c]		.57[a]	.56[a]	-.19[c]	-.32[a]			-.58[a]	-.61[a]
Self acceptance	.30[a]		.63[a]	.47[a]		-.34[a]		-.33[a]	-.51[a]	-.46[a]
Sense of well being			.27[b]		-.57[a]	-.49[a]	.44[a]	.25[b]	-.72[a]	-.71[a]
Responsibility		-.30[a]	.34[a]		-.32[a]	-.33[a]	.27[b]	.33[a]	-.23[c]	-.38[a]
Socialization	-.24[c]			-.29[a]	-.43[a]		.23[c]	.31[a]	-.31[a]	
Self control	-.38[a]	-.24[b]			-.39[a]	-.27[b]	.37[a]			-.40[a]
Tolerance			.51[a]	.42[a]	-.38[a]	-.44[a]	.23[c]	.24[b]	-.38[a]	-.66[a]
Good impression	-.21[c]		.27[b]		-.36[a]	-.34[a]	.18[c]		-.48[a]	-.53[a]
Communality			-.35[a]				.23[c]			
Achievement conformity		-.25[b]	.46[a]	.27[b]	-.41[a]	-.37[a]			-.56[a]	-.64[a]
Achievement independence			.52[a]	.42[a]		-.24[b]	-.32[a]		-.49[a]	-.52[a]
Intellectual efficiency			.52[a]	.49[a]	-.37[a]	-.48[a]	-.23	-.22[b]	-.34[a]	-.76[a]
Psychological mindedness			.56[a]	.50[a]	-.19	-.29[a]	-.46[a]			-.61[a]
Flexibility			.33[a]	.45[a]					.22[c]	
Femininity	-.19[c]			-.26[b]		.27[b]	-.26[b]		.28[b]	.42[a]

	Projection		Regression		Displacement		Reaction formation		Repression	
	Male	Female	Male	Female	Male	Female	Male	Female	Male	Female
Dominance		$-.20^c$	$-.47^a$	$-.20^c$	$-.30^a$	$-.27^b$		$.22^b$	$-.35^a$	$-.57^a$
Capacity for status	$-.46^a$	$-.35^a$	$-.39^a$	$-.24^b$	$-.49^a$	$-.41^a$		$.29^a$	$-.49^a$	$-.62^a$
Sociability	$-.21^c$	$-.30^a$	$-.33^a$	$-.39^a$	$-.35^a$	$-.49^a$		$.26^b$	$-.32^a$	$-.56^a$
Social presence	$-.24^c$	$-.40^a$		$-.19^c$		$-.34^a$		$.35^a$	$-.45^a$	$-.71^a$
Self acceptance		$-.21^c$				$-.22^b$		$.28^a$	$-.48^a$	$-.63^a$
Sense of well being	$-.36^a$	$-.45^a$	$-.64^a$	$-.60^a$	$-.63^a$	$-.68^a$	$.24^c$			
Responsibility	$-.47^a$	$-.39^a$	$-.46^a$	$-.42^a$	$-.46^a$	$-.48^a$		$.27^b$	$-.32^a$	$-.23^b$
Socialization	$-.32^a$	$-.18^c$	$-.67^a$	$-.39^a$	$-.50^a$	$-.26^b$				$.22^b$
Self control	$-.39^a$	$-.28^a$	$-.60^a$	$-.55^a$	$-.57^a$	$-.65^a$	$.19^c$	$.21^c$	$.24^c$	$.29^a$
Tolerance	$-.57^a$	$-.57^a$	$-.41^a$	$-.42^a$	$-.59^a$	$-.60^a$			$-.23^c$	$-.32^a$
Good impression	$-.34^a$	$-.34^a$	$-.63^a$	$-.56^a$	$-.58^a$	$-.65^a$	$.19^c$	$.19^c$		
Communality				$-.18^c$			$.25^b$		$.33^a$	
Achievement conformity	$-.59^a$	$-.45^a$	$-.72^a$	$-.56^a$	$-.65^a$	$-.71^a$			$-.19^c$	$-.21^c$
Achievement independence	$-.64^a$	$-.57^a$		$-.26^b$	$-.44^a$	$-.57^a$			$-.32^a$	$-.34^a$
Intellectual efficiency	$-.62^a$	$-.55^a$	$-.47^a$	$-.45^a$	$-.56^a$	$-.65^a$		$-.22^b$	$-.39^a$	$-.53^a$
Psychological mindedness	$-.53^a$	$-.36^a$	$-.23^c$	$-.26^b$	$-.38^a$	$-.52^a$	$-.37^a$		$-.31^a$	$-.34^a$
Flexibility	$-.34^a$	$-.32^a$	$.36^a$	$.26^b$			$-.48^a$	$-.35^a$	$-.39^a$	$-.40^a$
Femininity				$.27^b$		$.29^a$		$-.22^b$		

Significance levels based on a two-tailed test.

[a] $\leq .001.$

[b] $\leq .01.$

[c] $\leq .05.$

Males: $N = 111$; Females: $N = 132.$

munality, which is the extreme positive direction indicates overly conventional attitudes (Megargee, 1972). Flexibility and femininity were negatively correlated with reaction formation. The findings for denial are consistent with negative correlations that have been found with indices of psychological distress (Naditch *et al.*, 1975). The correlations with reaction formation are consistent with the vigilant, rigid, and overdetermined aspects of the ego defense.

The correlations between the CPI scales and the ego scales, based on the factor scores and on the summed ratings for coping and defense are shown in Table XXVI. The reader can consider these relationships in detail if he is so inclined. However the patterns are as expected coping scales generally have positive and defense scales generally have negative relationships with the CPI scales. The less differentiated nature of these ego scales probably accounts for the great number of significant relationships with the standard CPI scales. Primitive defense for men and structured defense for women are most frequently and strongly related to the standard CPI scales with controlled coping following closely behind for both sexes. Structured defense has many positive and strong associations with the men's CPI scales, but generally negative relations with the women's, while primitive defense is generally negatively related to the CPI scales for both sexes. If these findings are valid, they suggest that males who successfully defend themselves in differentiated ways are counted as well functioning people according to the CPI's prescriptions. The scales for expressive coping have the fewest and weakest associations with the CPI scales for both sexes, suggesting that intraceptive ego processing represents a different area of functioning than do the standard scales; its strongest relationships are with the men's scale for flexibility and the women's scales for social presence and self acceptance.

Correlations calculated between the MMPI-based ego scales and standard MMPI scales appear in Table XXVII. Concentration and suppression had large negative correlations with most of the MMPI scales. Regression correlated positively with many MMPI scales, most strongly with depression, hypochondriasis, psychopathic deviancy, psychasthenia, and schizophrenia. The absence of significant correlations between MMPI scales and projection is not surprising considering the projector's suspiciousness and unwillingness to admit pathology (Alker, 1971).

NORMS AND ITEM COMPOSITION

Normative means and standard deviations were computed for two samples: (*1*) the Oregon students, and (*2*) the Oakland Growth subjects (see Appendix D). Items listings for the new scales may also be found in Appendix E.

Discussion

The work described in this chapter involved the creation of a series of paper-and-pencil measures of ego functioning. A factor analysis was performed on the

Table XXVI
Correlations between Standard CPI Scales and CPI-based Summary Scales

	Summed coping		Summed defense		Controlled coping		Expressive coping		Structured defense		Primitive defense	
	Male	Female	Male	Female	Male	Female	Male	Female	Male	Female	Male	Female
Dominance	$.40^a$	$.39^a$	$-.31^a$	$-.43^a$	$.33^a$	$.62^a$		$.47^a$	$.23^c$	$-.30^a$	$-.62^a$	$-.60^a$
Capacity for status		$.46^a$	$-.34^a$	$-.37^a$	$.51^a$	$.53^a$		$.42^a$	$.27^b$	$-.27^b$	$-.46^a$	$-.49^a$
Sociability		$.34^a$	$-.20^c$	$-.52^a$	$.26^b$	$.51^a$		$.45^a$	$.37^a$	$-.46^a$	$-.40^a$	$-.59^a$
Social presence	$.24^c$	$.43^a$		$-.37^a$	$.24^c$	$.52^a$		$.54^a$	$.50^a$	$-.24^b$	$-.32^a$	$-.57^a$
Self acceptance	$.26^b$	$.46^a$		$-.52^a$	$.24^c$	$.58^a$		$.54^a$	$.43^a$	$-.26^b$	$-.34^a$	$-.62^a$
Sense of well being			$-.46^a$	$-.42^a$	$.48^a$	$-.24^c$				$-.56^a$	$-.66^a$	
Responsibility	$.37^a$	$.26^b$	$-.43^a$	$-.42^a$	$.52^a$	$.26^b$				$-.41^a$	$-.35^a$	$-.23^b$
Socialization		$-.19^c$	$-.46^a$		$.50^a$	$-.19^c$	$-.28^b$	$-.27^b$	$-.34^a$	$-.31^a$	$-.49^a$	
Self control		$-.19^c$	$-.36^a$	$-.21^c$	$.44^a$	$-.20^c$	$-.30^a$	$-.35^a$	$-.35^a$	$-.42^a$	$-.33^a$	$.23^b$
Tolerance	$.25^b$	$.31^a$	$-.29^b$	$-.40^a$	$.51^a$	$.34^a$		$.23^a$	$.20^c$	$-.42^a$	$-.37^a$	$-.29^a$
Good impression			$-.35^a$	$-.31^a$	$.44^a$		$-.29^b$			$-.53^a$	$-.52^a$	
Communality	$-.28^b$						$-.37^a$					
Achievement conformity	$.19^c$	$.24^b$	$-.49^a$	$-.40^a$	$.72^a$	$.27^b$	$-.20^c$		$.25^a$	$-.52^a$	$-.68^a$	$-.27^b$
Achievement independence	$.38^a$	$.41^a$		$-.24^b$	$.53^a$	$.29^a$	$.33^a$			$-.24^b$		$.22^b$
Intellectual efficiency	$.37^a$	$.51^a$	$-.38^a$	$-.53^a$	$.57^a$	$.50^a$		$.44^a$		$-.50^a$	$-.48^a$	$-.49^a$
Psychological mindedness	$.34^a$	$.22^b$	$-.20^c$	$-.32^a$	$.47^a$	$.36^a$		$.20^c$	$.22^c$	$-.27^b$	$-.32^a$	$-.30^a$
Flexibility	$.45^a$	$.43^a$	$.20^c$			$.27^b$	$.62^a$	$.26^b$	$.31^a$	$.22^b$	$.34^a$	$-.24^b$
Femininity				$.21^c$		$-.30^a$				$.28^a$		

Significance levels based on a two-tailed test.
[a] $\leq .001$.
[b] $< .01$.
[c] $< .05$.

Males: $N = 111$; Females: $N = 132$.

Table XXVII
Correlations between Standard MMPI Scales and MMPI-based Ego Scales

	Concentration		Suppression		Projection		Regression	
	Male	Female	Male	Female	Male	Female	Male	Female
F		$-.56^a$		$-.53^a$				$.54^a$
L					$.35^b$			
K				$.50^a$				$-.35^b$
Hs	$-.29^c$		$-.35^b$	$-.41^b$			$.42^b$	$.44^a$
D		$-.50^a$		$-.62^a$				$.56^a$
Hy	$-.57^a$	$-.43^a$	$-.56^a$	$-.70^a$			$.53^a$	$.67^a$
Pd	$-.53^a$	$-.52^a$	$-.61^a$	$-.57^a$			$.33^b$	$.59^a$
Mf		$-.50^a$		$-.36^b$				$.43^a$
Pa								$.35^b$
Pt		$-.54^a$		$-.72^a$				$.65^a$
Sc	$-.34^c$	$-.60^a$	$-.30^c$	$-.71^a$				$.70^a$
Ma	$-.52^a$	$-.45^a$	$-.63^a$	$-.36^b$			$.49^a$	$.40^b$
Si	$.30^c$		$.39^b$	$-.44^a$				$.37^b$

Significance levels based on a two-tailed test.
$^a \leqslant .001.$
$^b \leqslant .01.$
$^c \leqslant .05.$
Males: $N = 46$; Females: $N = 49$.

individual processes, and four additional scales were developed. A total of 30 measures were created, 26 on the CPI and 4 on the MMPI. For the most part, the scales had acceptable validity and reliability coefficients.

Haan's (1965) previous finding concerning the superiority of the CPI for the development of coping as opposed to defense scales was not confirmed here. Three coping scales and two defense scales could not be created for men. While three coping scales did not attain acceptable validity coefficients, all the defense scales did for women. A breakdown of the median validity coefficients for defense and coping reveals no stable differences. While the median validity coefficient for the male coping process was greater ($r = .40$) than that of defense ($r = .33$), this pattern was reversed for females (coping, $r = .34$; defense, $r = .38$). Haan's (1965) specific finding was that the CPI was more productive of items that differentiated highs from lows on the coping processes than it was for the defense processes. Although these data do not directly address this finding, they do suggest that the CPI is as stable across samples for defense as it is for coping.

The combined results of the validation, reliability, and the patterns of intercorrelation point to the strength and weakness of a number of scales. For men intellectuality, intellectualization, logical analysis, tolerance of ambiguity, doubt, projection, regression in service of ego, regression, summed coping, and the four MMPI scales can probably be regarded as acceptable by existing standards. Scales for isolation, rationalization, sublimation, substitution, summed defense, expressive coping, and primitive defenses have less acceptable qualifications and should be administered and interpreted cautiously. Among females these analyses suggest that intellectuality, intellectualization, logical analysis, tolerance of ambiguity, doubt, denial, regression in service of ego, regression, displacement, summed coping, structured and primitive defenses as well as the four MMPI scales are acceptable. Rationalization, projection (CPI), sublimation, and substitution should be used with caution among female subjects. Thus rationalization, sublimation, and substitution are weak indices for both sexes.

These new measures of ego functioning are not suited for all subjects. Ideally the best subjects would be those who are similar to the creation subjects in terms of age, race, and general background. These results represent an initial step in the validation of these measures. Norms need to be established on more and varied types of subjects. Further studies concerning construct validity are currently underway.

Appendix A. Procedures of Ego Rating

Preliminary Instructions

The 30 ratings represent a map of the most common ego processes (no claim is made that the set is complete), so that the array needs first to be viewed as a whole and the following decisions made in sequence.

1. What are the most salient and characteristic ways that the *S* handles conflict, perturbations, difficulties in terms of the generic ego processes?

2. What are his characteristic and most salient ways of *cognitive* reaction (the first three ratings: Discrimination, Detachment, and Means–End Symbolization)?

3. What are his characteristic and most salient ways of handling *affect* and *impulse* (Diversion, Transformation and Restraint).

4. What are his more characteristic and salient ways of handling the *immediate impact of environmental perturbations* (Selective Attention).

5. What are his most characteristic and salient intraceptive reactions, ways of handling others and their feelings, and himself and his feelings (Sensitivity, Temporal Reversals, Delayed Response).

6. Finally, are these most characteristic and salient modes usually and most characteristically coping, defensive, or fragmenting?

The balance in any one of these modes will depend upon the sample in question. It is logically and conceptually possible, within the framework of this model for a person to cope and defend within the same general process, for example, a university professor may make coping use of Intellectuality in many sectors of his life but under personal stress and with emotionally significant people he may Intellectualize. Fragmentations would not be expected to be extensive except in stressed, neurotic, or psychotic samples, and their extensive and intensiveness *may* preclude coping in some ways.

Most subjects could be expected to have some 4 or 5 ratings (see rating sheet in this appendix); however, an impoverished, self-limiting person in a bland, non-demanding environment might not have any 5s and maybe no 4s.

After the most characteristic and salient ways are rated, one can go back to make decisions about the functions that are of lesser importance. The resulting 30 ratings should be reviewed in order to consider whether their overall pattern reflects a picture of the subject's ego processes as he presented himself in interacting within the observational situation.

Definitions of Ego Processes

COGNITIVE FUNCTIONS

Discrimination

Process of separating idea from feeling, idea from idea, and feeling from feeling by the utilization of cognitive functioning. Its manifestations are mostly within the cognitive realm.

a. *Objectivity:* Subject separates his ideas from his feelings and his ideas from each other so that he achieves objective evaluations when situations require this sort of behavior. Subject separates his feelings from each other when he is of two minds and cognizes that fact.

Subjects with low ratings habitually give affective, emotional, noncognitive responses and balk at describing their behavior, their children's behavior, and so on. They personalize situations.

Persons with high ratings will be rated for their "justness" and "fairness" in emotionally laden situations. In a child, being a "good sport" would be a coping manifestation of this ego process.

b. *Isolation:* Subject's affect seems not to be related to his ideas, and/or he seems not to be able to put his ideas together.

Subjects with high ratings can't generalize, synthesize, or integrate meaningfully because they keep apart ideas and concomitant affects that belong together. Isolated affect may occur after some delay or diffuseness and is unfocused on the real causation.

c. *Tangentiality, concretisms:* Subject separates, concretizes, and reifies his ideas so thoroughly that he becomes fixed on some part or subordinated idea that is part of a large context and to the detriment of his handling the context, for example, one subject, anticipating stress, reported "he kept thinking about a little hole in the plaster"; another reported he was oblivious to the coming stress and instead thought of problems of methodology, probability, and so on.

Rating Form for Ego Processes

Interviewer____Date____Name____Case#____Rater____

(Minimal or Absent) (High)

Discrimination	Cognitive functions				
Objectivity	1	2	3	4	5
Isolation	1	2	3	4	5
Tangentiality, concretisms	1	2	3	4	5
Detachment					
Intellectuality	1	2	3	4	5
Intellectualizing	1	2	3	4	5
Neologisms, word salads	1	2	3	4	5
Means–end symbolization					
Logical analysis	1	2	3	4	5
Rationalization	1	2	3	4	5
Confabulation, autistic logic	1	2	3	4	5
	Attention-focusing functions				
Selective awareness					
Concentration	1	2	3	4	5
Denial	1	2	3	4	5
Pollyannish, silly	1	2	3	4	5
	Self-reflexive, intraceptive functions				
Sensitivity					
Empathy	1	2	3	4	5
Projection	1	2	3	4	5
Delusional, ideas of reference	1	2	3	4	5
Delayed response					
Tolerance of ambiguity	1	2	3	4	5
Doubt and indecision	1	2	3	4	5
Immobilized	1	2	3	4	5
Time reversion					
Regress. serv. ego	1	2	3	4	5
Regression	1	2	3	4	5
Decompensation	1	2	3	4	5
Affective diversion	Affective regulations				
Sublimation	1	2	3	4	5
Displacement	1	2	3	4	5
Impulse preoccupation	1	2	3	4	5
Affective transformation					
Substitution	1	2	3	4	5
Reaction formation	1	2	3	4	5
Unstable alternation	1	2	3	4	5
Affective restraint					
Suppression	1	2	3	4	5
Repression	1	2	3	4	5
Depersonalization, amnesic, withdrawal	1	2	3	4	5

Detachment

Ability to let mind "roam freely," speculate, analyze, without a sense of forbiddance. This process would be positively related to high intellectual level, but a high intellectual level does not compel high ratings.

a. *Intellectuality:* Subject is capable of detachment in an affect-laden situation which requires impartial analysis and awareness and is so detached from restrictions of the environment and self that he is able to give his thoughts free rein. Subject articulates and symbolizes his feelings, so that they contribute to the wealth and richness of his cognitive processes.

Subjects with low ratings are overinvolved with their present experiencing and consequently personalize most events.

b. *Intellectualization:* (a subcategory of Isolation) Subjects with high ratings retreat from affect to formulations of words and abstractions. Subject thinks and talks on a level of abstraction not quite appropriate to the situation, uses jargon, and does not specify how these ideas relate to context. Subject is overdetailed, overprecise, and pseudointellectual.

c. *Neologisms, word salads:* Subject uses words in a disconnected, odd fashion with a great show of precision, knowingness, and detachment. One psychotic psychiatrist explained his state of mind to his colleagues with all the jargon but used it erroneously.

Means—End Symbolization (Causal): Capacity to Analyze
Causal Texture of Experience, to Anticipate Outcomes, to
Analyze Alternative Choices

a. *Logical Analysis:* Subject is interested in analyzing thoughtfully, carefully, and cogently the causal aspects of situations, personal or otherwise. He proceeds systematically in his exposition, or if he backtracks, he still manages to reorganize the material well. Motivational explanations are one kind of causal reasoning.

Subjects with low ratings will view their life as a series of fortuitous and discontinuous incidents and phases and will tend to act as if their life experience had merely "come about." They will be bound by the present, will jump around in their explanations, leave "loose ends," or otherwise show little order to their presentations.

Subjects high on this variable will tend to use high points of their memory as launching pads for deducing the answer to questions. If they backtrack or associate freely they will tend to resummarize.

b. *Rationalization:* Subject offers superficially plausible reasons to explain his behavior and/or intentions, which allows his sub rosa self-gratification to escape attention, but he omits crucial aspects of situations, or is otherwise inexact. He needs to offer causal explanations, but they do not hang together. He needs to justify himself in terms of fortuitous circumstances: "fate just came out that way."

c. *Confabulations, autistic logic:* Subject offers explanations, but they do not hold together and they appear to be partly or mostly made up. One subject, anticipating stress, described his intention of not experiencing the shock, if it turned out to be powerful! More often, confabulations can be directly seen as ritualistic intentions to justify oneself that are based on privatistic assumptions.

INTRACEPTIVE FUNCTIONS

Delayed Response: Ability to Hold Up Decision, to Time-bind Tension due to Personal or Situational Complexities or Lack of Clarity

a. *Tolerance of ambiguity:* Subjects are able to cope with cognitive and affective complexity or dissonance. Subject is capable of qualified judgment; he is able to think in terms of grays rather than in blacks and whites. Subject does not need to commit himself to clearcut choices, in complicated situations where choice is impossible, and he can handle being of two minds. When answering memory questions, *Subject* seems comfortable with the inevitable uncertainties of his recall. He tolerates inevitably complex negative and positive feelings toward others.

b. *Doubt and indecision:* Subject is unable to resolve ambiguity. He doubts the validity of his own perceptions or judgments, is unable to make up his mind, and is unable to commit himself to a course of action or presentation of incidents. He hopes that problems will solve themselves or that someone will solve them for him. He states his problem and then qualifies it to death. He worries about whether he has answered questions correctly and is uncertain about whether he has treated others the way they should be treated. He makes strenuous efforts to avoid uncertain situations because he is aware that he becomes easily stalemated.

c. *Immobilized, vague, frozen:* Subject cannot move on without external aid; he handles situations by doing nothing. When one subject anticipating stress was questioned as to whether he thought about quitting, he said he did not know how to quit, that the room just closed in on him.

Sensitivity: In Direct Relationships, Subject Apprehends and Is Sensitively Aware of Others' Often Unexpressed Feelings or Ideas

a. *Empathy:* Subject sensitively puts himself in the other person's boots; he takes the other's role; he is able to imagine how the other person feels and thinks. In his interpersonal relationships he takes account of others' feelings and ideas.

Subjects with high ratings will be interested in the feelings of others. They will comment that they know how others feel about certain situations, how their parents must have felt when dealing with subject himself, how the interviewer or observer might be experiencing the situation and will at the same time have relatively accurate assessment of the other person's reactions to them.

Subjects with low ratings will be a system unto themselves and will have little interest in or awareness of others' reactions. Observers will be seen as scientists, not people.

b. *Projection:* Subject attributes an objectionable tendency to another person, or persons, instead of recognizing it as part of himself. The projected contents may involve either accusation or power. Subject is suspicious about what scientific study will find about him, perceives the world as a jungle, and feels he needs to be constantly on guard or he will be made a "sucker."

c. *Delusional, ideas of reference:* Subject invests himself in closed, airtight formulations that serve to explain his relationship to others and are based on privatistic assumptions that he is special in others' eyes (e.g., powerful or weak) and that they are reacting to him.

Time Reversion: Subject *Replays or Recaptures Experiences, Feelings, Attitudes, Ideas of the Past*

a. *Regression in the service of the ego (playfulness):* Subject utilizes feelings and ideas that are not directly ordered or required by the practical immediate elements of the situation to add to his understanding of problems, his handling of situations, and his enjoyment of life. He essentially utilizes his preconscious functioning in a rich and flexible way because his ego boundaries allow rapid and productive reversal of the time frame. He indicates a comfortable and optimistic expectancy that his products are likely to be good (resolved omnipotence), but he can stand the possibility that they may not be (laughs at his own bad wit).

Subjects with high ratings will "play" with ideas, feelings, and motoric expressions without being stifled by concerns over their practicality, reality allegiance, or appropriateness. Their approach may initially be disorderly. Subjects' humor should be more situational than a recounting of stock jokes.

Subjects with low ratings will be propelled forward, unwilling to take time out and unable to let their preconscious work for them, that is, if they cannot remember a fact immediately, they have no conviction that it will come and no way of facilitating the recall.

b. *Regression:* Subject resorts to evasive, wistful, demanding, dependent, ingratiating, non–age appropriate behavior to avoid responsibility, aggression, and unpleasant demands from others and self. He encourages others to indulge him. Nonproductive fantasy in adults would be part of this process, particularly if the fantasy is used defensively against action, effort, and real accomplishment.

c. *Decompensation:* Subject gives up, puts himself in the hands of the others and the situation.

ATTENTION-FOCUSING FUNCTION

Selective Awareness: Ability to Focus Attention

a. *Concentration:* Subject is able to set aside disturbing or attractive feelings or thoughts in order to concentrate on the task at hand.

Subjects with high ratings will be efficiently productive in difficult situations—resisting either pleasurable or painful thoughts. They are work oriented.

Subjects with low ratings will be easily distracted by the immediate requirements or attractions of the situation. Subjects will talk ad infinitum about what happened that particular day or is happening right now with their lives, and so on.

b. *Denial:* Denial of present or past facts and feelings that would be painful to acknowledge and focusing instead on the benign or pleasant. Basic formula: there is no pain, no anticipation of pain, no danger, no conflict.

c. *Silly, pollyannish, hebephrenic responses:* Subject is laughing, giggling, as an automatic reaction in regard to matters that are not apparent nor funny or pleasurable to others. Subject *attends* only to thoughts that please him.

AFFECTIVE REGULATIONS

Diversion

Subject modifys or *redirects* (but does *not* change or transform) the expression, the aim, or the situation of his affect.

a. *Sublimation:* Subject finds alternate channels and means, which are self-satisfying, socially accepted, and tempered for the expression of affect which can sometimes be basically "primitive."

Subjects with high ratings should give evidence of a wealth of situations and interests for the expression of basic feelings, for example, sports, sewing, painting, cooking, card playing, chess, investments, gardening, refinishing furniture, mountain trips, and so on. Subjects' immediate behavior in some situations may not give these clues but overall these *subjects* will arrange their lives to provide a variety of diversions that satisfy and permit acceptable self-expression.

Subjects with low ratings will seem to have limited and conventional means of self-expression. They will appear to constrict their feelings.

b. *Displacement:* Subject temporarily and unsuccessfully attempts to control unacceptable affects or impulses in relation to their original objects or situations, and then expresses them in a situation of greater internal or external tolerance. *Situational* displacement may occur as a *temporal* displacement (e.g., carrying frustrations home from office) or as an *object* displacement (e.g., repressed resentment toward parents or authorities is expressed in hostility toward weaker or defenseless persons). Subject may sexualize neutral situations, but find himself inhibited or hostile in situations of sexual permissiveness. Transference in psychotherapy can be a manifestation of displacement.

c. *Preoccupation:* Subject is directly focused, in thought and behavior, on "primitive" impulses to the exclusion of other aspects of life—for example, he is consumed by anger; preoccupied with sex. One subject anticipating stress occupied himself with the "performance" of different girls in bed; another fantasized wiring and shocking a child he knew.

Transformation

The change is from unmodulated expression of an affect to a transformed, reversed, and altered version. Within the *defensive realm* transformation involves Frenkel–Brunswick's (1942) notions of the affinity of opposites and may likewise be involved with Jungian notions of the "light" and the "dark" side. Within the *coping realm* this process expresses autonomous conflict—free alternation of impulse that is based upon constitutional propensities and/or more or less complete socialization, e.g., Rapaport's (1954) "good reaction formations."

a. *Substitution* ("good reaction formations"): Subject expresses tempered, domesticated feelings. The distinction between strong reaction formations and strong substitutions must be made on the basis of the appropriateness, flexibility, metering, and purposiveness of the coping process and on the rigidity, compulsion, self-righteousness, and "magic" involved in the defense mechanism.

Subjects with high ratings would appear to be genuinely civilized people with interests that extend beyond their own immediate spheres. (An objective abstract painting would be evidence of coping substitution, whereas an emotional, subjective abstract painting would be more in the realm of coping sublimation).

Subjects with high ratings may be seen as symbolic men whose functioning betrays little *direct* affective expression, but who are more concerned with the rational, objective matters (e.g., mathematics as opposed to jet airplanes).

Subjects with low ratings will be affectively involved people, for example, emotional temperature-takers.

b. *Reaction formation:* Subject appears to have transformed his impulses and affects into their opposites, with resulting alteration of behavior which may, nevertheless, occasionally break down so that the original impulse is in evidence. Subject is excessively or brittlely kind, altruistic, or submissive as a defense against hostile impulses. Subject is excessively clean and orderly as a defense against impulses to dirt and disorder. Subject is excessively self-sufficient as a defense against underlying dependency. Subject is excessively tough and masculine as a defense against underlying passive—feminine tendencies. Reaction formations are often accompanied by a smug righteousness.

Subjects with high ratings "protest too much" against the impulse (excessive talk about cleanliness).

Subjects with low ratings may admit all kinds of impulses (e.g., a wish to submit totally to drugs) or may not seem to have impulse problems because they use other means for regulating feelings, such as sublimation, effective suppression or substitution.

c. *Unstable alternation:* Subject vacillates back and forth between "morality and sin"—acting out followed by self castigation.

Restraint

Subject restrains the expression of his feelings in situations where they might be expected to occur.

a. *Suppression:* Subjects' infeasible and inappropriate feelings and affective responses are held in abeyance and controlled until the proper time and place and with the proper object. At the same time, affect can be expressed when it is appropriate.

Subjects with low ratings act out: for example, sexual promiscuity, unrefined aggression, flights from responsibility. Or they could be highly repressed and constrained persons with little suppression.

b. *Regression:* Subject unconsciously and purposefully forgets. He has gaps in recall of the past and just can't remember or elaborate. His constriction in thinking is not due to low IQ, but is rather manifested as a naive, oblivious, unthinking attitude.

c. *Depersonalization, amnesic, withdrawal:* Subject controls, inhibits, and withdraws from an effective life to the point where he does not "exist" as an entity believable to himself. This kind of failure is to be distinguished from decompensation where identity is altered in form; he's younger, hapless, and so forth.

Appendix B. Q Sort of Ego Processes: Coping and Defense

Item Listing

COGNITIVE FUNCTIONS

Objectivity

1. Distinguishes between his own feelings and the facts of situations
2. Views self in an objective light
3. Evaluates both sides of arguments, including those contrary to his own point of view

Isolation

4. Fails to see connections between related ideas
5. Compartmentalizes his feelings
6. Misses connections between feelings and ideas

Intellectuality

7. Lets mind roam freely to consider possibilities (low if restricted in range)
8. Applies abstract, formal ideas in solving problems (low if thinks concretely)
9. Attempts to get at the "truth," even if it is against his own self-interest

Intellectualization

10. Produces intellectualizations rather than cogent solutions
11. Applies abstract ideas and terms to situations to avoid feelings
12. Produces intellectualizations which seem self-serving

Logical Analysis

13. Deduces seemingly accurate consequences of an event (place low if either not interested or inaccurate)
14. "Backtracks" to reconstruct a plausible chain of events (low if doesn't use past to understand present)
15. Gives seemingly accurate reasons as to why interpersonal events arose (low if not interested, or inaccurate)

Rationalization

16. Deduces unlikely and possibly self-serving consequences of events (low if rational)
17. Offers unlikely reasons for his past actions (low if not interested or accurate)
18. Reconstructs implausible chains of events (low if not interested or accurate)

INTRACEPTIVE FUNCTIONS

Tolerance of Ambiguity

19. Can defer decisions in complicated situations (low if unable to make decisions *or* acts on spur of moment)
20. Tolerates uncertainty in the structure and rules of situations (low if needs certainty)
21. Able to wait for other people to make up their minds in complicated situations; tolerates indecision or slowness in others

Doubt and Indecision

22. Unable to commit self to personal courses of action even when possible to do so (place low if action oriented)
23. Rethinks what he or she has already decided (low if decisive)
24. Has a tentative attitude toward problems and human relations

Empathy

25. Tries to understand others' feelings and perceptions (low if oblivious to others' feelings)
26. Reacts sensitively to others' feelings
27. Anticipates others' reactions to situations with accuracy, that is, can put himself in other fellow's boots

Projection

28. Preoccupied with the possibility that others will act badly
29. Feels accused and criticized by others
30. Vigilant in "ferreting" out others' reactions

Regression in Service of Ego (Playfulness)

31. Enjoys surprising aspects of situations, for example, situational humor, or sudden insights
32. Plays with ideas, and feelings without being constrained by situational demands (low if constrained by situations)
33. Integrates past memories with present to enhance his understandings

Regression

34. Seems to expect that he will be cared for in difficult situations
35. Acts non-age-appropriate in some situations or in important relationships (low if in charge of self and situation)
36. Views self as not being responsible in difficult situations

ATTENTION-FOCUSING FUNCTIONS

Concentration

37. Focuses attention and effort on most relevant problems of situations
38. Completes tasks even if he must set aside interesting distractions (low if acts on whims)
39. Organizes self to complete tasks according to work plans

Denial

40. Oblivious to complex, problematic nuances of situations
41. Ignores aspects of his situations that are potentially threatening
42. Focuses attention on the pleasant aspects of problems and ignores others, for example, "Every cloud has a silver lining"

Sublimation

43. Can express aggressive, even hostile feelings when the situation needs and warrants it
44. Expresses warm feelings toward a variety of activities and people
45. Expresses feelings in a variety of satisfying, socially tolerated ways

Displacement

46. Displaces feelings in form (e.g., stomach ache instead of temper tantrum) or in object (kicks dog instead of boss)
47. Misdirects positive, warm feelings from original aims or object (e.g., dogs are better than people)
48. Expresses aggressive, even hostile feelings in nonrelevant contexts and objects (irrelvant irritability)

Substitution

49. Acts fairly, even in trying circumstances
50. Acts civilly even in trying circumstances
51. Regulates expression of feelings proportionate to the situation

Reaction Formation

52. Acts with conformity in most circumstances
53. Acts with such fairness that legitimate self-interest seems negated (e.g., masochistic)
54. Acts with excessive moderation in circumstances that seem to warrant expression of feeling

Suppression

55. Suppresses, but is aware of feelings and thoughts in most circumstances (low if expresses or unaware of feelings)
56. Controls expression of affective reactions when not appropriate to express them, for example, older person not hurting children even when provoked
57. Inhibits his reactions for the time being when appropriate

Repression

58. Constricts and inhibits his cognitive associations
59. Forgets aspects of trying circumstances
60. Unable to recall painful experiences

	Suggested Distribution of Items								
	Most uncharacteristic					Most characteristic			
Steps	1	2	3	4	5	6	7	8	9
# Items	3	5	7	9	12	9	7	5	3

Formula for Q Correlation for this distribution between two sorts:

$$r = 1.00 - \frac{\Sigma d^2}{520}$$

Appendix C

Multiple Regression Models of Parents' Ego Processes to Predict Their Offspring's (F = father; M = mother)

Girls' process	Processes	F Ratio	β	%	r	Boys' process	Parents' processes	F Ratio	β	%	r
Objectivity	F Intellectualizing	11.28[a]	.42	12	.28	Objectivity	F Doubt	9.31[b]	-38	-12	-35
	F Doubt	6.33[b]	-31	-4	28		F Reaction formation	7.51[b]	-32	-6	-34
	Model df 2/68	6.27[b]		16	39		M Displacement	7.84[b]	-34	-6	-22
Isolation	F Regression	29.91[a]	57	14	38		M Isolation	5.51[c]	+29	+5	09
	M Substitution	8.24[b]	28	14	27		F Rationalization	3.26	+24	+4	-08
	F Tolerance/ambiguity	6.18[c]	-25	-4	-21		Model df 5/63	6.05[a]		32	57
	F Regression	7.49[b]	-30	-4	00	Isolation	M Reaction formation	4.81[c]	32	+7	26
	M Doubt	5.49[c]	-23	-4	-14		M Empathy	6.99[b]	40	+5	04
	F Reaction formation	5.33[c]	.23	+5	.27		M Isolation	3.59	29	+5	23
	Model df 6/64	8.38[b]		44	66		Model df 3/65	4.29[b]		17	41
Intellectuality	SES	8.27[b]	-32	11	-33	Intellectuality	F Reaction formation	14.01[a]	-43	-17	-42
	M Sublimation	5.49[c]	.26	+7	28		M Regression	10.14[b]	-32	-9	-28
	Model df 2/68	7.27[a]		18	.42		F Concentration	11.00[b]	39	+4	29
Intellectualizing	F Suppression	6.52[b]	-29	-9	-29		F Rationalization	13.69[a]	46	+4	-02
	Model df 1/79	6.52[b]		-9	-29						
Logical analysis	F Intellectualizing	10.74[b]	35	10	31		F Substitution	9.72[b]	-37	-5	04
	F Sublimation	5.58[c]	25	+7	21	Intellectualizing	F Regression/Ego	4.31[c]	25	+4	26
	F Projection	7.13[b]	-28	-6	-22		M Objectivity	3.81	-20	-3	-02
	M Intellectualizing	4.48	23	5	23		F Doubt	3.64	-22	-3	-28
	Model df 4/66	6.42[a]		28	53		Model df 8/60	7.08[a]		49	70
Rationalization	M Empathy	7.68[b]	-38	-4	-20		M Tolerance/Ambiguity	3.65	-21	-4	-20
	M Rationalization	5.06[c]	-31	-5	-08		M Denial	16.69	-49	-6	-17
	F Denial	3.11	20	4	.15		M Empathy	11.55[a]	-45	-5	-12
	Model df 3/67	3.42[c]		13	.36	F Logical analysis	F Logical analysis	13.19[a]	40	+8	21
Tolerance ambiguity	F Intellectualizing	25.87[a]	56	20	44		F Isolation	17.58[a]	48	+12	24
	M Tolerance/ambiguity	15.92[a]	39	12	41		M Sublimation	4.83[c]	27	+2	08
	F Isolation	7.11[b]	-33	-6	01		M Substitution	3.03	-20	-1	-01
	F Projection	9.35[b]	-34	-4	-22	Logical analysis	Model df 7/61	6.01[a]		41	64
	F Displacement	4.92[c]	.25	+3	-04		F Reaction formation	6.21[c]	-29	-10	-31
	F Repression	3.91[c]	22	+3	-09		M Tolerance/ambiguity	3.99[c]	-23	-5	-26

continued

	Predictor	F			
Doubt	F Regression/Ego	3.42	.18	+3	24
	Model df 7/63	8.75^a	49	.70	
	F Suppression	6.98^b	-28	-9	-29
	M Regression	9.30^b	35	+4	25
	M Suppression	9.09^b	35	+6	13
	F Substitution	8.52^b	32	+5	13
	F Concentration	7.41^b	-29	-8	-23
	Model df 5/65	6.23^a	32	57	
Concentration	F Regression	7.21^b	-31	-7	-26
	F Intellectualizing	5.28^c	26	+7	20
	Model df 2/68	5.23^b	13	37	
Denial	F Regression	17.16^a	44	+14	31
	F Regression/Ego	16.65^a	-42	-15	-35
	M Doubt	6.95^b	-28	-3	-12
	F Intellectualizing	3.39	-19	-2	-08
	Model df 4/66	8.14^a	33	.57	
Empathy	F Intellectualizing	26.45^a	58	+18	42
	M Intellectualizing	8.27^b	26	+9	30
	F Concentration	6.77^b	26	+8	27
	M Tolerance ambiguity	9.12^b	29	+3	30
	F Repression	15.09^a	44	6	12
	F Rationalization	4.49^c	-24	-4	-04
	F Isolation	4.00^c	-23	-3	.13
	Model df 7/63	9.47^a	51	.72	
Projection	M Projection	14.00^a	44	6	24
	M Intellectualizing	3.79	-2	-6	-14
	F Substitution	14.54^a	42	6	22
	F Regression	12.95^a	39	7	18
	F Regression/Ego	9.09^b	-34	-6	-16
	M Regression	5.79^c	-31	-6	-05
	Model df 6/64	6.18^a	37	61	
Regression	F Reaction formation	3.68	-22	-6	-24
	M Displacement	3.56	-22	-5	-24

	Predictor	F				
Rationalization	Model df 2/62	5.79^b	30	15	39	
	M Reaction formation	7.52^b	25	+13	36	
	M Doubt	5.19^c	25	+5	29	
	F Denial	5.81^c	28	+4	23	
	F Projection	3.20	-21	-4	-06	
	Model df 4/64	5.55^a	26	51		
	F Tolerance ambiguity	12.31^a	29	17	41	
Doubt	M Intellectuality	3.98^c	22	5	26	
	Model df 2/66	9.02^a	21	46		
	F Doubt	9.46^b	35	+9	30	
Concentration	F Objectivity	15.14^a	48	+10	19	
	F Reaction formation	5.42^c	28	+5	19	
	M Reaction formation	4.97^c	24	+5	20	
	Model df 4/64	6.69^a	29	54		
Denial	M Regression	13.34^a	-41	-8	-29	
	F Isolation	9.65^b	-37	-12	-25	
	F Concentration	6.48^c	36	+4	27	
	F Objectivity	3.09	-26	-3	12	
	Model df 4/64	6.20^a	28	52		
	M Reaction formation	6.16^c	33	+8	28	
	M Objectivity	10.64^b	45	7	.06	
	M Suppression	7.20^b	-36	-8	-27	
	F Doubt	4.17^c	22	5	23	
Empathy	Model df 4/64	5.84^a	27	52		
	F Reaction formation	7.18^b	-35	-10	-32	
	F Rationalization	9.94^b	38	8	12	
	F Tolerance ambiguity	8.88^b	37	4	28	
	F Intellectuality	9.36^b	-39	-8	-07	
	F Isolation	4.56^c	-27	-5	-20	
	Model df 4/63	6.53^a	34	58		
Projection	M Reaction formation	5.56^c	28	8	28	
	Model 1/62	5.56^c	28	8	28	

Appendix C—Continued

Girls' process	Processes	F Ratio	β	%	r	Boys' process	Parents' processes	F Ratio	β	%	r
Repression	Model df 2/68	3.95^c		10		Repression/ego	F Tolerance/ambiguity	11.21^a	38	16	40
	F Objectivity	4.03^c	-23	-6	.23		M Projection	10.76^b	-32	-9	-32
	Model	4.03^c	-23	-6	.23		F Denial	11.07^a	-37	-7	-37
Sublimation	M Projection	7.69^b	-30	-15	-39		F Rationalization	7.97^b	31	4	03
	F Regression	5.90^c	-26	-7	-27		F Substitution	4.09^c	-23	-4	12
	F Sublimation	5.16^c	24	+4	29		F Projection	3.28	-20	-3	-29
	F Intellectualizing	3.19	20	+3	18		Model df 6/62	7.91^a		43	66
	Model df 4/66	6.91^a		30	54	Regression	F Doubt	12.70^a	37	+17	41
Displacement	F Empathy	11.05^b	-37	-13	-36		M Reaction formation	10.68^b	34	+12	38
	F Substitution	31.39^a	57	+7	15		Model df 2/66	13.11^a		28	53
	F Intellectuality	7.29^b	-32	-9	-35	Sublimation	M Displacement	12.47^a	-38	-15	-39
	M Suppression	11.11^a	44	+5	12		F Doubt	5.99^c	-27	-7	-27
	M Projection	6.30^c	29	+4	17		Model df 2/66	9.33^a		22	47
	F Repression	19.55^a	47	+5	27	Displacement	(Not significant)				
	M Regression/ego	3.73	-22	-5	-04	Substitution	F Reaction formation	8.12^b	-26	-11	-33
	F Repression	9.16^b	-37	-4	20		M Displacement	17.71^a	-51	-9	-28
	M Regression	6.29^c	-29	-3	-06		M Suppression	17.07^a	-55	-12	-18
	F Regression/ego	4.71^c	-26	-3	-23		M Rationalization	6.82^b	-34	-4	-23
	M Empathy	3.47	-22	-2	-07		M Isolation	7.11^b	34	+4	08
	Model df 11/59	7.62^a		59	77		M Logical analysis	7.96^b	34	+4	05
Substitution	F Intellectualizing	7.55^b	33	+8	29		M Tolerance ambiguity	5.06^c	-23	-4	-22
	M Regression	10.30^b	-40	-6	-28		Model df 7/61	8.58^a		50	70
	F Regression/ego	11.24^a	-40	-5	-18	Reaction formation	M Reaction formation	12.50^a	41	+12	34
	F Doubt	3.40	-23	-4	-08		M Denial	4.43^c	-25	-6	-13
	M Suppression	6.66^c	-32	-5	00		Model df 2/66	6.89^b		17	42
	F Logical analysis	3.39	22	+4	.07	Suppression	F Logical analysis	10.59^b	36	+16	40
	Model df 6/64	5.01^a	22	32	57		M Regression	10.22^b	-36	-4	-20
							F Isolation	5.70^c	-27	-8	-32

		F	β		r
Reaction formation	M Substitution	8.90[b]	.35	+4	21
	M Tolerance ambiguity	6.70[c]	-31	-6	-18
	SES	4.64[c]	-25	-5	-14
	F Regression	3.61	22	+4	14
	Model df 4/66	3.98[b]		19	44
						Repression
	M Empathy	6.73[b]	-32	-4	-12
	M Denial	3.17	-21	-3	-07
	Model df 5/63	6.82[a]		35	59
	(Not significant)				
Suppression	M Suppression	17.60[a]	-49	-11	-22
	F Regression/ego	20.81[a]	-52	-11	-22
	M Regression	16.17[a]	-50	-3	-06
	M Intellectualizing	7.72[b]	30	+6	20
	F Logical analysis	13.27[a]	40	+6	15
	Model df 5/65	7.74[a]		37	61
Repression	F Suppression	10.68[b]	-39	-10	-31
	M Tolerance	5.74[c]	-26	-7	-29
	F Regression	13.49[a]	-44	-7	-04
	F Regression	9.40[b]	34	+4	21
	F Intellectualizing	3.80	-21	-5	-14
	F Substitution	5.12[c]	24	+3	02
	F Tolerance/ambiguity	4.34[c]	-25	-4	-29
	Model df 7/63	5.79[a]		39	63

Note: Decimals are not shown for the beta and correlation coefficients

Appendix D

Means and standard deviations:

adult subjects

	Males		Females	
CPI based scales	Mean	SD	Mean	SD
Objectivity	20.68	4.06	16.39	3.14
Isolation	13.90	3.22	12.83	2.70
Intellectuality	17.34	5.16	15.69	5.14
Intellectualization	18.76	5.52	14.05	4.74
Logical analysis	16.28	4.34	15.07	3.43
Rationalization	12.33	3.20	13.61	3.49
Concentration	21.65	3.54	19.95	3.20
Denial	18.62	4.26	19.98	4.10
Tolerance ambiguity	18.20	4.66	16.47	4.88
Doubt	8.22	5.41	13.36	6.03
Empathy	18.73	3.51	19.48	3.13
Projection	10.61	3.83	7.69	2.82
Regression ego	13.66	4.42	14.40	4.49
Regression	10.29	4.92	11.59	4.54
Sublimation	22.04	2.86	22.45	3.40
Displacement	11.82	4.48	9.48	4.56
Substitution	20.32	3.07	17.11	3.61
Reaction formation	18.95	3.78	14.80	4.13
Suppression	23.77	3.62	24.41	3.21
Repression	15.07	3.64	14.90	4.22
Summed coping	18.42	3.83	18.49	3.81
Summed defense	12.75	3.63	10.10	3.46
Controlled coping	28.49	5.65	19.43	4.91
Expressive coping	18.99	5.64	17.83	4.43
Structured defense	21.99	4.98	15.61	5.44
Primitive defe	10.59	4.93	15.56	5.04
MMPI based scales				
Concentration	29.59	5.94	20.22	3.95
Projection	21.35	4.17	17.45	4.18
Regression	8.89	4.40	10.98	4.80
Suppression	24.89	4.83	23.06	4.43

Note: CPI   sample size: Males   N = 111; Females   N = 132.
        MMPI sample size: Males   N = 46; Females   N = 49.

Means and standard deviations:

student subjects

	Males		Females	
CPI based scales	Mean	SD	Mean	SD
Objectivity	19.74	2.97	17.03	2.32
Isolation	13.73	2.47	13.88	2.56
Intellectuality	17.60	3.79	17.73	3.59
Intellectualization	18.28	3.97	16.14	4.05
Logical analysis	16.25	3.78	16.44	2.48
Rationalization	12.47	2.70	13.04	2.90
Concentration	21.18	2.48	20.78	2.69
Denial	18.15	3.14	20.12	3.73
Tolerance ambiguity	20.88	3.74	18.33	3.36
Doubt	9.68	4.88	14.41	5.20
Empathy	18.88	2.57	18.88	2.55
Projection	11.25	3.37	7.69	2.37
Regression ego	15.85	3.55	15.47	3.52
Regression	12.32	3.71	12.26	3.78
Sublimation	22.34	2.79	23.04	2.69
Displacement	13.04	4.06	10.64	3.33
Substitution	20.44	2.63	18.78	2.72
Reaction formation	16.88	2.17	13.66	2.93
Suppression	23.36	3.11	23.65	2.53
Repression	15.21	3.13	13.86	3.21
Summed coping	19.76	2.91	19.28	2.82
Summed defense	13.83	2.97	10.59	2.84
Controlled coping	26.83	4.47	21.47	3.77
Expressive coping	19.73	4.16	18.99	3.20
Structured defense	23.05	3.75	16.72	4.07
Primitive defense	11.21	3.18	14.13	3.74
MMPI based scales				
Concentration	27.34	3.64	18.87	2.82
Projection	19.01	2.42	15.73	2.76
Regression	10.01	2.93	11.52	3.04
Suppression	24.43	3.12	23.06	2.55

Note: CPI sample size: Males N = 95; Females N = 108.
       MMPI sample size: Males N = 79; Females N = 108.

Appendix E

Item composition of the CPI based ego scales

Objectivity: Male (36 items).
    True: 7 18 140 154 197 200 211 215 227 234 292 295 303 373 375 401 407
           445

    False: 41 45 55 73 74 76 116 121 125 133 143 170 238 257 299 382 417
           436

Objectivity: Female (31 items).
    True: 18 140 147 154 197 200 211 215 234 292 295 303 315 375 401 407 445

    False: 41 45 55 73 76 116 121 125 143 170 238 313 417 436

Isolation: Male (31 items).
    True: 19 42 80 102 109 143 253 257 258 316 330 393 397 403 404 412 416
           455

    False: 69 86 106 120 128 201 213 232 290 322 368 418 466

Isolation: Female (32 items).
    True: 19 42 80 102 109 143 253 257 258 314 316 393 397 403 404 412 416
           463

    False: 60 69 86 106 120 201 213 232 260 290 322 368 418 466

Intellectuality: Male (35 items).
    True: 17 31 46 85 103 160 172 179 200 211 215 239 303 320 403 407 418

    False: 41 45 55 73 116 141 144 230 238 241 255 258 263 340 357 371 436
           452

Intellectuality: Female (35 items).
    True: 17 46 57 60 103 160 172 179 200 211 215 239 243 303 320 403 407

    False: 41 45 55 73 116 141 144 230 238 241 255 258 263 340 357 371 436
           452

Intellectualization: Male (35 items).
    True: 46 102 172 179 200 215 234 239 278 355 376 403 420 448

    False: 7 25 31 65 116 186 230 241 255 263 266 293 302 333 340 367 371
          385 387 443 466

Intellectualization: Female (35 items).
    True: 46 102 159 172 179 200 215 234 239 355 376 403 420 448

    False: 7 25 31 37 65 116 133 186 230 241 255 263 293 333 340 367 371
          385 387 443 466

Logical analysis: Male (33 items).
    True: 38   46 112 135 140 160 179 204 211 215 225 227 378 407 418

    False: 22   41   45   55   73   89 116 121 143 165 170 238 241 253 255 326 340
             357

Logical analysis: Female (32 items).
    True: 46   57 112 135 140 160 179 204 209 211 215 225 226 378 407 418

    False: 41   45   55   73   89 116 121 143 165 238 241 253 255 326 340 357

Rationalization: Male (34 items).
    True: 27   55   79   94 102 121 125 144 165 252 253 258 307 337 341 372 411
             417 429 430 463 477

    False: 13   16   37   54   70 168 169 197 322 329 356 367

Rationalization: Female (34 items).
    True: 27   55   79   94 102 121 125 144 165 252 253 258 307 337 341 372 411
             417 429 430 463 477

    False: 11   16   37 137 168 169 197 225 322 329 356 367

Concentration: Male (33 items).
    True: 53   54   70 129 135 139 179 197 225 245 256 290 292 359 378 407 418
             445

    False: 92 143 238 252 270 279 339 369 383 422 431 438 449 465 472

Concentration: Female (34 items).
    True: 53   71   94 129 135 139 160 179 197 225 245 256 290 292 359 407 418
             445 453

    False: 92 143 238 252 270 279 339 369 383 422 431 438 449 465 472

Denial: Male (34 items).
    True: 3   8   36   41   45 121 131 143 229 230 245 253 263 312 357 404 467

    False: 18   32   54   70 128 152 180 186 243 285 289 309 327 373 375 378 444

Denial: Female (37 items).
    True: 3   8   36   41   45   88 121 131 143 229 230 245 253 263 312 357 404
             456 ·

    False: 18   32   54   70   86 114 128 152 243 285 289 309 327 373 375 378 380
             395 444

Tolerance of ambiguity: Male (38 items).
    True: 14   17   46   62 152 185 211 213 234 243 292 295 296 303 305 335 378
             399

    False: 5   45   73 121 123 134 141 176 230 255 340 361 370 371 387 391 397
             400 404 463

Tolerance of ambiguity: Female (32 items).
    True: 17   25   46   62 152 185 211 213 243 264 295 296 303 380 399

    False: 45   73 121 123 134 141 176 230 255 340 361 370 371 387 397 400 404

Doubt: Male (33 items).
   True: 13 38 40 54 76 94 111 144 177 227 279 284 335 341 344 351 369
          416 419 422 429 449 452 456 467

   False: 37 129 161 202 245 264 305 368

Doubt: Female (38 items).
   True: 13 38 40 54 66 76 94 97 111 144 177 192 227 239 252 279 284
          335 341 344 351 369 373 383 416 419 422 429 449 452 456 467

   False: 37 129 202 245 367 368

Empathy: Male (35 items).
   True: 1 18 28 30 32 110 180 185 213 217 218 221 244 292 303 334 368
          385 433

   False: 45 49 87 123 141 156 168 171 202 210 239 249 253 307 397 404

Empathy: Female (29 items).
   True: 18 28 30 32 37 110 185 213 217 244 292 303 380 433

   False: 45 49 87 123 141 156 168 171 202 210 239 249 307 397 404

Projection: Male (33 items).
   True: 41 59 63 67 76 90 98 121 125 143 153 173 220 257 258 270 282
          355 404 405 436 474

   False: 62 83 133 168 186 197 212 259 362 368 418

Projection: Female (27 items).
   True: 41 59 63 67 76 90 98 125 143 153 173 220 258 270 355 405 436
          474

   False: 58 133 168 182 197 212 259 362 368

Regression in service of ego: Male (34 items).
   True: 4 28 29 62 86 114 211 213 229 231 243 250 262 306 311 335 375
          378 399 423

   False: 45 55 71 88 141 149 174 230 255 316 347 397 408 451

Regression in service of ego: Female (35 items).
   True: 4 28 29 44 62 86 114 211 213 231 243 250 262 306 311 335 354
          375 378 399

   False: 42 45 88 124 141 149 174 180 230 255 316 347 397 408 451

Regression: Male (35 items).
   True: 5 13 44 47 71 76 81 91 121 143 238 252 257 262 341 369 416
          419 429 467

   False: 24 54 83 149 150 168 197 212 221 245 246 367 368 380 451

Regression: Female (37 items).
   True: 5 13 44 47 71 76 81 91 121 143 238 252 257 262 341 369 416 41
          429 467

   False: 24 35 37 149 168 187 197 212 221 245 246 273 361 367 368 380 451

Sublimation: Male (35 items).
    True: 23   86 130 152 160 166 172 197 240 280 322 349 368 378 380 399 418
             445 466

    False: 27   61   67   73   76 144 187 273 299 301 344 390 404 416 436 449

Sublimation: Female (34 items).
    True: 86 110 130 152 160 166 172 197 209 280 322 349 368 378 380 389 399
             418 445 466

    False: 27   67   73   76 144 187 273 299 301 344 390 416 436 449

Displacement: Male (36 items).
    True: 5   71   76   77   81   94 102 121 153 161 214 232 247 248 252 257 258
             262 340 369 416 417 419 436 450 456 463 471

    False: 37   54   70 149 224 243 407 413

Displacement: Female (30 items).
    True: 5   71   76   77   81   94 121 153 161 214 232 247 248 252 257 258 262
             340 369 416 419 436 456 463 471

    False: 25   32 149 224 407

Substitution: Male (31 items).
    True: 19   60   61 133 223 225 231 256 310 401 411 447

    False: 55   94 119 165 173 174 232 258 270 301 340 347 379 397 404 416 430
             477 479

Substitution: Female (32 items).
    True: 19   60   61 133 225 231 256 284 310 331 401

    False: 55   94 119 165 173 174 228 232 258 270 301 340 344 347 379 397 404
             416 430 477 479

Reaction formation: Male (33 items).
    True: 19   75   87   88 100 113 121 123 141 210 249 258 269 389 400 404

    False: 1   11   18   92 128 152 160 186 211 217 219 244 264 293 395 418 443

Reaction formation: Female (35 items).
    True: 19   75   87   88 100 113 121 123 141 210 249 258 269 389 400 404 480

    False: 1   11   18   37   92 152 160 161 163 186 211 217 244 264 293 322 395
             443

Suppression: Male (37 items).
    True: 4   18   70 154 160 175 225 311 407

    False: 3   76   94   96 143 161 168 176 198 206 214 239 253 267 270 316 337
             341 369 390 393 416 431 436 449 453 463 465

Suppression: Female (35 items).
    True: 4   18   32 154 160 225 243 311 351 407

    False: 3   76   94   96 143 176 198 206 214 253 267 270 316 337 341 369 390
             393 416 431 436 449 453 463 465

Repression: Male (33 items).
   True: 5   7   25   41   45   73   76   88   89 121 124 187 210 242 305 361 429
   False: 4 17 18 28 86 97 152 159 211 213 229 244 292 295 320 399

Repression: Female (31 items).
   True: 5   7   25   41   45   73   76   88 121 124 187 210 361 429
   False: 4 17 18 28 86 97 152 209 211 213 244 284 292 295 320 399 459

Summed coping: Male (35 items).
   True: 18 30 69 103 114 152 160 211 213 219 223 225 292 375 378 407 418
   False: 41 45 55 73 76 141 143 165 230 253 255 258 340 347 397 404 436
          463

Summed coping: Female (34 items).
   True: 18 25 30 103 114 152 160 209 211 213 225 292 375 378 407 418
   False: 41 45 55 73 76 101 141 143 165 230 253 255 258 340 347 397 404
          436

Summed defense: Male (37 items).
   True: 76 94 121 143 165 252 253 257 258 341 416 417 419 420 429 431 436
          463 474
   False: 18 32 37 54 86 186 197 201 212 213 217 245 322 368 380 418 445
          466

Summed defense: Female (35 items).
   True: 76 94 121 143 165 252 253 257 258 341 416 417 419 420 429 431 436
          463 474
   False: 18 32 37 60 86 192 197 212 213 225 245 322 368 380 445 466

Controlled coping: Male (41 items).
   True: 69 114 212 215 225 246 268 317 368
   False: 5 29 39 41 55 71 94 119 121 143 147 165 170 173 191 214 220
          238 248 253 257 270 299 308 340 357 369 417 431 436 467 474

Controlled coping: Female (39 items).
   True: 18 53 86 103 129 133 148 160 179 197 211 213 224 225 243 249 256
          280 281 292 295 403 407 418 445 454
   False: 7 67 73 116 143 144 149 263 305 394 429 436 452

Expressive coping: Male (42 items).
   True: 18 30 31 54 114 122 201 221 237 243 250 360 378 399 418 471
   False: 5 41 45 55 68 88 138 141 165 168 195 202 210 230 253 340 361
          371 376 386 397 404 419 442 463 479

Expressive coping: Female (38 items).
   True: 4 19 25 29 32 37 44 130 148 160 179 189 209 211 213 232 243
          244 275 281 292 311 327 373 375 407
   False: 76 124 141 144 177 273 301 316 416 452 456 477

Structured defense: Male (45 items).
    True: 28   55   77   80 102 103 109 138 143 159 165 191 222 248 307 324 386
               391 417 429

    False: 7   38   69   83 106 124 128 149 168 186 197 201 212 219 227 229 300
               302 333 368 378 394 418 441 442

Structured defense: Female (44 items).
    True: 13   81 101 144 175 176 177 252 257 258 268 341 353 369 372 416 419
               422 429 440 452 456

    False: 25   32   37   86 126 133 168 187 197 224 225 232 245 249 276 322 329
               367 368 380 408 413

Primitive defense: Male (34 items).
    True: 13   27   40   43   47   71   76   94 238 335 341 344 369 416 419 422 429
               449 477

    False: 54   83 112 135 166 197 212 245 246 254 305 320 359 368 418

Primitive defense: Female (36 items).
    True: 7   67   88 121 134 141 177 258 263 404 429 436 456

    False: 1   4   18   25   52   60   86 148 152 211 213 222 244 256 264 280 292
               375 395 412 418 433 445

Item composition of MMPI based ego scales

Concentration: Male (42 items).
   True: 37 51 55 183 302 379 384 387 460 466

   False: 27 38 41 72 97 98 101 118 140 156 189 198 205 215 222 224 231
           239 241 254 268 275 311 352 373 399 400 410 421 475 514 519

Concentration: Female (30 items).
   True: 14 37 51 55 183 302 379 384 387 437 460

   False: 38 41 72 97 98 101 118 140 156 215 222 231 254 352 399 410 421
           475 519

Projection: Male (41 items).
   True: 5 31 37 54 73 170 194 204 220 240 264 348 355 385 400 406 426
           494 534 554

   False: 12 45 89 128 139 215 248 250 258 271 296 305 307 419 428 467 487
           504 513 540 549

Projection: Female (38 items).
   True: 5 73 82 86 170 194 204 220 240 264 267 348 355 385 400 406 426
           494 534 554

   False: 12 45 89 128 139 215 248 258 296 305 307 419 467 487 504 513 540
           549

Regression: Male (32 items).
   True: 14 62 69 72 98 101 115 133 140 156 189 212 224 249 251 254 322
           334 404 483 489 519

   False: 37 55 148 230 302 379 384 442 466 496

Regression: Female (35 items).
   True: 14 62 72 98 101 103 115 140 156 189 212 224 249 251 254 322 324
           334 337 352 404 483 489 519 528

   False: 37 55 148 230 302 379 384 466 496 504

Suppression: Male (36 items).
   True: 9 36 152 284 294 302 374 416 460 551

   False: 22 33 38 41 62 72 98 101 140 156 160 189 215 240 241 244 251
           254 322 337 351 397 421 483 489 519

Suppression: Female (31 items).
   True: 36 294 302 374 416 460

   False: 22 38 41 62 72 98 140 156 160 189 215 240 241 244 251 254 322
           324 337 351 397 421 483 489 519

References

Alker, H. A. Item characteristics for measuring primary and secondary processes. Paper presented at the convention of the American Psychological Association, New York, September 1966.

Alker, H. A. Cognitive controls and the Haan-Kroeber model of ego functioning. *Journal of Abnormal Psychology*, 1967, *72*(5), 434–440.

Alker, H. A. Coping, defense and socially desirable responses. *Psychological Reports*, 1968, *22*, 985–988.

Alker, H. A. A quasi-paranoid feature of students' extreme attitudes against colonialism. *Behavioral Science*, 1971, *16*(3), 218–227.

Alker, H. A., & Poppen, P. J. Personality and ideology in university students. *Journal of Personality*, 1973, *41*, 653–671.

Anchor, K. N., & Cross, H. J. Maladaptive aggression, moral perspective, and the socialization process. *Journal of Personality and Social Psychology*, 1974, *30*, 163–168.

Antonovsky, A. Conceptual and methodological problems in the study of resistance resources and stressful life events. In B. S. Dohrenwend & B. P. Dohrenwend (Eds.), *Stressful life events: Their nature and effects.* New York: Wiley, 1974.

Antonovsky, A., Maoz, B., Dowty, N., & Wijsenbeck, H. Twenty-five years later: A limited study of the sequelae of the concentration camp experience. *Social Psychiatry*, 1971, *6*(4), 186–193.

Arbuthnot, J. Relationships between maturity of moral judgment and measures of cognitive abilities. *Psychological Reports*, 1973, *33*, 945–946.

Arbuthnot, J. Modification of moral judgment through role playing. *Developmental Psychology*, 1975, *11*, 319–324.

Argyris, C. Dangers in applying results from experimental social psychology. *American Psychologist*, 1975, *30*, 469–485.

Arnold, M. Human emotion and action. In T. Mischel (Ed.), *Human action.* New York: Academic Press, 1969. Pp. 167–198.

Aronfreed, J. *Conduct and conscience.* New York: Academic Press, 1968.

Bales, R. F. *Interaction process analysis: A method for the study of small groups.* Reading, Massachusetts: Addison-Wesley, 1950.

Barclay, A.M., Weissman, H. N., Riter, K., & Gordon, R. M. Reliability study of the Defense Mechanism Inventory. *Psychological Reports,* 1971, *29,* 1237–1238.

Becker, W. C. Consequences of different kinds of parental discipline. In M. L. Hoffman & L. W. Hoffman (Eds.), *Review of the child development research.* New York: Russell Sage Foundation, 1964. Pp. 169–208.

Bell, R. Q. A reinterpretation of the directions of effects in studies of socialization. *Psychological Review,* 1968, *75*(2), 81–95.

Bellak, L., & Hurvich, M. A systematic study of ego function. *Journal of Nervous and Mental Diseases,* 1969, *148*(6), 569–585.

Bem, D. J., & Allen, A. On predicting some of the people some of the time. *Psychological Review,* 1974, *81,* 506–520.

Berlyne, D. *Conflict arousal and curiosity.* New York: McGraw-Hill, 1960.

Berman, E. Regrouping for survival: Approaching dread and three phases of family interaction. *Journal of Comparative Family Studies,* 1973, *4,* 63–87.

Bettelheim, B. *New York Review of Books,* September 10, 1964, 1.

Block, J. *The Q sort method in personality assessment and psychiatric research.* Springfield, Illinois: Charles C. Thomas, 1962.

Bloom, B. S. *Stability and change in human characteristics.* New York: Wiley, 1964.

Bodin, A. M. Family interaction: A social-clinical study of synthetic, normal, and problem family triads. In W. D. Winter & A. J. Ferreira (Eds.), *Research in family interaction.* Palo Alto, California: Science and Behavior Books, 1969. Pp. 125–127.

Bouchard, T. J., Jr. Personality, problem-solving procedure, and performance in small groups. *Journal of Applied Psychology Monograph,* 1969, *53*(1, Pt. 2), 1–29.

Braungart, R. Family status, socialization and student politics: A multivariate analysis. Paper presented at the meeting of American Sociological Association, San Francisco, September 2, 1969.

Brehm, J. V. *A theory of psychological reactance.* New York: Academic Press, 1966.

Bruner, J. S., Olver, R. R., & Greenfield, P. M. *Studies in cognitive growth.* New York: Wiley, 1966.

Brunswik, E. The conceptual framework of psychology. In O. Neurath (Ed.), *International encyclopedia of Unified Science,* 1950, *1*(Whole No. 10), 1–102.

Campagna, A. F., & Harter, S. Moral judgment in sociopathic and normal children. *Journal of Personality and Social Psychology,* 1975, *31,* 199–205.

Campbell, D. T., & Fiske, D. W. Convergent and discriminant validation by the multitrait–multimethod matrix. *Psychological Bulletin,* 1959, *56,* 81–105.

Campbell, S. B. Mother-child interaction in reflective, impulsive, and hyperactive children. *Developmental Psychology,* 1973, *8*(3), 341–349.

Chilman, C. S. Families in development at mid-stage of the family life cycle. *The family coordinator,* 1968, 297–312.

Christie, P., & Geis, F. *Studies in Machiavellianism.* New York: Academic Press, 1970.

Clum, G. A., & Clum, J. Choice of defense mechanisms and their relationship to mood level. *Psychological Reports,* 1973, *32,* 507–510.

Cobb, S. A model for life events and their consequences, In B. S. Dohrenwend & B. P. Dohrenwend (Eds.), *Stressful life events.* New York: Wiley, 1974. Pp. 151–156.

Cobb, B., Clark, R., Carson, M., & Howe, C. Patient-responsible delay of treatment in cancer. *Cancer,* 1954, *7,* 920–926.

Cohen, F., & Lazarus, R. S. Active coping processes, coping dispositions, and recovery from surgery. *Psychosomatic Medicine,* 1973, *35,* 375–389.

Colby, K. M. *Energy and structure in psychoanalysis.* New York: Ronald Press, 1955.

Coleman, J., Hobson, C. J., McPartland, J., Mood, A. M., Weinfeld, F. D., & York, R. L. *Equality of educational opportunity.* Washington, D.C.: U. S. Government Printing Office, 1966.

Crites, J. O., Bechtoldt, H. P., Goodstein, L. D., & Heilbrun, A. B., Jr. A factor analysis of the California Psychological Inventory. *Journal of Applied Psychology*, 1961, *45*, 408–414.

Cronbach, L. J. *Essentials of psychological testing*. New York: Harper, 1970.

Dahlstrom, W. G. Whither the MMPI? In J. N. Butcher (Ed.), *Objective personality assessment*. New York: Academic Press, 1972.

Darlington, R. B., & Bishop, H. Increasing test validity by considering interitem correlation. *Journal of Applied Psychology*, 1966, *50*(4), 322–330.

Dember, W. N. Motivation and the cognitive revolution. *American Psychologist*, 1974, *29*(3), 161–168.

Dohrenwend, B. P. Problems in defining and sampling the relevant population of stressful life events. In B. S. Dohrenwend & B. P. Dohrenwend (Eds.), *Stressful life events*. New York: Wiley, 1974. Pp. 275–312.

Dohrenwend, B. S. Social status and stressful life events. *Journal of Personality and Social Psychology*, 1973, *28*(2), 225–235.

Dohrenwend, B. S., & Dohrenwend, B. P. (Eds.) *Stressful life events*. New York: Wiley, 1974.

Drabek, T. E. Social processes in disaster: Family evacuation. *Social Problems*, 1969, *16*, 336–349.

Erikson, E. H. *Childhood and society*. New York: Norton, 1950.

Erikson, E. H. Identity and the life cycle. *Psychological Issues*, 1959, *1*(1, Whole No. 1).

Erikson, E. H. *Childhood and society* (2nd ed.). New York: Norton, 1963.

Erikson, E. H. *Gandhi's truth*. New York: Norton, 1969.

Fenichel, O. *The psychoanalytic theory of neurosis*. New York: Norton, 1945.

Festinger, L. *A theory of cognitive dissonance*. Stanford, California: Stanford Univ. Press, 1964.

Flacks, R. "The liberated generation": An exploration of the roots of student protest. *Journal of Social Issues*, 1967, *23*(3), 52–75.

Folkins, C. Temporal factors and the cognitive mediators of stress reactions. *Journal of Personality and Social Psychology*, 1970, *14*(2), 173–184.

French, J., Rodgers, W., & Cobb, S. Adjustment as person-environment fit. In G. Coelho, D. Hamburg, J. Adams (Eds.), *Coping and adaptation*. New York: Basic Books, 1974. Pp. 316–333.

Frenkel-Brunswik, E. Motivation and behavior. *Genetic Psychology Monographs*, 1942, *26*, 121–265.

Frenkel-Brunswik, E. Social research and the problem of values. *Journal of Abnormal and Social Psychology*, 1954, *49*, 466–471.

Freud, A. *The ego and the mechanisms of defense*. London: Hogarth Press, 1937.

Freud, A., & Burlingham, D. *Infants without families*. New York: International Universities Press, 1944.

Freud, S. *The ego and the id*. New York: Norton, 1923, 1960.

Freud, S. *New introductory lectures*. London: Hogarth Press, 1946.

Freud, S. *Outline of psychoanalysis*. New York: Norton, 1949.

Gleser, G., & Ihilevich, D. An objective instrument for measuring defense mechanisms. *Journal of Consulting and Clinical Psychology*, 1969, *33*, 51–60.

Gleser, G., & Sucks, M. Ego defenses and reaction to stress: A validation study of the Defense Mechanism Inventory. *Journal of Consulting and Clinical Psychology*, 1973, *40*, 181–187.

Goldberg, L. In O. K. Buros (Ed.) *Seventh mental measurements yearbook*. Highland Park, New Jersey: Gryphon Press, 1972.

Goldstein, M. J., & Adams, J. N. Coping style and behavioral response to stress. *Journal of Experimental Research in Personality*, 1967, *2*(4), 239–251.

Goldstein, M. J., Judd, L. L., Rodnick, E. H., Alkire, A., & Gould, E. A method for studying social influence and coping patterns within families of disturbed adolescents. *Journal of Nervous and Mental Disease,* 1968, *147*(3), 233–251.

Gough, H. *Manual for the California psychological inventory.* Palo Alto, California: Consulting Psychologists' Press, 1957.

Goulet, L. R., & Baltes, P. B. Status and issues of a life-span developmental psychology. In L. R. Goulet & P. B. Baltes (Eds.), *Life-span developmental psychology: Research and theory.* New York: Academic Press, 1970. Pp. 3–21.

Gounin-Decarie, T. *Intelligence and affectivity in early childhood.* New York: International Universities Press, 1966.

Haan, N. Proposed model of ego functioning: Coping and defense mechanisms in relationship to I.Q. change. *Psychological Monographs,* 1963, 77(8, Whole No. 571).

Haan, N. The relationship of ego functioning and intelligence to social status and social mobility. *Journal of Abnormal and Social Psychology,* 1964, *69,* 594–605. (a)

Haan, N. An investigation of the relationship of Rorschach scores, patterns and behavior to coping and defense mechanisms. *Journal of Projective Techniques,* 1964, *28,* 429–441. (b)

Haan, N. Coping and defense mechanisms related to personality inventories. *Journal of Consulting Psychology,* 1965, *29,* 373–378.

Haan, N. A tripartite model of ego functioning, values and clinical and research applications. *Journal of Nervous and Mental Disease,* 1969, *148,* 14–30.

Haan, N. Moral redefinition in the family as the critical aspect of the generation gap. *Youth and Society,* 1971, *2*(3), 259–283.

Haan, N. The adolescent antecedants of an ego model of coping and defense and comparisons with Q-sorted ideal personalities. *Genetic Psychology Monographs,* 1974, *89,* 273–306. (a)

Haan, N. Changes in young adults after Peace Corps experience. *Journal of Youth and Adolescence,* 1974, *3,* 177–194. (b)

Haan, N. The implications of family ego patterns for adolescent members. Unpublished doctoral dissertation, California School of Professional Psychology, 1974. (c)

Haan, N. Personality organizations of well functioning younger people and older adults. Symposium on the middle years, Gerontological Society Meeting, Portland, Oregon, October 28, 1974. (d)

Haan, N. Moral reasoning in hypothetical and an actual situation of civil disobedience. *Journal of Personality and Social Psychology,* 1975, *32,* 255–270.

Haan, N., & Day, D. Change and sameness in personality development: Adolescence to adulthood. *International Journal of Aging and Human Development,* 1974, *5,* 11–39.

Haan, N., Langer, J., & Kohlberg, L. Family moral patterns. *Child Development,* 1976, *47*(No. 4).

Haan, N., Smith, M. B., & Block, J. Moral reasoning of young adults: Political-social behavior, family background, & personality correlates. *Journal of Personality and Social Psychology,* 1968, *10,* 183–201.

Haan, N., Stroud, J., & Holstein, C. Moral and ego stages in relationship to ego processes: A study of "hippies." *Journal of Personality,* 1973, *41,* 596–612.

Handel, A. Attitudinal orientations and cognitive functioning among adolescents. *Developmental Psychology,* 1975, *11*(6), 667–675.

Hartmann, H. *Ego psychology and the problem of adaptation.* New York: International Universities Press, 1958.

Hartmann, H. *Psychoanalysis and moral values.* New York: International Universities Press, 1960.

Hartmann, H. *Essays on ego psychology.* New York: International Universities Press, 1964.

Hartmann, H., & Kris, E. The genetic approach in psychoanalysis. *The psychoanalytic study of the child.* Vol. 1. New York: International Universities Press, 1945. Pp. 11–30.

Hill, R., & Hansen, D. A. The identification of conceptual frameworks utilized in family study. *Marriage and Family Living*, 1960, *22*, 299–311.

Hinkle, L. E. The effect of exposure to cultural change, social change, and changes in interpersonal relationship on health. In B. S. Dohrenwend & B. P. Dohrenwend (Eds.), *Stressful life events*. New York: Wiley, 1974, Pp. 9–44.

Hoffman, M. Moral development. In P. Mussen (Ed.), *Carmichael's manual of child psychology* (Vol. III, 3rd ed.). New York: Wiley, 1970. Pp. 261–360.

Holmes, T. S., & Rahe, R. H. The social readjustment rating scale. *Journal of Psychosomatic Research*, 1967, *11*, 213–218.

Holstein, C., Stroud, J., & Haan, N. Alienated and non alienated youth. *Youth and Society*, 1974, *5*, 279–298.

Holt, R. Competence on competence. *Contemporary Psychology*, 1964, *9*(11), 433–434.

Holt, R. Ego autonomy: Re-evaluated. *International Journal of Psychiatry*, 1967, *3*(6), 481–536.

Hosack, A. A comparison of crises: Mothers' early experiences with normal and abnormal first-born infants. Unpublished doctoral dissertation, Harvard School of Public Health, 1968.

Houston, R. K. Trait and situational denial and performance under stress. *Journal of Personality and Social Psychology*, 1971, *18*(3), 289–293.

Hunter, C. G., & Goodstein, L. D. Ego strength and types of defensive and coping behavior. *Journal of Consulting Psychology*, 1967, *31*, 432.

Inhelder, B., & Piaget, J. *The growth of logical thinking from childhood and adolescence*. New York: Basic Books, 1958.

Jackson, D. D. (Ed.) *The etiology of schizophrenia*. New York: Basic Books, 1960.

Jahoda, M. *Current concepts of positive mental health*. New York: Basic Books, 1958.

Janis, I. Psychodynamic aspects of stress tolerance. In S. Klausner (Ed.), *The quest for self-control*. New York: Free Press, 1965. Pp. 215–246.

Janis, I. Vigilance and decision making in personal crises. In G. Coelho, D. Hamburg, & J. Adams (Eds.), *Coping and adaptation*. New York: Basic Books, 1974. Pp. 139–175.

Kagan, J., & Moss, H. *Birth to maturity*. New York: Wiley, 1962.

Katz, J. L., Weiner, H., Gallagher, T. F., & Hellman, L. Stress, astress and ego defenses. *Archives of General Psychiatry*, 1970, *23*, 131–142.

Kelley, E. L. In O. K. Buros (Ed.), *Personality tests and reviews*. Highland Park, New Jersey: Gryphon Press, 1970.

Kelman, H. *A time to speak; on human values and social research*. San Francisco: Jossey-Bass, 1968.

Kohlberg, L. Stage and sequence: The cognitive-developmental approach to socialization. In P. Goslin (Ed.), *Handbook of socialization theory and research*. New York: Rand McNally, 1969. Pp. 347–480.

Kroeber, T. C. The coping functions of the ego mechanisms. In R. White (Ed.), *The study of lives*. New York: Atherton, 1963.

Kubie, L. S. *The neurotic distortion of the creative process*. Lawrence, Kansas: Univ. of Kansas Press, 1958.

Kuhn, D. Inducing development experimentally: Comments on a research paradigm. *Developmental Psychology*, 1974, *10*, 590–600.

Kuhn, D., Langer, J., Kohlberg, L., & Haan, N. Logical operational foundation of moral judgment. *Genetic Psychology Monographs* (to appear 1977).

Kuypers, J. A. Internal-external locus of control, ego functioning and personality characteristics in old age. *Gerontologist*, 1972, *12*, 168–173.

Kuypers, J. A. Ego functioning in old age: Early adult life antecedants. *International Journal of Aging and Human Development*, 1974, *5*, 157–179.

Lane, M. *Introduction to structuralism*. New York: Basic Books, 1970.

Langer, J. *Theories of development.* New York: Holt, 1969.

Langer, J. Personal communication, 1973.

Lazarus, R. *Psychological stress and the coping process.* New York: McGraw-Hill, 1966.

Lazarus, R., Averill, J., & Opton, E. The psychology of coping: Issues of research and assessment. In G. Coelho, D. Hamburg, & J. Adams (Eds.), *Coping and adaptation.* New York: Basic Books, 1974, Pp. 249–315.

Lazarus, R. S. The psychology of stress and coping: With particular reference to Israel. Address at international conference on psychological stress and adjustment in time of war and peace, Tel Aviv, Israel, January 6–10, 1973.

Lazarus, R. S. Personal communication, January 15, 1976.

Lefcourt, H. The function of illusions of control and freedom. *American Psychologist,* 1973, *28*(3), 417–425.

Lenneberg, E. *Biological foundations of language.* New York: Wiley, 1967.

Levi, L. (Ed.) *Society, stress, disease.* Vol. I. New York: Oxford Univ. Press, 1971.

Livson, N., & Peskin, H. Prediction of adult psychological health in a longitudinal study. *Journal of Abnormal Psychology,* 1967, *72*(6), 509–518.

Loevinger, J. Three principles for a psychoanalytic psychology. *Journal of Abnormal Psychology,* 1966, *71*(6), 432–443. (a)

Loevinger, J. The meaning and measurement of ego development. *American Psychologist,* 1966, *21*(3), 195–206. (b)

Loevinger, J. Recent research on ego development. *Society of Research in Child Development,* Biennal meeting, Philadelphia, March, 31, 1973. (a)

Loevinger, J. Ego development: Syllabus for a course. *Psychoanalysis and Contemporary Science,* 1973, *2,* 77–97. (b)

Loevinger, J., Wessler, R., & Redmore, C. *Measuring ego development.* San Francisco: Jossey-Bass, 1970.

London, P. *The modes and morals of psychotherapy.* New York: Holt, 1964.

Mackinnon, D. W. The creativity of architects. In D. W. Taylor and F. Barron (Eds.), *Widening horizons in creativity.* New York: Wiley, 1964. Pp. 359–378.

Macklin, R. Mental problems and mental illness: Some problems of definition and concept formation. *Philosophy of Science,* 1972, *39,* 341–365.

Maguire, G. P., Maclean, A. W., & Aitken, R. C. B. Adaptation on repeated exposure to film-induced stress. *Biological Psychology,* 1973, *1,* 43–51.

Margolis, C. G. Coping and defense responses in four role-playing situations. *Journal of Consulting and Clinical Psychology,* 1970, *35,* 427.

Maruyama, M. The second cybernetics: Deviation-amplifying mutual causal processes. In W. Buckley (Ed.), *Modern systems research for the behavioral scientist.* Chicago: Aldine, 1968. Pp. 304–313.

Maslow, A. *Toward a psychology of being.* New York: D. Van Nostrand, 1962.

McGrath, J. E. Settings, measures and themes: An integrative review of some research on social-psychological factors in stress. In J. E. McGrath (Ed.), *Social & psychological factors in stress.* New York: Holt, 1970. Pp. 58–96.

Mechanic, D. Social structure and personal adaptation. In G. Coelho, D. Hamburg, & J. Adams (Eds.), *Coping and adaptation.* New York: Basic Books, 1974. Pp. 32–46. (a)

Mechanic, D. Discussion of research programs on relations between stressful life events and episodes of physical illness. In B. S. Dohrenwend & B. P. Dohrenwend (Eds.), *Stressful life events.* New York: Wiley, 1974. Pp. 87–98. (b)

Megargee, M. I. *The California psychological inventory handbook.* San Francisco: Jossey-Bass, 1972.

Melden, A. I. The conceptual dimensions of emotions. In T. Mischel (Ed.), *Human action.* New York: Academic Press, 1969. Pp. 167–198.

Milgram, S. *Obedience to authority.* New York: Harper, 1974.

Miller, F. T., Bentz, W. K., Aponte, J. F., & Brogan, D. R. Perception of life crises events: A comparative study of rural and urban samples. In B. S. Dohrenwend & B. P. Dohrenwend (Eds.), *Stressful life events*. New York: Wiley, 1974. Pp. 259–274.

Miller, D., & Swanson, G. E. *Inner conflict and defense*. New York: Holt, 1960.

Miller, G. A., Galanter, E. & Pribram, K. *Plans and the structure of behavior*. New York: Holt, 1960.

Mischel, W. *Personality and assessment*. New York: Wiley, 1968.

Mischel, W. Continuity and change in personality. *American Psychologist*, 1969, *24*, 1012–1018.

Moir, D. J. Egocentricism and the emergence of conventional morality in preadolescent girls. *Child Development*, 1974, *45*, 299–304.

Moore, H. E. *Before the wind*. National Academy of Sciences-National Research Council, Washington, D. C., 1963.

Murphy, L. B. *The widening world of childhood*. New York: Basic Books, 1962.

Murphy, L. B. Coping, vulnerability, and resilience in childhood. In G. Coelho, D. Hamburg, & J. Adams (Eds.), *Coping and adaptation*. New York: Basic Books, 1974. Pp. 69–100.

Naditch, M. P. Acute adverse reactions to psychoactive drugs, drug usage and psychopathology. *Journal of Abnormal Psychology*, 1974, *83*, 394–403.

Naditch, M. P. Relation of motives for drug use and psychopathology in the development of acute adverse reactions to psychoactive drugs. *Journal of Abnormal Psychology*, 1975, *84*, 374–385. (a)

Naditch, M. P. Ego functioning and acute adverse reactions to psychoactive drugs. *Journal of Personality*, 1975, *43*, 305–320. (b)

Naditch, M. P. Ego mechanisms and marijuana usage. In D. J. Lettieri (Ed.), *Predicting adolescent drug abuse: A review of issues, methods and correlates*. Washington, D. C.: U.S. Government Printing Office, 1975. (c)

Naditch, M. P. *A causal model of personality and problem drinking behavior*. Unpublished manuscript, 1975. (d)

Naditch, M. P., Gargan, M. A., & Michael, L. B. Denial, anxiety, locus of control, and the discrepancy between aspirations and achievements as components of depression. *Journal of Abnormal Psychology*, 1975, *84*, 1–9.

Naditch, M. P., & Naditch, S. F. LSD flashbacks and ego functioning. Unpublished manuscript, 1975.

Natanson, M. *The journeying self*. Reading, Massachusetts: Addison-Wesley, 1970.

Nesselroade, J., & Baltes, P. Adolescent personality development and historical change: 1970–1972. *Monograph of the Society for Research in Child Development*, 1974, *39*(1, Serial No. 154), 1–80.

Neugarten, B. (Ed.) *Middle age and aging*. Chicago: Univ. of Chicago Press, 1968.

O'Rourke, J. F. Field and laboratory: The decision-making behavior of family groups in two experimental conditions. *Sociometry*, 1963, *26*(4), 422–435.

Parloff, M. B., Datta, L. E., Kleman, M., & Handlon, H. H. Personality characteristics which differentiate creative male adolescents and adults. *Journal of Personality*, 1968, *36*, 528–552.

Parsons, T., & Bales, R. F. *Family, socialization and interaction process*. Glencoe, Illinois: Free Press, 1955.

Peskin, H. Multiple prediction of adult psychological health from preadolescent and adolescent behavior. *Journal of Consulting and Clinical Psychology*, 1972, *38*, 155–160.

Peters, R. S. Motivation, emotion, and the conceptual schemes of common sense. In T. Mischel (Ed.), *Human action*. New York: Academic Press, 1969. Pp. 135–166.

Piaget, J. *The psychology of intelligence*. London: Routledge & Kegan Paul, 1950.

Piaget, J. *The child's conception of physical causality*. Paterson, New Jersey: Littlefield, Adams, 1960.

Piaget, J. *Play, dreams and imitation in childhood.* New York: Norton, 1962.

Piaget, J. *The moral judgment of the child.* Glencoe, Illinois: Free Press, 1965.

Piaget, J. *The mechanisms of perception.* New York: Norton, 1969.

Piaget, J. *Structuralism.* New York: Basic Books, 1970.

Piaget, J. *Insights and illusions of philosophy.* New York: World Publishing, 1971.

Piaget, J. *The child and reality.* New York: Grossman, 1973.

Piaget, J., & Inhelder, B. *Memory and intelligence.* New York: Basic Books, 1973.

Podd, M. H. Ego identity status and morality. *Developmental Psychology,* 1972, *6,* 497–507.

Powers, R. W. Jr., & Alker, H. A. Coping suppression, defensive repression and reports about dirty words. *Cornell Journal of Social Relations,* 1968, *3*(2), 124–128.

Pribram, K. H. Emotion: Steps toward a neurophysiological theory. In D. C. Glass (Ed.), *Neurophysiology and emotion.* New York: Rockfeller Univ. Press, 1967. Pp. 3–39.

Quine, W. V. *From a logical point of view.* New York: Harper, 1963.

Quine, W. V. *Ontological relativity and other essays.* New York: Columbia Univ. Press, 1969.

Rahe, R. H. The pathway between subjects' recent life change and their near-future illness reports. In B. S. Dohrenwend & B. P. Dohrenwend (Eds.), *Stressful life events.* New York: Wiley, 1974. Pp. 73–86.

Rapaport, D. The autonomy of the ego. In R. Knight & C. Friedman (Eds.), *Psychoanalytic psychiatry and psychology.* New York: International Universities Press, 1954. Pp. 248–258.

Rawls, J. *The theory of justice.* Cambridge, Massachusetts: Harvard Univ. Press, 1971.

Reiss, D. Individual thinking and family interaction. *Journal of Nervous and Mental Disease,* 1970, *151*(3), 187–202.

Reiss, D. Varieties of consensual experience. I. A theory for relating family interaction to individual thinking. *Family Process,* 1971, *10*(1), 1–28.

Rest, J. R. Longitudinal study of the defining issues test of moral judgment. *Developmental Psychology,* 1975, *11,* 738–748.

Ricoeur, P. *Freud and philosophy.* New Haven, Connecticut: Yale Univ. Press, 1970.

Rieff, P. *Freud: The mind of the moralist.* New York: Viking Press, 1959.

Riskin, J., & Faunce, E. E. An evaluative review of family interaction research. *Family Process,* 1972, *11*(4), 365–456.

Rogers, C. R. *On becoming a person.* Boston: Houghton-Mifflin, 1961.

Rosenberg, M. J. The conditions and consequences of evaluation apprehension. In R. Rosenthal & R. Rosnow (Eds.), *Artifacts in behavioral science.* New York: Academic Press, 1969. Pp. 280–348.

Rosenthal, R., & Rosnow, R. *Artifact in behavioral research.* New York: Academic Press, 1969.

Rosten, L. *Captain Newman, M.D.* New York: Harper, 1956.

Rotter, J. B. Generalized expectancies for internal vs. external control reinforcement. *Psychological Monographs,* 1966, *80*(Whole No. 609), 1–28.

Rudner, R. S. The scientist qua scientist makes value judgments. *Philosophy of Science,* 1953, *20.*

Rudner, R. S. *Philosophy of social science.* Englewood Cliffs, New Jersey: Prentice-Hall, 1966.

Saffer, J. B. Coping mechanisms of obese men: A psychometric and behavioral study. Unpublished doctoral dissertation, Illinois Institute of Technology, 1968.

Saltzstein, H., Diamond, R. M., & Belenky, M. Moral judgment level and conformity behavior. *Developmental Psychology,* 1972, *7,* 327–336.

Selman, R. The relation of role taking to the development of moral judgment in children. *Child Development,* 1971, *42,* 79–92.

Selman, R., & Damon, W. The necessity (but insufficiency) of social perspective taking for conception of justice at three early levels. In D. DePalma & J. Foley (Eds.), *Moral development.* New York: Erlbaum Assoc., 1975. Pp. 57–74.

Selye, H. *Stress without distress.* Philadelphia: Lippincott, 1974.

Shaver, K. G. Defensive attribution: Effects of severity and relevance on responsibility assigned for an accident. *Journal of Personality and Social Psychology,* 1970, *14*(2), 101–113.

Shaw, G. B. *Selected prose.* New York: Dodd, Mead, 1952.

Shure, G. F., & Rogers, M. S. Personality Factor stability for three ability levels. *Journal of Psychology,* 1963, *55,* 445–456.

Siegelman, E., Block, J., Block, J. H., & von der Lippe, A. Antecedents of optimal adjustment. *Journal of Consulting and Clinical Psychology,* 1970, *35,* 283–289.

Silber, E., Coeltto, G. V., Murphey, E. B., Hamburg, D., Pearlin, L., & Rosenberg, M. Competent adolescents coping with college decisions. *Archives of General Psychiatry,* 1961, *5,* 517–527.

Singer, M. T., & Wynne, L. C. Thought disorder and family relations of schizophrenics. *Archives of General Psychiatry,* 1965, *12,* 201–212. (a)

Singer, M. T., & Wynne, L. C. Thought disorder and family relations of schizophrenics. *Archives of General Psychiatry,* 1965, *12,* 187–200. (b)

Singer, M. T., & Wynne, L. C. Communication styles in parents of normals, neurotics and schizophrenics. *Psychiatric Research Reports,* 1966, *20,* 25–38. (a)

Singer, M. T., & Wynne, L. C. Principles of scoring communication defects and deviances in parents of schizophrenics: Rorschach and TAT scoring manuals. *Psychiatry,* 1966, *24,* 260–288. (b)

Skinner, B. F. *Walden II.* New York: Macmillan, 1948.

Skinner, B. F. *Beyond freedom and dignity.* New York: Kropf, 1971.

Smith, M. B. Optima of mental health, *Psychiatry,* 1950, *13,* 503–510.

Smith, M. B. Research strategies toward a conception of positive mental health. *American Psychologist,* 1959, *14,* 673–681.

Smith, M. B. "Mental health" reconsidered: A special case of the problem of values in psychology. *American Psychologist,* 1961, *16,* 299–306.

Smith, M. B. *Social psychology and human values.* Chicago: Aldine, 1969.

Smith, M. B. *Humanizing social psychology.* San Francisco: Jossey-Bass, 1974.

Spiegel, J. *Transactions: The interplay between individual, family and society.* New York: Jason Aronson, 1972.

Spiegel, J. P., & Bell, N. W. Family of the psychiatric patient. In S. Arieti (Ed.), *American handbook of psychiatry.* Vol. I. New York: Basic Books, 1959. Pp. 114–149.

Stack, C. *All our kin: Strategies for survival in a black community.* New York: Harper, 1974.

Steiner, G. On the psychological reality of cognitive structures: A tentative synthesis of Piaget's and Bruner's theories. *Child Development,* 1974, *45,* 891–899.

Steiner, I. D. Strategies for controlling stress in interpersonal situations. In J. E. McGrath (Ed.), *Social-psychological factors in stress.* New York: Holt, 1970. Pp. 140–158.

Strodtbeck, F. L. Husband-wife interaction over revealed differences. *American Sociological Review,* 1951, *16,* 468–473.

Strodtbeck, F. L. The family as a three-person group. *American Sociological Review,* 1954, *19,* 23–29.

Swanson, G. E. Determinants of the individual's defense against inner conflict: Review and reformulation. In J. C. Glidewell (Ed.), *Parental attitudes and child behavior.* Springfield, Illinois: Charles C. Thomas, 1961. Pp. 5–41.

Swanson, G. E. The routinization of love: Structure and process in primary relations. In S. Klausner (Ed.), *The quest for self control.* Glencoe, Illinois: Free Press, 1965. Pp. 160–209.

Swanson, G. E. Self processes and social organization: An interpretation of the mechanisms of coping and defense, unpublished manuscript, 1968.

Swanson, G. E. Family structures and the reflective intelligence of children. *Sociometry,* 1974, *37,* 459–490.

Szasz, T. S. *The myth of mental illness.* New York: Harper, 1961.

Thelen, M. H., & Varble, D. L. Comparison of college students seeking psychotherapy with nontherapy students on coping and defense scales. *Journal of Clinical Psychology,* 1970, *26,* 123–124.

Thorndike, R. L. Personality tests and reviews. In O. K. Buros (Ed.) *Fourth Mental Measurements Yearbook,* Highland Park, New Jersey: Gryphon Press, 1970. Pp. 632.

Tomlinson-Keasey, C., & Keasey, C. B. The mediating role of cognitive development in moral judgment. *Child Development,* 1974, *45,* 291–298.

Trilling, L. *Freud and the crisis of our culture.* Boston: Beacon Press, 1955.

Tryon, C. Evaluations of adolescent personality by adolescents. *Monograph of Society for Research in Child Development,* 1939, *4*(4), 83.

Turiel, E. Conflict and transition in adolescent moral development. *Child Development,* 1974, *45,* 14–29.

Turiel, E. The development of social concepts: Mores, customs, and conventions. In D. DePalma & J. Foley (Eds.), *Moral development.* Hillsdale, New Jersey: Lawrence Erlbaum, 1975. Pp. 7–38.

Twelker, P., & Layden, K. *Humanus.* La Jolla, California: Simile II, 1973.

Ullman, L. P. An empirically derived MMPI scale which measures facilitation-inhibition of recognition of threatening stimuli. *Journal of Clinical Psychology,* 1962, *18,* 127–132.

Viney, L. L., & Clarke, A. M. Children coping with crisis: An analogue study. *British Journal of Social and Clinical Psychology,* 1974, *13,* 305–313.

Watson, J. Depression and the perception of control in early childhood. Unpublished manuscript, 1975.

Watts, W., & Whittaker, D. Profile of a non-conformist youth culture: A study of Berkeley non-students. *Sociology of Education,* 1968, *41*(2), 178–200.

Weick, K. E. The "Ess" in stress: Some conceptual and methodological problems. In J. E. McGrath (Ed.), *Social and psychological factors in stress.* New York: Holt, 1970. Pp. 287–347.

Weinstock, A. Family environment and the development of defense and coping mechanisms. *Journal of Personality and Social Psychology,* 1967, *5,* 67–75. (a)

Weinstock, A. R. Longitudinal study of social class and defense preferences. *Journal of Consulting Psychology,* 1967, *31,* 539–541. (b)

Weisbroth, S. P. Moral judgment, sex, and parental identification in adults. *Developmental Psychology,* 1970, *2,* 396–402.

Weisman, A. D. *On dying and denying.* New York: Behavioral Publications, 1972.

White, R. Ego and reality in psychoanalytic theory. *Psychological Issues,* 1963, *3*(3, Whole No. 11).

White, R. Strategies of adaptation: An attempt at systematic description. In G. Coelho, D. Hamburg, & J. Adams (Eds.), *Coping and adaptation.* New York: Basic Books, 1974. Pp. 47–68.

Wilden, A. Piaget and the structure as law and order. In K. Riegel & G. Rosenwald (Eds.), *Structure and transformation.* New York: Wiley, 1975. Pp. 83–118.

Witkin, H. A. Social influences in the development of cognitive style. In D. Goslin (Ed.), *The handbook of socialization.* Chicago: Rand McNally, 1969. Pp. 687–706.

Witkin, H. A., Goodenough, D. R. & Karp, S. H. Stability of cognitive style from childhood to young adulthood. *Journal of Personality and Social Psychology,* 1967, *7,* 291–300.

Wohlwill, J. F. Methodology and research strategy in the study of developmental change. In L. R. Goulet & P. B. Baltes (Eds.), *Life span developmental psychology.* New York: Academic Press, 1970. Pp. 150–193.

Subject Index